Hana-Kimi

For You in Full Blossom

22

story and art by
HISAYA NAKAJO

HANA-KIMI
For You in Full Blossom
VOLUME 22

STORY & ART BY HISAYA NAKAJO

Translation & English Adaptation/David Ury
Touch-Up Art & Lettering/Primary Graphix
Design/Izumi Evers
Editor/Jason Thompson

Editor in Chief, Books/Alvin Lu
Editor in Chief, Magazines/Marc Weidenbaum
VP of Publishing Licensing/Rika Inouye
VP of Sales/Gonzalo Ferreyra
Sr. VP of Marketing/Liza Coppola
Publisher/Hyoe Narita

Printed in the U.S.A.

Published by VIZ Media, LLC, P.O. Box 77010, San Francisco, CA 94107

Shôjo Edition
10 9 8 7 6 5 4 3 2 1

First printing, February 2008

T 251605

www.viz.com
store.viz.com

CONTENTS

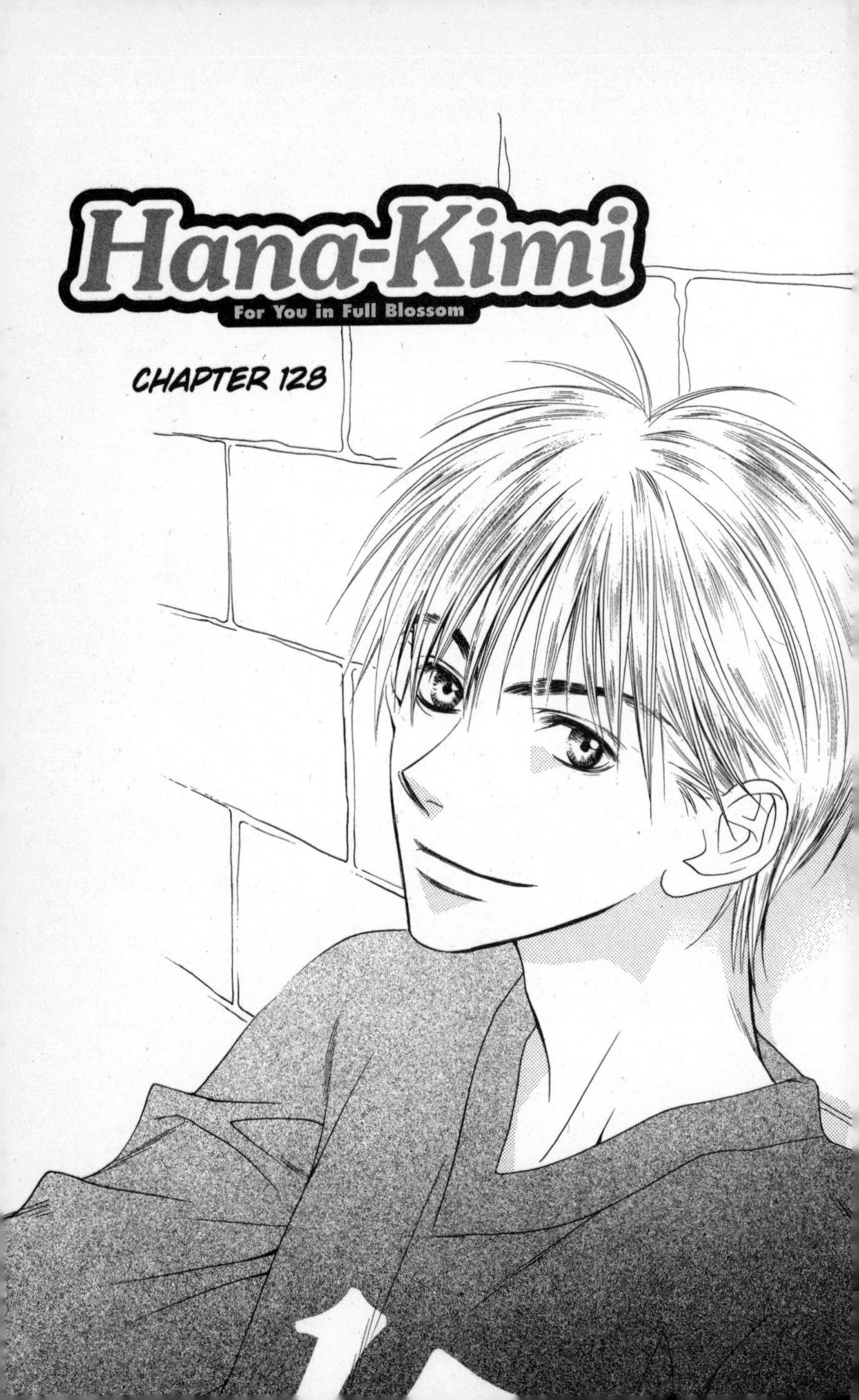
Hana-Kimi
For You in Full Blossom
CHAPTER 128

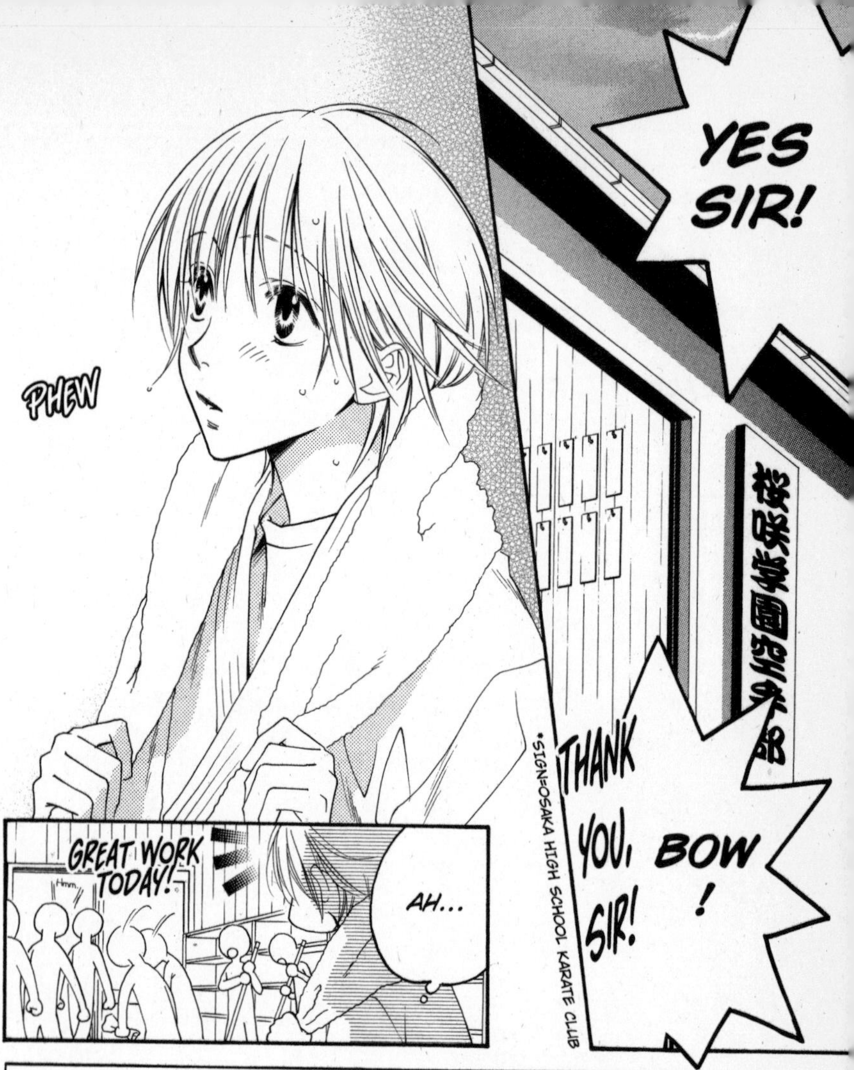
YES SIR!
桜咲学園空手部
THANK YOU, SIR!
BOW!
*SIGN: OSAKA HIGH SCHOOL KARATE CLUB
PHEW
AH...
GREAT WORK TODAY!
Hmm.

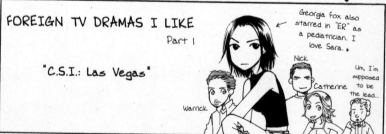

FOREIGN TV DRAMAS I LIKE

Part 1

"C.S.I.: Las Vegas"

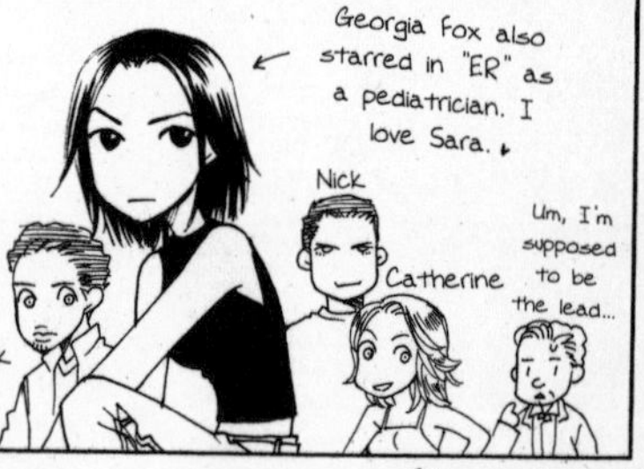
Georgia Fox also starred in "ER" as a pediatrician. I love Sara.
Nick
Um, I'm supposed to be the lead...
Catherine
Warrick
Grissom, the real main character

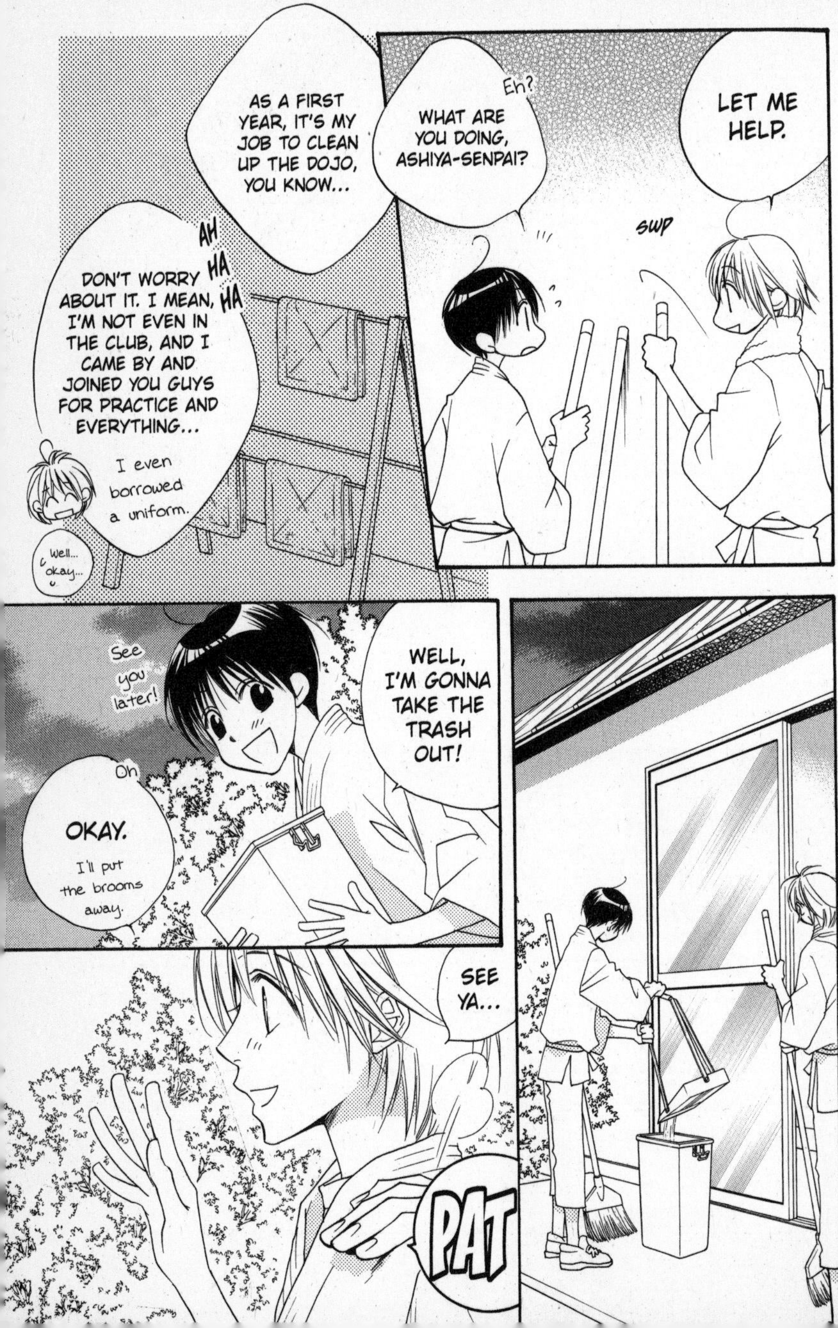
LET ME HELP.
SWP
Eh?
WHAT ARE YOU DOING, ASHIYA-SENPAI?
AS A FIRST YEAR, IT'S MY JOB TO CLEAN UP THE DOJO, YOU KNOW...
AH HA HA
DON'T WORRY ABOUT IT. I MEAN, I'M NOT EVEN IN THE CLUB, AND I CAME BY AND JOINED YOU GUYS FOR PRACTICE AND EVERYTHING...
I even borrowed a uniform.
Well... okay...
WELL, I'M GONNA TAKE THE TRASH OUT!
See you later!
Oh
OKAY.
I'll put the brooms away.
SEE YA...
PAT

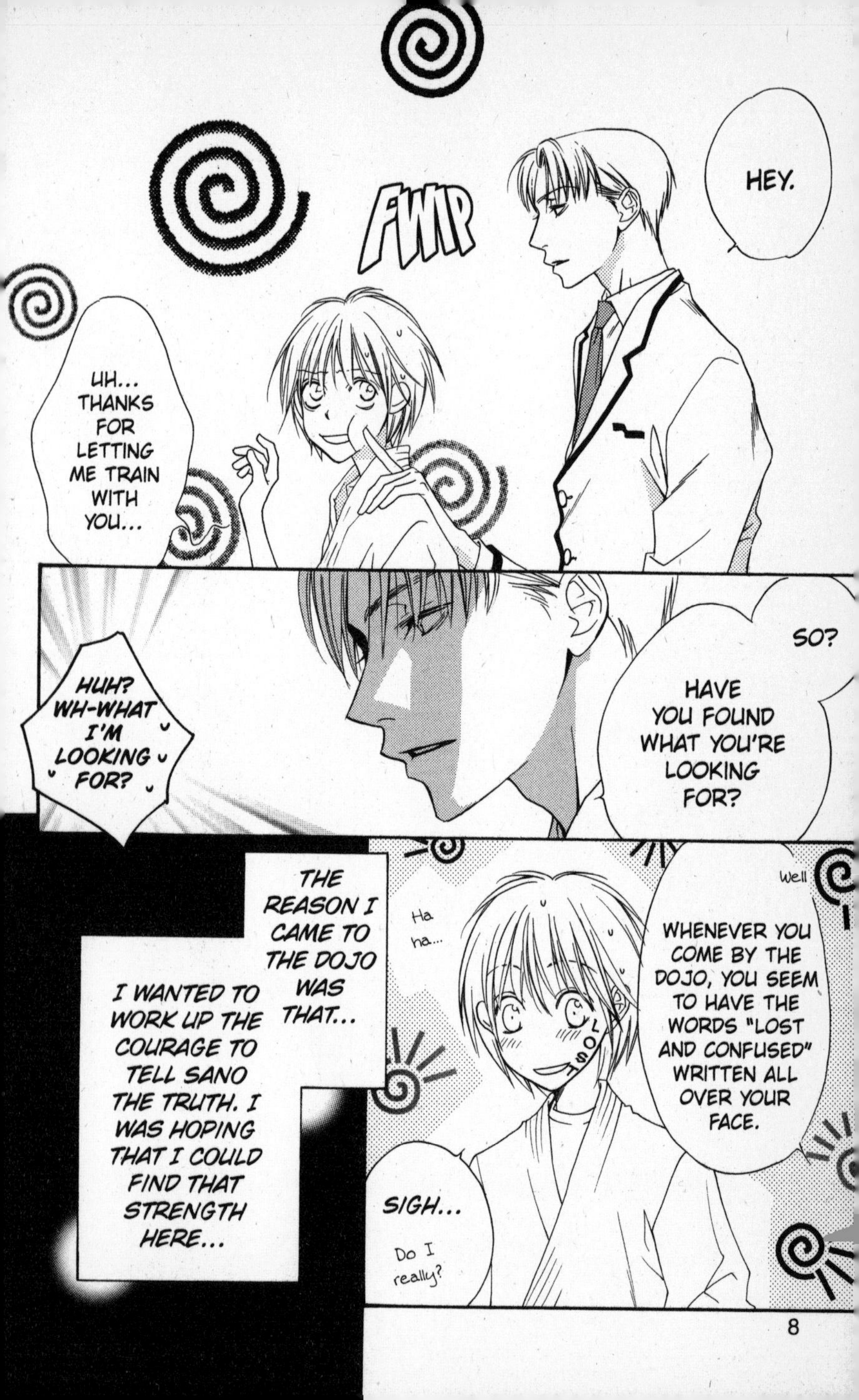

HEY.
FWIP
UH... THANKS FOR LETTING ME TRAIN WITH YOU...
SO?
HAVE YOU FOUND WHAT YOU'RE LOOKING FOR?
HUH? WH-WHAT I'M LOOKING FOR?
Well
WHENEVER YOU COME BY THE DOJO, YOU SEEM TO HAVE THE WORDS "LOST AND CONFUSED" WRITTEN ALL OVER YOUR FACE.
LOST
Ha ha...
SIGH...
Do I really?
THE REASON I CAME TO THE DOJO WAS THAT...
I WANTED TO WORK UP THE COURAGE TO TELL SANO THE TRUTH. I WAS HOPING THAT I COULD FIND THAT STRENGTH HERE...

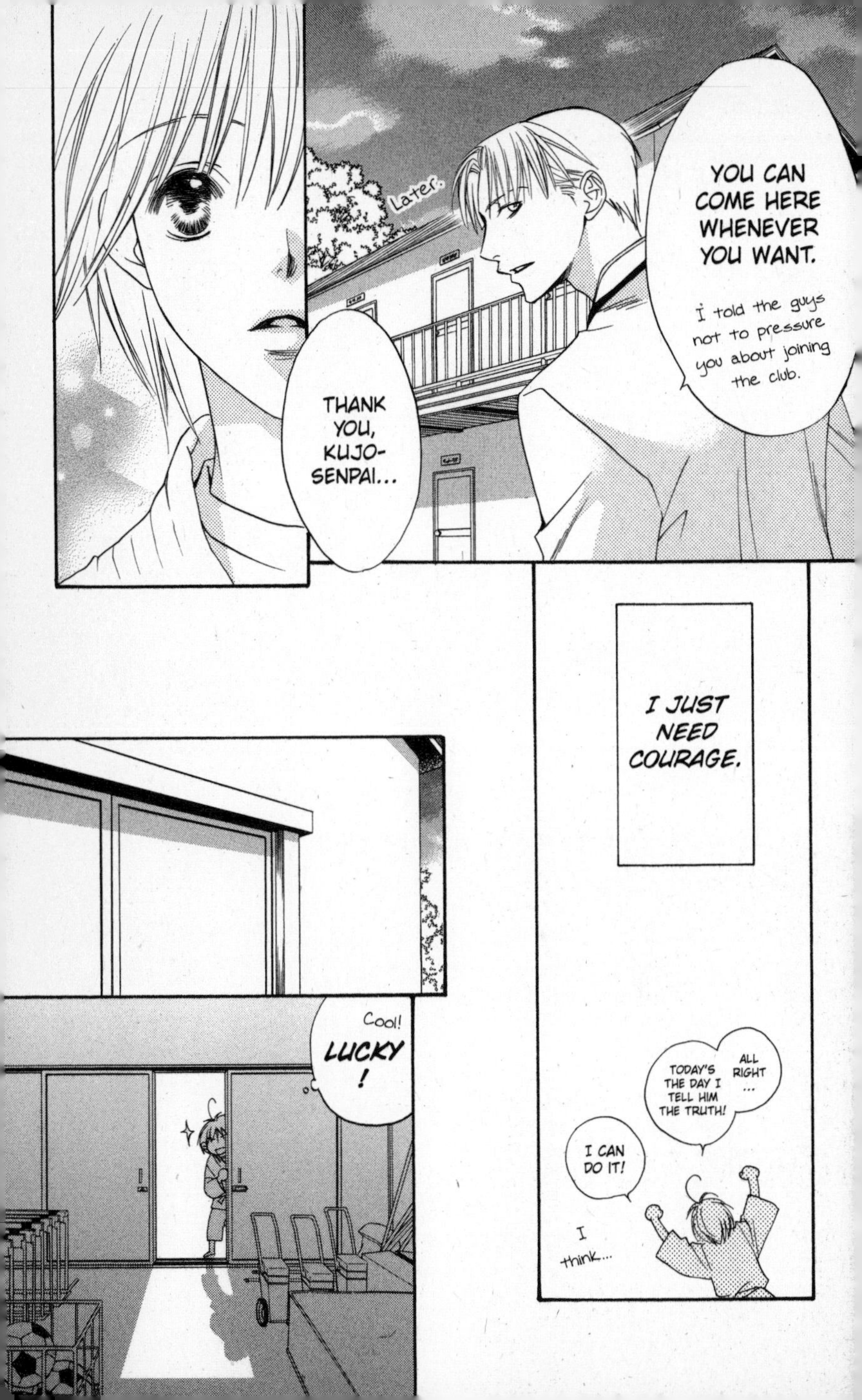
YOU CAN COME HERE WHENEVER YOU WANT.
I told the guys not to pressure you about joining the club.
Later.
THANK YOU, KUJO-SENPAI...
I JUST NEED COURAGE.
ALL RIGHT...
TODAY'S THE DAY I TELL HIM THE TRUTH!
I CAN DO IT!
I think...
Cool!
LUCKY!

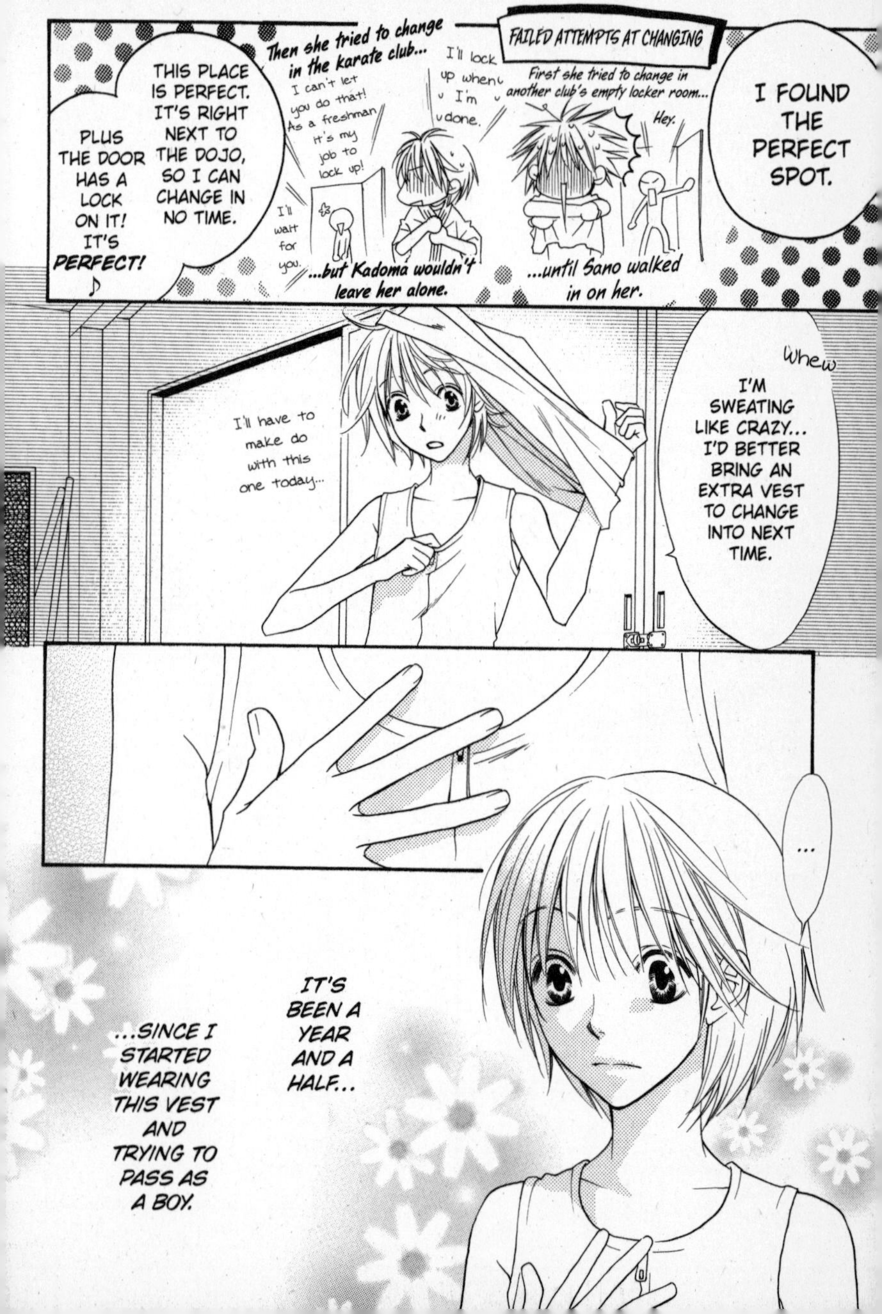
I FOUND THE PERFECT SPOT.
FAILED ATTEMPTS AT CHANGING
First she tried to change in another club's empty locker room...
Hey.
...until Sano walked in on her.
Then she tried to change in the karate club...
I'll lock up when I'm done.
I can't let you do that! As a freshman it's my job to lock up!
I'll wait for you.
...but Kadoma wouldn't leave her alone.
THIS PLACE IS PERFECT. IT'S RIGHT NEXT TO THE DOJO, SO I CAN CHANGE IN NO TIME.
PLUS THE DOOR HAS A LOCK ON IT! IT'S PERFECT! ♪
Whew
I'M SWEATING LIKE CRAZY... I'D BETTER BRING AN EXTRA VEST TO CHANGE INTO NEXT TIME.
I'll have to make do with this one today...
...
IT'S BEEN A YEAR AND A HALF...
...SINCE I STARTED WEARING THIS VEST AND TRYING TO PASS AS A BOY.

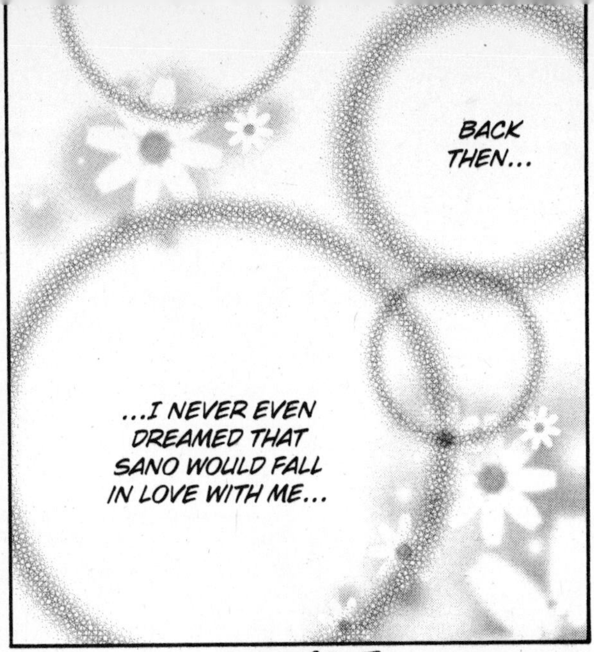
BACK THEN...
...I NEVER EVEN DREAMED THAT SANO WOULD FALL IN LOVE WITH ME...

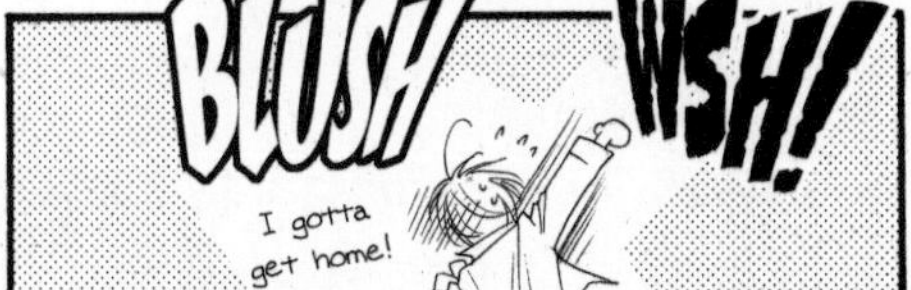
WSH!
BLUSH
I gotta get home!

*SIGN=OSAKA HIGH SCHOOL DORMS

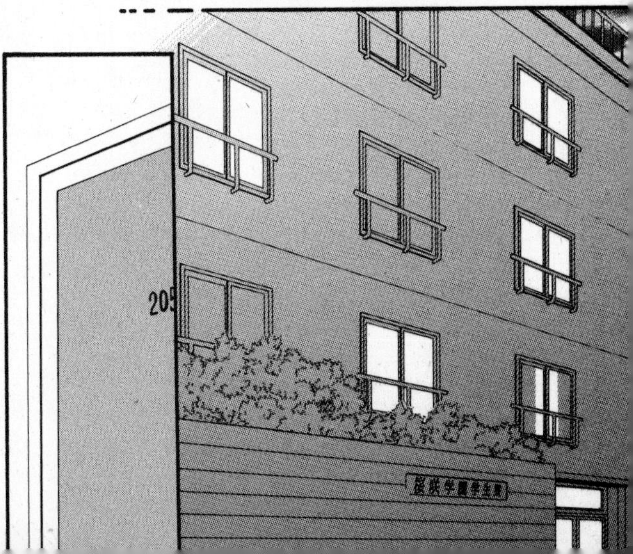
205

22

GREETINGS

Thanks for reading. This is Hana-Kimi volume 22. Waagh! In the last volume, I remember writing "There's gonna be more romance in book 22." So, what did you guys think? Did I keep my promise? I'll let you guys be the judge of that. (I'm not much of a judge.)

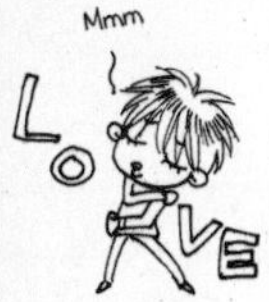
Mmm
LOVE

22

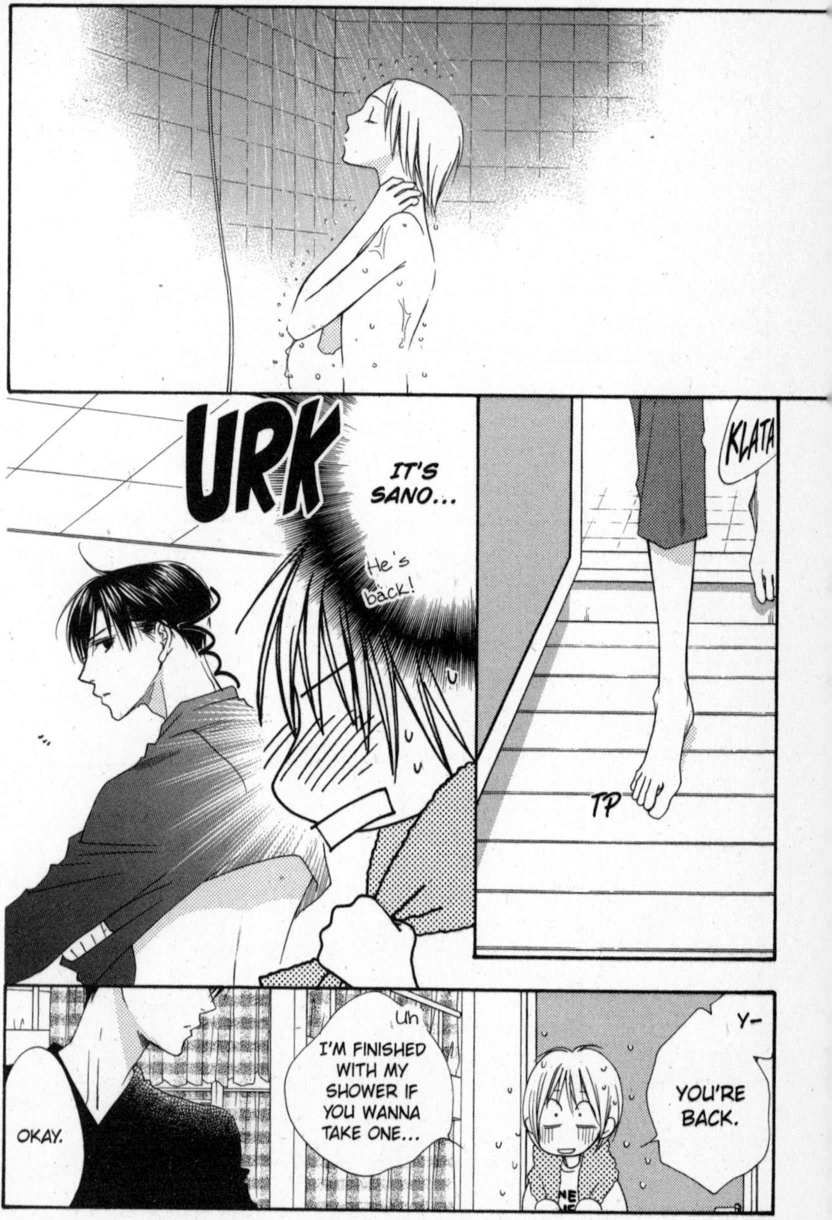
KLATA
TP
URK
IT'S SANO...
He's back!
...
Y-
YOU'RE BACK.
Uh
I'M FINISHED WITH MY SHOWER IF YOU WANNA TAKE ONE...
OKAY.

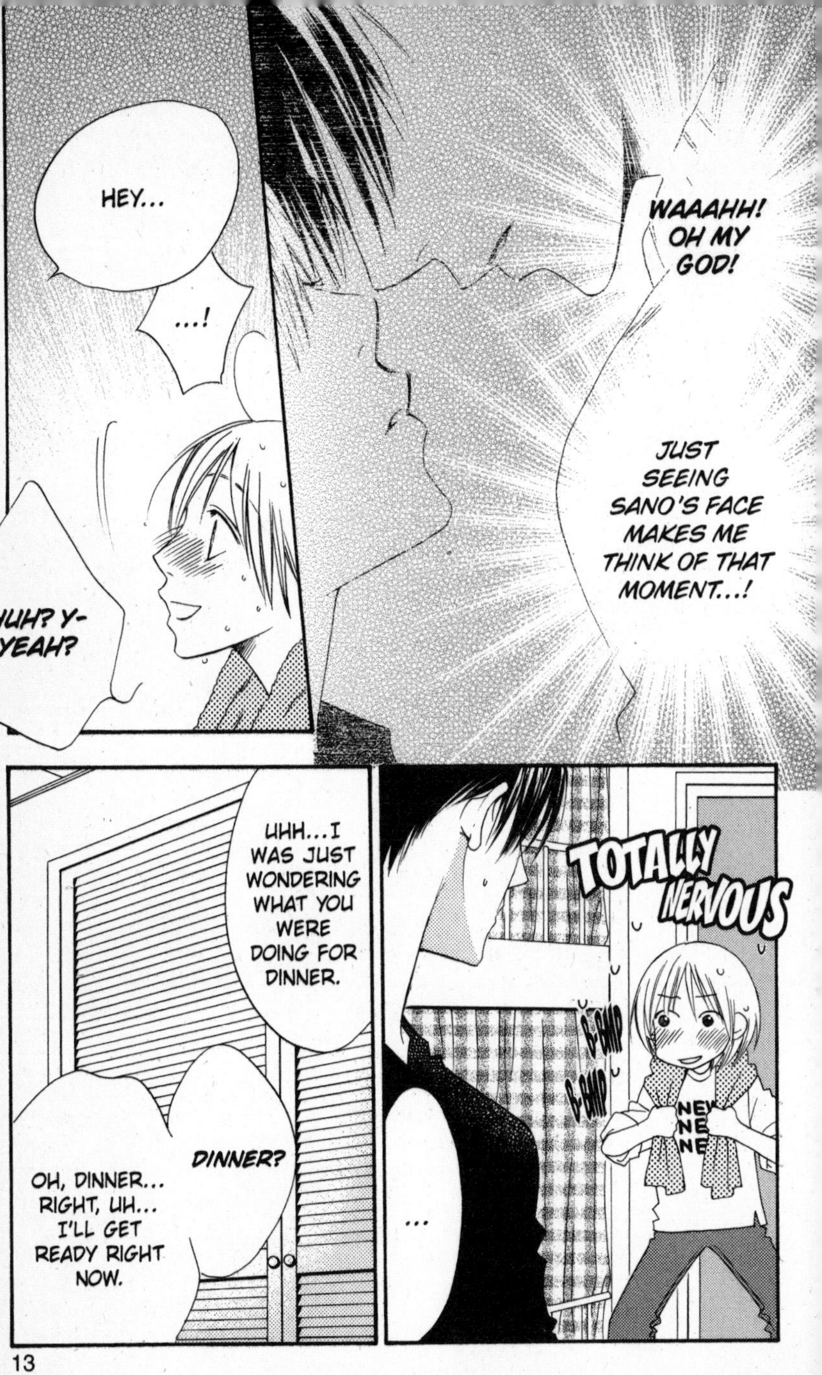
WAAAHH! OH MY GOD!
JUST SEEING SANO'S FACE MAKES ME THINK OF THAT MOMENT...!
HEY...
...!
HUH? Y-YEAH?
TOTALLY NERVOUS
B-BMP
B-BMP
...
UHH...I WAS JUST WONDERING WHAT YOU WERE DOING FOR DINNER.
DINNER?
OH, DINNER... RIGHT, UH... I'LL GET READY RIGHT NOW.

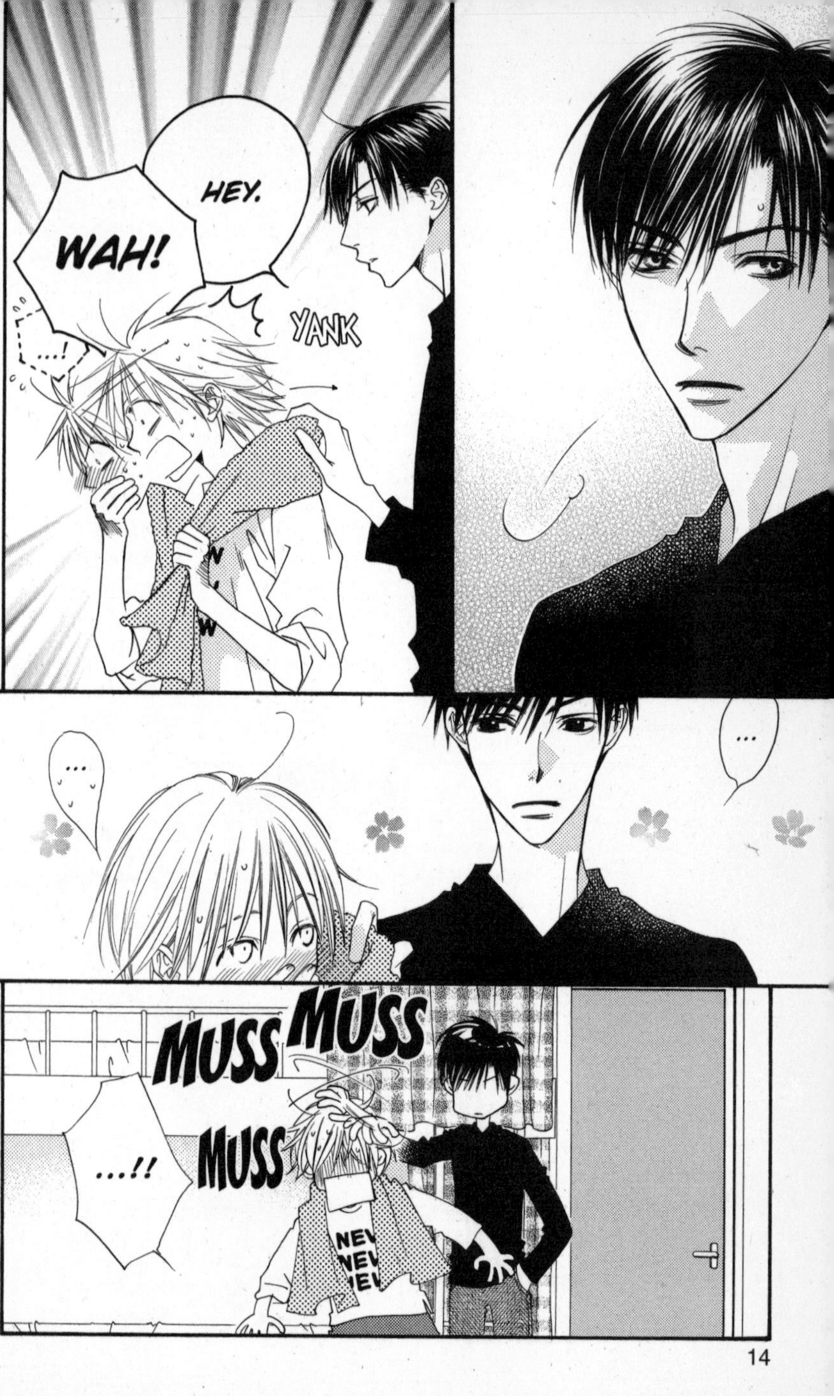

HEY.
WAH!
YANK
...!
...
...
MUSS
MUSS
MUSS
...!!

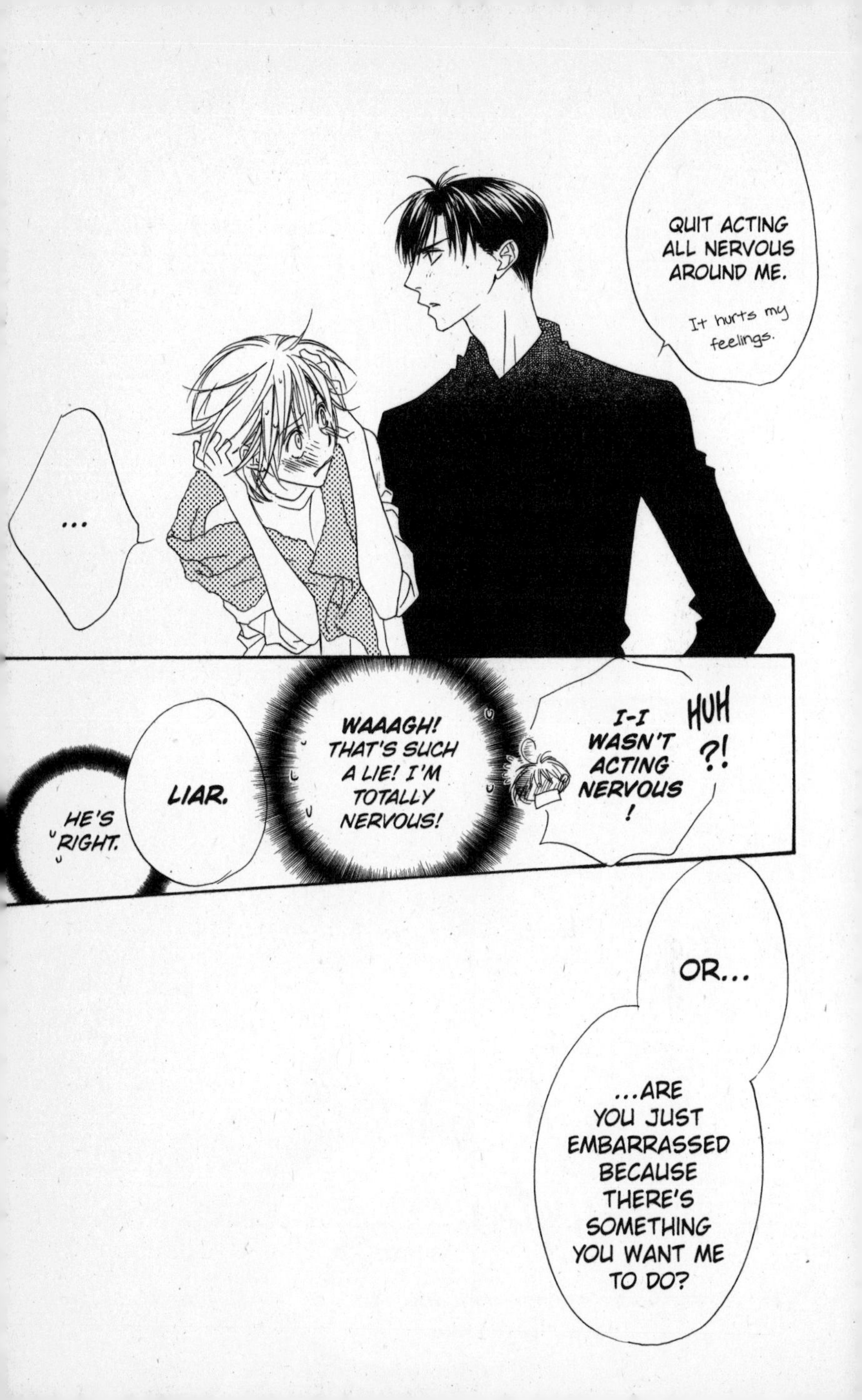
QUIT ACTING ALL NERVOUS AROUND ME.
It hurts my feelings.
...
HUH ?!
I-I WASN'T ACTING NERVOUS!
WAAAGH! THAT'S SUCH A LIE! I'M TOTALLY NERVOUS!
LIAR.
HE'S RIGHT.
OR...
...ARE YOU JUST EMBARRASSED BECAUSE THERE'S SOMETHING YOU WANT ME TO DO?

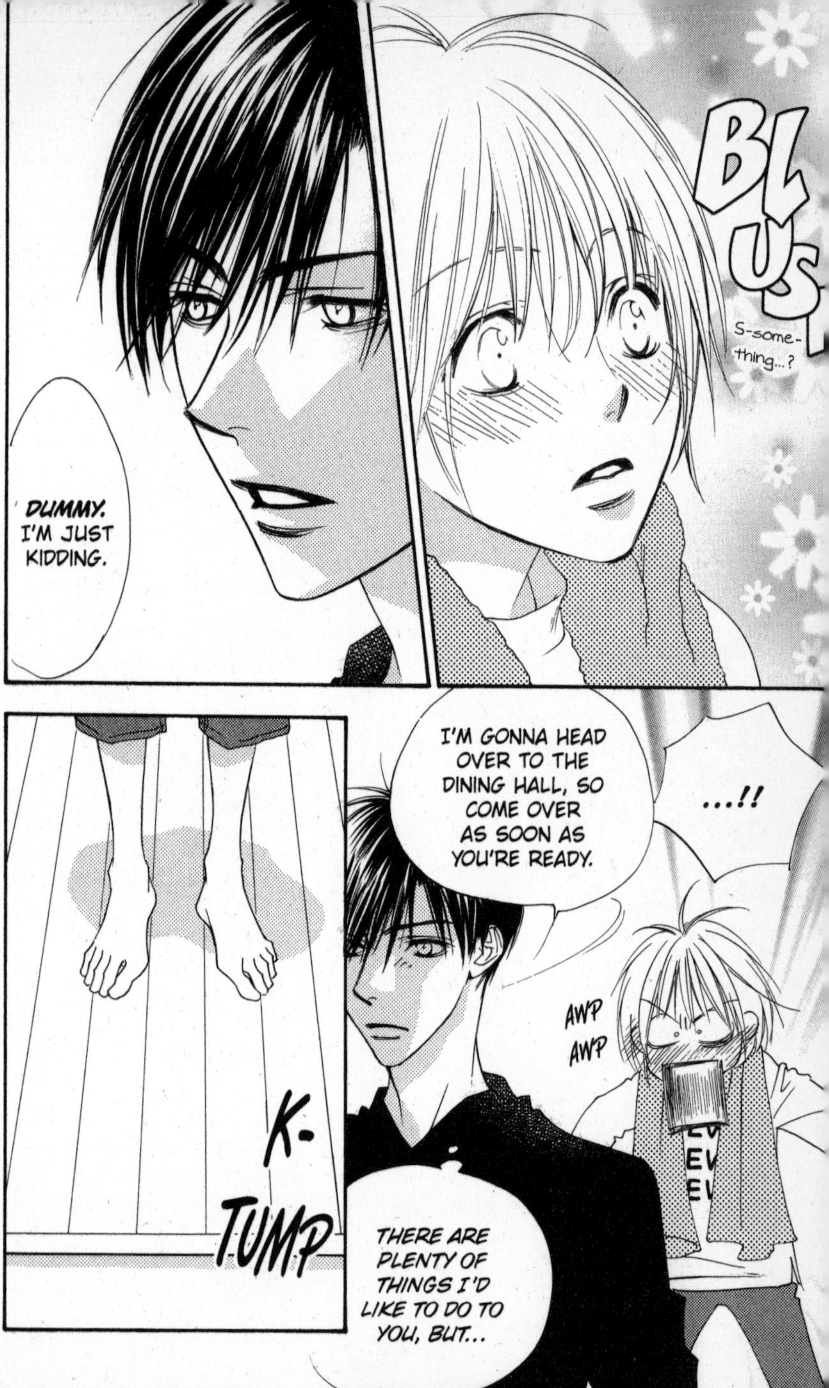
BLUSH
S-some-thing...?
DUMMY. I'M JUST KIDDING.
...!!
I'M GONNA HEAD OVER TO THE DINING HALL, SO COME OVER AS SOON AS YOU'RE READY.
AWP AWP
THERE ARE PLENTY OF THINGS I'D LIKE TO DO TO YOU, BUT...
K-TUMP

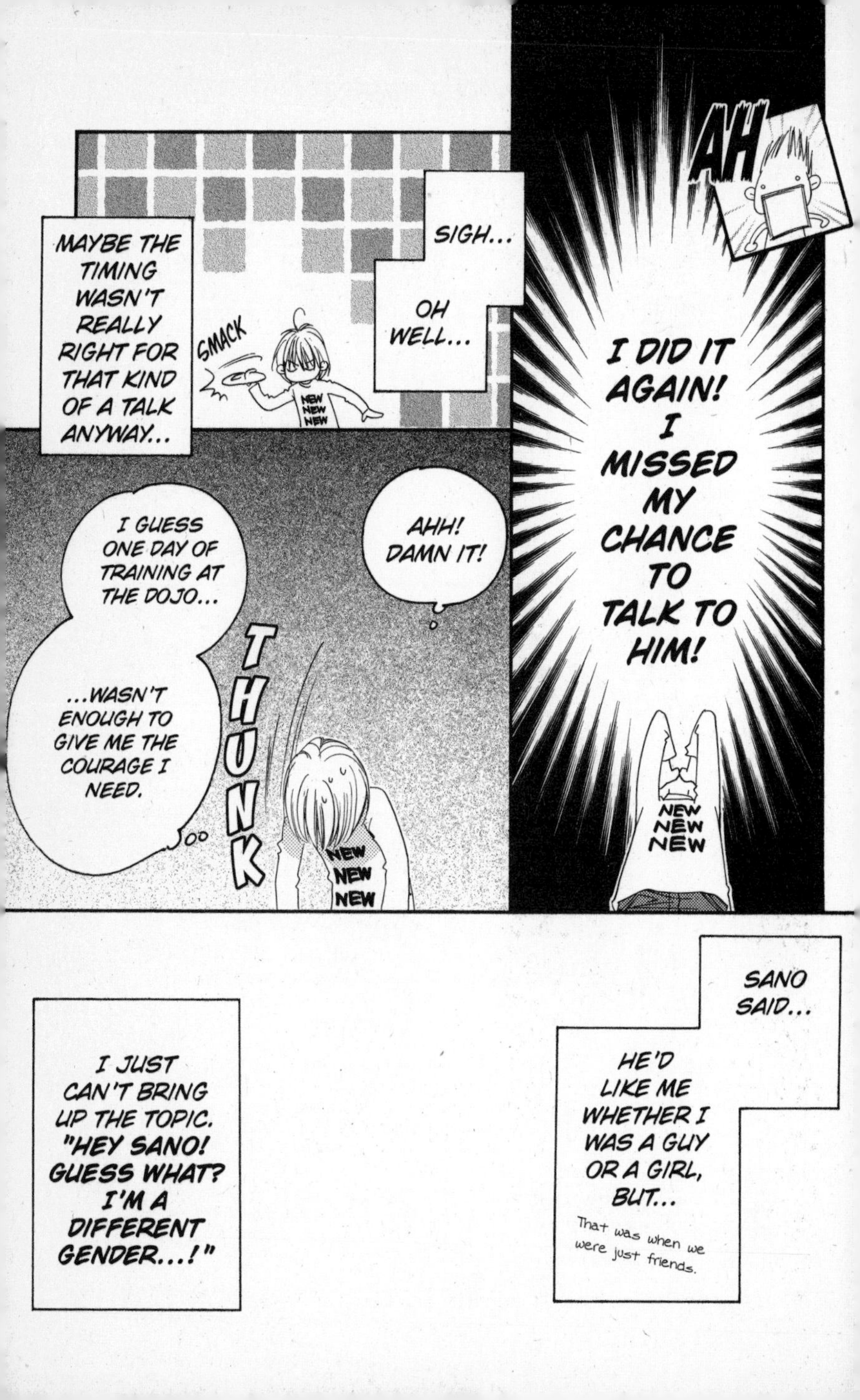
AH
I DID IT AGAIN! I MISSED MY CHANCE TO TALK TO HIM!
NEW NEW NEW
SIGH...
OH WELL...
MAYBE THE TIMING WASN'T REALLY RIGHT FOR THAT KIND OF A TALK ANYWAY...
SMACK
NEW NEW NEW
AHH! DAMN IT!
I GUESS ONE DAY OF TRAINING AT THE DOJO...
...WASN'T ENOUGH TO GIVE ME THE COURAGE I NEED.
THUNK
NEW NEW NEW
SANO SAID...
HE'D LIKE ME WHETHER I WAS A GUY OR A GIRL, BUT...
That was when we were just friends.
I JUST CAN'T BRING UP THE TOPIC. "HEY SANO! GUESS WHAT? I'M A DIFFERENT GENDER...!"

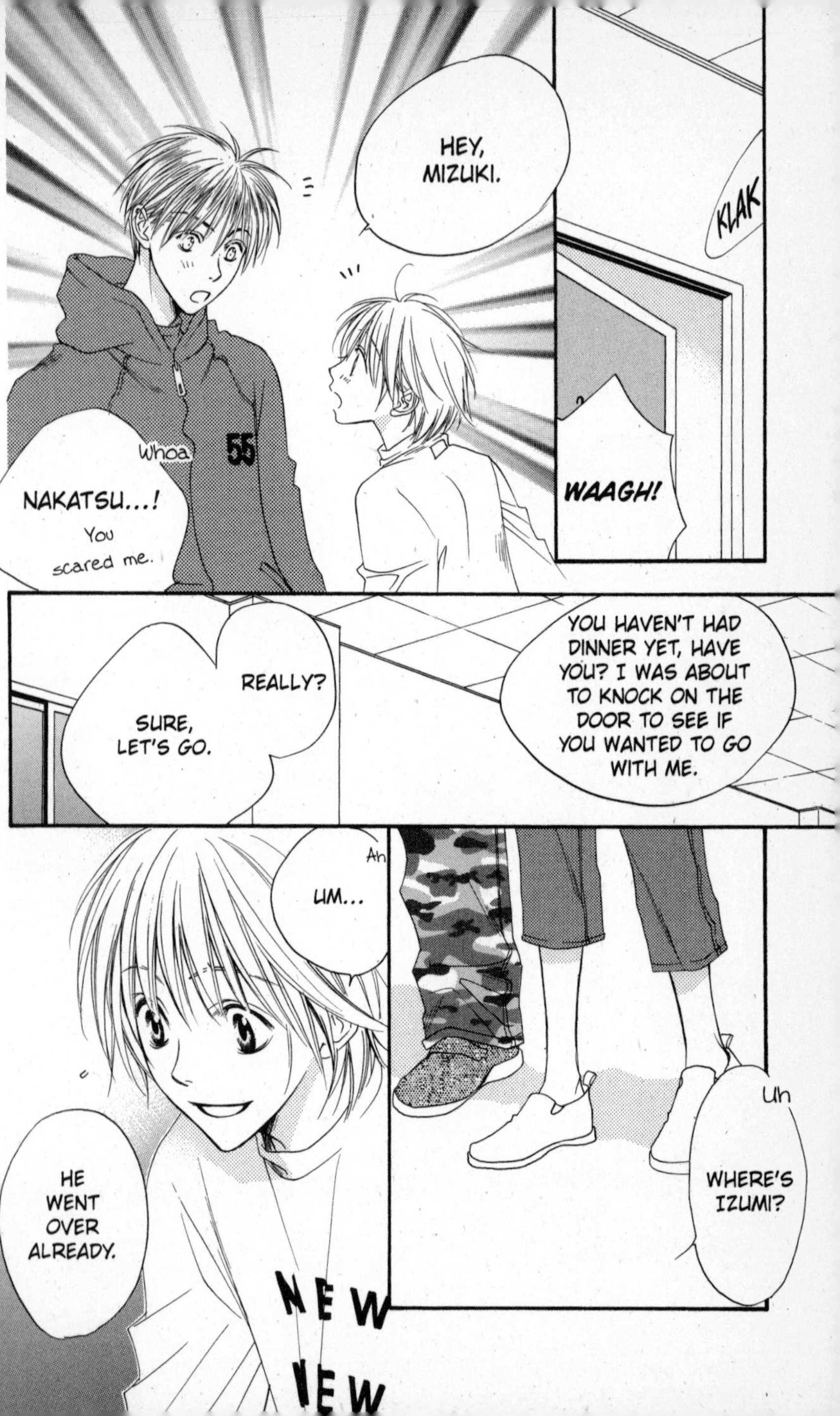
KLAK
WAAGH!
HEY, MIZUKI.
Whoa
NAKATSU...! You scared me.
YOU HAVEN'T HAD DINNER YET, HAVE YOU? I WAS ABOUT TO KNOCK ON THE DOOR TO SEE IF YOU WANTED TO GO WITH ME.
REALLY? SURE, LET'S GO.
Uh
WHERE'S IZUMI?
An
UM...
HE WENT OVER ALREADY.
NEW
NEW

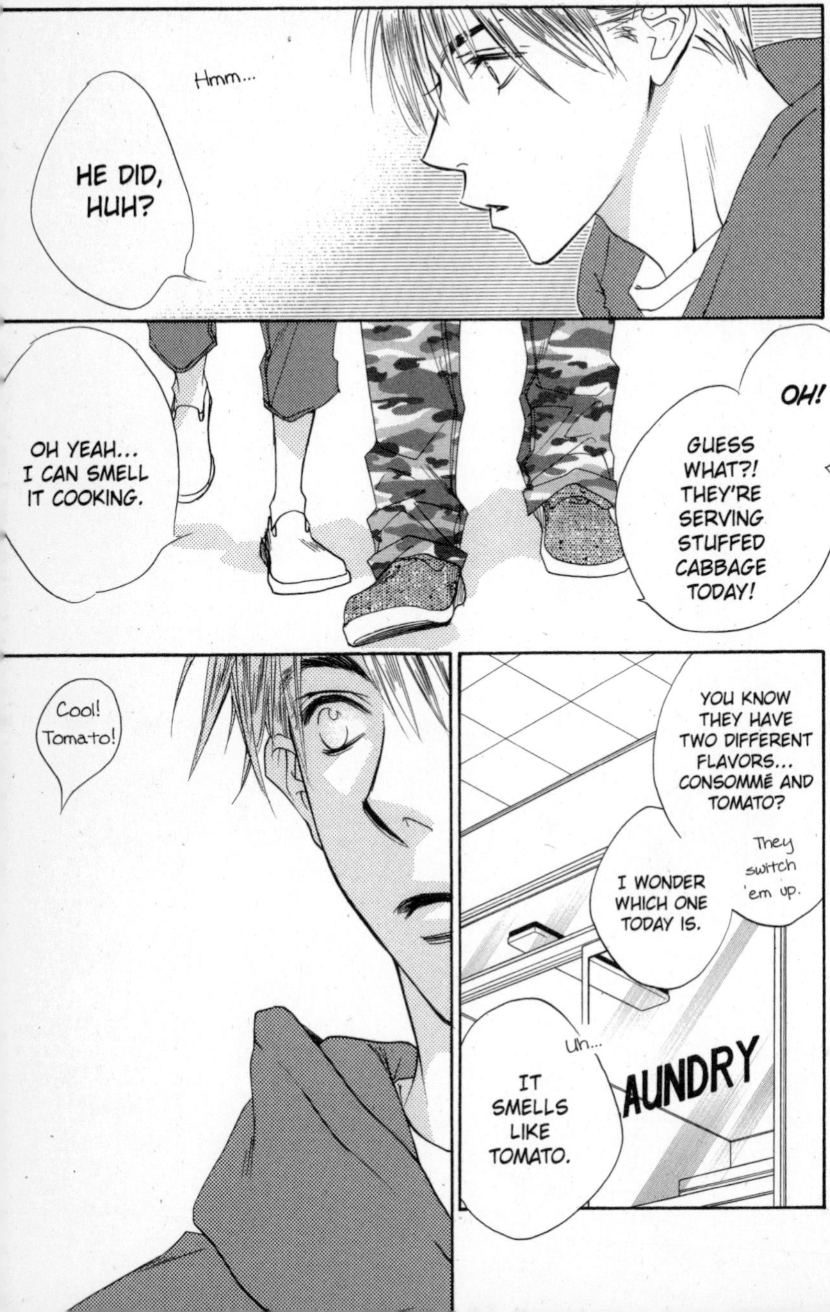
Hmm...
HE DID, HUH?
OH! GUESS WHAT?! THEY'RE SERVING STUFFED CABBAGE TODAY!
OH YEAH... I CAN SMELL IT COOKING.
YOU KNOW THEY HAVE TWO DIFFERENT FLAVORS... CONSOMMÉ AND TOMATO?
They switch 'em up.
I WONDER WHICH ONE TODAY IS.
Uh...
AUNDRY
IT SMELLS LIKE TOMATO.
Cool! Tomato!

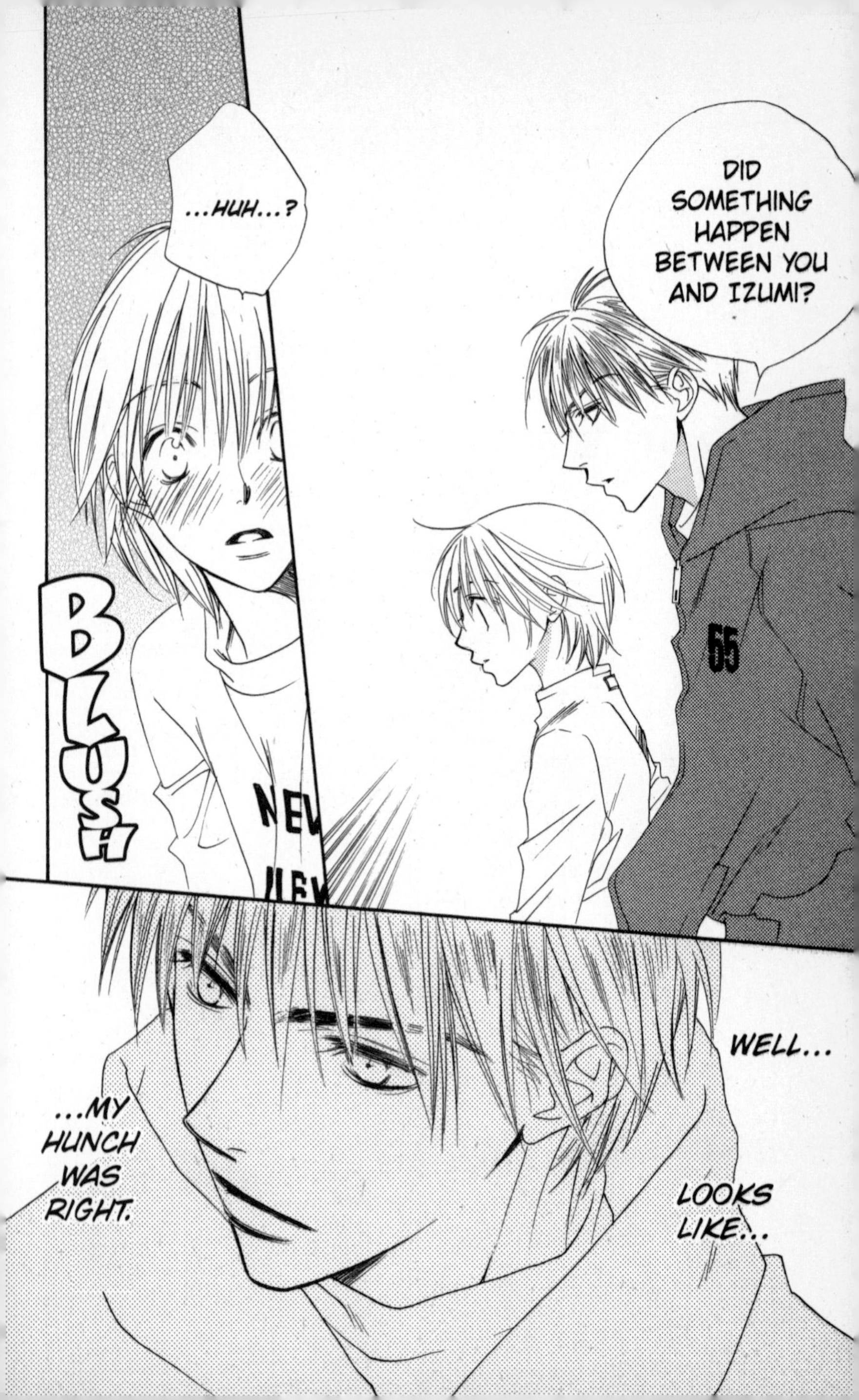
DID SOMETHING HAPPEN BETWEEN YOU AND IZUMI?
55
...HUH...?
BLUSH
WELL...
LOOKS LIKE...
...MY HUNCH WAS RIGHT.

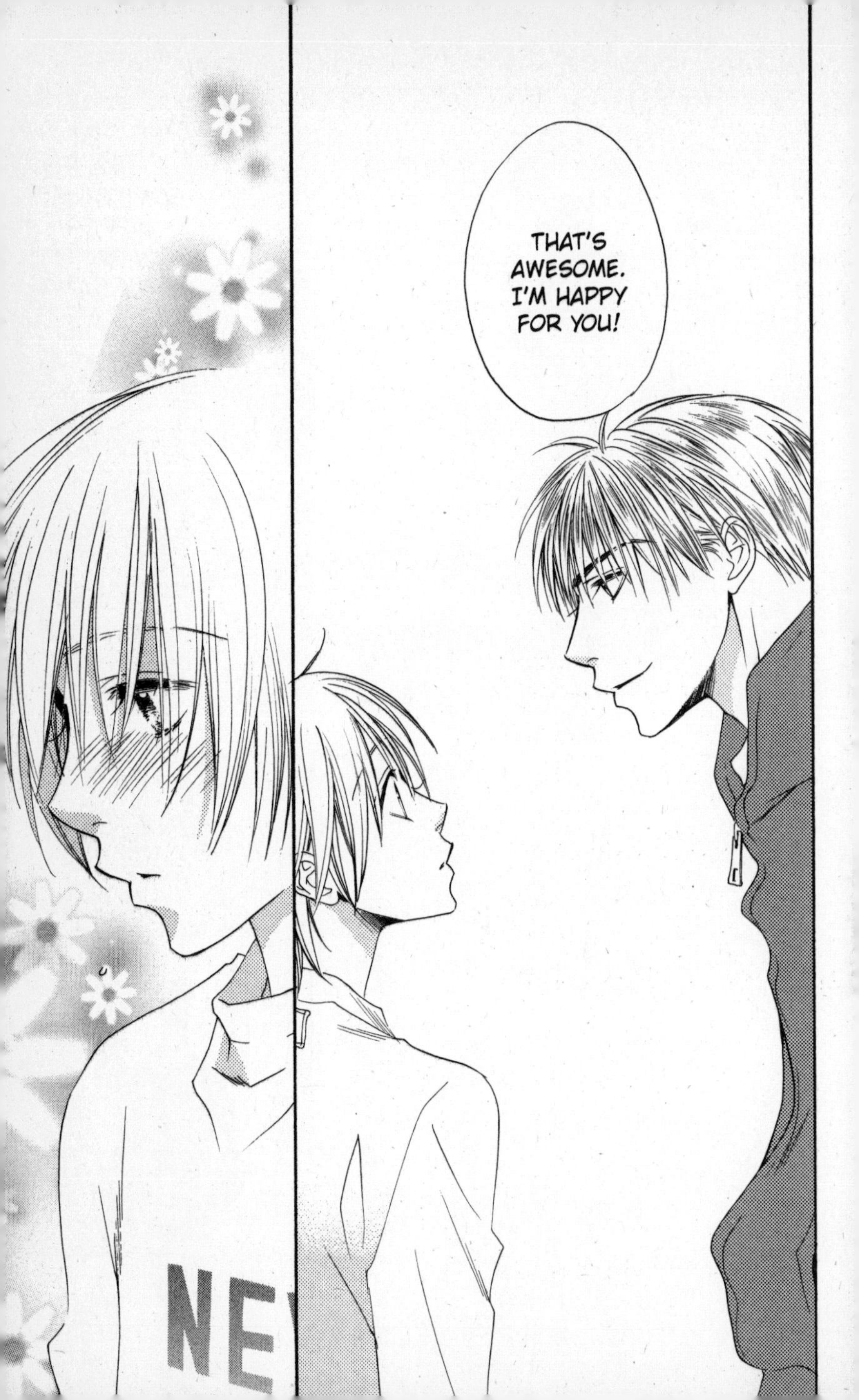
THAT'S AWESOME. I'M HAPPY FOR YOU!
NE

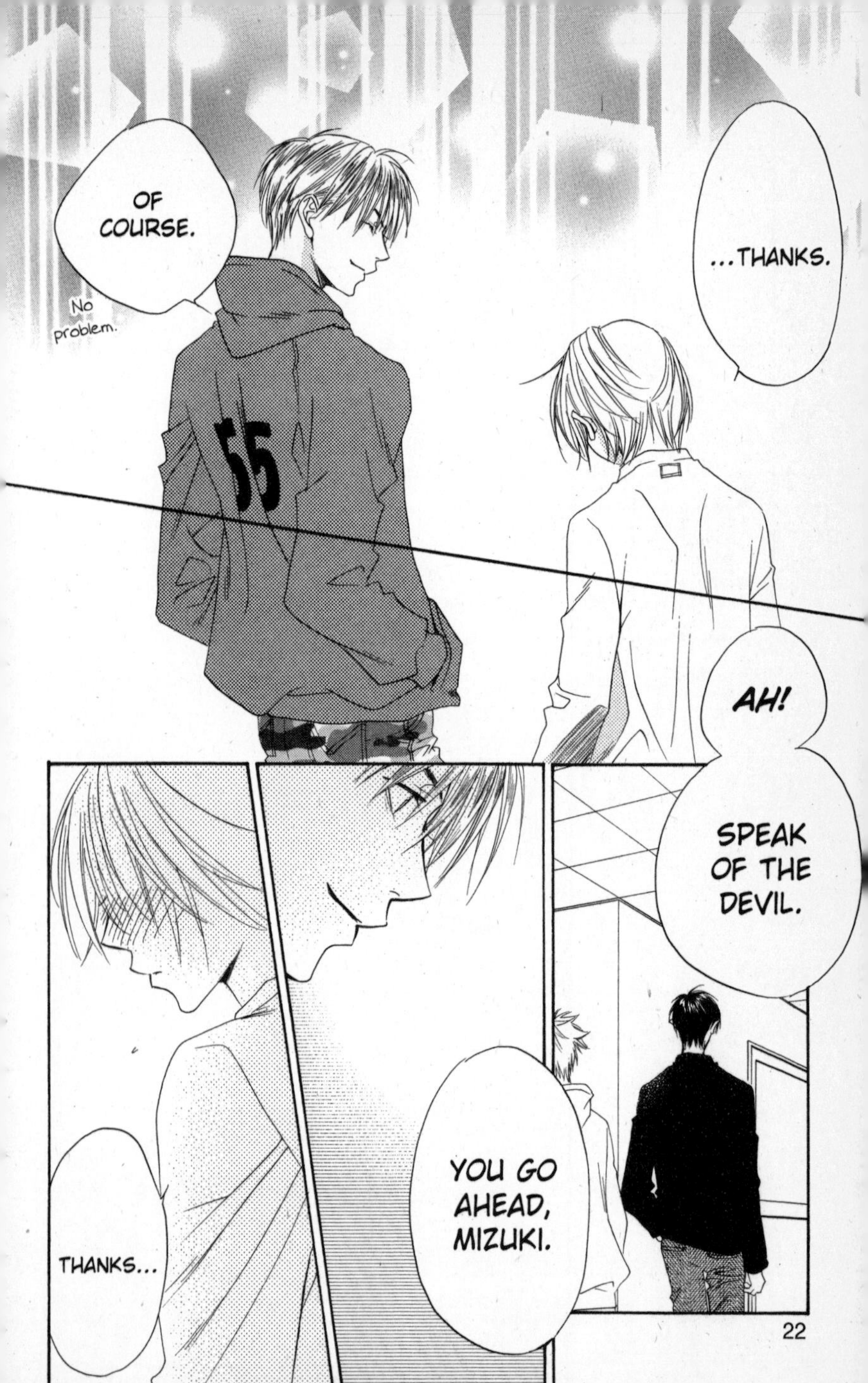
...THANKS.
OF COURSE.
No problem.
AH!
SPEAK OF THE DEVIL.
YOU GO AHEAD, MIZUKI.
THANKS...

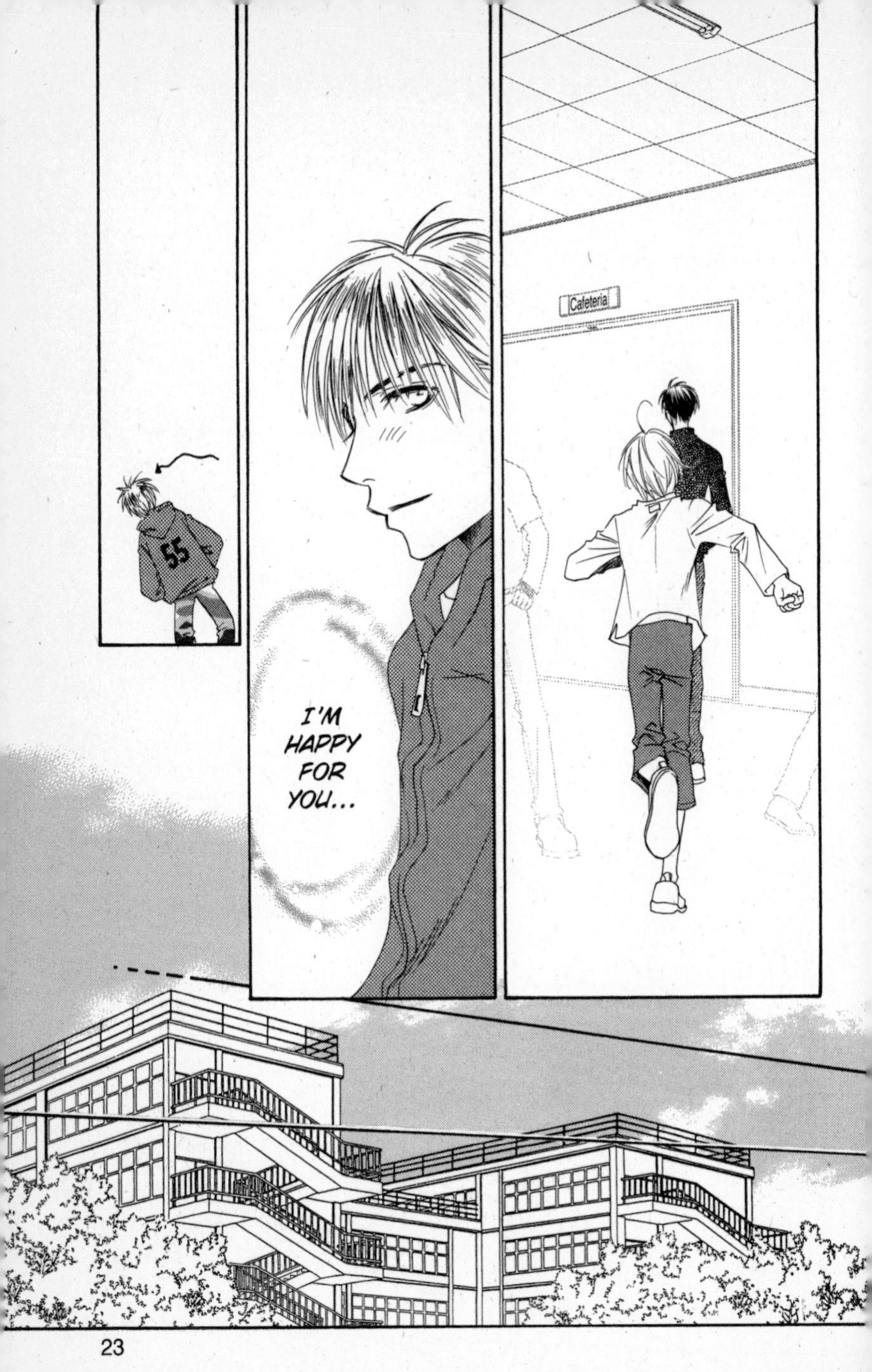
Cafeteria
I'M HAPPY FOR YOU...

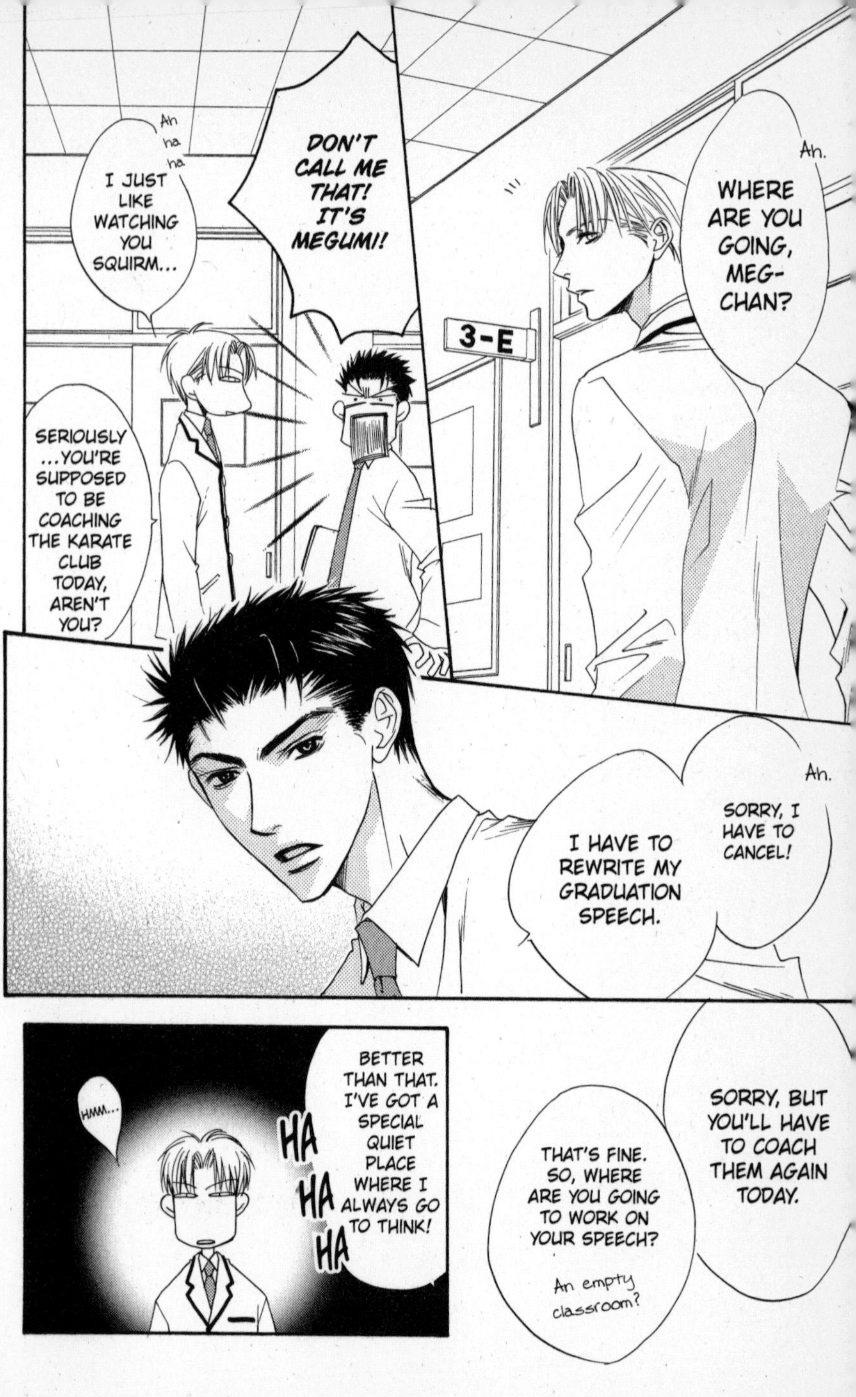
Ah.
WHERE ARE YOU GOING, MEG-CHAN?
DON'T CALL ME THAT! IT'S MEGUMI!
Ah ha ha
I JUST LIKE WATCHING YOU SQUIRM...
SERIOUSLY ...YOU'RE SUPPOSED TO BE COACHING THE KARATE CLUB TODAY, AREN'T YOU?
Ah.
SORRY, I HAVE TO CANCEL!
I HAVE TO REWRITE MY GRADUATION SPEECH.
SORRY, BUT YOU'LL HAVE TO COACH THEM AGAIN TODAY.
THAT'S FINE. SO, WHERE ARE YOU GOING TO WORK ON YOUR SPEECH?
An empty classroom?
BETTER THAN THAT. I'VE GOT A SPECIAL QUIET PLACE WHERE I ALWAYS GO TO THINK!
HA HA HA
HMM...

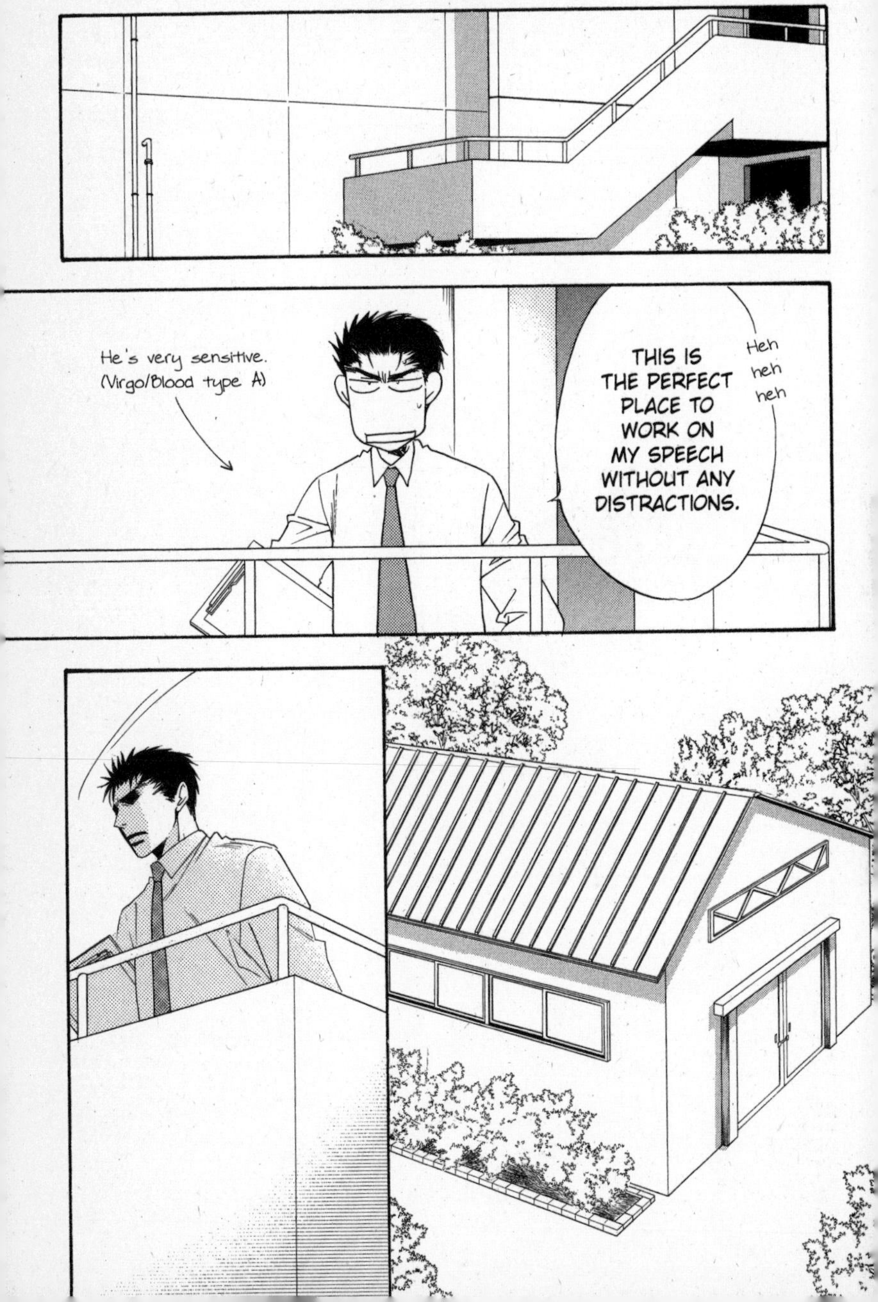
THIS IS THE PERFECT PLACE TO WORK ON MY SPEECH WITHOUT ANY DISTRACTIONS.
Heh heh heh
He's very sensitive. (Virgo/Blood type A)

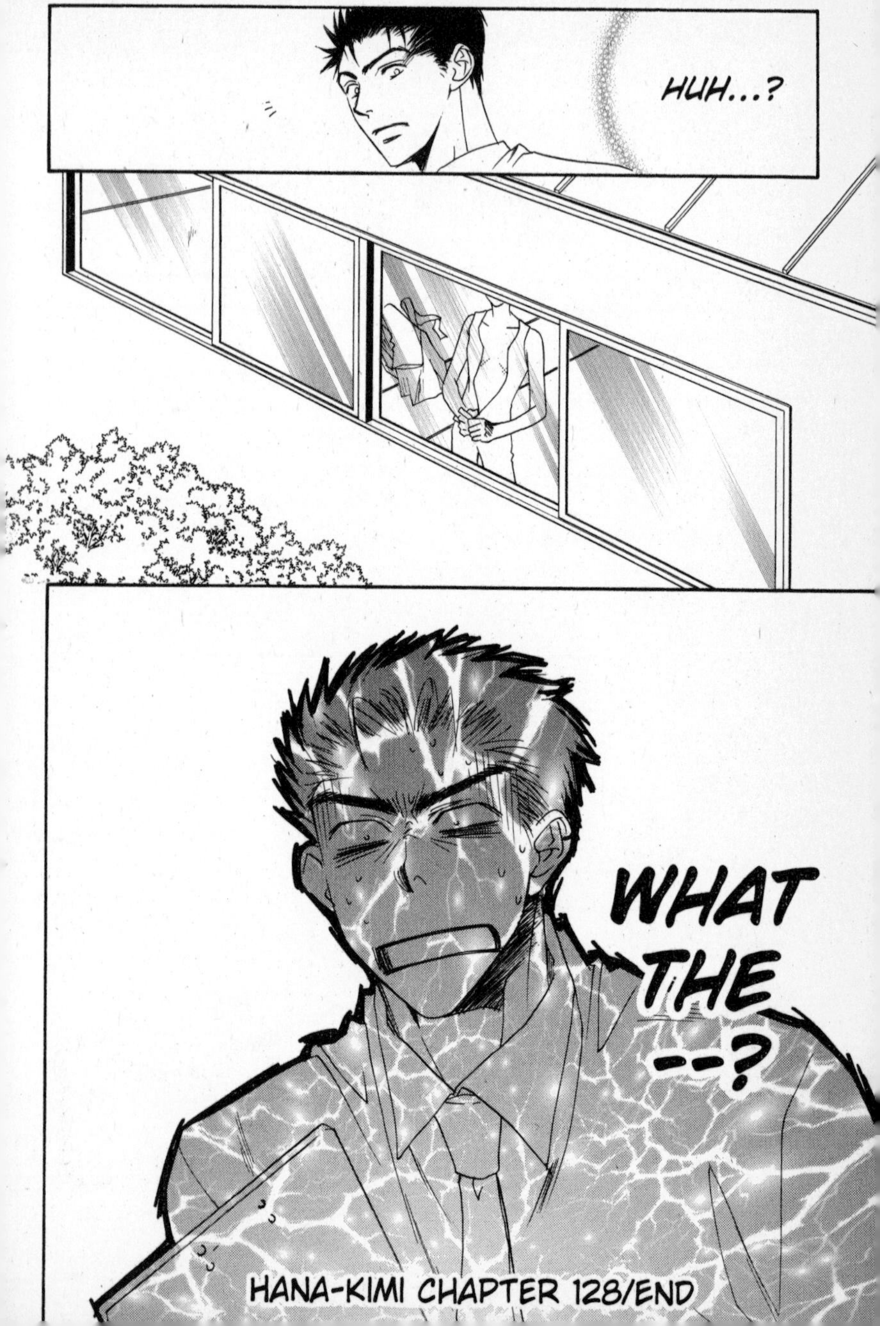
HUH...?
WHAT THE --?
HANA-KIMI CHAPTER 128/END

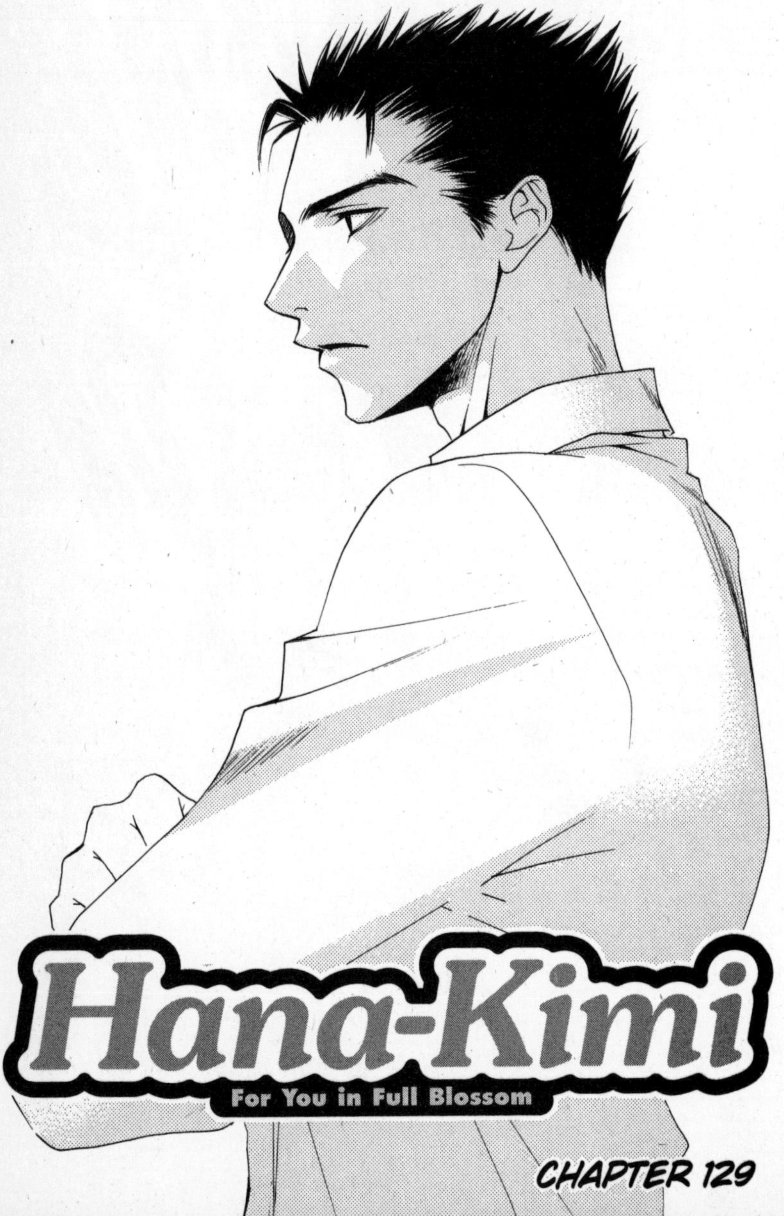
Hana-Kimi
For You in Full Blossom
CHAPTER 129

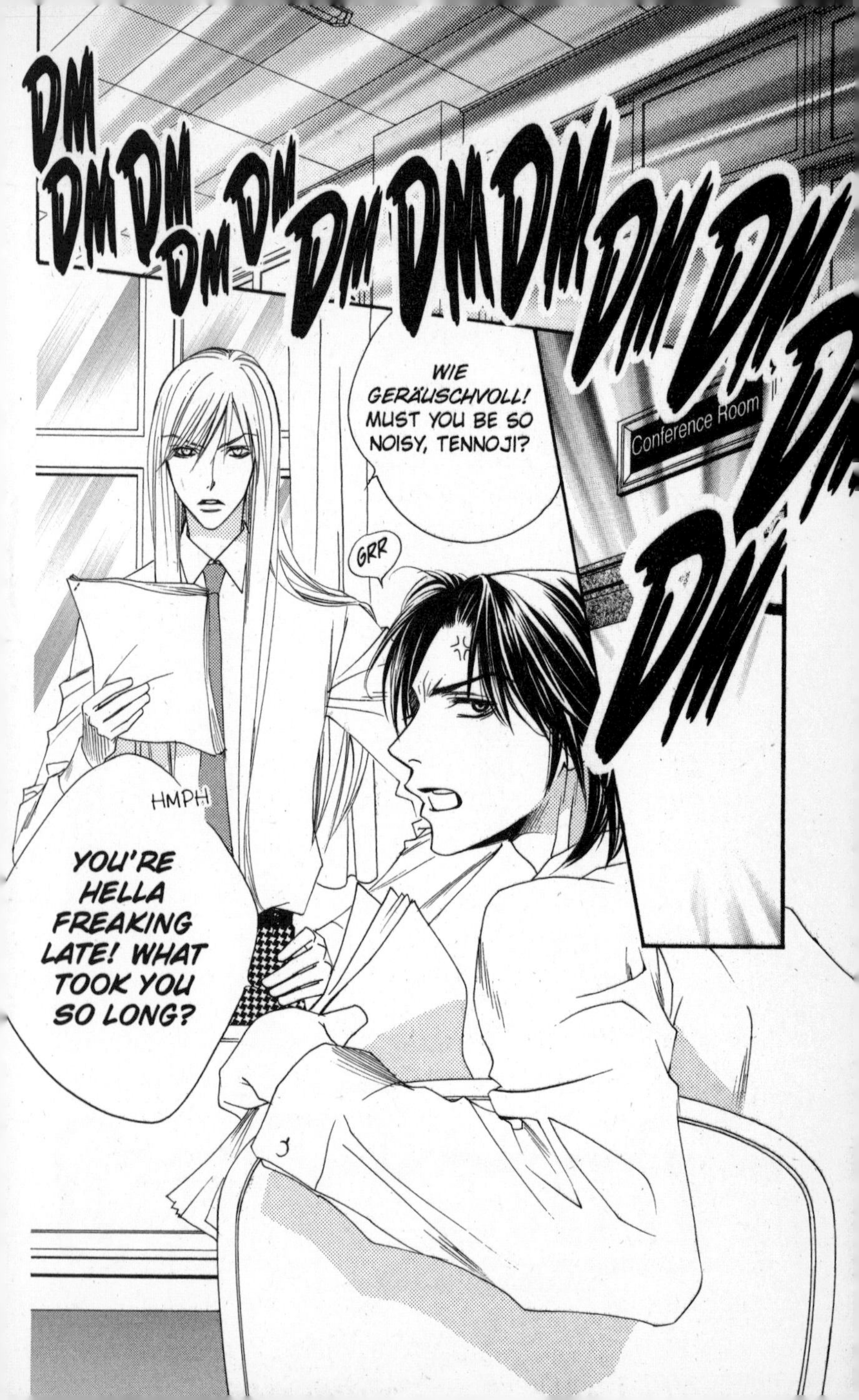
DM DM DM DM DM DM DM DM DM DM DM DM DM
Conference Room
WIE GERÄUSCHVOLL! MUST YOU BE SO NOISY, TENNOJI?
GRR
HMPH
YOU'RE HELLA FREAKING LATE! WHAT TOOK YOU SO LONG?

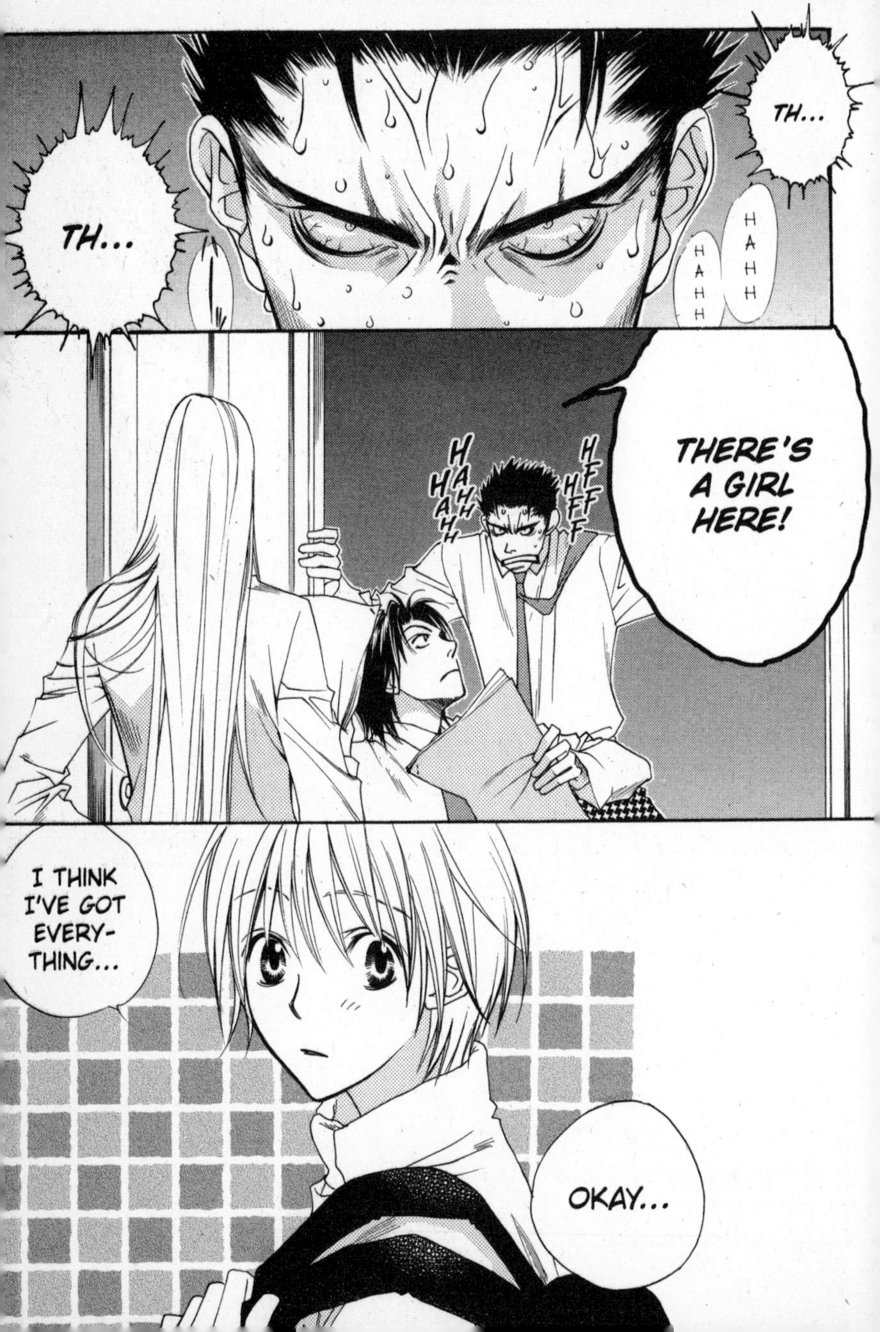
TH...
HAHH
HAHH
TH...
THERE'S A GIRL HERE!
HFF HFF
HAHH HAHH
I THINK I'VE GOT EVERY-THING...
OKAY...

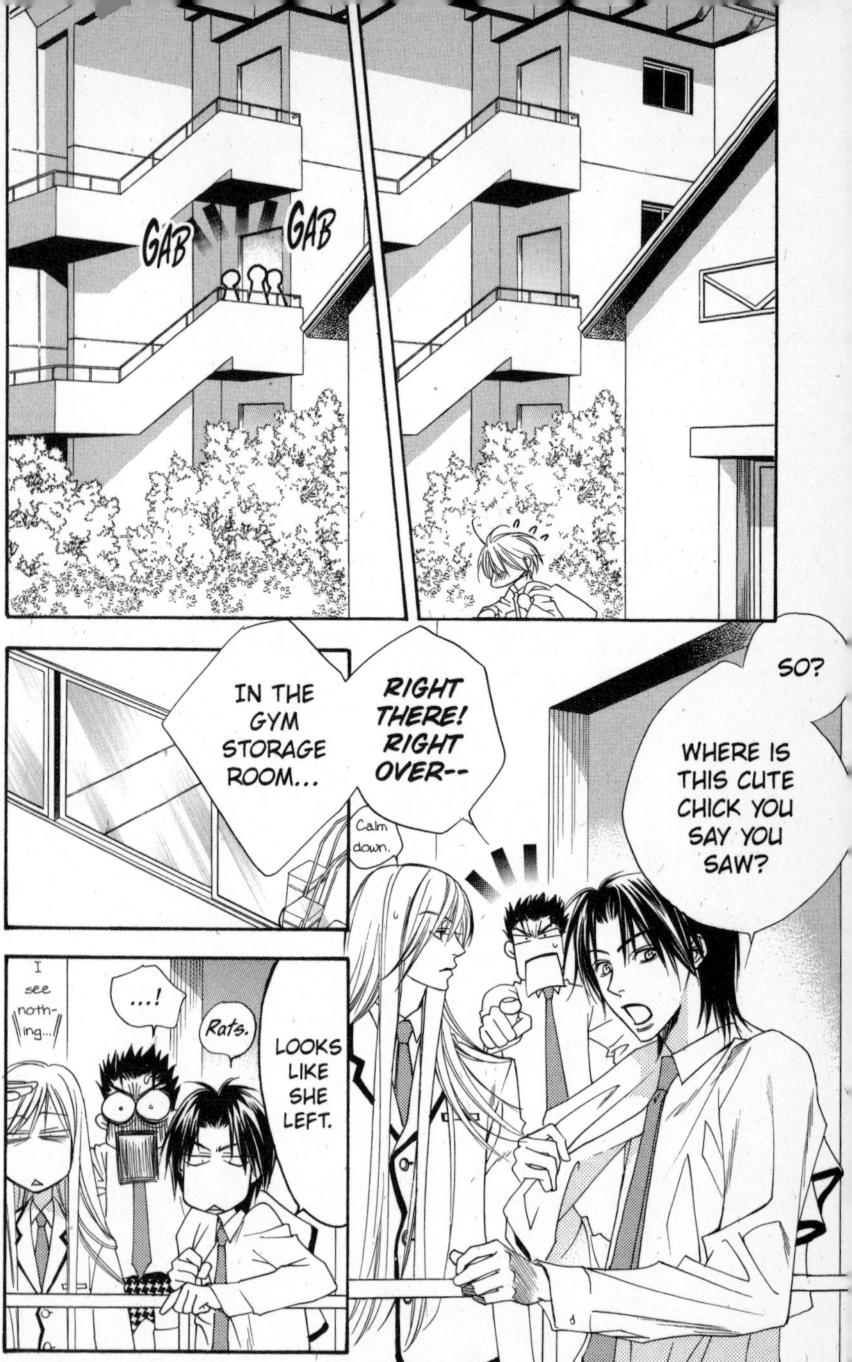
GAB GAB
SO?
WHERE IS THIS CUTE CHICK YOU SAY YOU SAW?
IN THE GYM STORAGE ROOM...
RIGHT THERE! RIGHT OVER--
Calm down.
LOOKS LIKE SHE LEFT.
Rats.
...!
I see nothing...

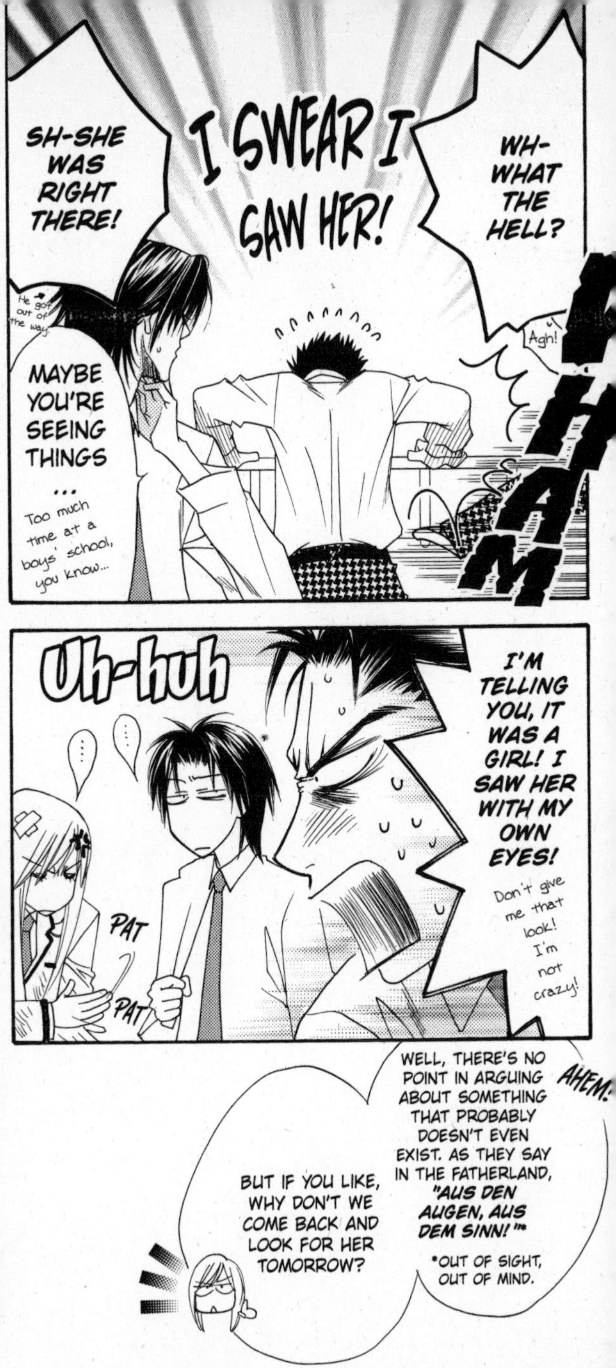
WH- WHAT THE HELL?
Agh!
I SWEAR I SAW HER!
SH-SHE WAS RIGHT THERE!
He got out of the way.
MAYBE YOU'RE SEEING THINGS...
Too much time at a boys' school, you know...
I'M TELLING YOU, IT WAS A GIRL! I SAW HER WITH MY OWN EYES!
Don't give me that look! I'm not crazy!
Uh-huh
...
...
PAT
PAT
AHEM!
WELL, THERE'S NO POINT IN ARGUING ABOUT SOMETHING THAT PROBABLY DOESN'T EVEN EXIST. AS THEY SAY IN THE FATHERLAND, "AUS DEN AUGEN, AUS DEM SINN!"*
*OUT OF SIGHT, OUT OF MIND.
BUT IF YOU LIKE, WHY DON'T WE COME BACK AND LOOK FOR HER TOMORROW?

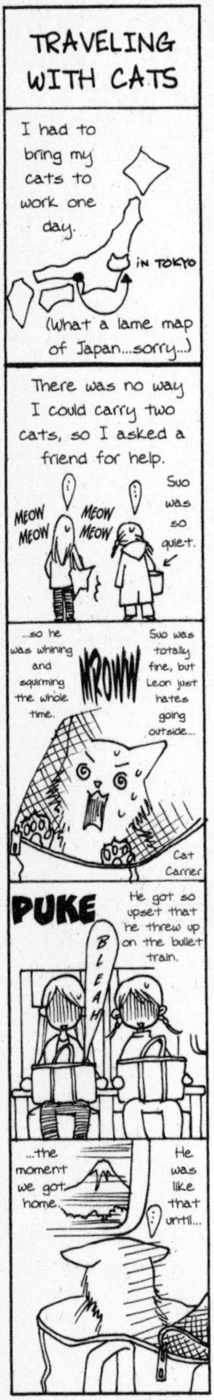
TRAVELING WITH CATS
I had to bring my cats to work one day.
IN TOKYO
(What a lame map of Japan...sorry...)
There was no way I could carry two cats, so I asked a friend for help.
MEOW MEOW
MEOW MEOW
Suo was so quiet.
Suo was totally fine, but Leon just hates going outside...
...so he was whining and squirming the whole time.
KROWW
Cat Carrier
He got so upset that he threw up on the bullet train.
PUKE
BLEAH
He was like that until...
...the moment we got home.

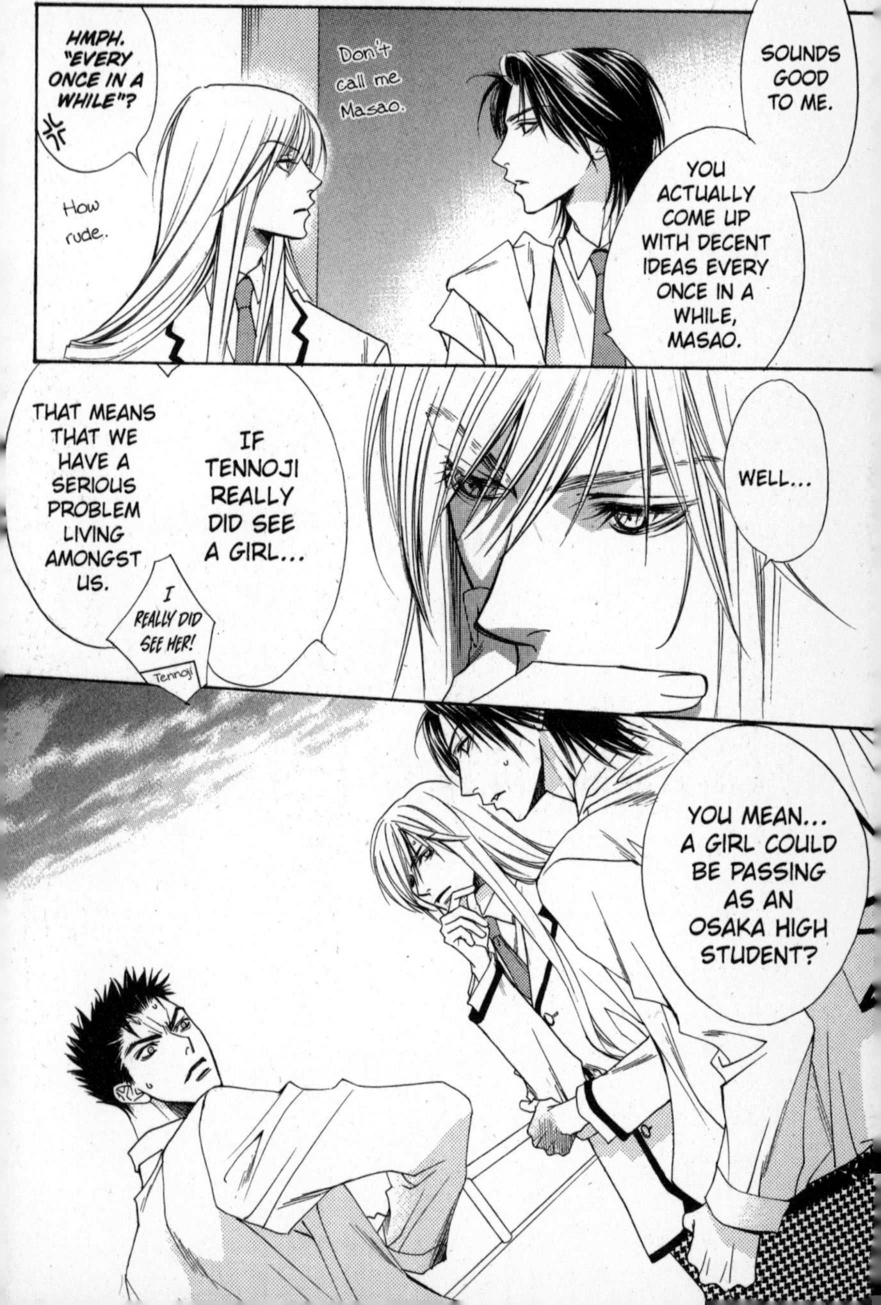
SOUNDS GOOD TO ME.
YOU ACTUALLY COME UP WITH DECENT IDEAS EVERY ONCE IN A WHILE, MASAO.
Don't call me Masao.
HMPH. "EVERY ONCE IN A WHILE"?
How rude.
WELL...
IF TENNOJI REALLY DID SEE A GIRL...
THAT MEANS THAT WE HAVE A SERIOUS PROBLEM LIVING AMONGST US.
I REALLY DID SEE HER!
Tennoji
YOU MEAN... A GIRL COULD BE PASSING AS AN OSAKA HIGH STUDENT?

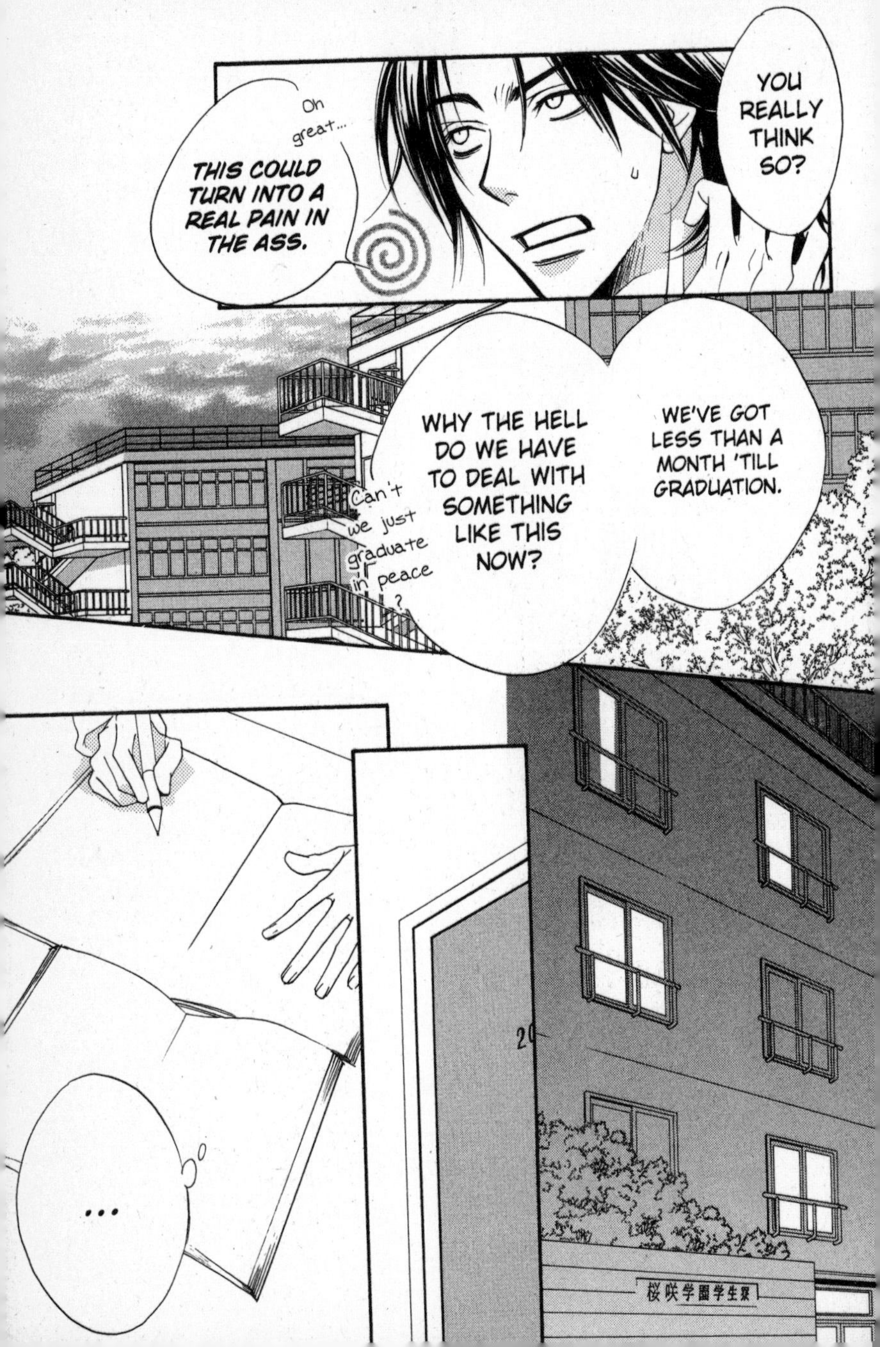
YOU REALLY THINK SO?
Oh great...
THIS COULD TURN INTO A REAL PAIN IN THE ASS.
WE'VE GOT LESS THAN A MONTH 'TILL GRADUATION.
WHY THE HELL DO WE HAVE TO DEAL WITH SOMETHING LIKE THIS NOW?
Can't we just graduate in peace?
桜咲学園学生寮
...

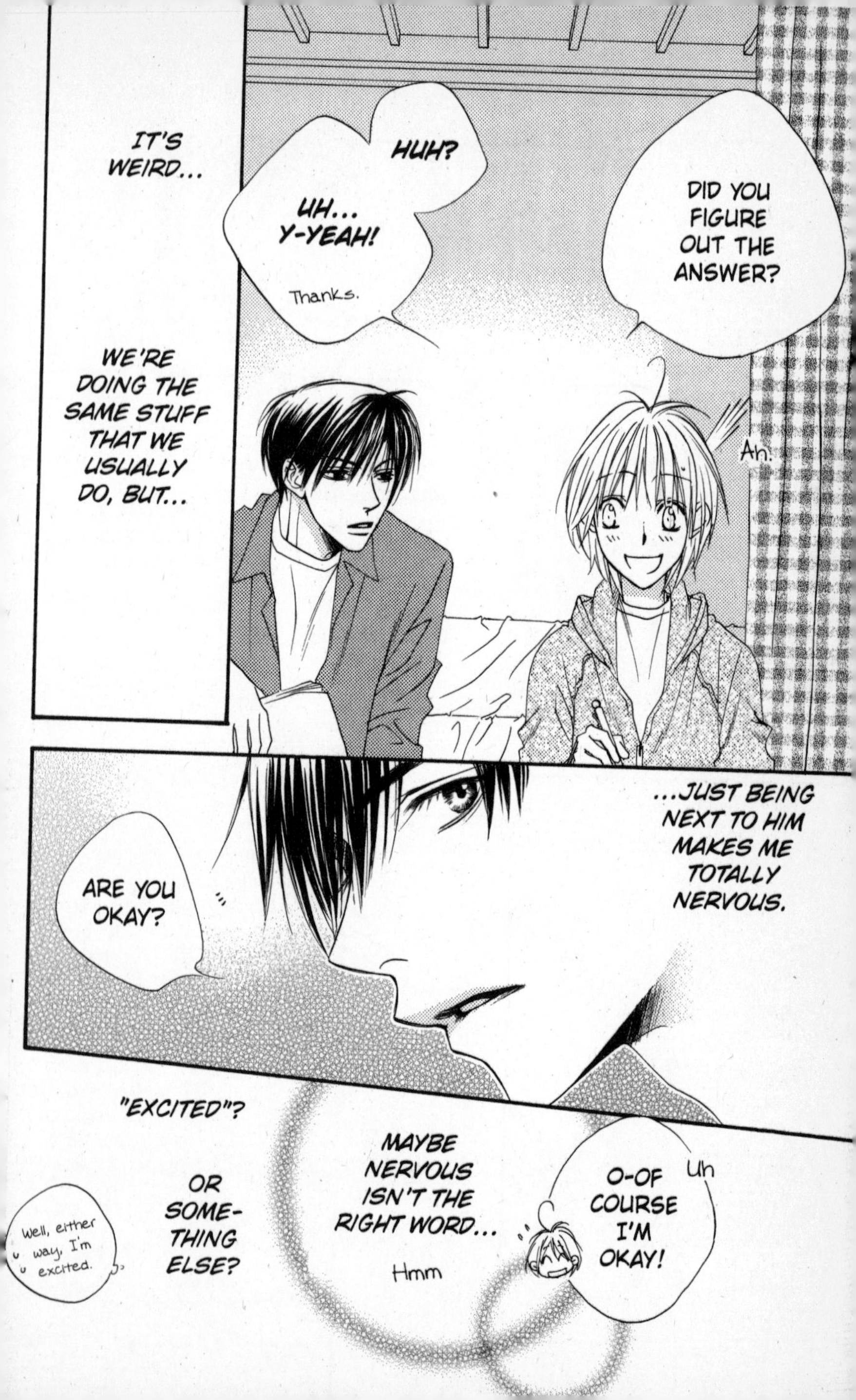
DID YOU FIGURE OUT THE ANSWER?
Ah.
HUH?
UH... Y-YEAH!
Thanks.
IT'S WEIRD...
WE'RE DOING THE SAME STUFF THAT WE USUALLY DO, BUT...
...JUST BEING NEXT TO HIM MAKES ME TOTALLY NERVOUS.
ARE YOU OKAY?
Uh
O-OF COURSE I'M OKAY!
MAYBE NERVOUS ISN'T THE RIGHT WORD...
Hmm
"EXCITED"?
OR SOME-THING ELSE?
Well, either way, I'm excited.

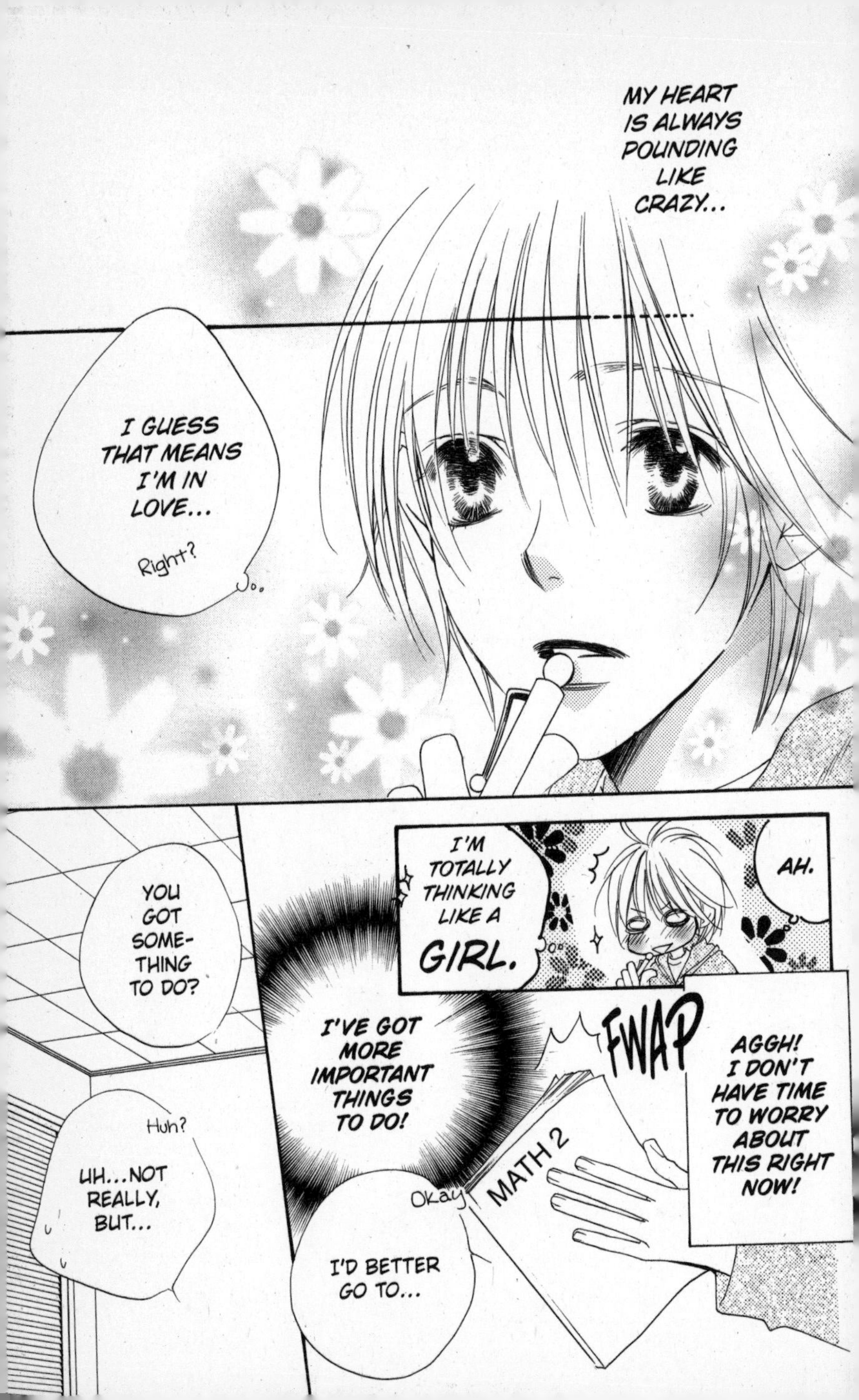
MY HEART IS ALWAYS POUNDING LIKE CRAZY...
I GUESS THAT MEANS I'M IN LOVE...
Right?
AH.
I'M TOTALLY THINKING LIKE A GIRL.
AGGH! I DON'T HAVE TIME TO WORRY ABOUT THIS RIGHT NOW!
FWAP
I'VE GOT MORE IMPORTANT THINGS TO DO!
MATH 2
Okay
I'D BETTER GO TO...
YOU GOT SOME-THING TO DO?
Huh?
UH...NOT REALLY, BUT...

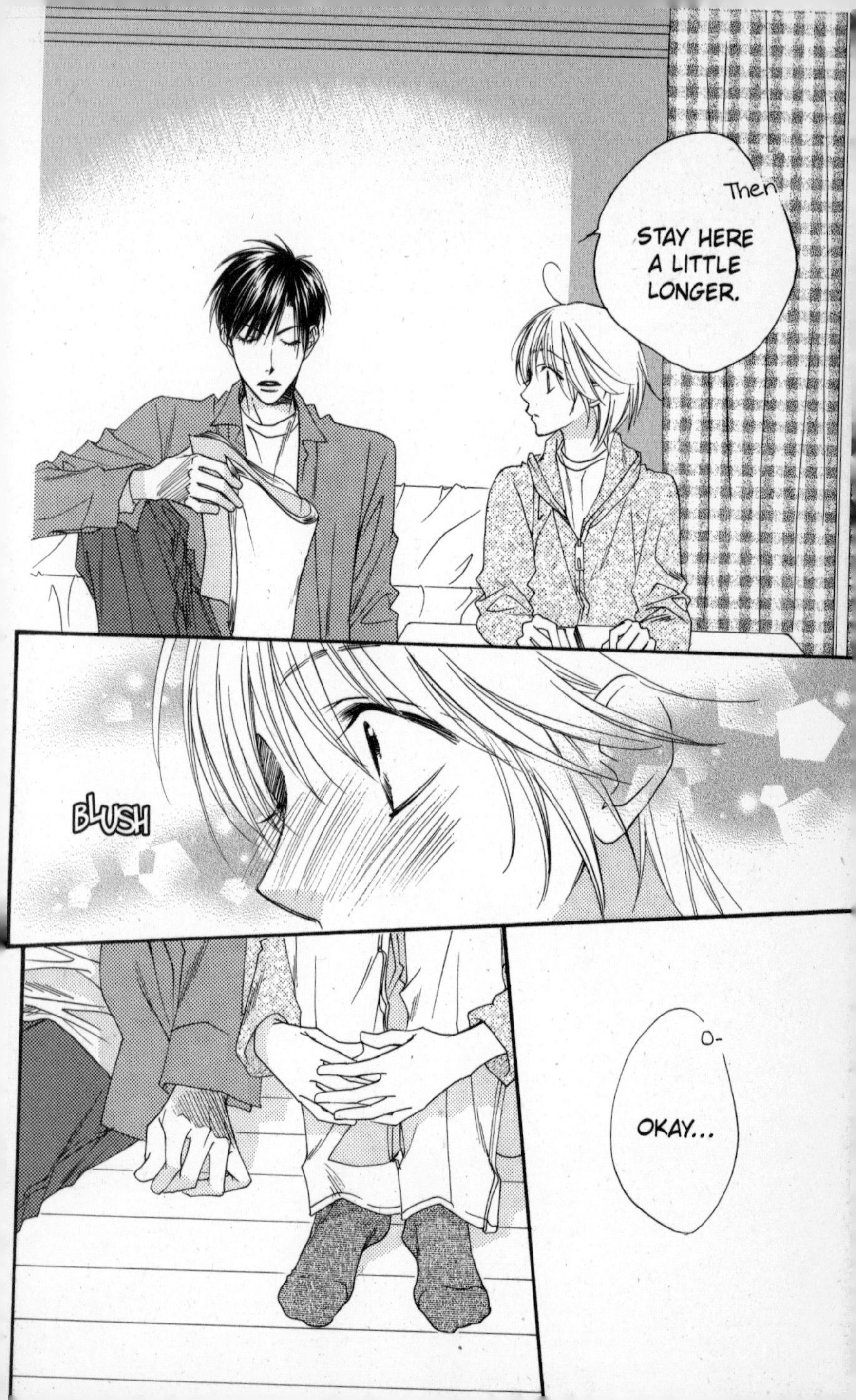
Then
STAY HERE A LITTLE LONGER.
BLUSH
O-
OKAY...

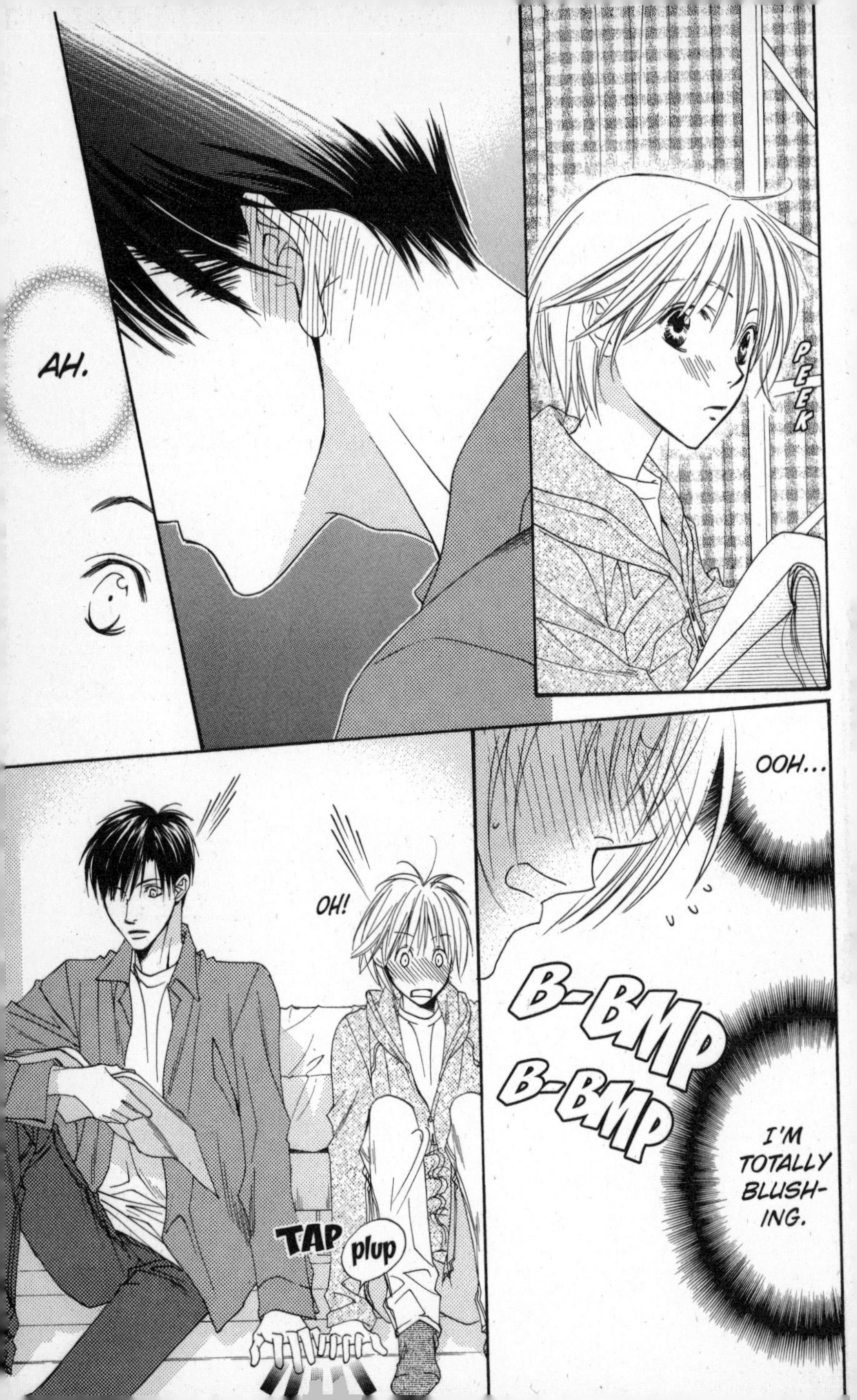
PEEK
AH.
OOH...
B-BMP
B-BMP
I'M TOTALLY BLUSH-ING.
OH!
TAP
plup

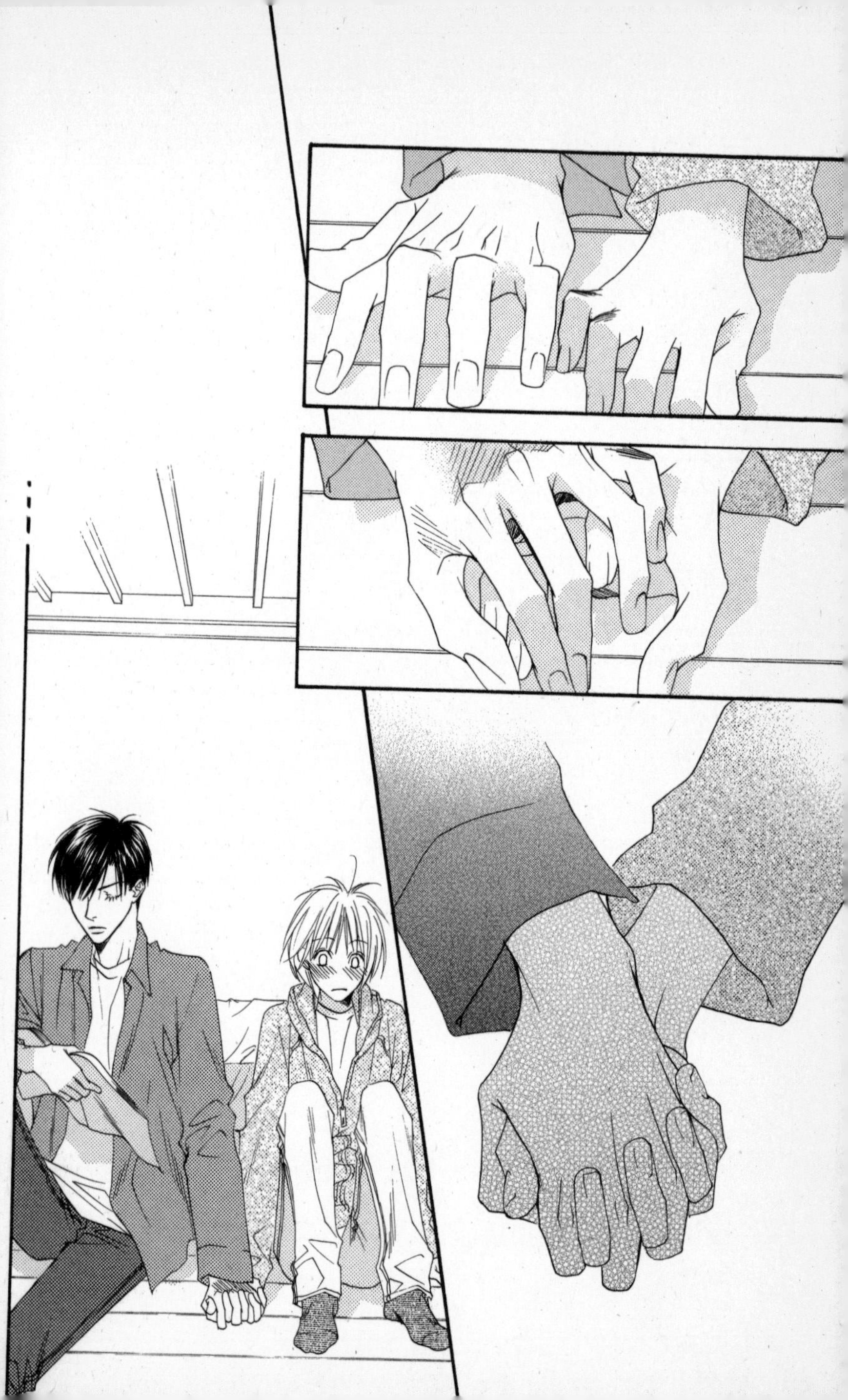

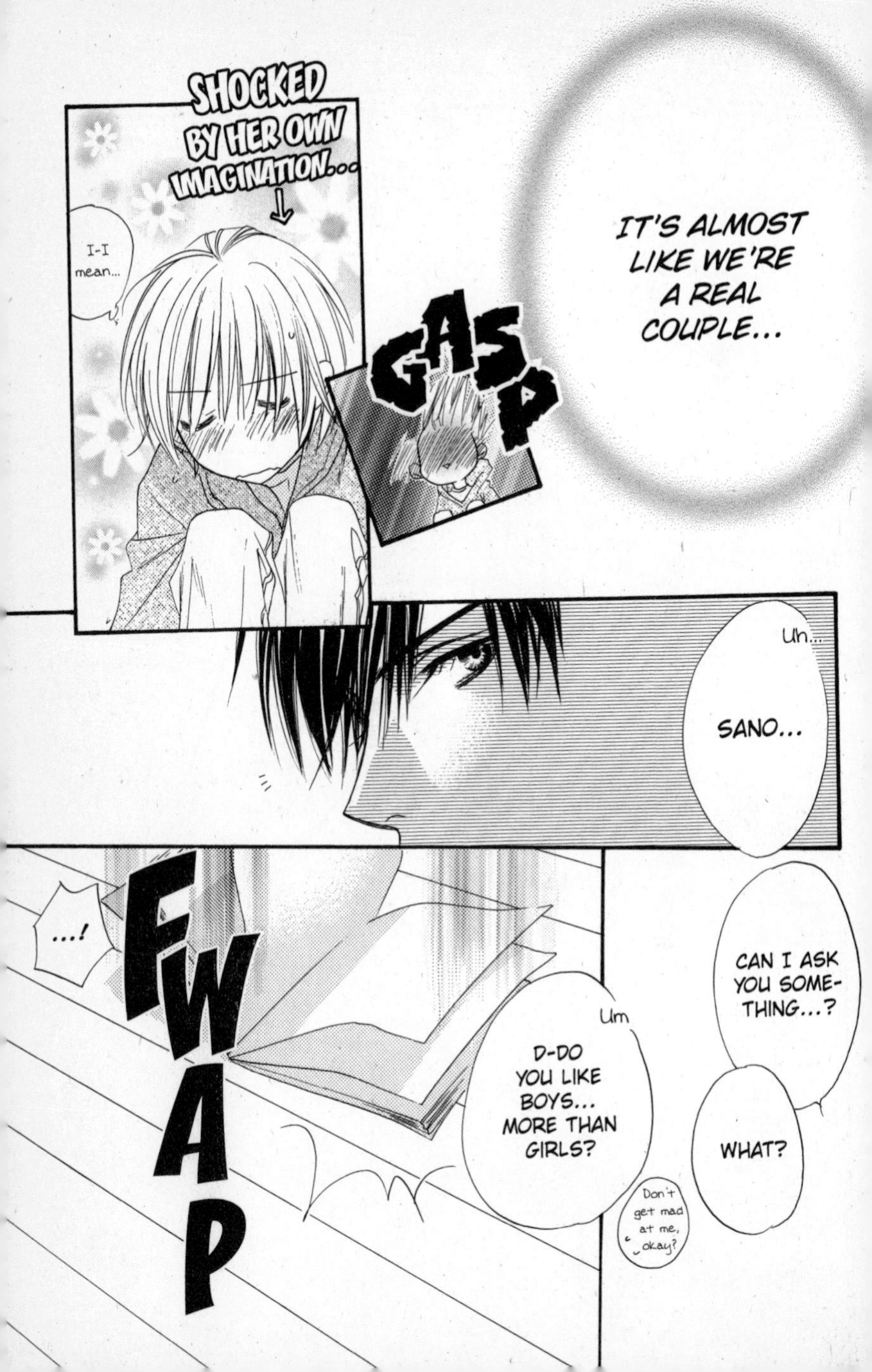
IT'S ALMOST LIKE WE'RE A REAL COUPLE...
GASP
SHOCKED BY HER OWN IMAGINATION...
I-I mean...
Uh...
SANO...
CAN I ASK YOU SOME-THING...?
WHAT?
Um
D-DO YOU LIKE BOYS... MORE THAN GIRLS?
Don't get mad at me, okay?
...!
FWAP

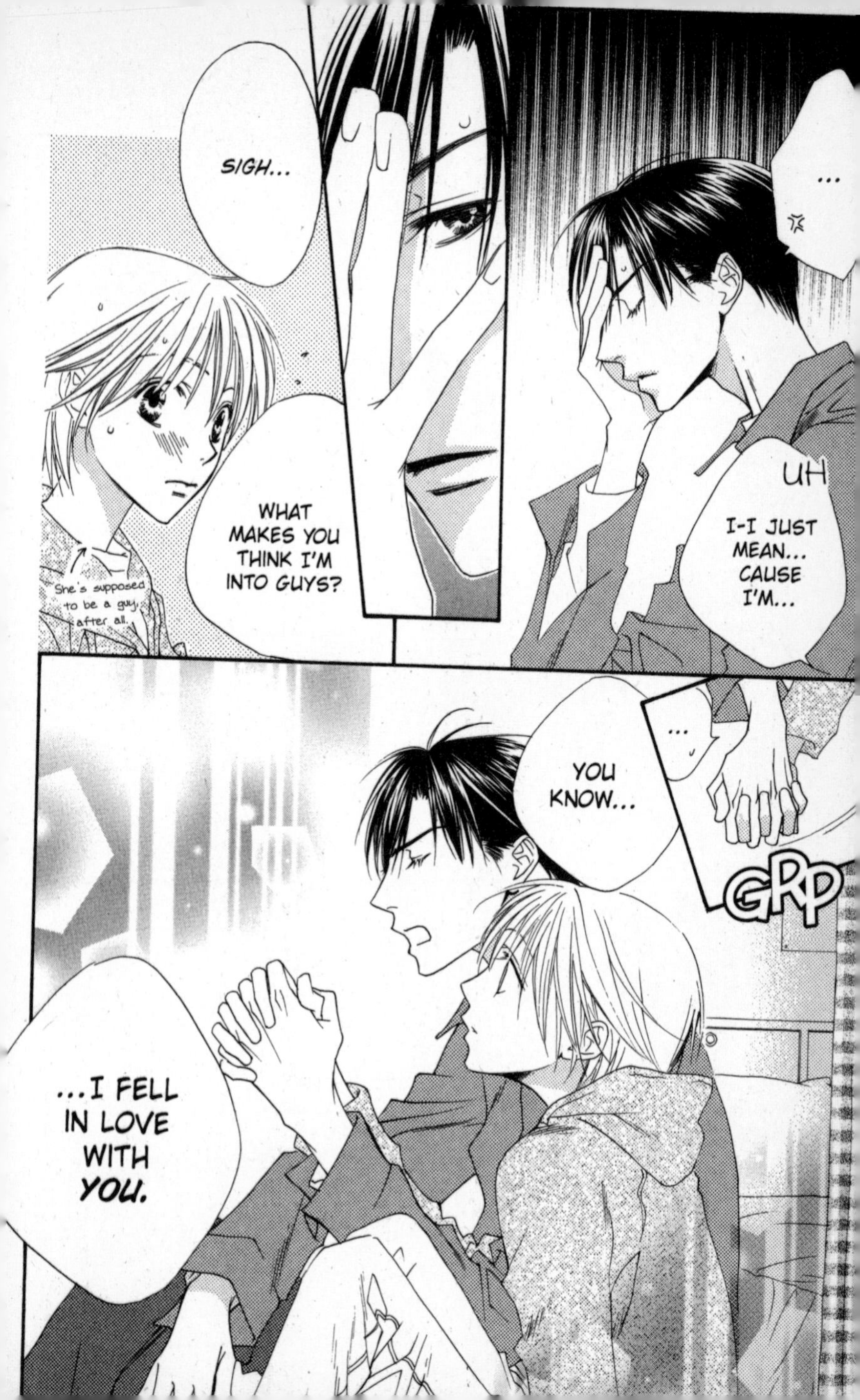
...
UH
I-I JUST MEAN... CAUSE I'M...
SIGH...
WHAT MAKES YOU THINK I'M INTO GUYS?
She's supposed to be a guy, after all.
...
YOU KNOW...
GRP
...I FELL IN LOVE WITH *YOU.*

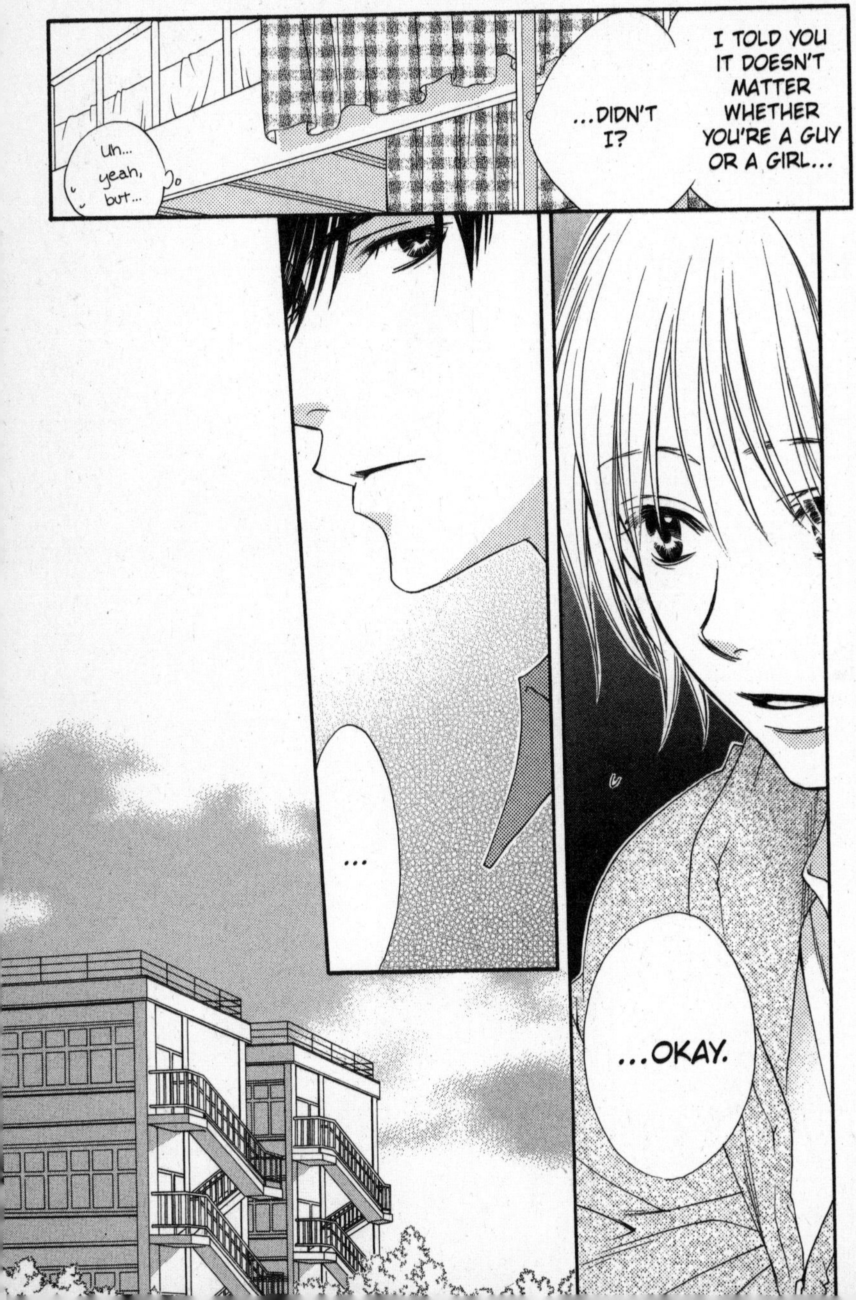
I TOLD YOU IT DOESN'T MATTER WHETHER YOU'RE A GUY OR A GIRL...
...DIDN'T I?
Uh... yeah, but...
...OKAY.
...

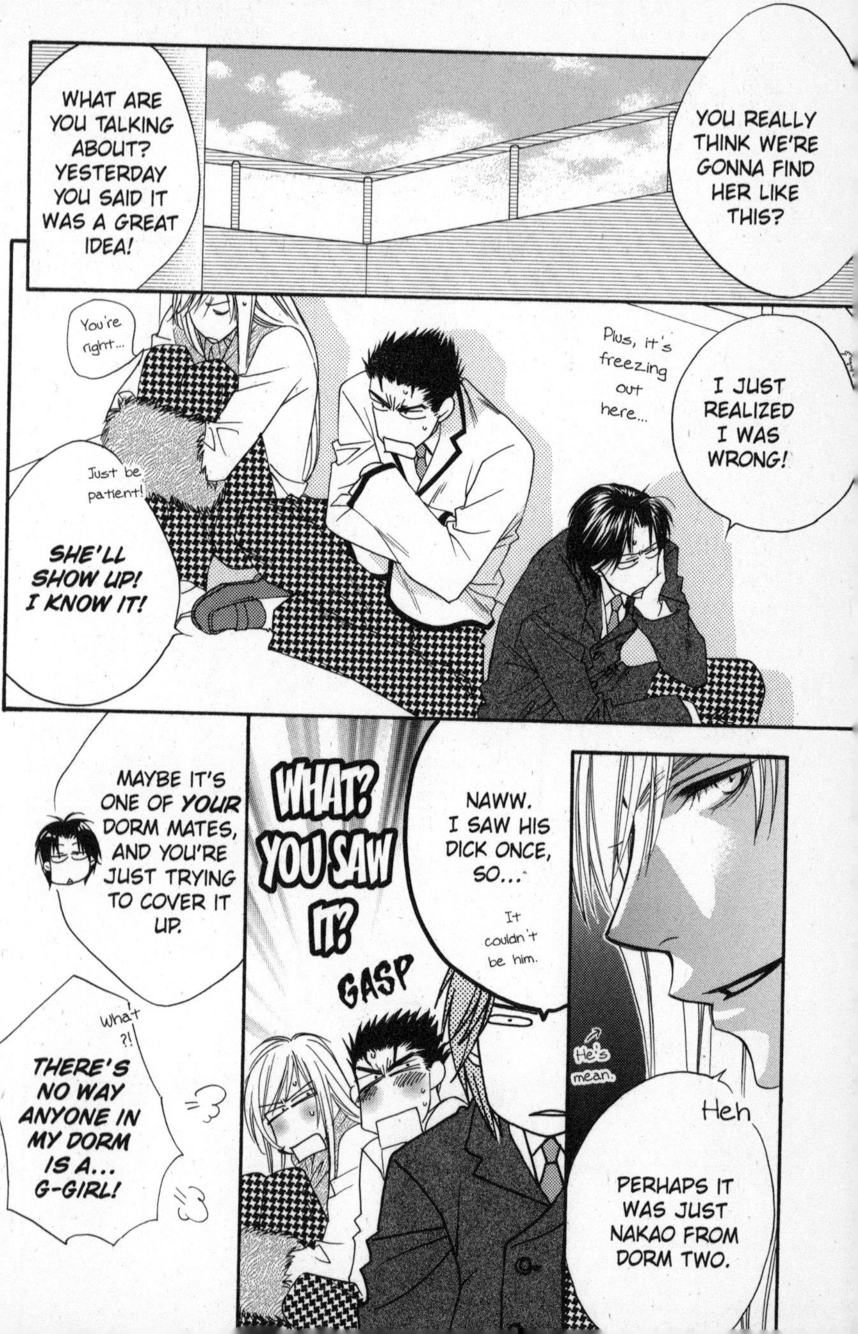
YOU REALLY THINK WE'RE GONNA FIND HER LIKE THIS?
WHAT ARE YOU TALKING ABOUT? YESTERDAY YOU SAID IT WAS A GREAT IDEA!
I JUST REALIZED I WAS WRONG!
Plus, it's freezing out here...
You're right...
Just be patient!
SHE'LL SHOW UP! I KNOW IT!
Heh
PERHAPS IT WAS JUST NAKAO FROM DORM TWO.
He's mean.
NAWW. I SAW HIS DICK ONCE, SO...
It couldn't be him.
WHAT? YOU SAW IT?
GASP
MAYBE IT'S ONE OF YOUR DORM MATES, AND YOU'RE JUST TRYING TO COVER IT UP.
What?!
THERE'S NO WAY ANYONE IN MY DORM IS A... G-GIRL!

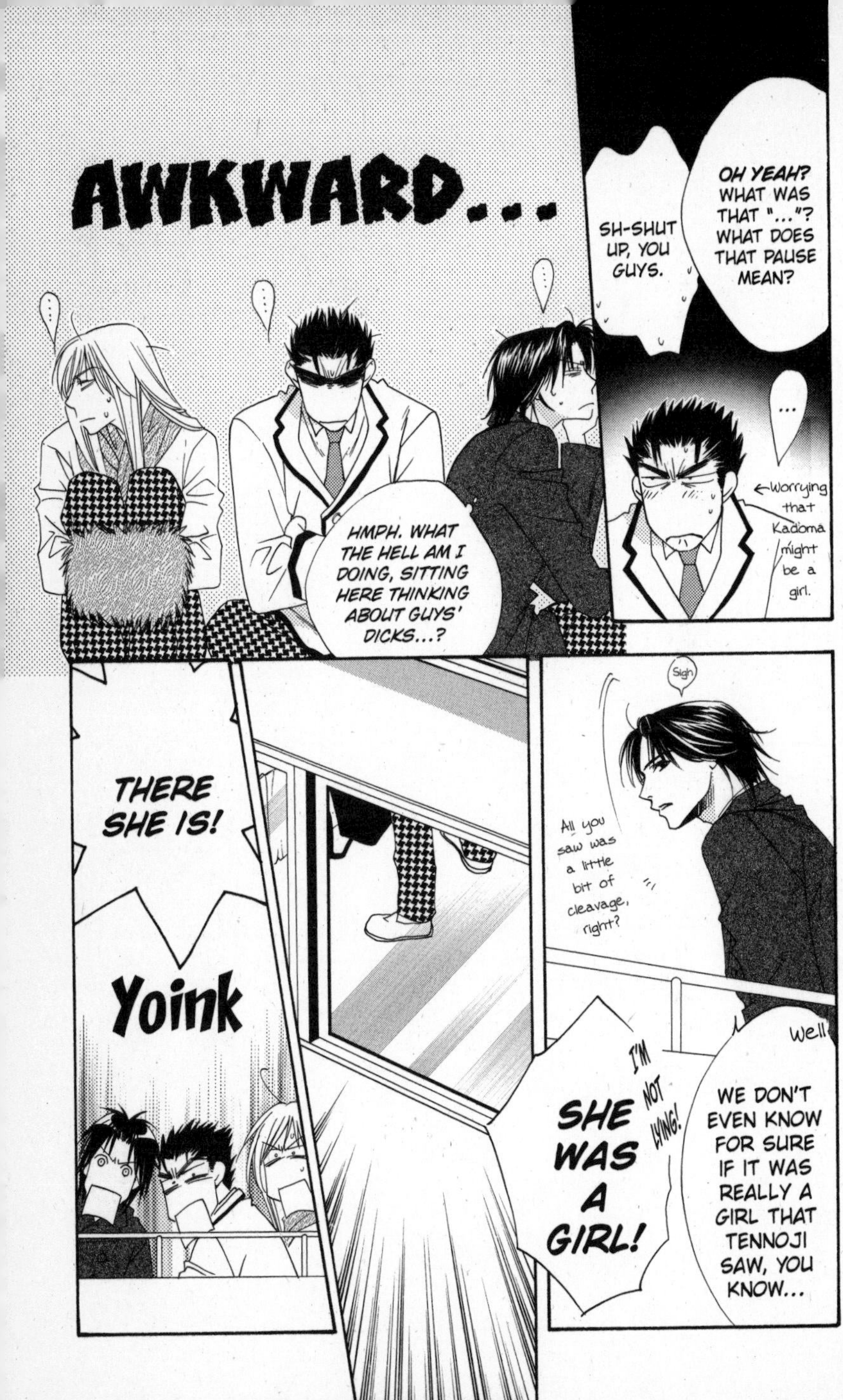
OH YEAH? WHAT WAS THAT "..."? WHAT DOES THAT PAUSE MEAN?
SH-SHUT UP, YOU GUYS.
...
←Worrying that Kadoma might be a girl.
AWKWARD...
HMPH. WHAT THE HELL AM I DOING, SITTING HERE THINKING ABOUT GUYS' DICKS...?
Sigh
Well
WE DON'T EVEN KNOW FOR SURE IF IT WAS REALLY A GIRL THAT TENNOJI SAW, YOU KNOW...
All you saw was a little bit of cleavage, right?
SHE WAS A GIRL!
I'M NOT LYING!
THERE SHE IS!
Yoink

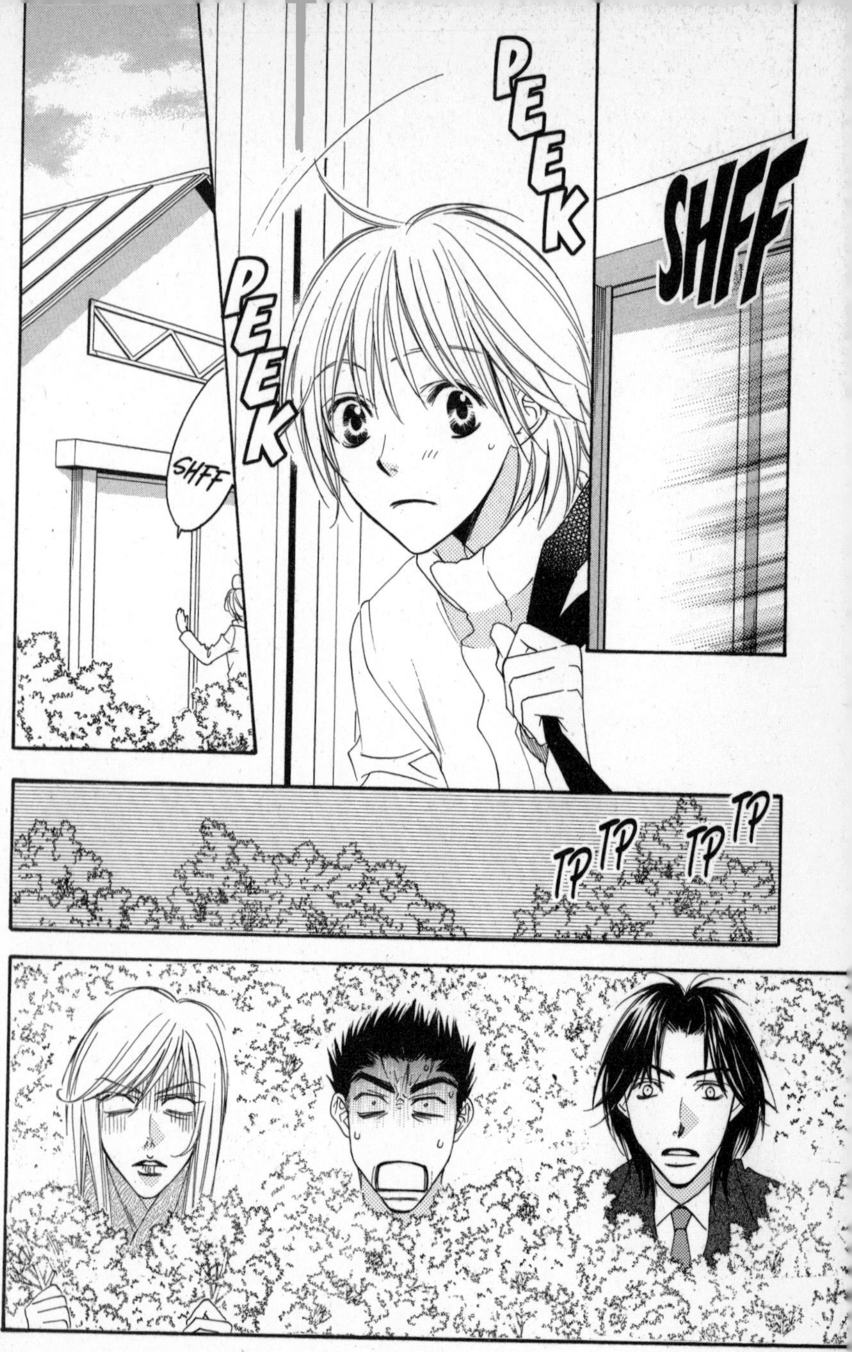
SHFF
PEEK
PEEK
SHFF
TP TP TP TP

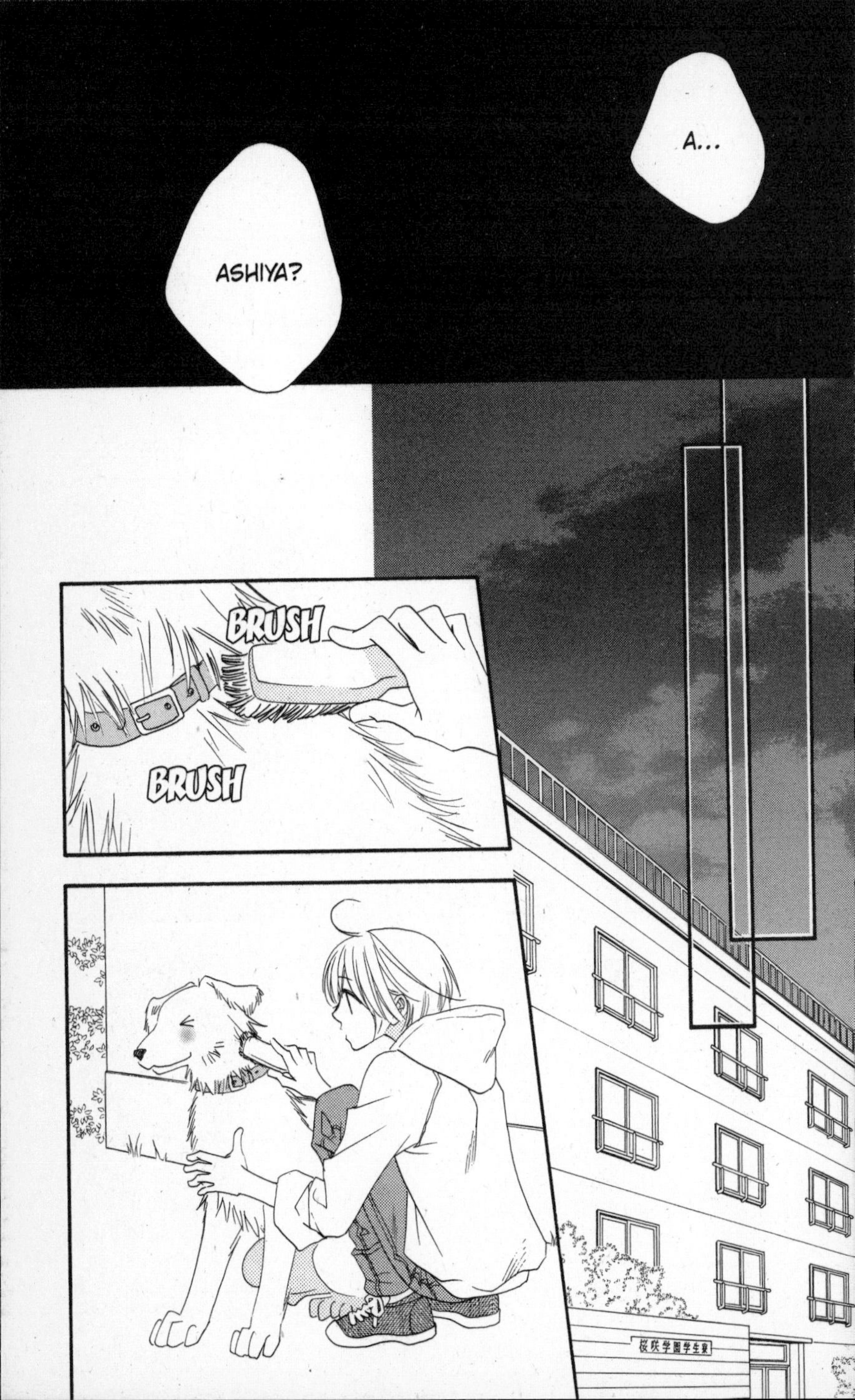
A...
ASHIYA?
桜咲学園学生寮
BRUSH
BRUSH

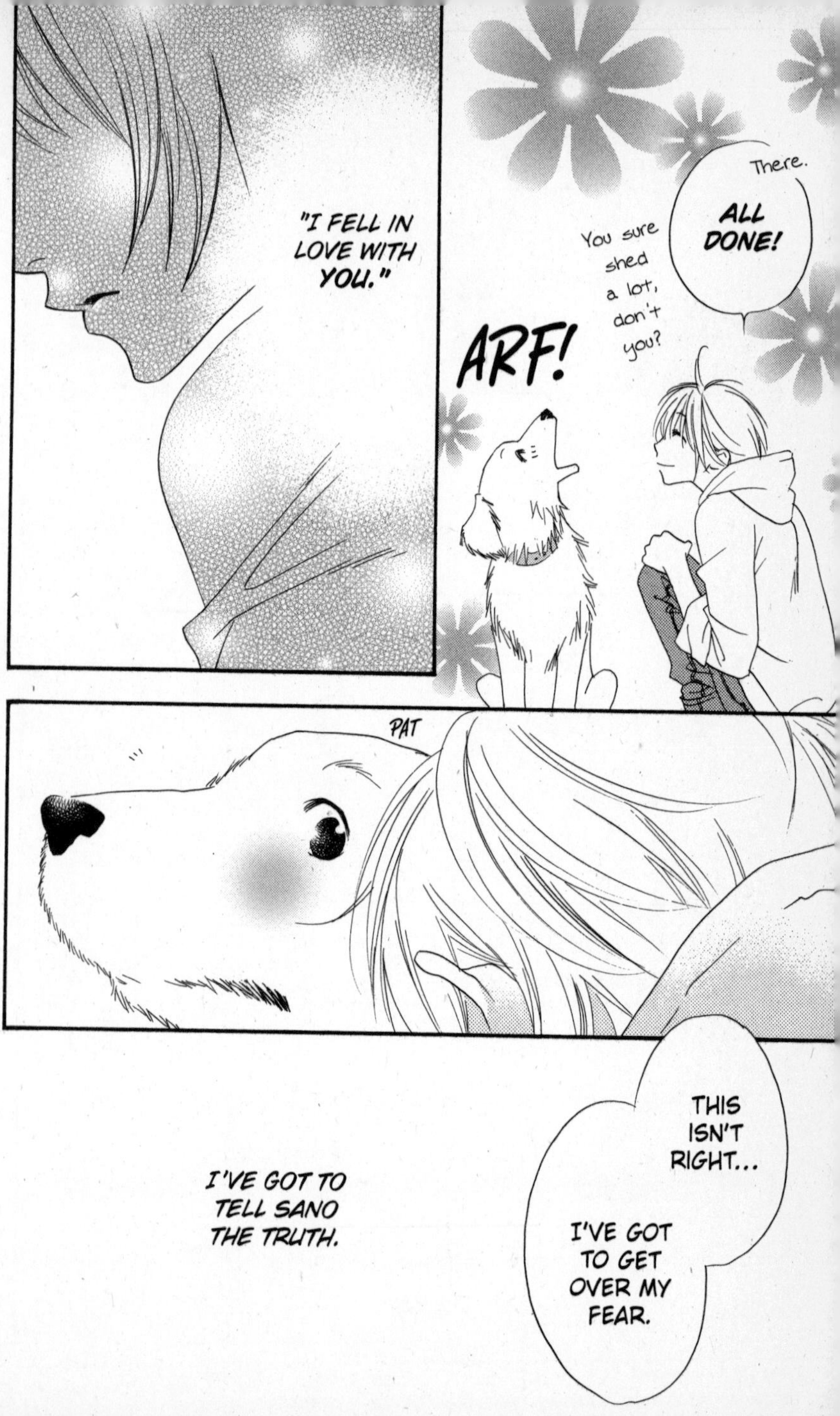
There.
ALL DONE!
You sure shed a lot, don't you?
ARF!
"I FELL IN LOVE WITH YOU."
PAT
THIS ISN'T RIGHT...
I'VE GOT TO GET OVER MY FEAR.
I'VE GOT TO TELL SANO THE TRUTH.

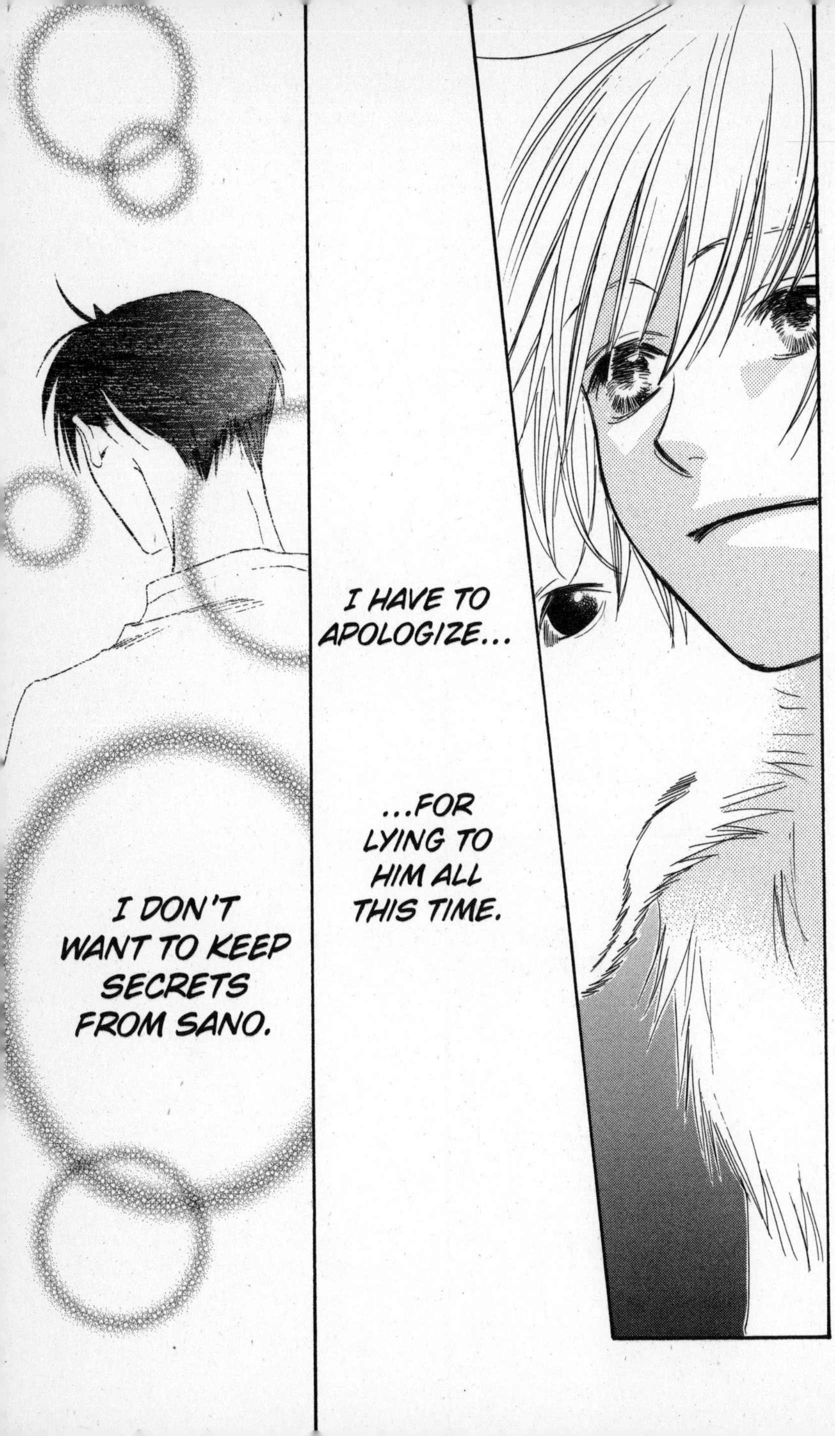
I HAVE TO APOLOGIZE...
...FOR LYING TO HIM ALL THIS TIME.
I DON'T WANT TO KEEP SECRETS FROM SANO.

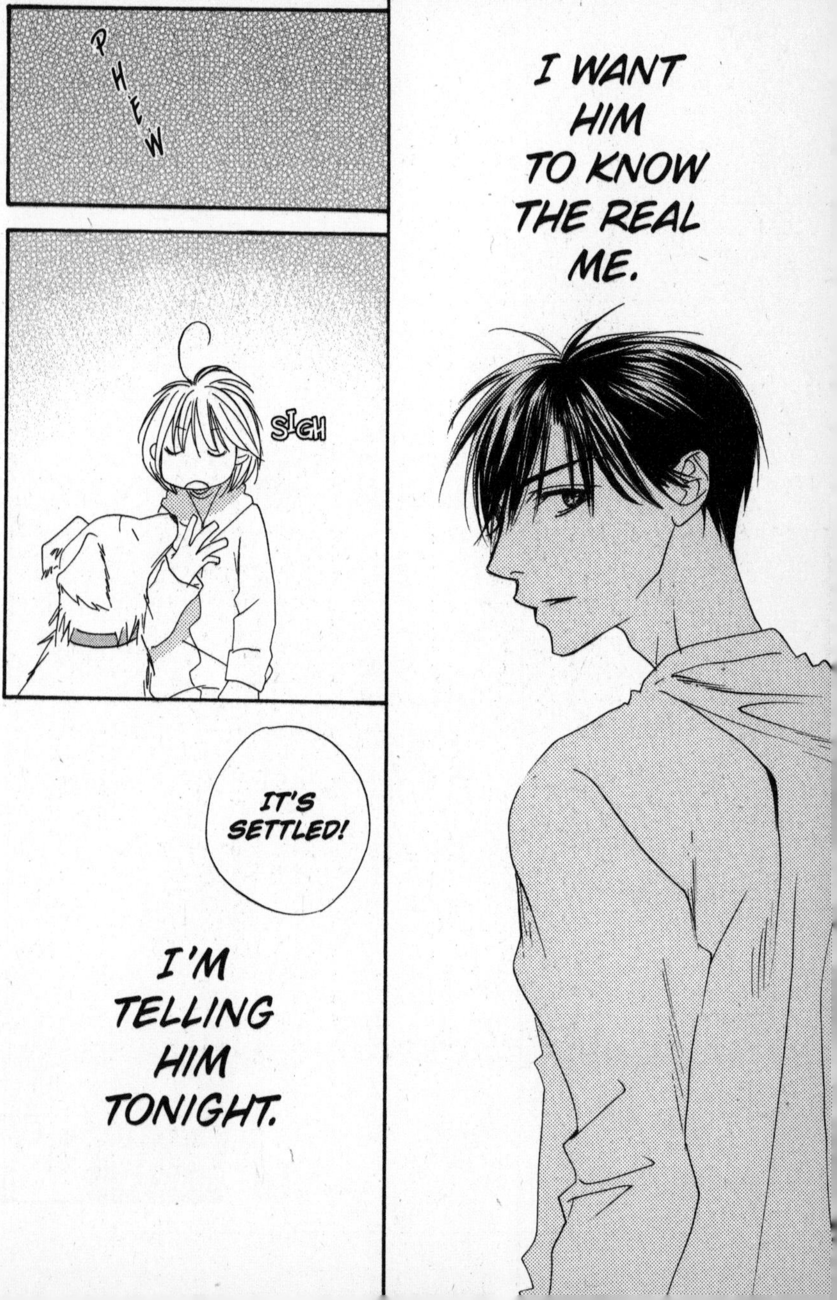
I WANT HIM TO KNOW THE REAL ME.
PHEW
SIGH
IT'S SETTLED!
I'M TELLING HIM TONIGHT.

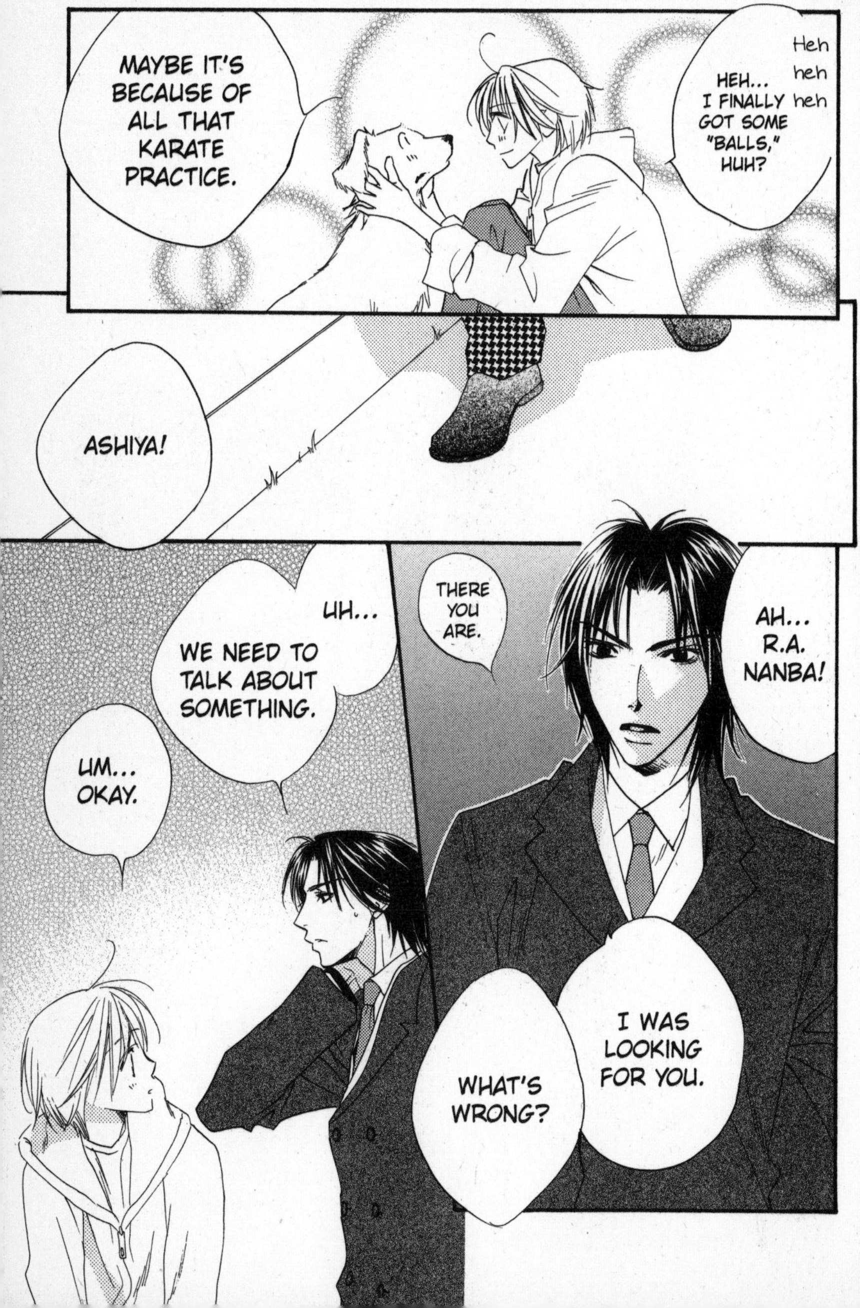
Heh heh heh
HEH... I FINALLY GOT SOME "BALLS," HUH?
MAYBE IT'S BECAUSE OF ALL THAT KARATE PRACTICE.
ASHIYA!
AH... R.A. NANBA!
THERE YOU ARE.
I WAS LOOKING FOR YOU.
WHAT'S WRONG?
UH...
WE NEED TO TALK ABOUT SOMETHING.
UM... OKAY.

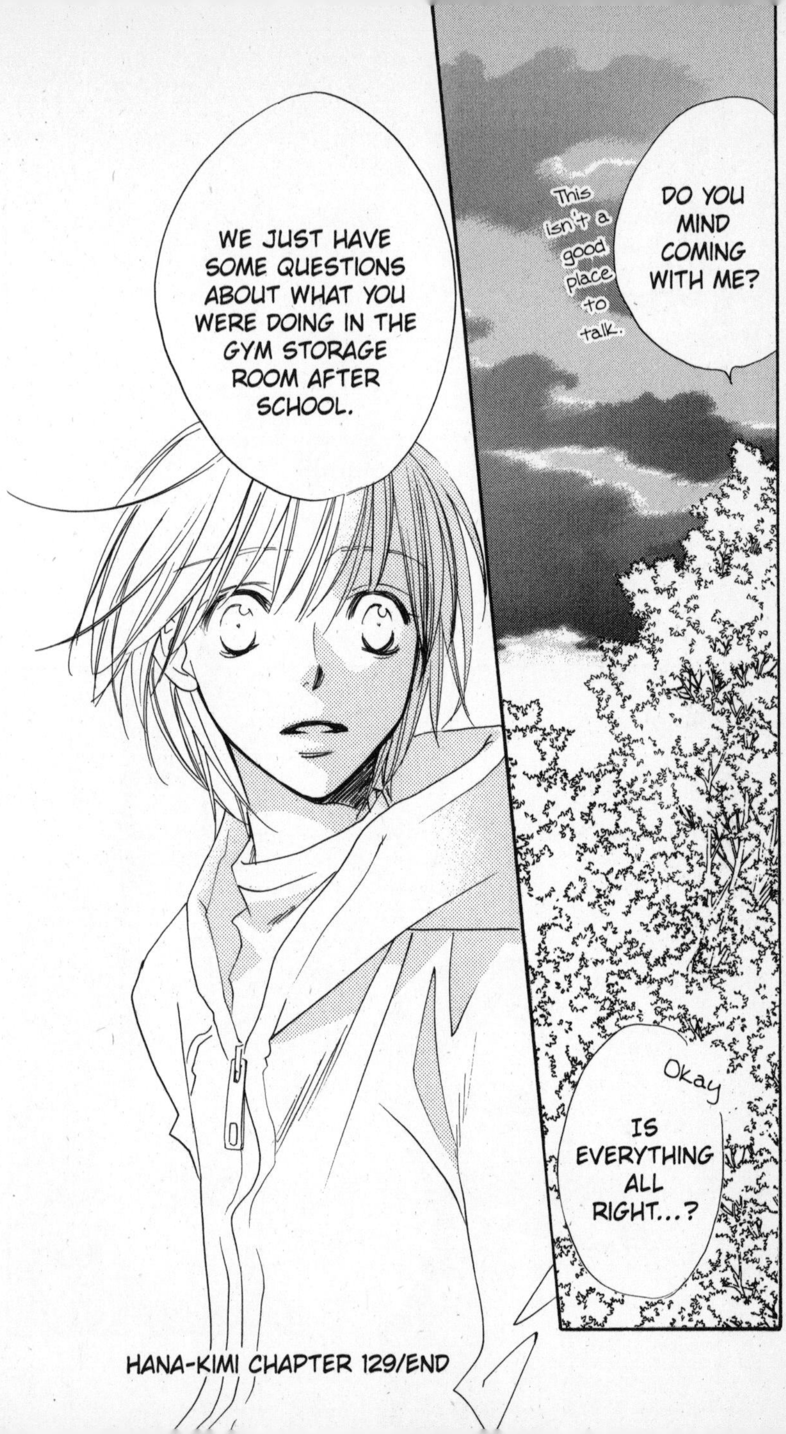
DO YOU MIND COMING WITH ME?
This isn't a good place to talk.
Okay
IS EVERYTHING ALL RIGHT...?
WE JUST HAVE SOME QUESTIONS ABOUT WHAT YOU WERE DOING IN THE GYM STORAGE ROOM AFTER SCHOOL.

HANA-KIMI CHAPTER 129/END

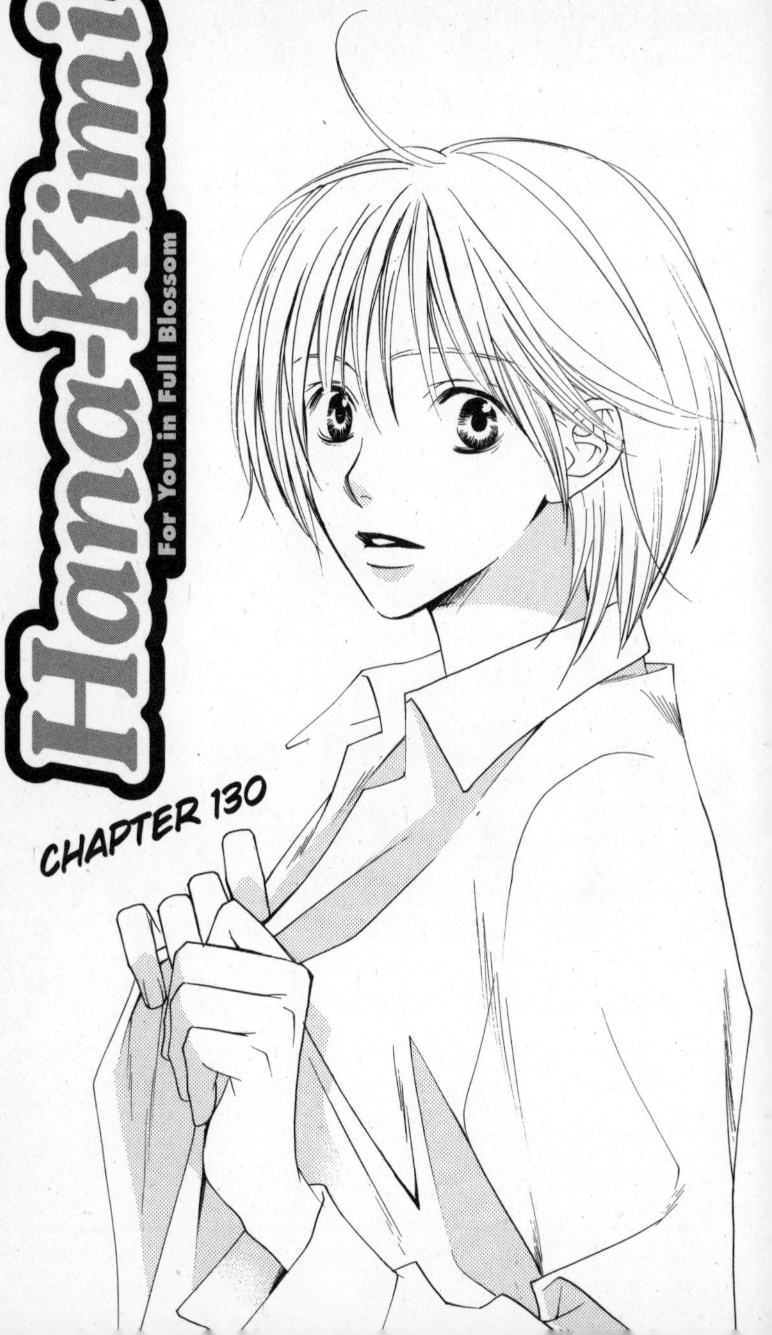
Hana-Kimi
For You in Full Blossom
CHAPTER 130

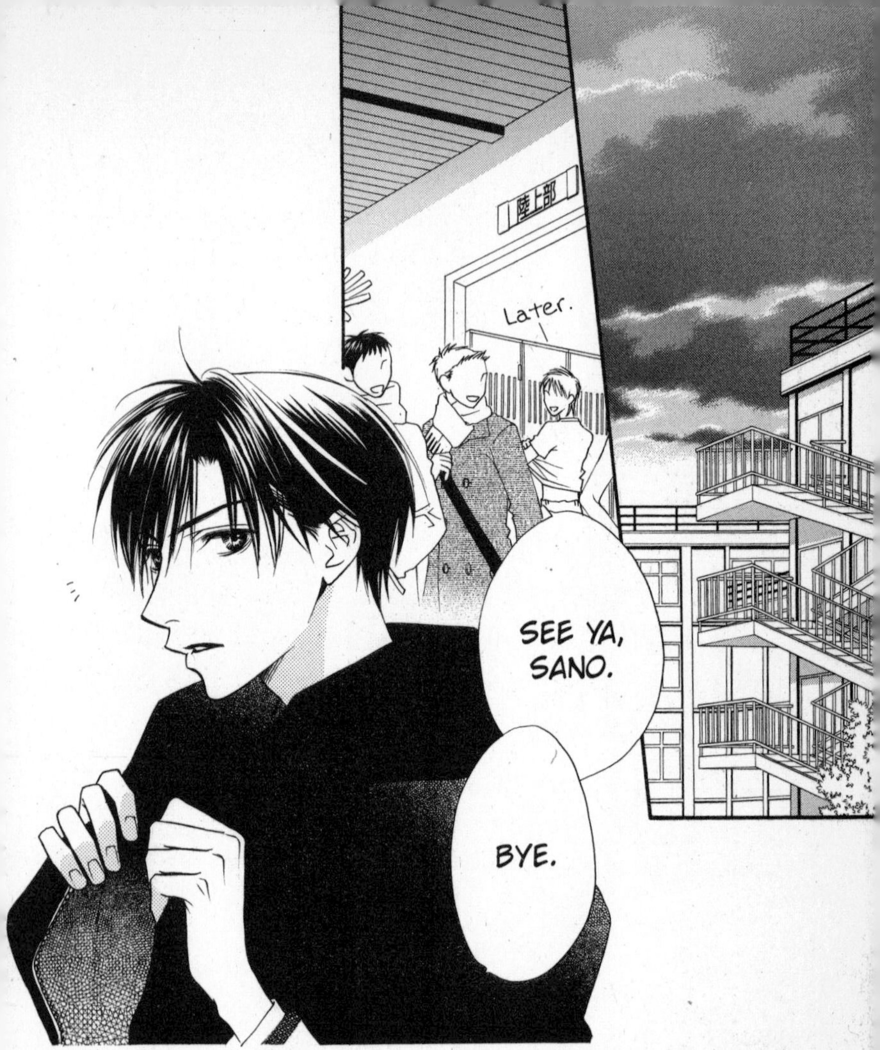
陸上部
Later.
SEE YA, SANO.
BYE.

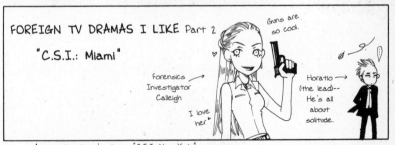

FOREIGN TV DRAMAS I LIKE Part 2

"C.S.I.: Miami"

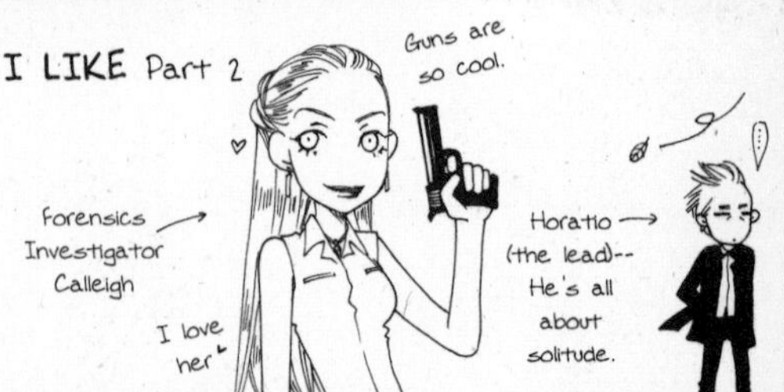
Guns are so cool.
Forensics Investigator Calleigh
I love her
Horatio (the lead)-- He's all about solitude.

Apparently, there's also a "C.S.I: New York"...

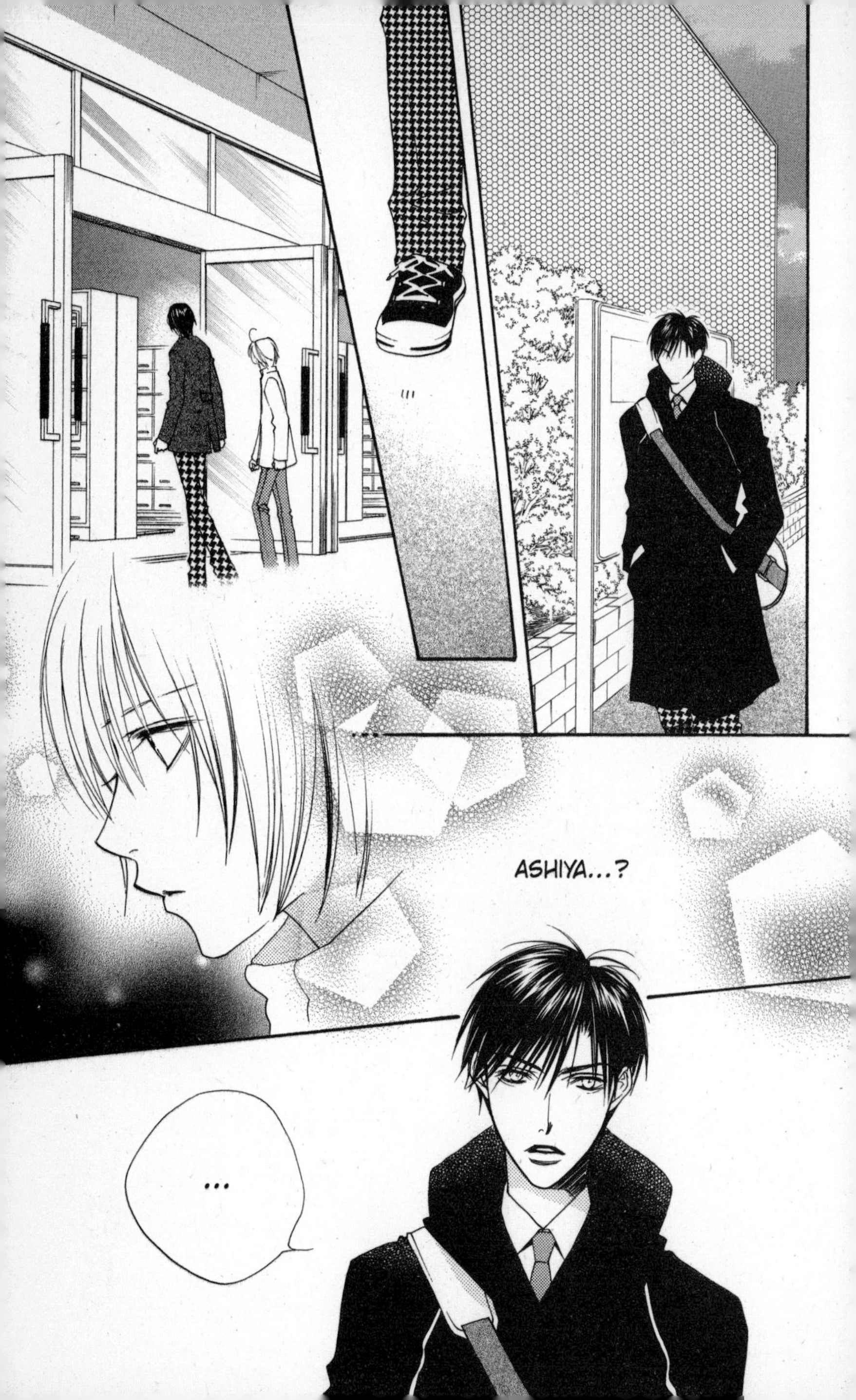
!!!
...
ASHIYA...?
...

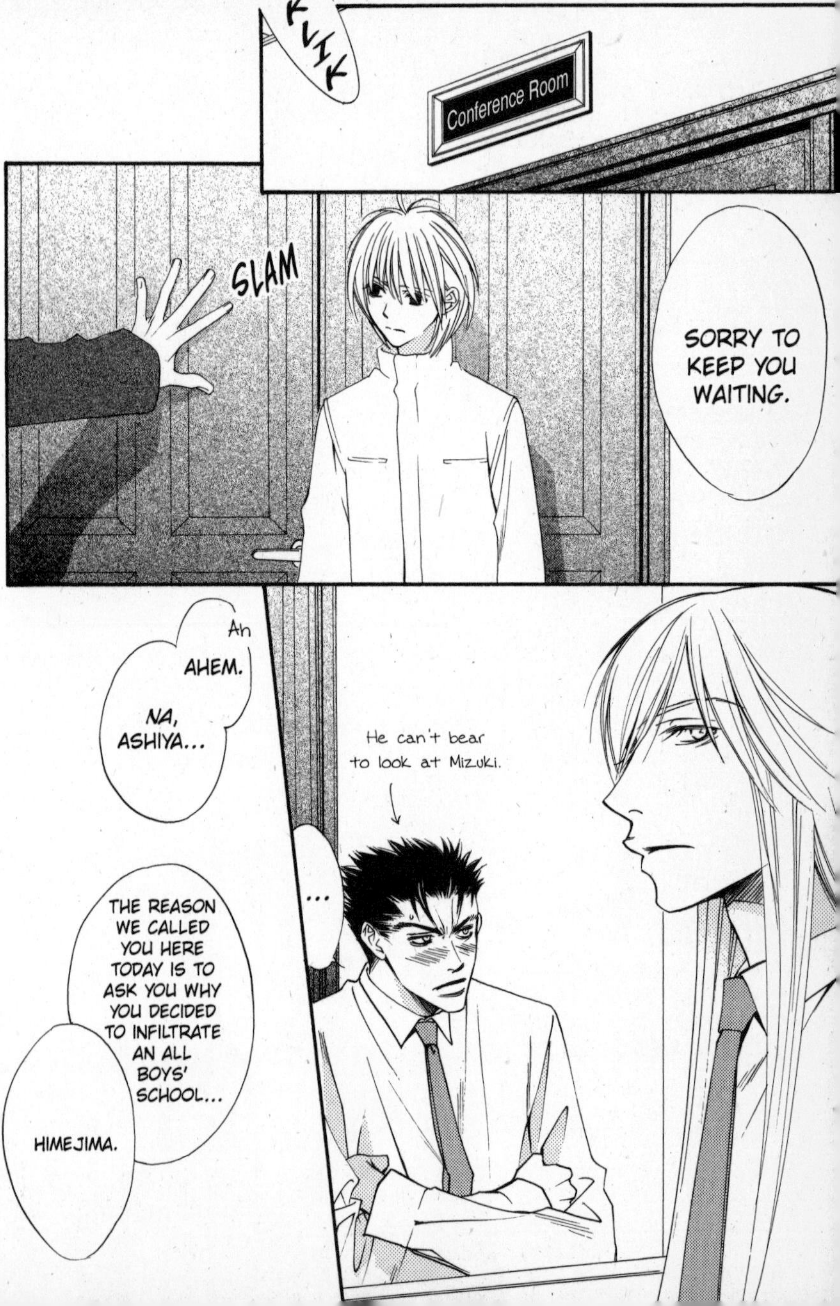
KLIK
Conference Room
SORRY TO KEEP YOU WAITING.
SLAM
He can't bear to look at Mizuki.
...
An AHEM.
NA, ASHIYA...
THE REASON WE CALLED YOU HERE TODAY IS TO ASK YOU WHY YOU DECIDED TO INFILTRATE AN ALL BOYS' SCHOOL...
HIMEJIMA.

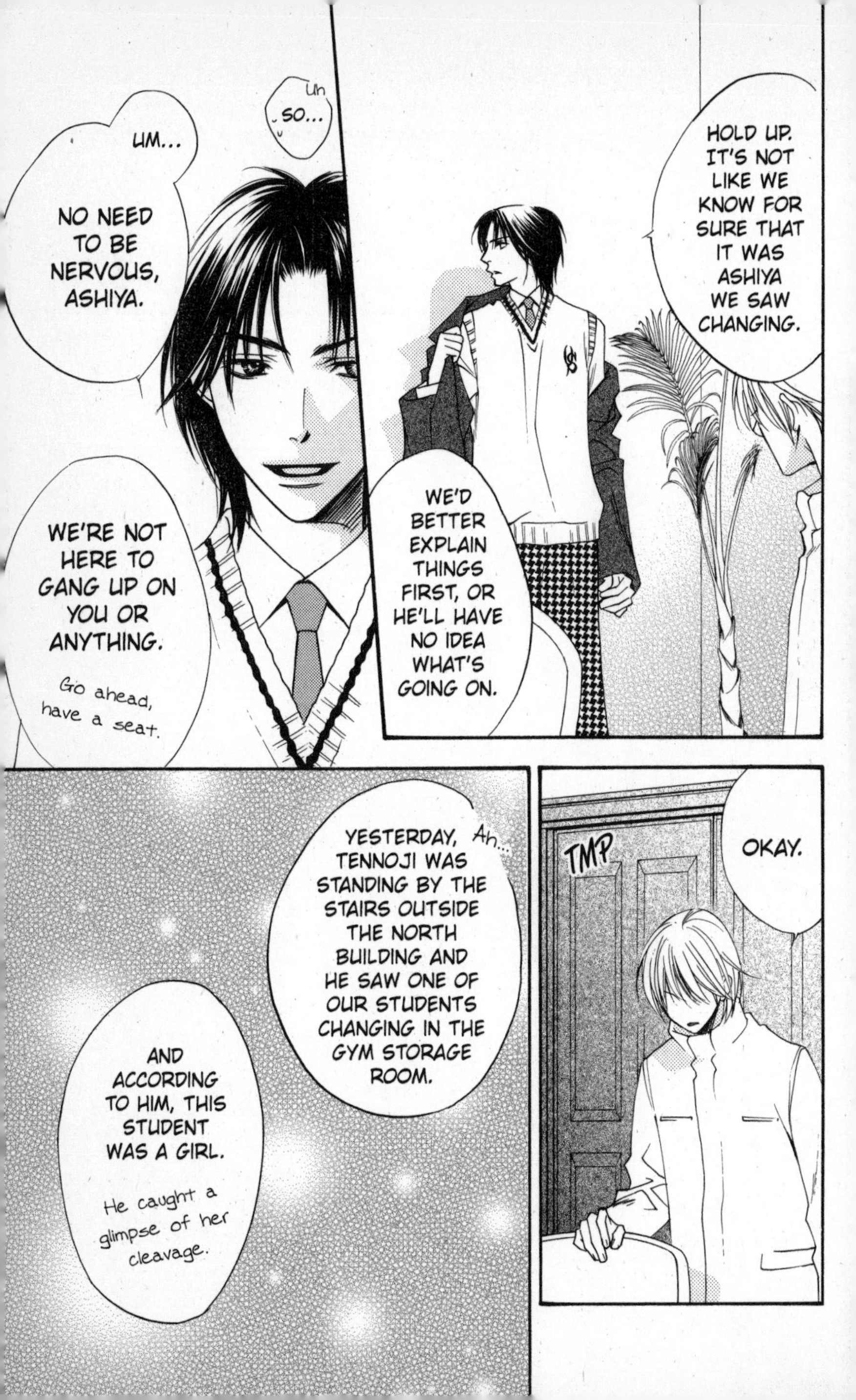
HOLD UP. IT'S NOT LIKE WE KNOW FOR SURE THAT IT WAS ASHIYA WE SAW CHANGING.
WE'D BETTER EXPLAIN THINGS FIRST, OR HE'LL HAVE NO IDEA WHAT'S GOING ON.
Un so...
UM...
NO NEED TO BE NERVOUS, ASHIYA.
WE'RE NOT HERE TO GANG UP ON YOU OR ANYTHING.
Go ahead, have a seat.
OKAY.
TMP
Ah...
YESTERDAY, TENNOJI WAS STANDING BY THE STAIRS OUTSIDE THE NORTH BUILDING AND HE SAW ONE OF OUR STUDENTS CHANGING IN THE GYM STORAGE ROOM.
AND ACCORDING TO HIM, THIS STUDENT WAS A GIRL.
He caught a glimpse of her cleavage.

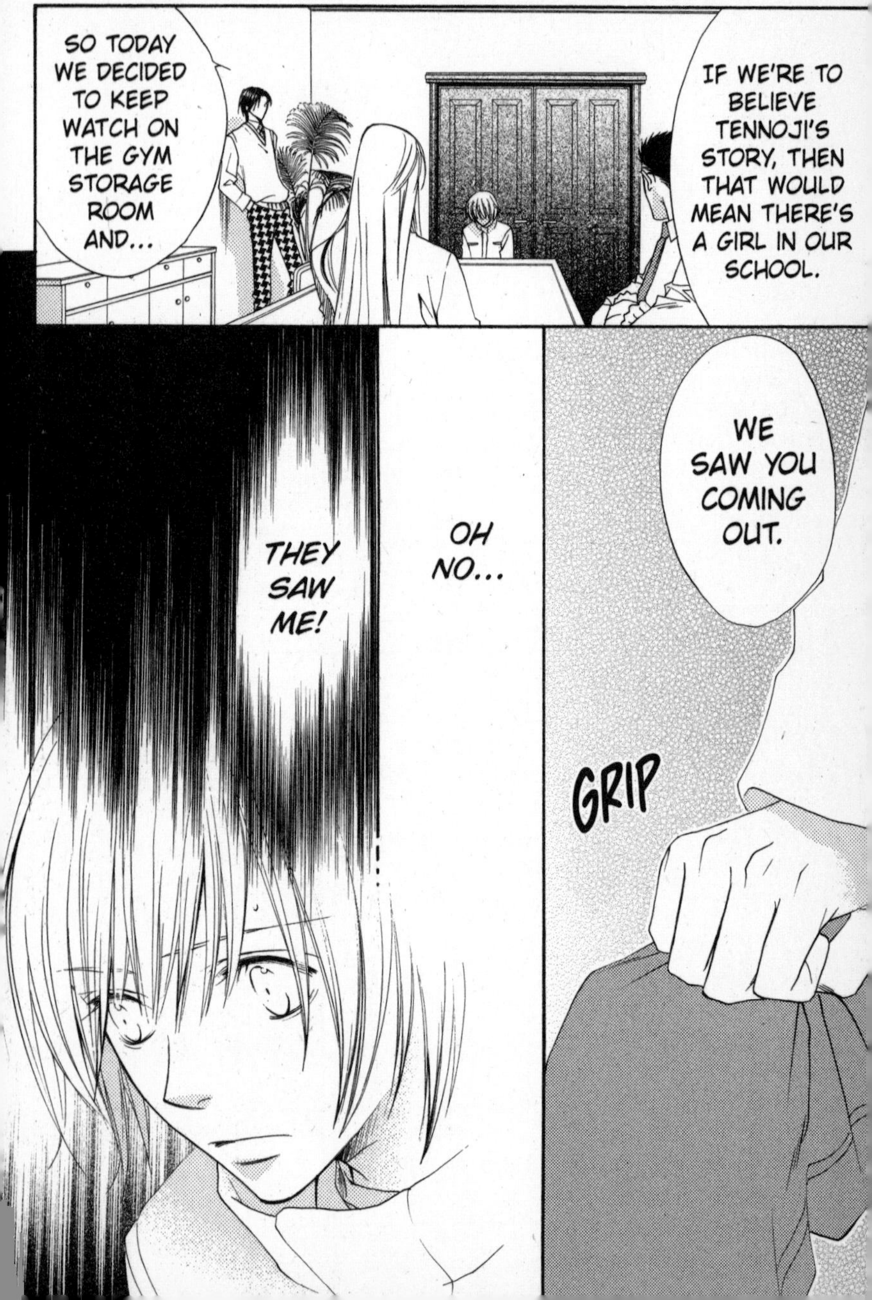
IF WE'RE TO BELIEVE TENNOJI'S STORY, THEN THAT WOULD MEAN THERE'S A GIRL IN OUR SCHOOL.
SO TODAY WE DECIDED TO KEEP WATCH ON THE GYM STORAGE ROOM AND...
WE SAW YOU COMING OUT.
GRIP
OH NO...
THEY SAW ME!

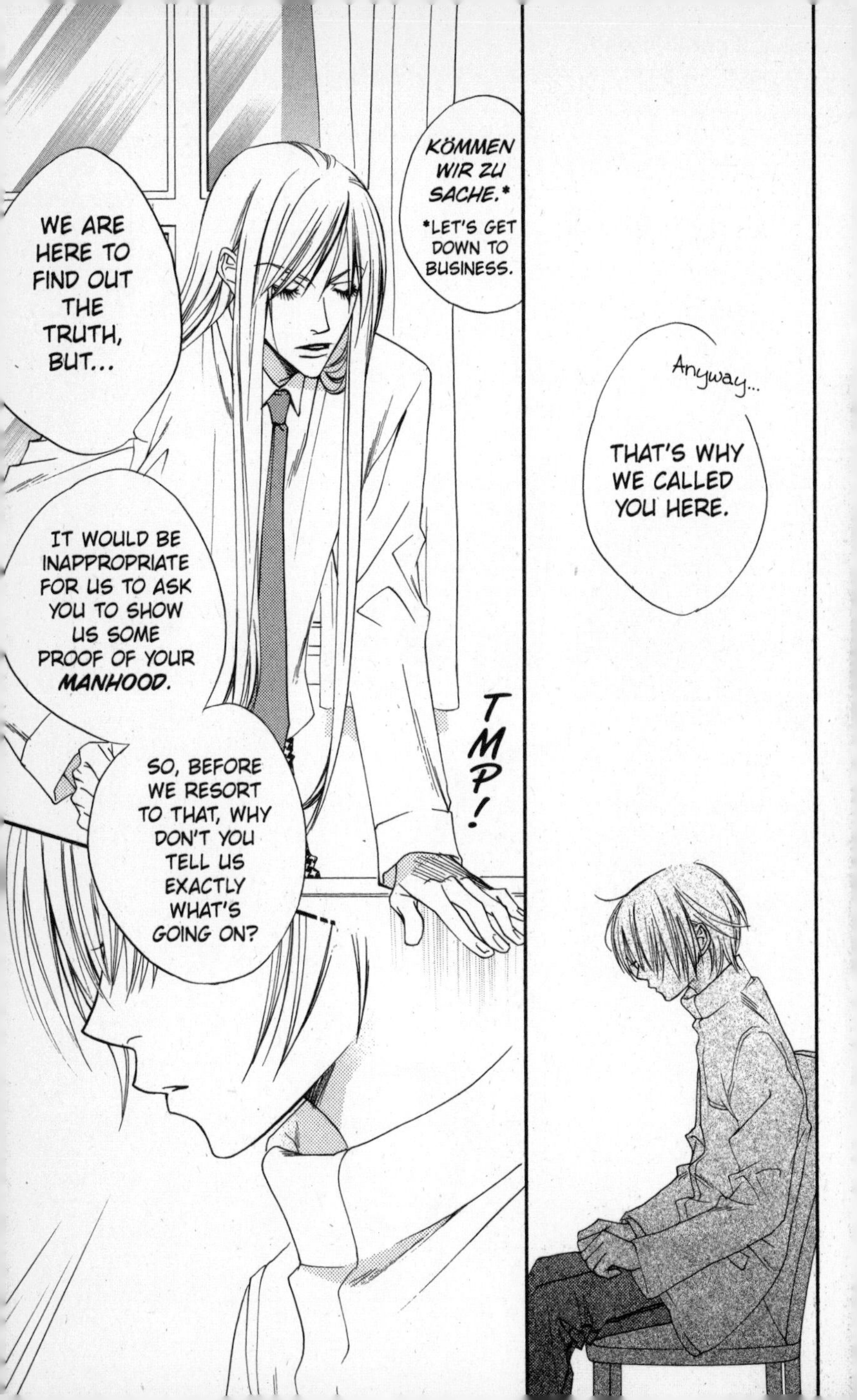
Anyway...
THAT'S WHY WE CALLED YOU HERE.
KÖMMEN WIR ZU SACHE.*
*LET'S GET DOWN TO BUSINESS.
WE ARE HERE TO FIND OUT THE TRUTH, BUT...
IT WOULD BE INAPPROPRIATE FOR US TO ASK YOU TO SHOW US SOME PROOF OF YOUR MANHOOD.
TMP!
SO, BEFORE WE RESORT TO THAT, WHY DON'T YOU TELL US EXACTLY WHAT'S GOING ON?

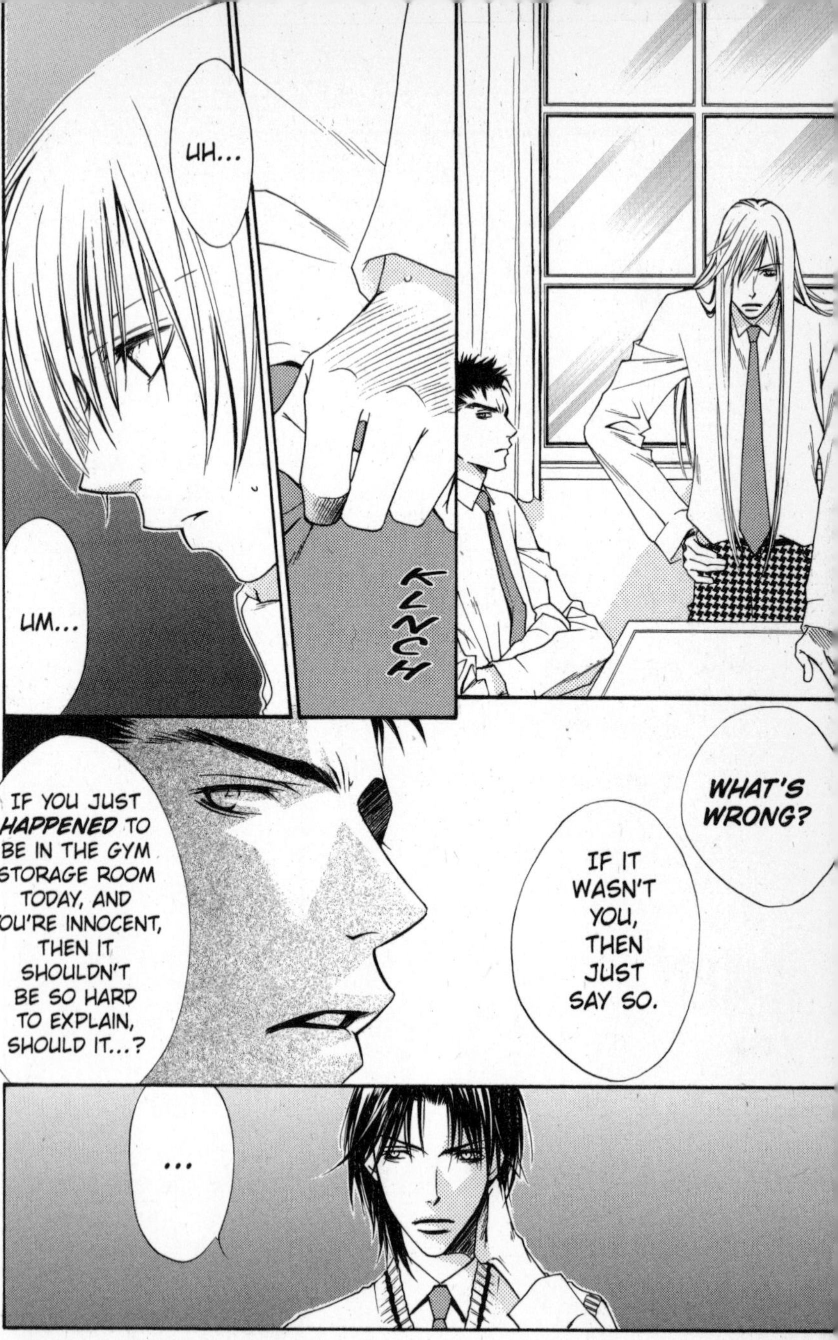
KINCH
UH...
UM...
WHAT'S WRONG?
IF IT WASN'T YOU, THEN JUST SAY SO.
IF YOU JUST HAPPENED TO BE IN THE GYM STORAGE ROOM TODAY, AND YOU'RE INNOCENT, THEN IT SHOULDN'T BE SO HARD TO EXPLAIN, SHOULD IT...?
...

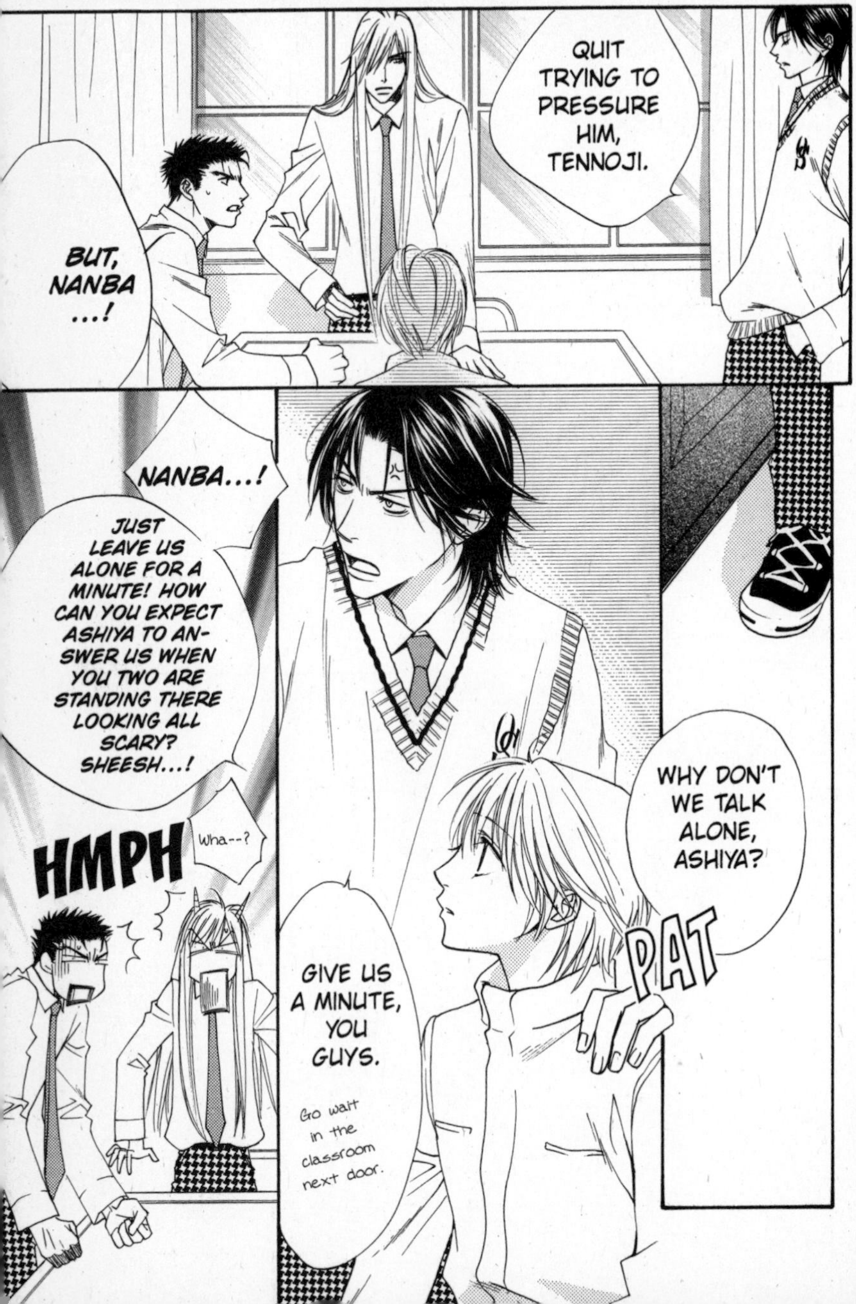
QUIT TRYING TO PRESSURE HIM, TENNOJI.
BUT, NANBA ...!
WHY DON'T WE TALK ALONE, ASHIYA?
PAT
GIVE US A MINUTE, YOU GUYS.
Go wait in the classroom next door.
NANBA...!
JUST LEAVE US ALONE FOR A MINUTE! HOW CAN YOU EXPECT ASHIYA TO AN-SWER US WHEN YOU TWO ARE STANDING THERE LOOKING ALL SCARY? SHEESH...!
Wha--?
HMPH

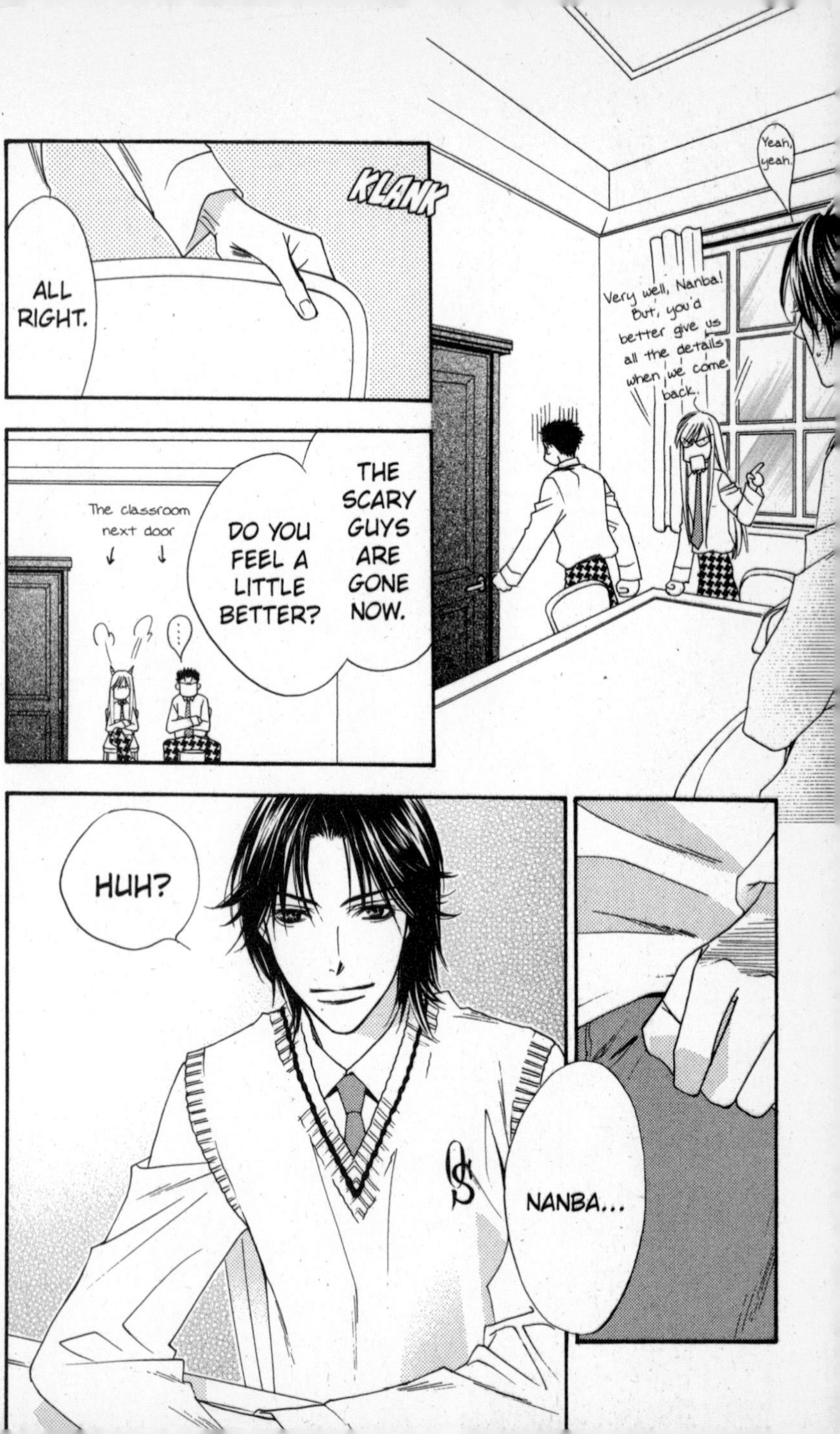
Yeah, yeah.
KLANK
Very well, Nanba! But, you'd better give us all the details when we come back.
ALL RIGHT.
THE SCARY GUYS ARE GONE NOW.
DO YOU FEEL A LITTLE BETTER?
The classroom next door
NANBA...
HUH?

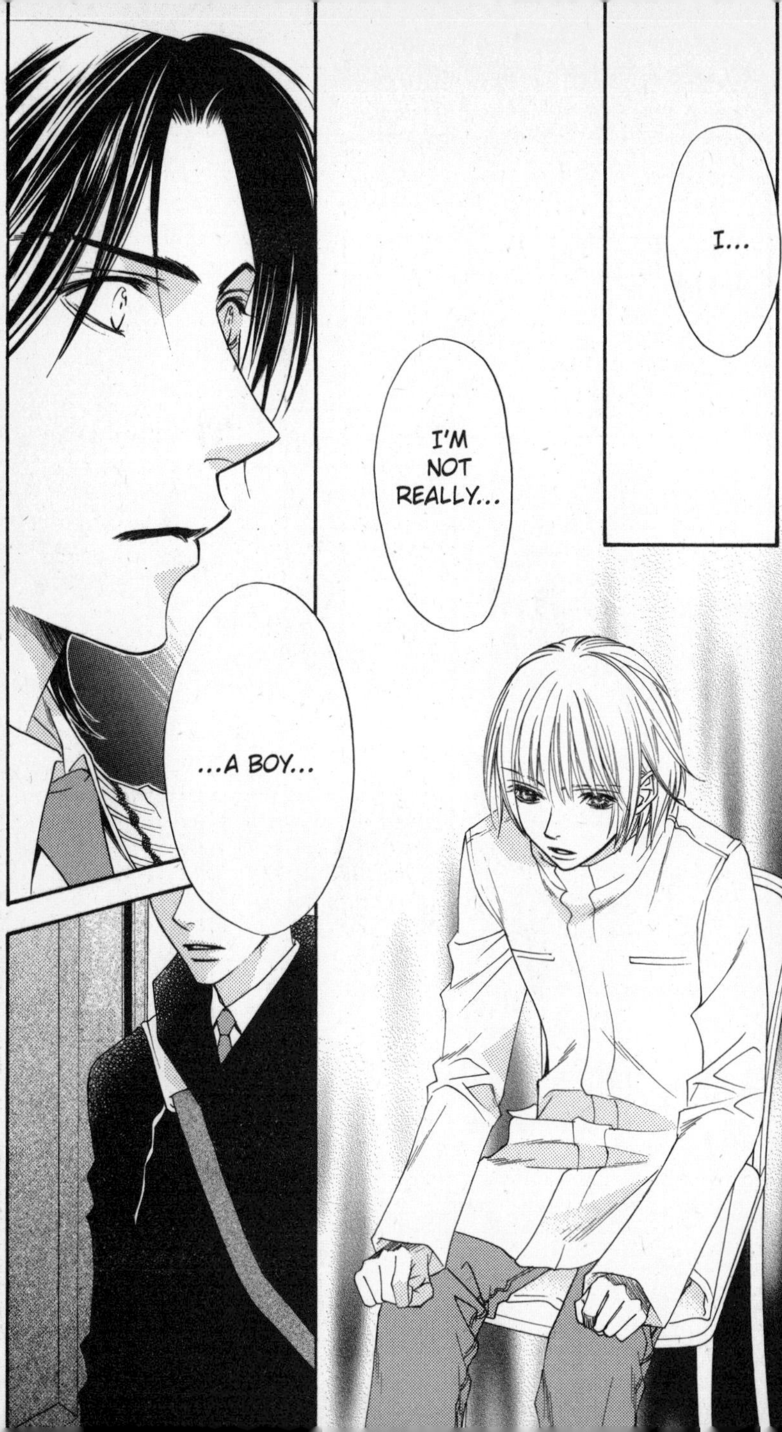
I...
I'M NOT REALLY...
...A BOY...

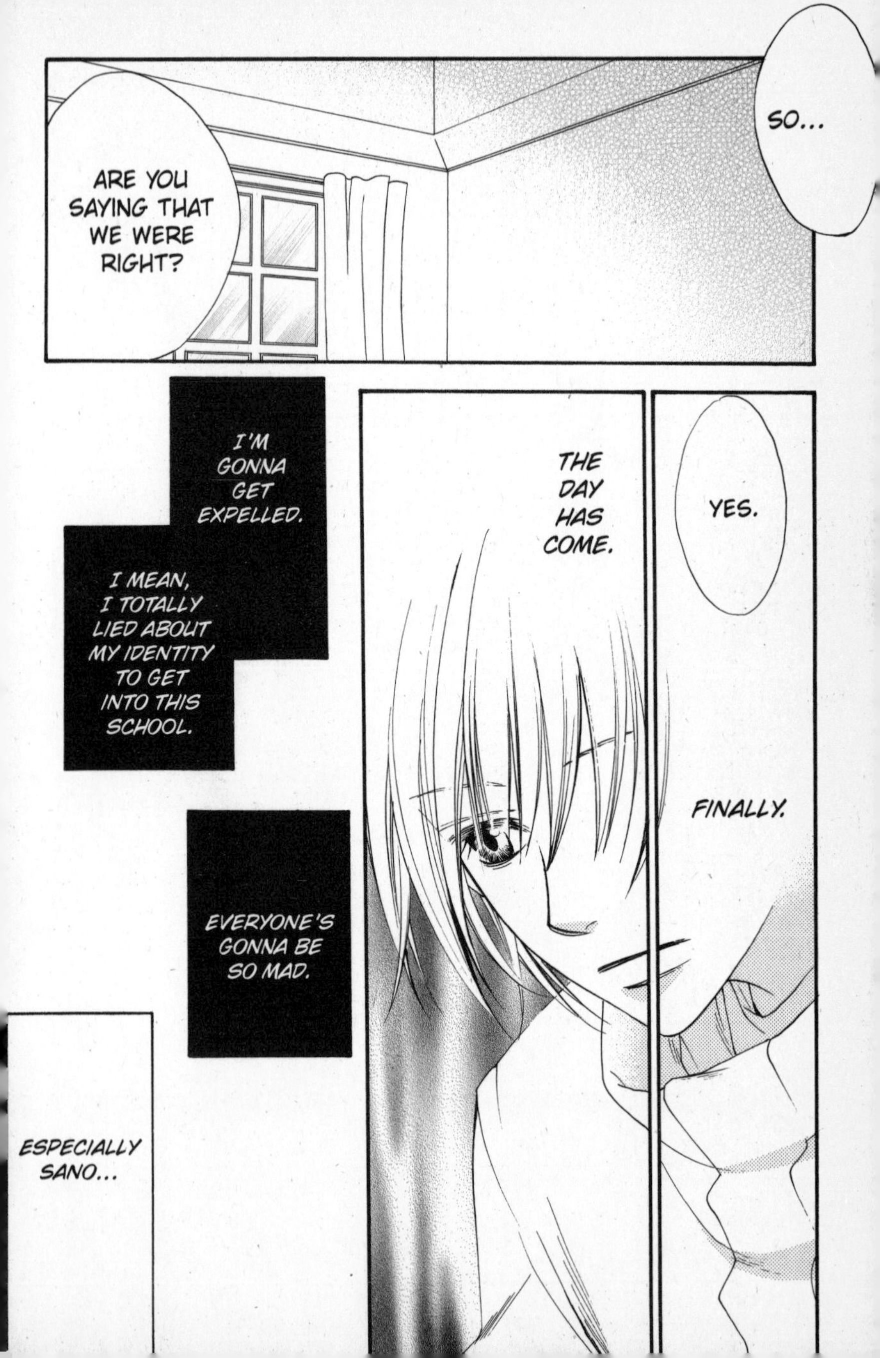

SO...
ARE YOU SAYING THAT WE WERE RIGHT?
YES.
FINALLY.
THE DAY HAS COME.
I'M GONNA GET EXPELLED.
I MEAN, I TOTALLY LIED ABOUT MY IDENTITY TO GET INTO THIS SCHOOL.
EVERYONE'S GONNA BE SO MAD.
ESPECIALLY SANO...

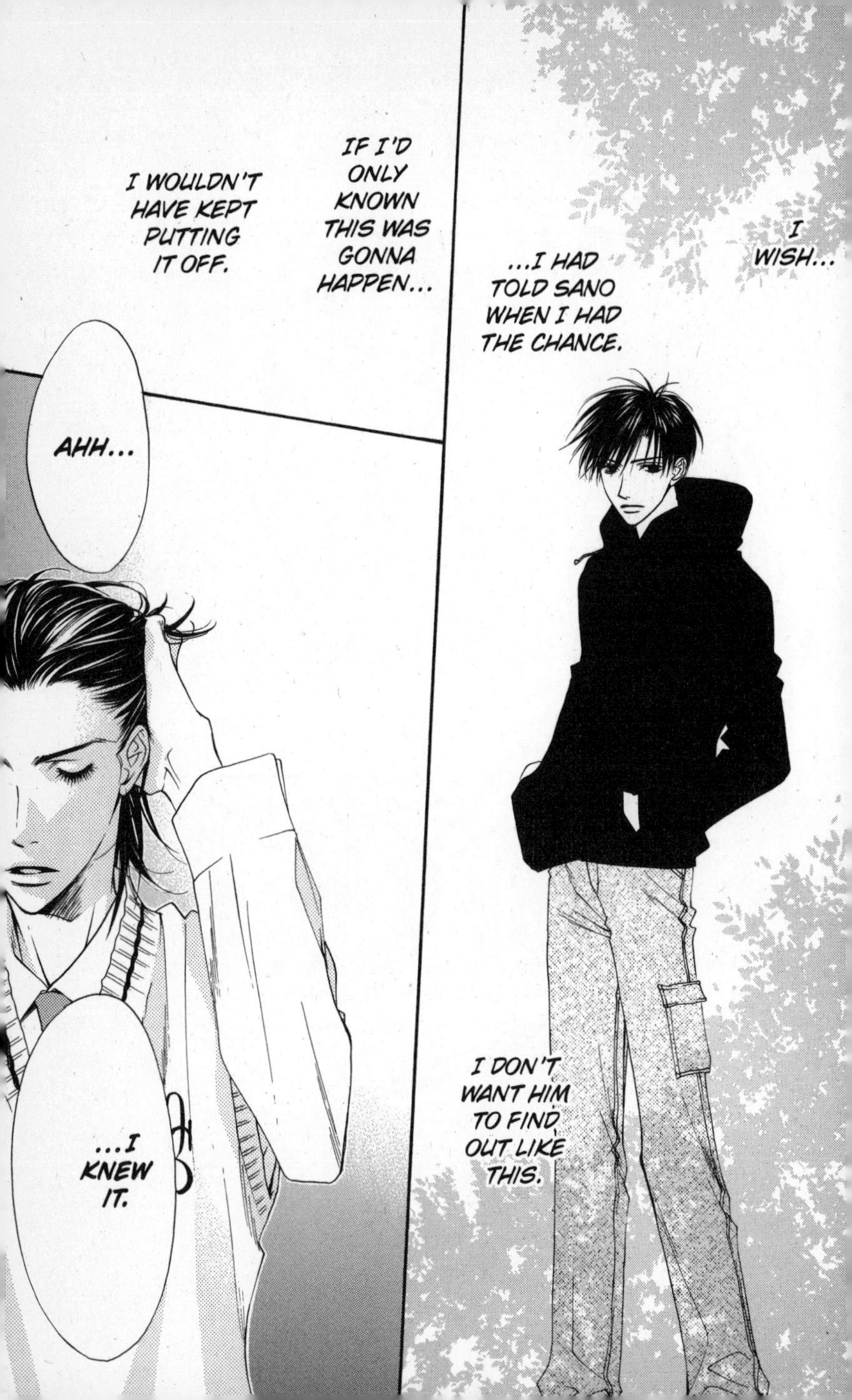
I WISH...
...I HAD TOLD SANO WHEN I HAD THE CHANCE.
I DON'T WANT HIM TO FIND OUT LIKE THIS.
IF I'D ONLY KNOWN THIS WAS GONNA HAPPEN...
I WOULDN'T HAVE KEPT PUTTING IT OFF.
AHH...
...I KNEW IT.

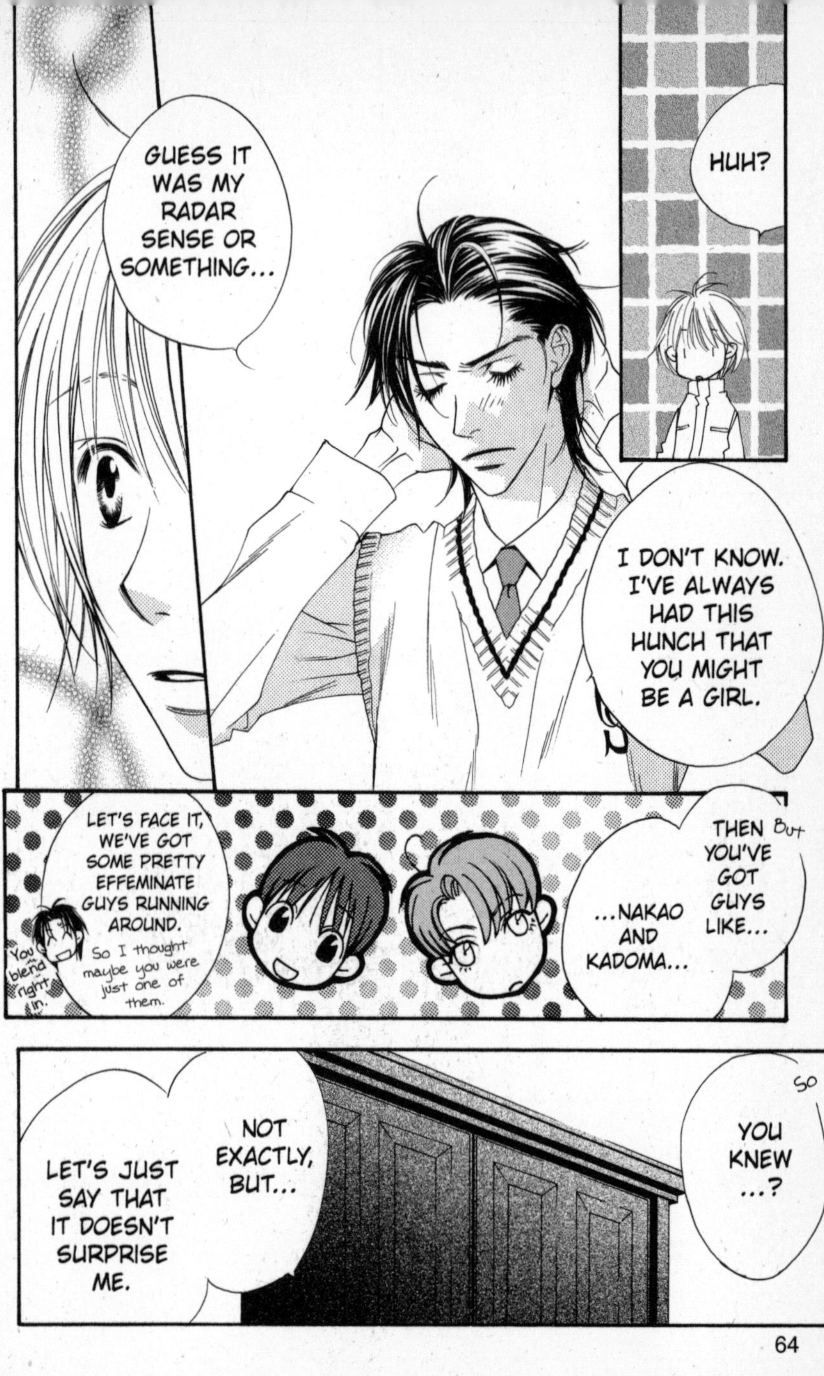
HUH?
GUESS IT WAS MY RADAR SENSE OR SOMETHING...
I DON'T KNOW. I'VE ALWAYS HAD THIS HUNCH THAT YOU MIGHT BE A GIRL.
But THEN YOU'VE GOT GUYS LIKE...
...NAKAO AND KADOMA...
LET'S FACE IT, WE'VE GOT SOME PRETTY EFFEMINATE GUYS RUNNING AROUND.
So I thought maybe you were just one of them.
You blend right in.
So YOU KNEW...?
NOT EXACTLY, BUT...
LET'S JUST SAY THAT IT DOESN'T SURPRISE ME.

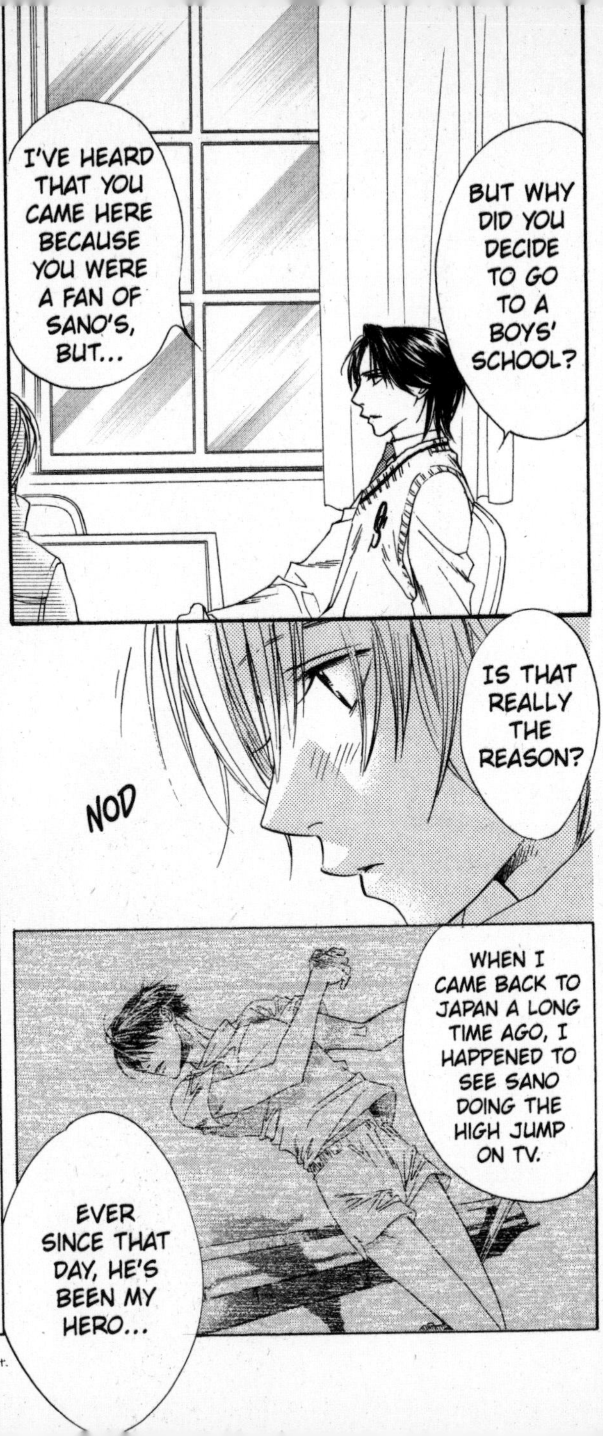
I'VE HEARD THAT YOU CAME HERE BECAUSE YOU WERE A FAN OF SANO'S, BUT...
BUT WHY DID YOU DECIDE TO GO TO A BOYS' SCHOOL?
IS THAT REALLY THE REASON?
NOD
WHEN I CAME BACK TO JAPAN A LONG TIME AGO, I HAPPENED TO SEE SANO DOING THE HIGH JUMP ON TV.
EVER SINCE THAT DAY, HE'S BEEN MY HERO...

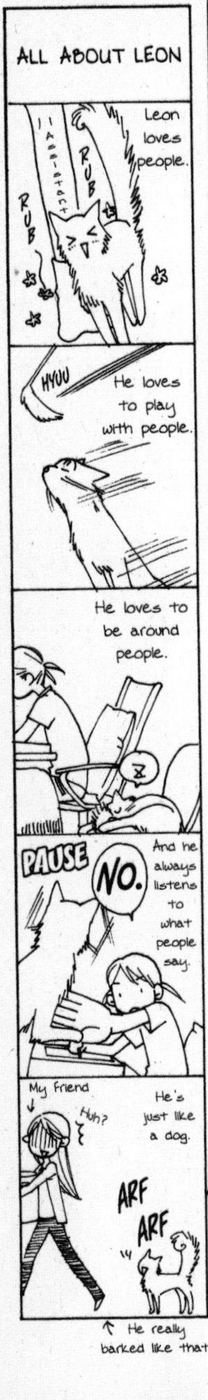
ALL ABOUT LEON
Leon loves people.
RUB
RUB
Assistant
HYUU
He loves to play with people.
He loves to be around people.
PAUSE
NO.
And he always listens to what people say.
My Friend
Huh?
He's just like a dog.
ARF
ARF
He really barked like that.

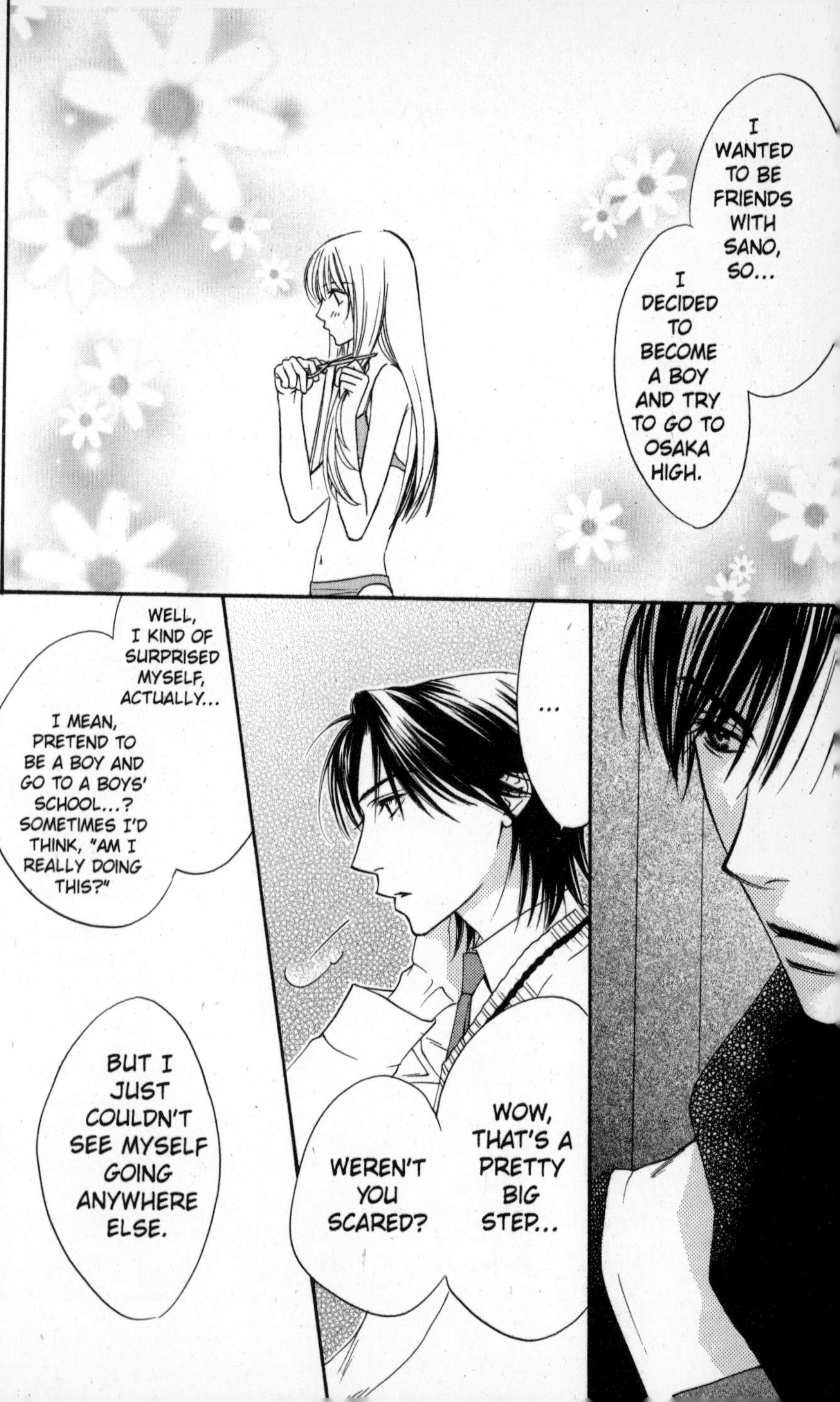
I WANTED TO BE FRIENDS WITH SANO, SO...
I DECIDED TO BECOME A BOY AND TRY TO GO TO OSAKA HIGH.
...
WOW, THAT'S A PRETTY BIG STEP...
WEREN'T YOU SCARED?
WELL, I KIND OF SURPRISED MYSELF, ACTUALLY...
I MEAN, PRETEND TO BE A BOY AND GO TO A BOYS' SCHOOL...? SOMETIMES I'D THINK, "AM I REALLY DOING THIS?"
BUT I JUST COULDN'T SEE MYSELF GOING ANYWHERE ELSE.

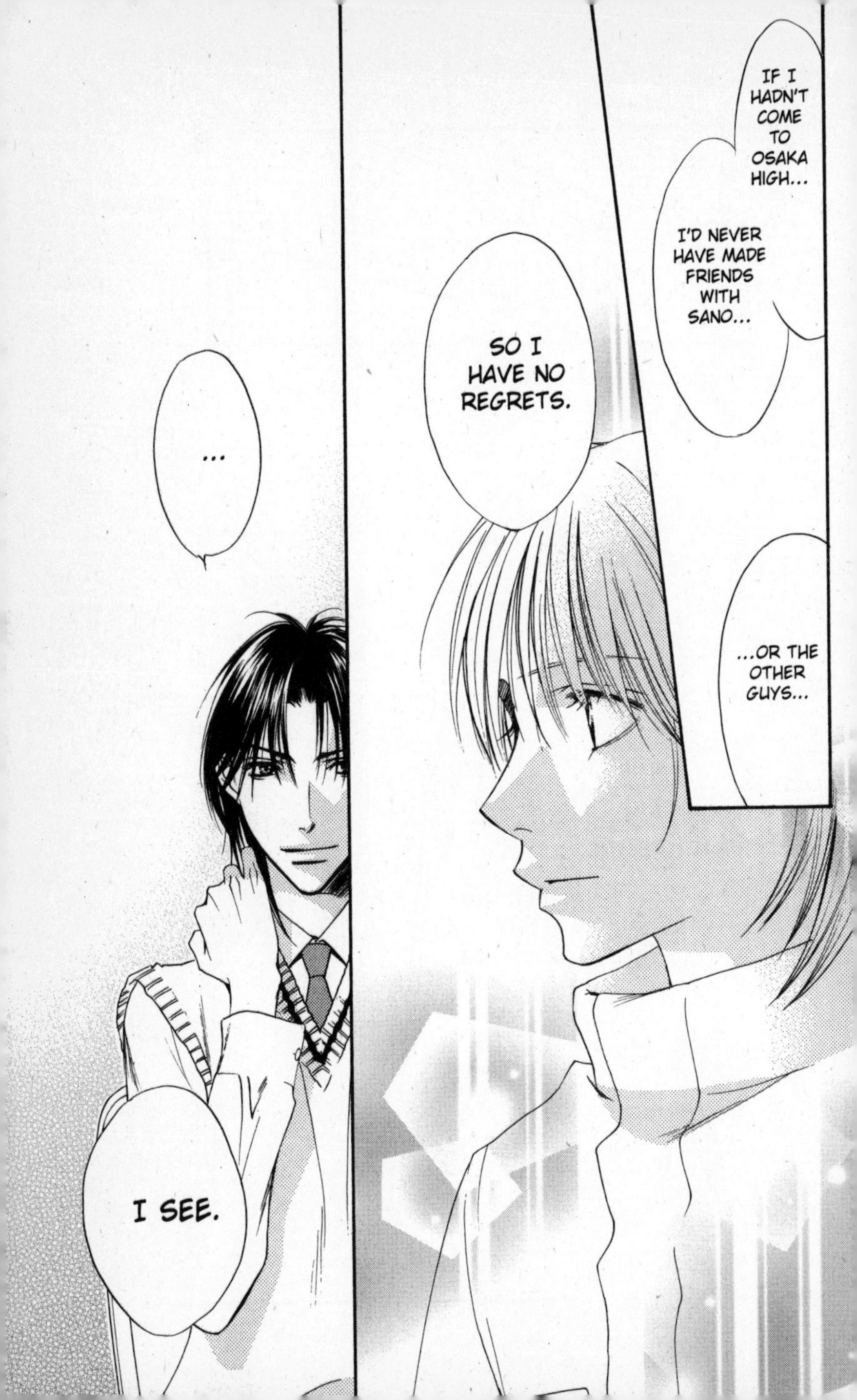
IF I HADN'T COME TO OSAKA HIGH...
I'D NEVER HAVE MADE FRIENDS WITH SANO...
...OR THE OTHER GUYS...
SO I HAVE NO REGRETS.
...
I SEE.

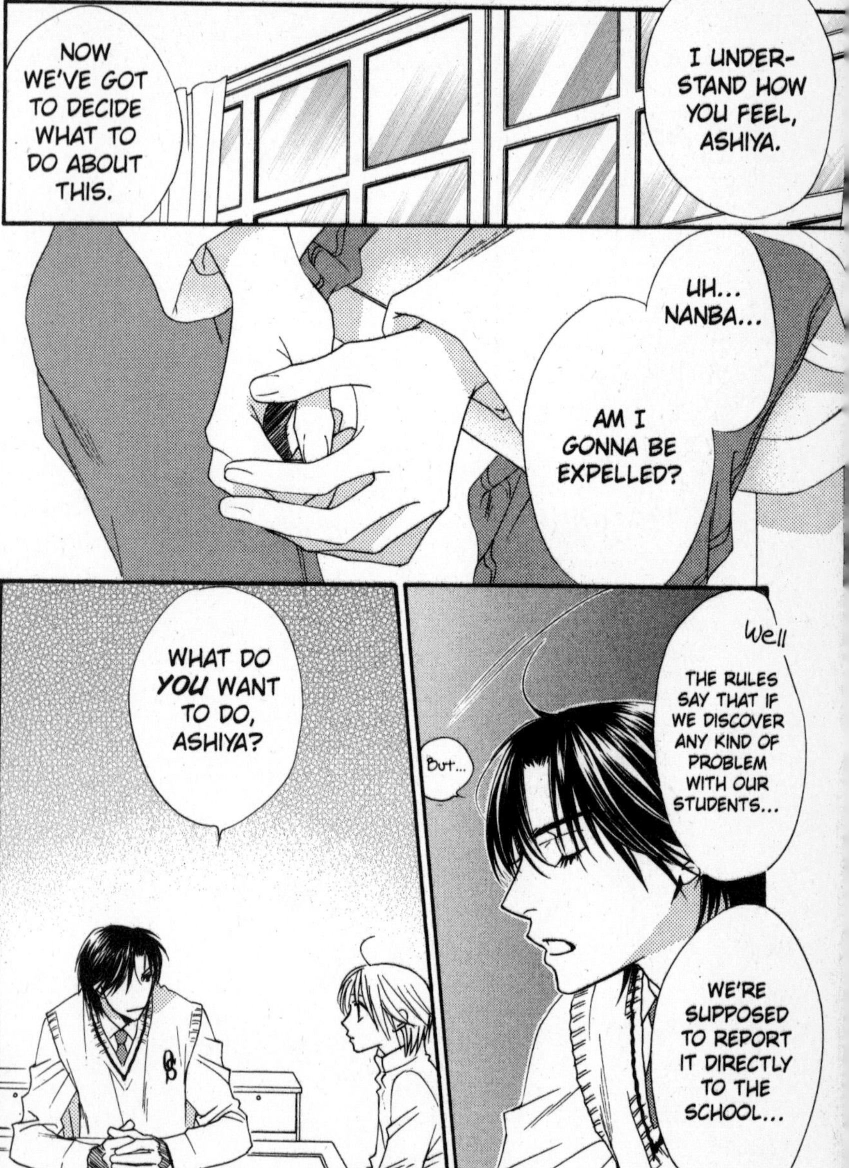
I UNDER-STAND HOW YOU FEEL, ASHIYA.
NOW WE'VE GOT TO DECIDE WHAT TO DO ABOUT THIS.
UH... NANBA...
AM I GONNA BE EXPELLED?
Well
THE RULES SAY THAT IF WE DISCOVER ANY KIND OF PROBLEM WITH OUR STUDENTS...
WE'RE SUPPOSED TO REPORT IT DIRECTLY TO THE SCHOOL...
But...
WHAT DO *YOU* WANT TO DO, ASHIYA?

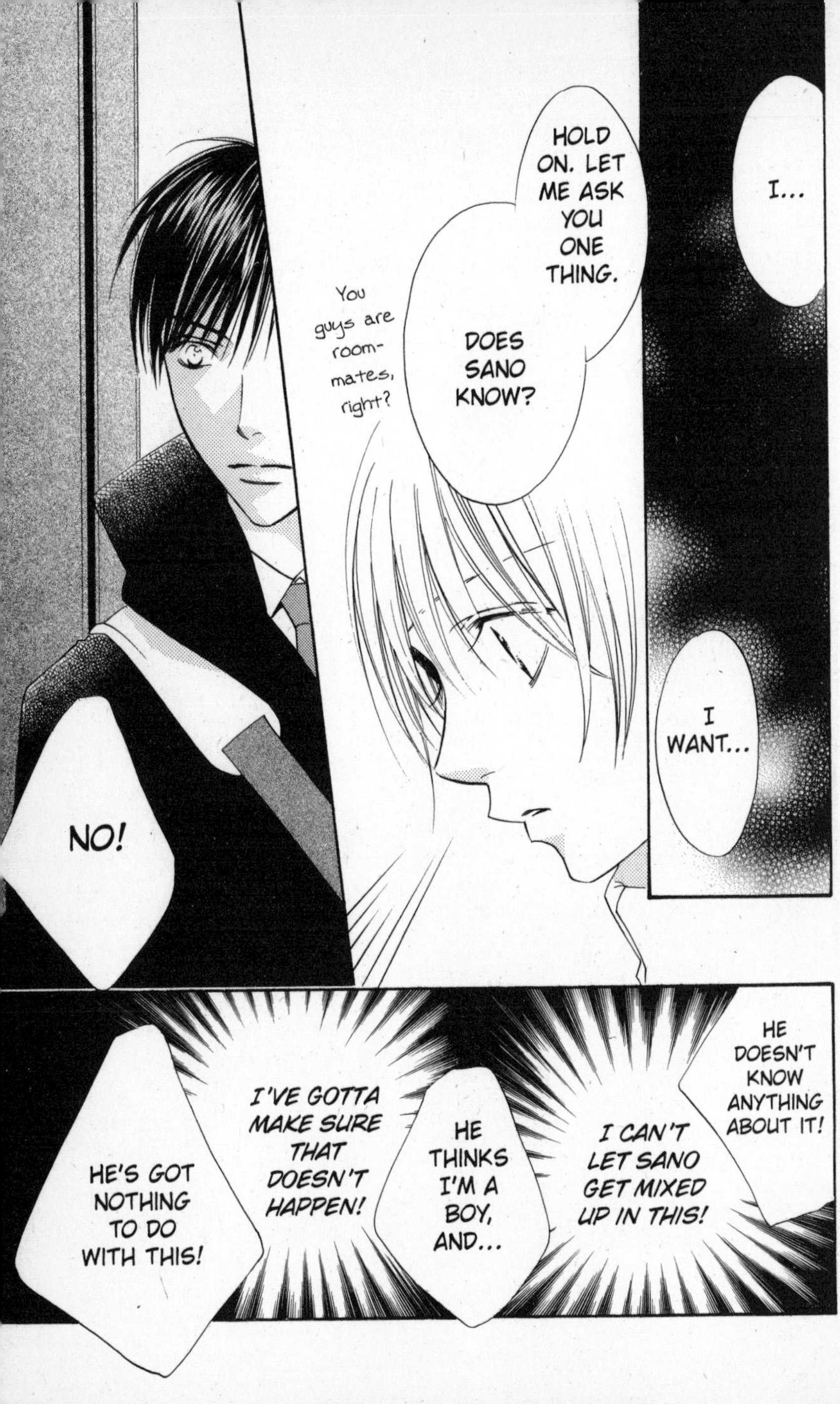
I...
I WANT...
HOLD ON. LET ME ASK YOU ONE THING.
DOES SANO KNOW?
You guys are room-mates, right?
NO!
HE DOESN'T KNOW ANYTHING ABOUT IT!
I CAN'T LET SANO GET MIXED UP IN THIS!
HE THINKS I'M A BOY, AND...
I'VE GOTTA MAKE SURE THAT DOESN'T HAPPEN!
HE'S GOT NOTHING TO DO WITH THIS!

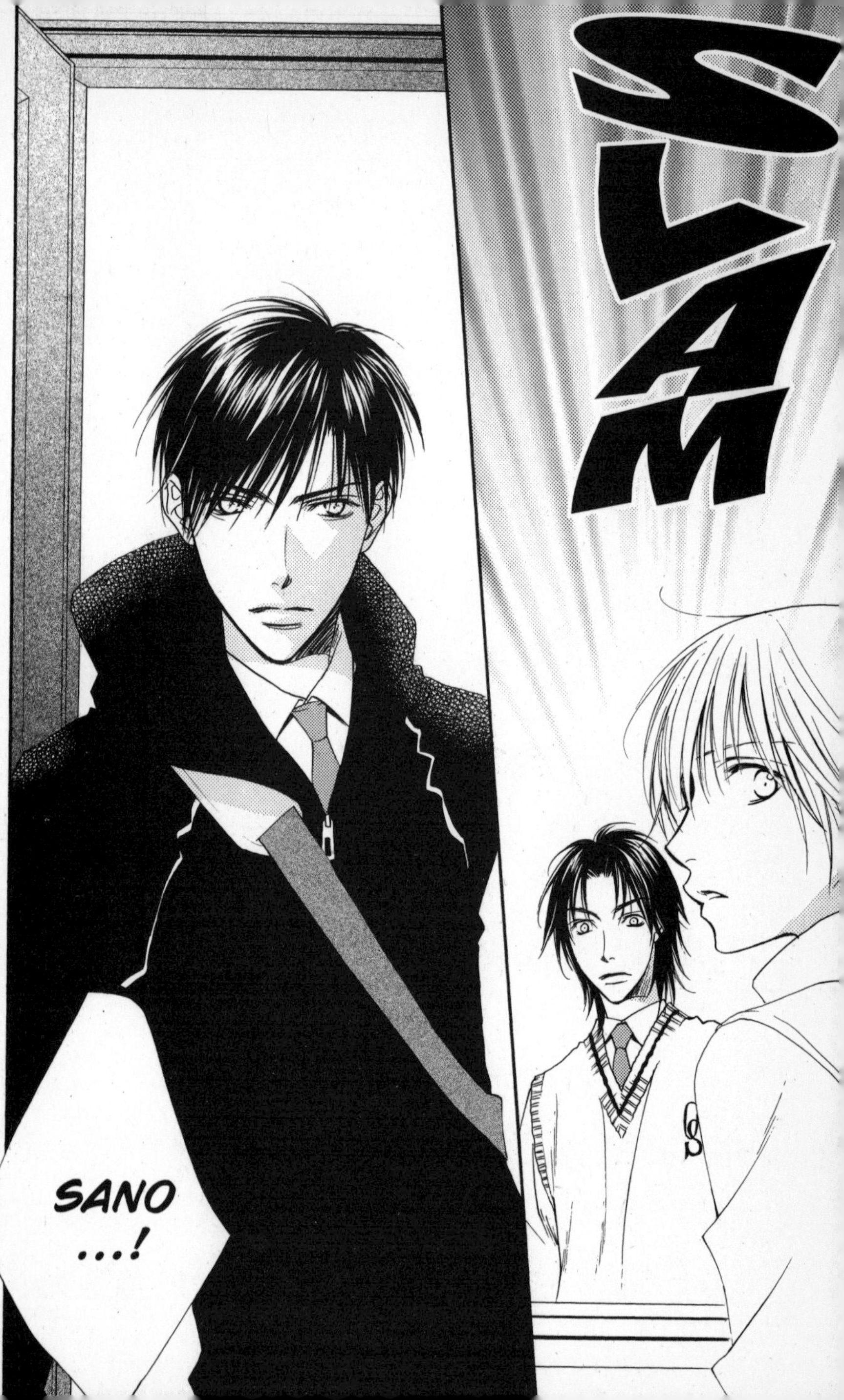
SLAM
SANO ...!

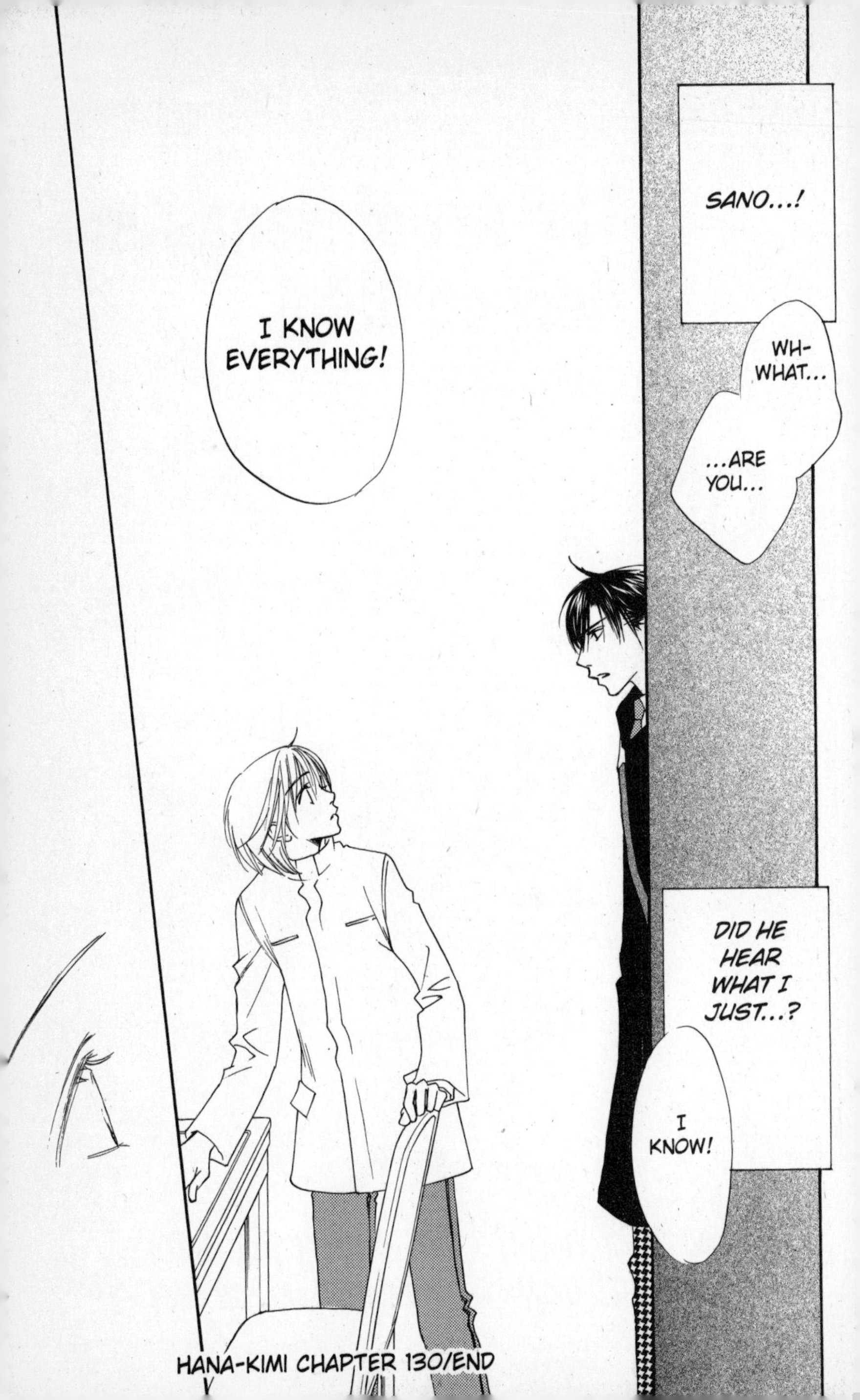
SANO...!
WH-WHAT...
...ARE YOU...
DID HE HEAR WHAT I JUST...?
I KNOW!
I KNOW EVERYTHING!

HANA-KIMI CHAPTER 130/END

The Art of Hana-Kimi Now on Sale!

Just $19.95!

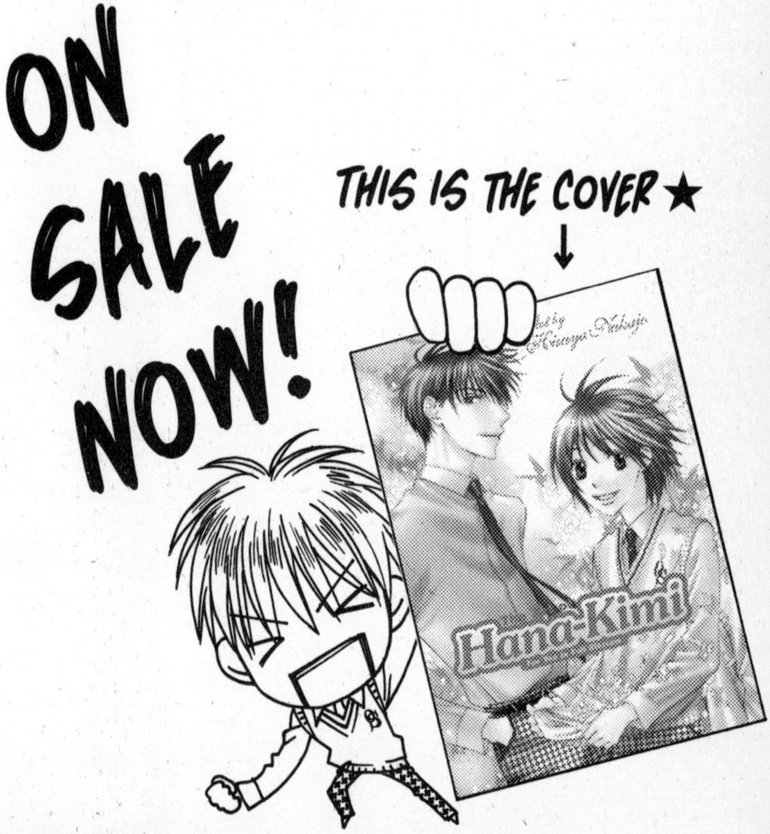
ON SALE NOW!
THIS IS THE COVER ★
Hana-Kimi

IF YOU CAN'T FIND IT AT YOUR LOCAL BOOKSTORE, PLEASE SPECIAL ORDER IT! NOW AVAILABLE IN ENGLISH!

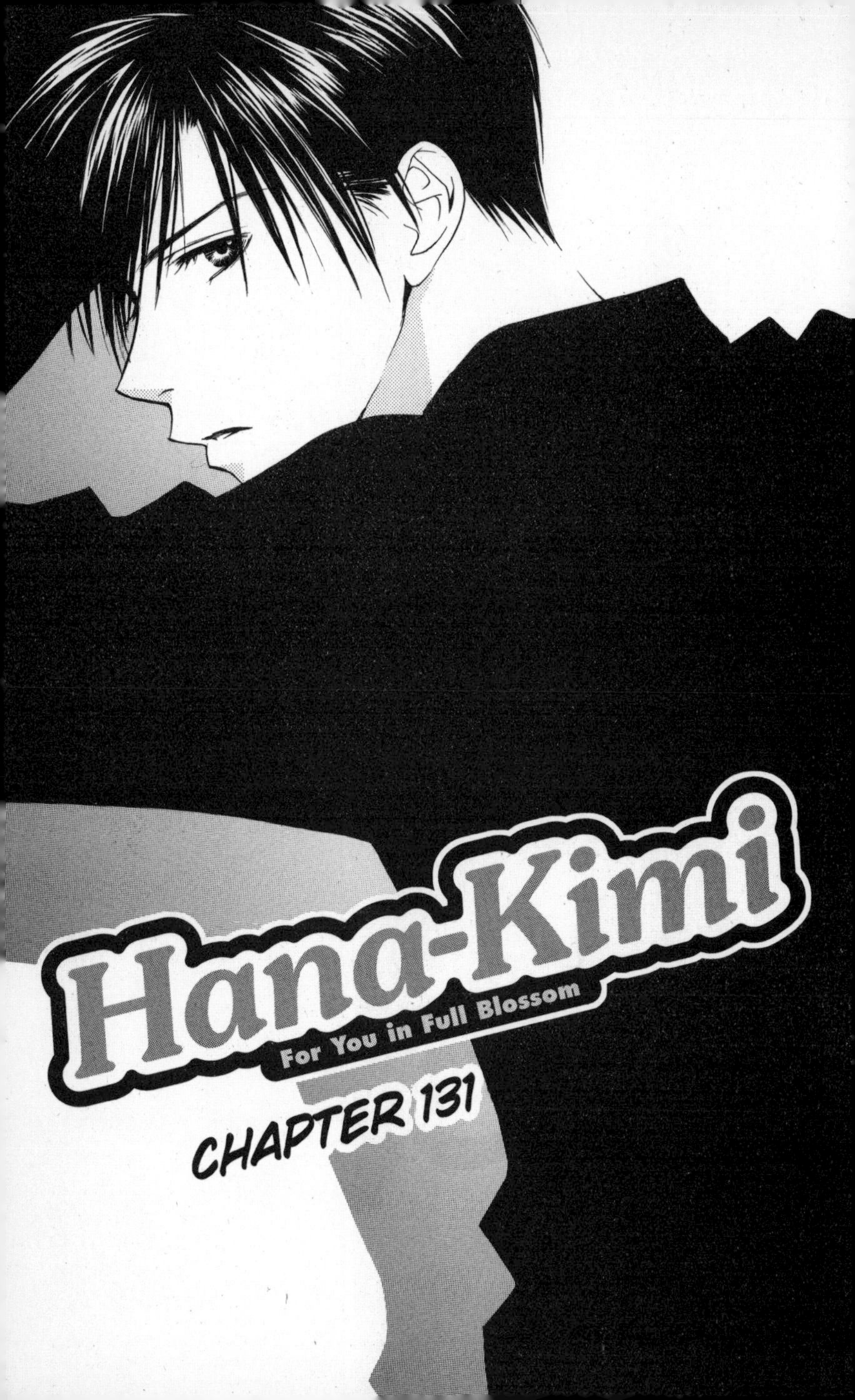
Hana-Kimi
For You in Full Blossom
CHAPTER 131

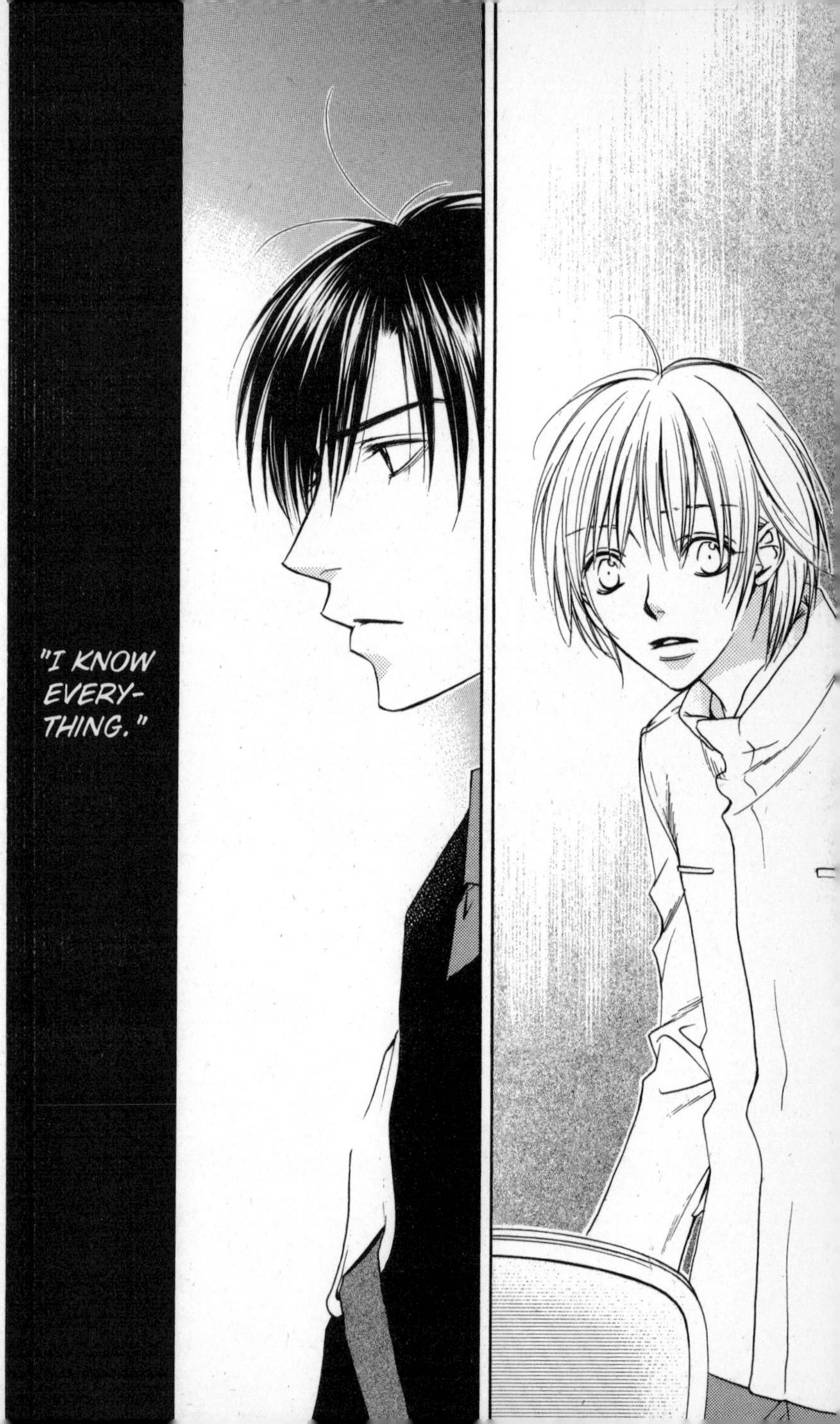
"I KNOW EVERY-THING."

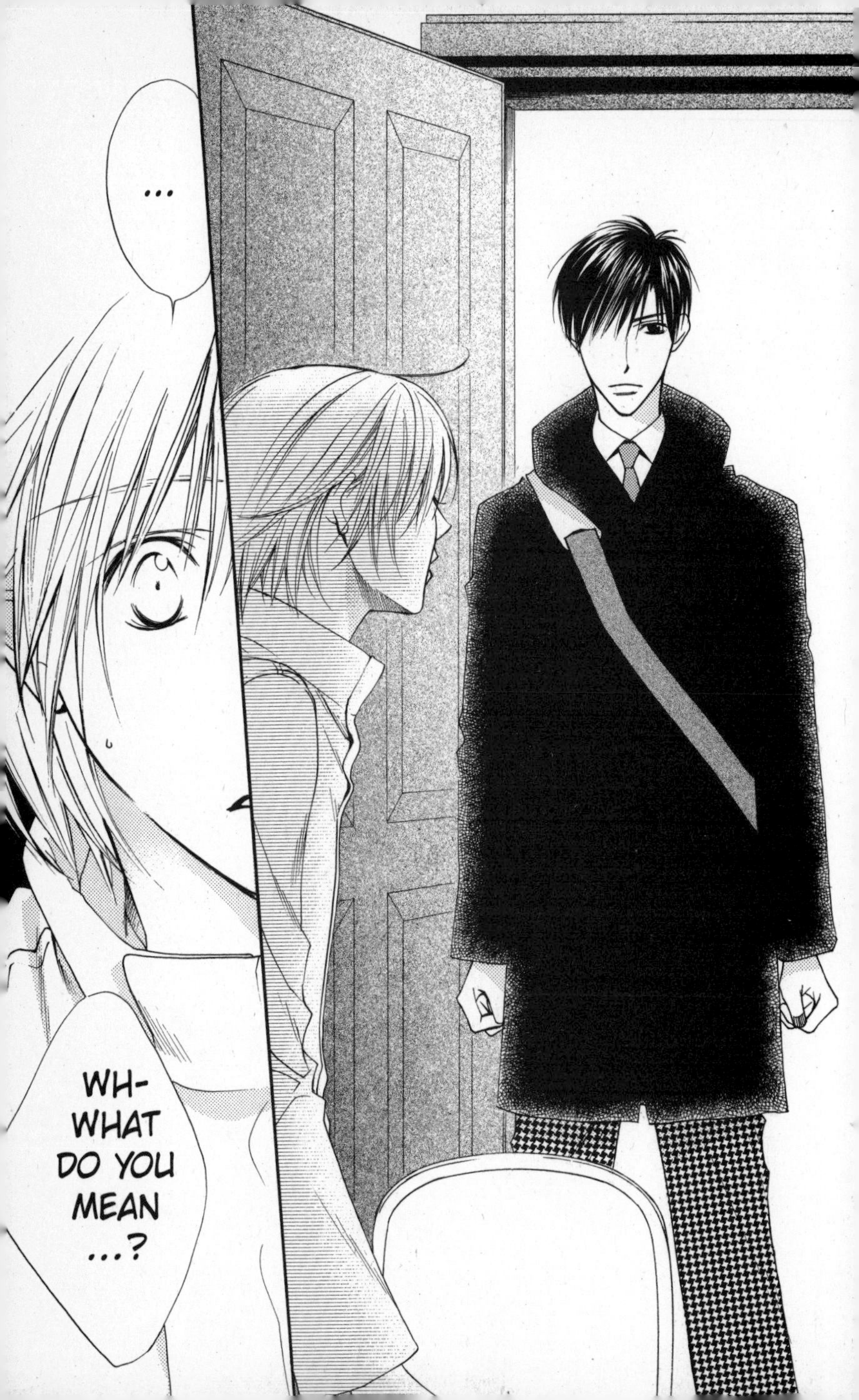
...
WH-WHAT DO YOU MEAN ...?

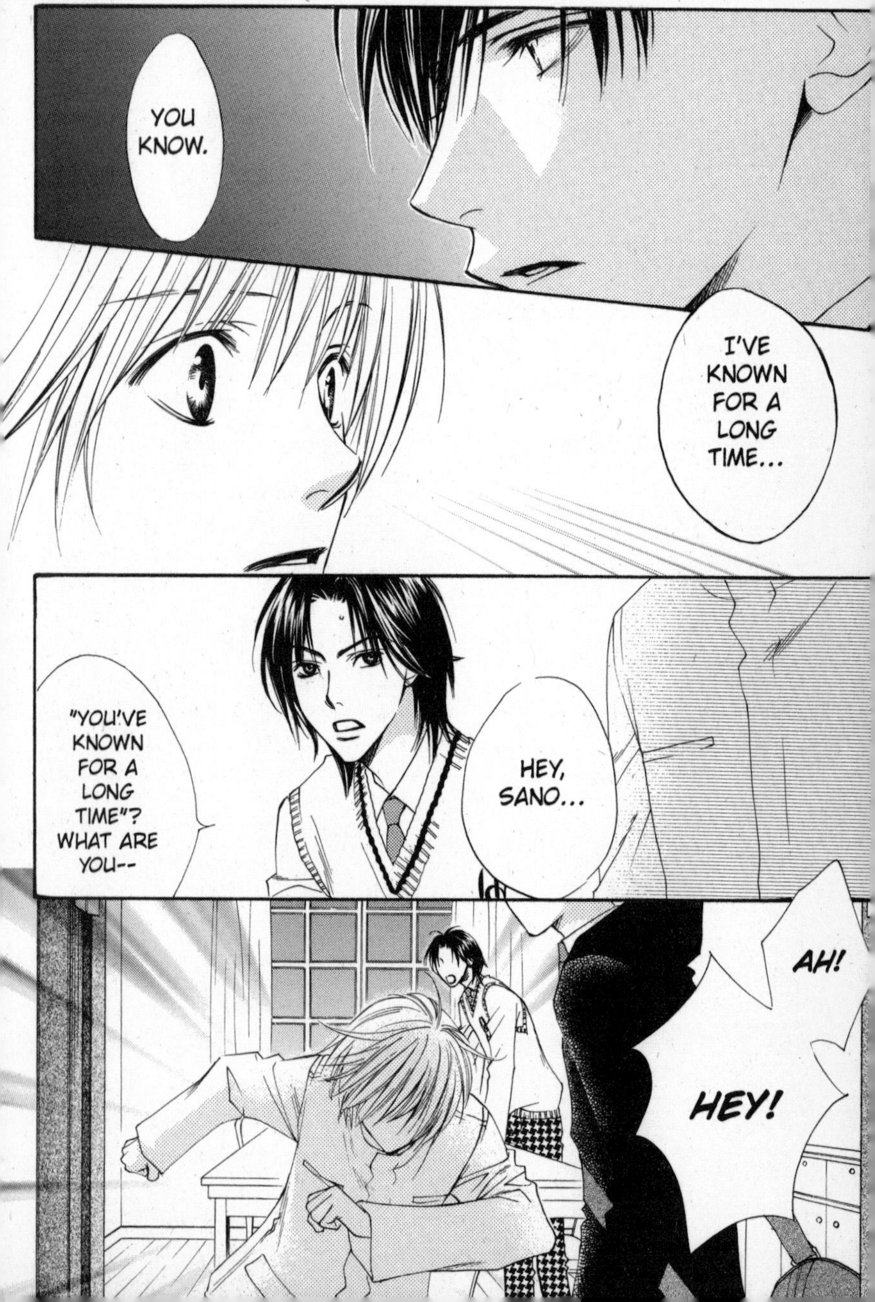
YOU KNOW.
I'VE KNOWN FOR A LONG TIME...
HEY, SANO...
"YOU'VE KNOWN FOR A LONG TIME"? WHAT ARE YOU--
AH!
HEY!

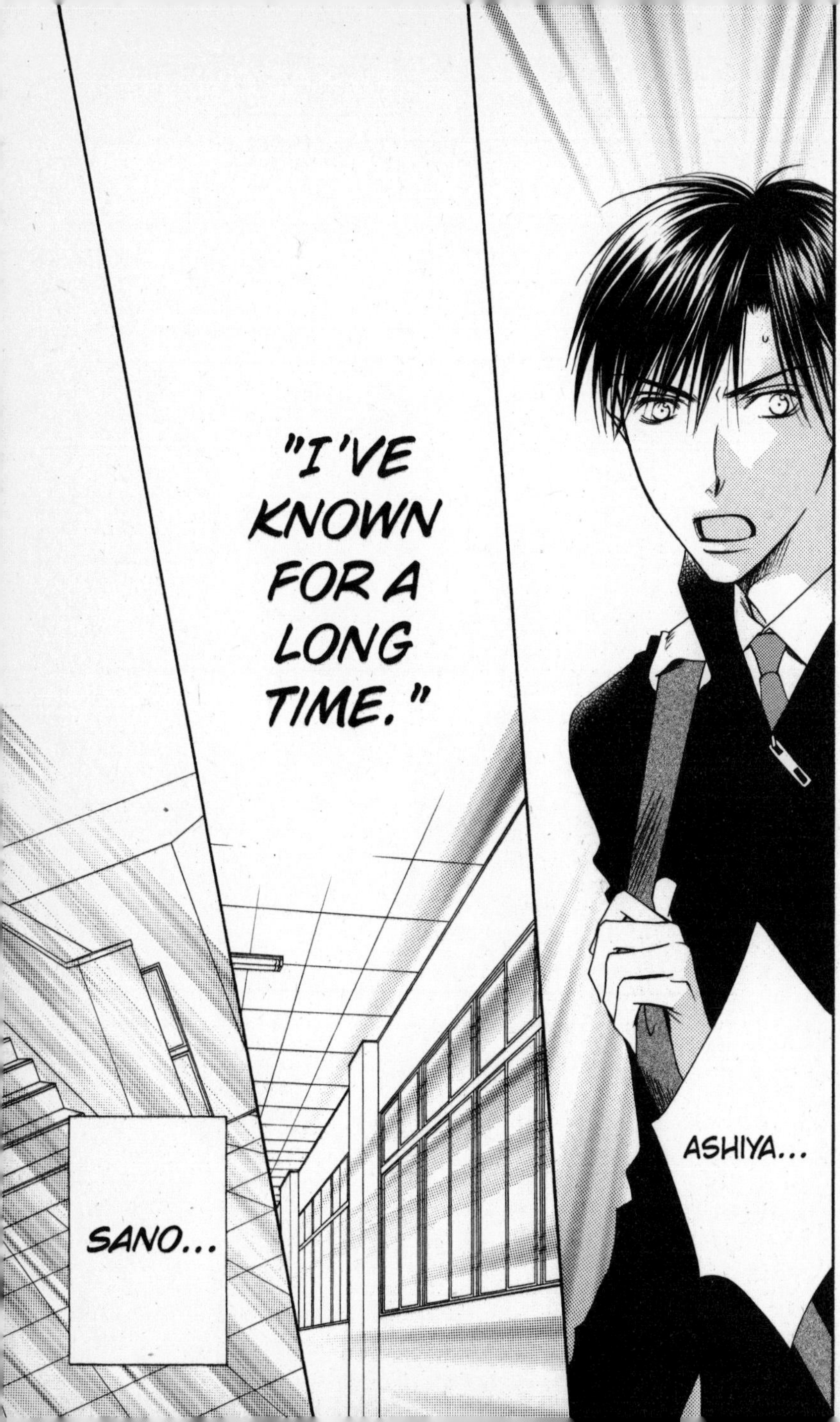
ASHIYA...
"I'VE KNOWN FOR A LONG TIME."
SANO...

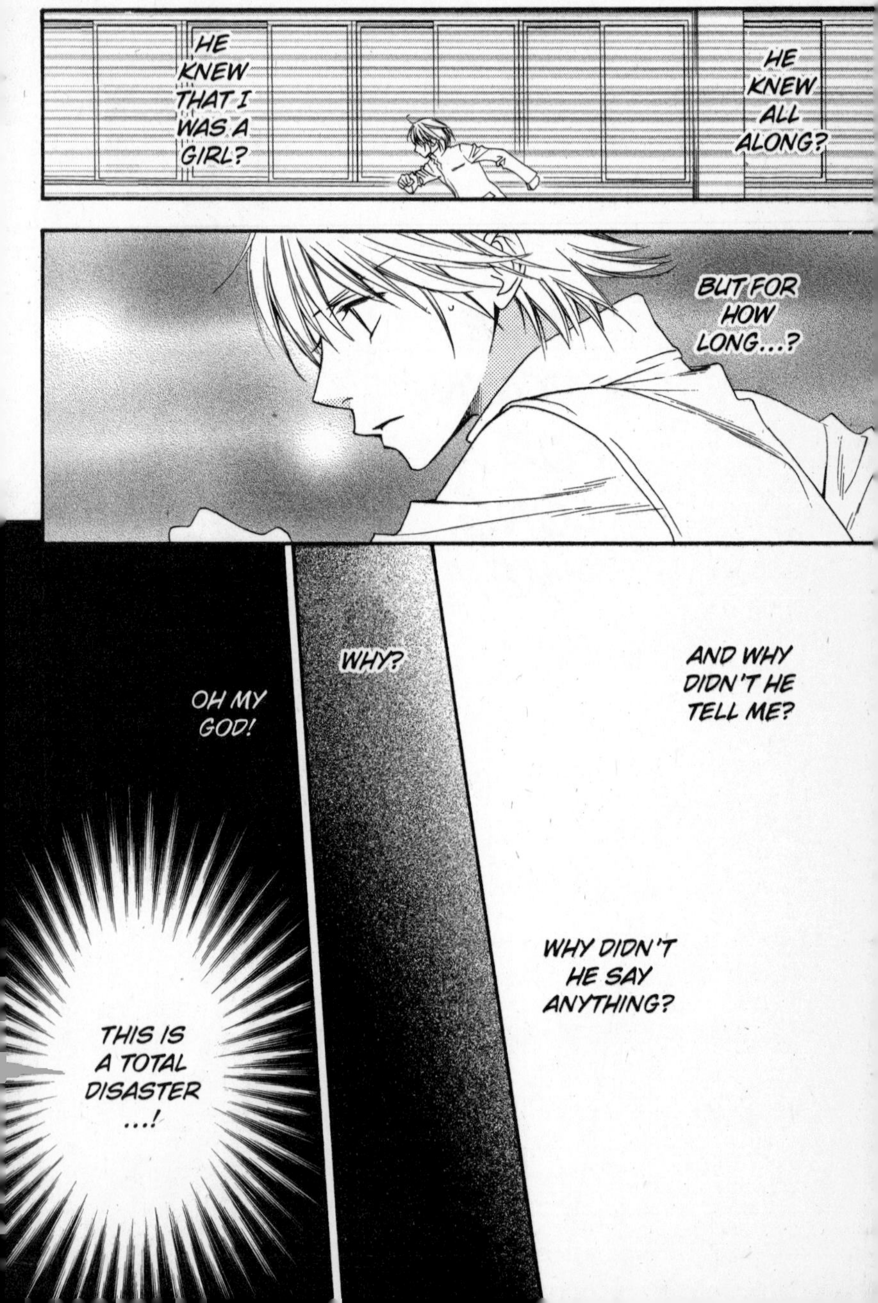
HE KNEW ALL ALONG?
HE KNEW THAT I WAS A GIRL?
BUT FOR HOW LONG...?
AND WHY DIDN'T HE TELL ME?
WHY DIDN'T HE SAY ANYTHING?
WHY?
OH MY GOD!
THIS IS A TOTAL DISASTER ...!

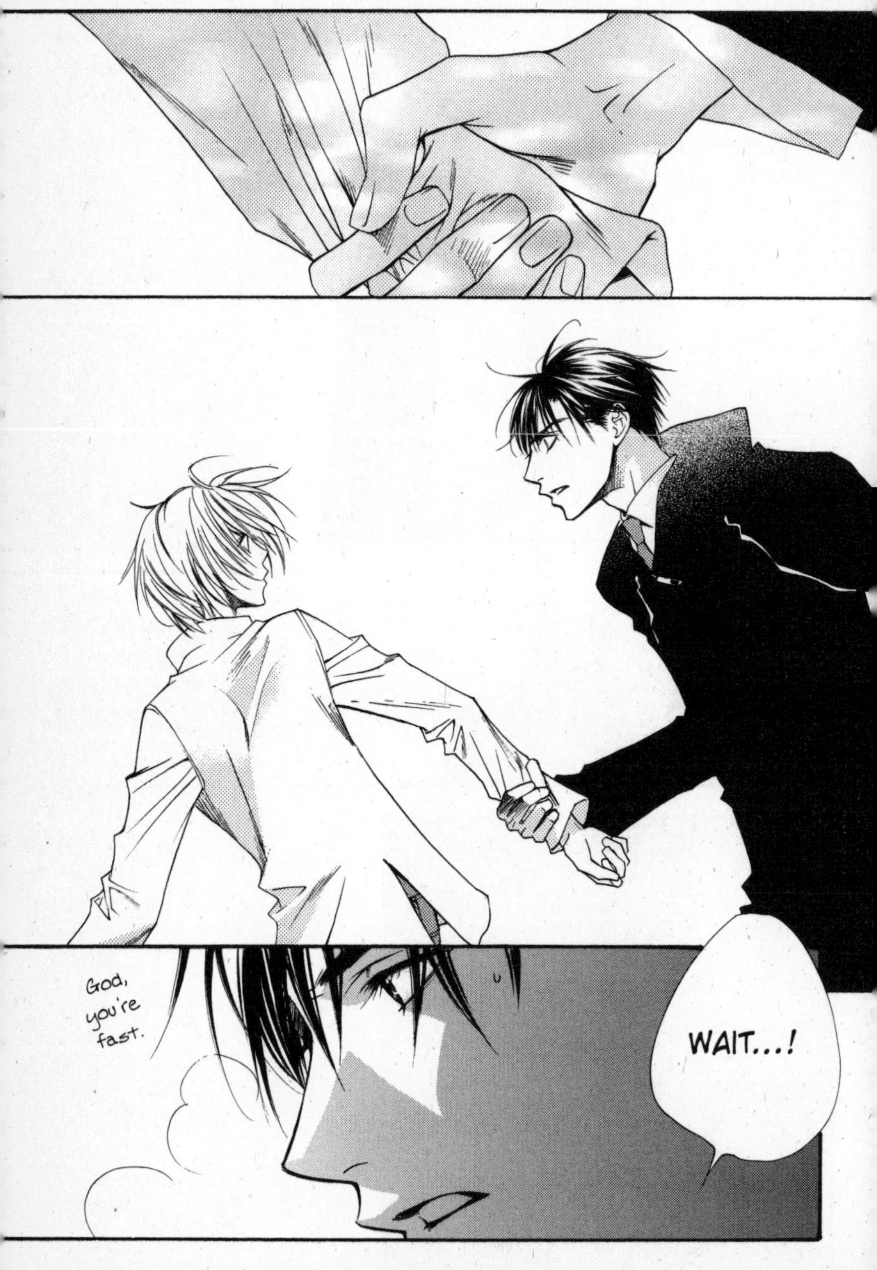
WAIT...!
God, you're fast.

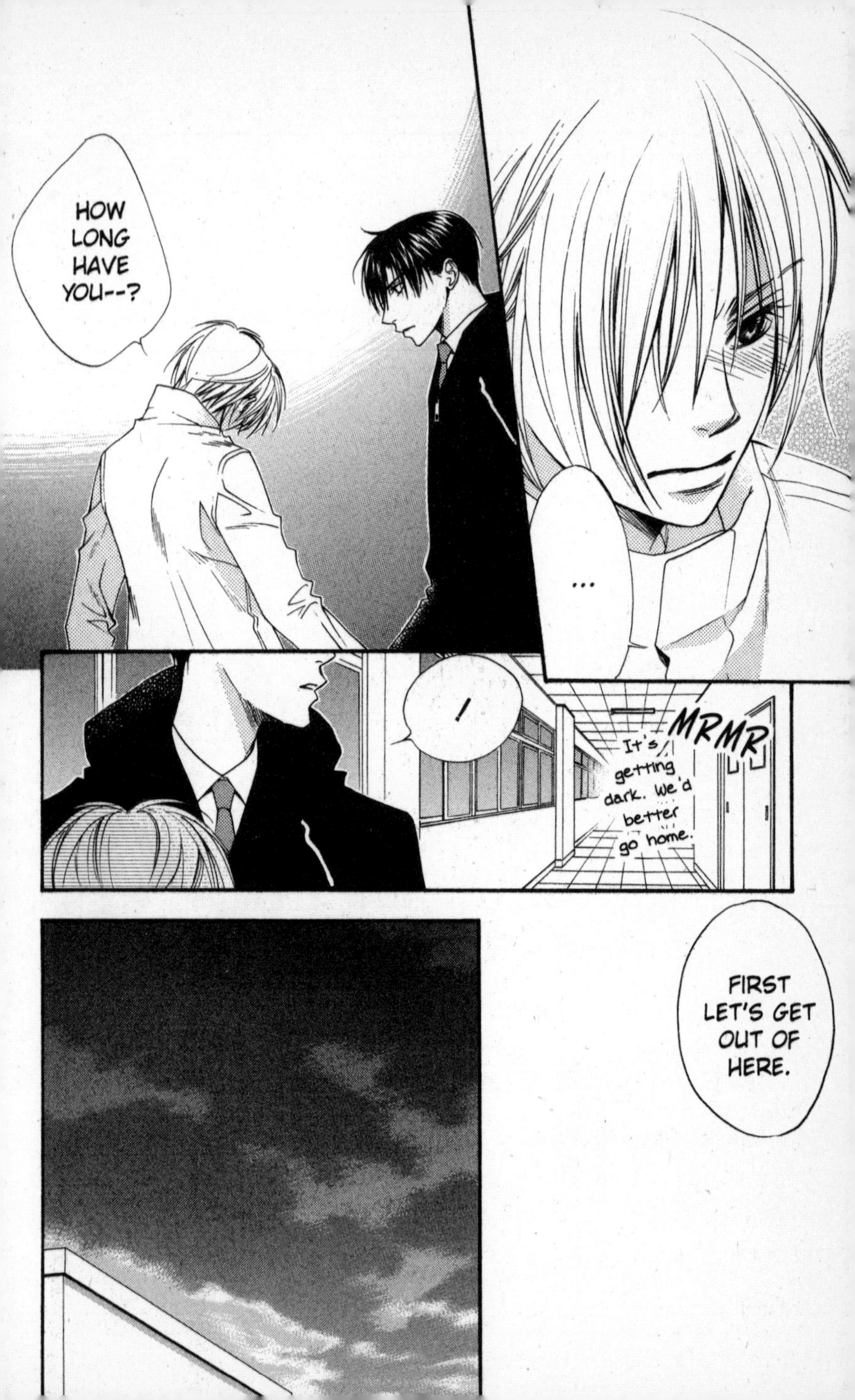
...
HOW LONG HAVE YOU--?
MRMR
It's getting dark. We'd better go home.
!
FIRST LET'S GET OUT OF HERE.

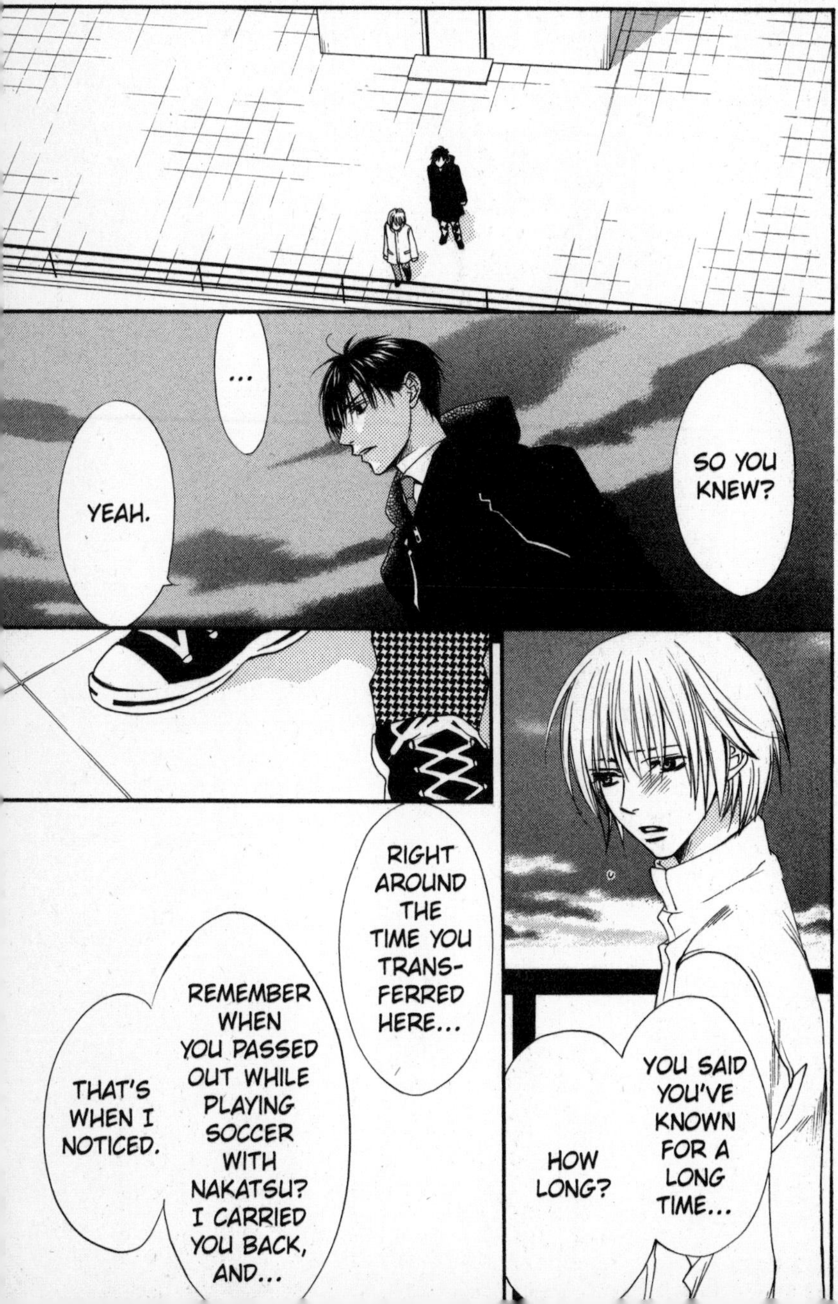
SO YOU KNEW?
...
YEAH.
YOU SAID YOU'VE KNOWN FOR A LONG TIME...
HOW LONG?
RIGHT AROUND THE TIME YOU TRANSFERRED HERE...
REMEMBER WHEN YOU PASSED OUT WHILE PLAYING SOCCER WITH NAKATSU? I CARRIED YOU BACK, AND...
THAT'S WHEN I NOTICED.

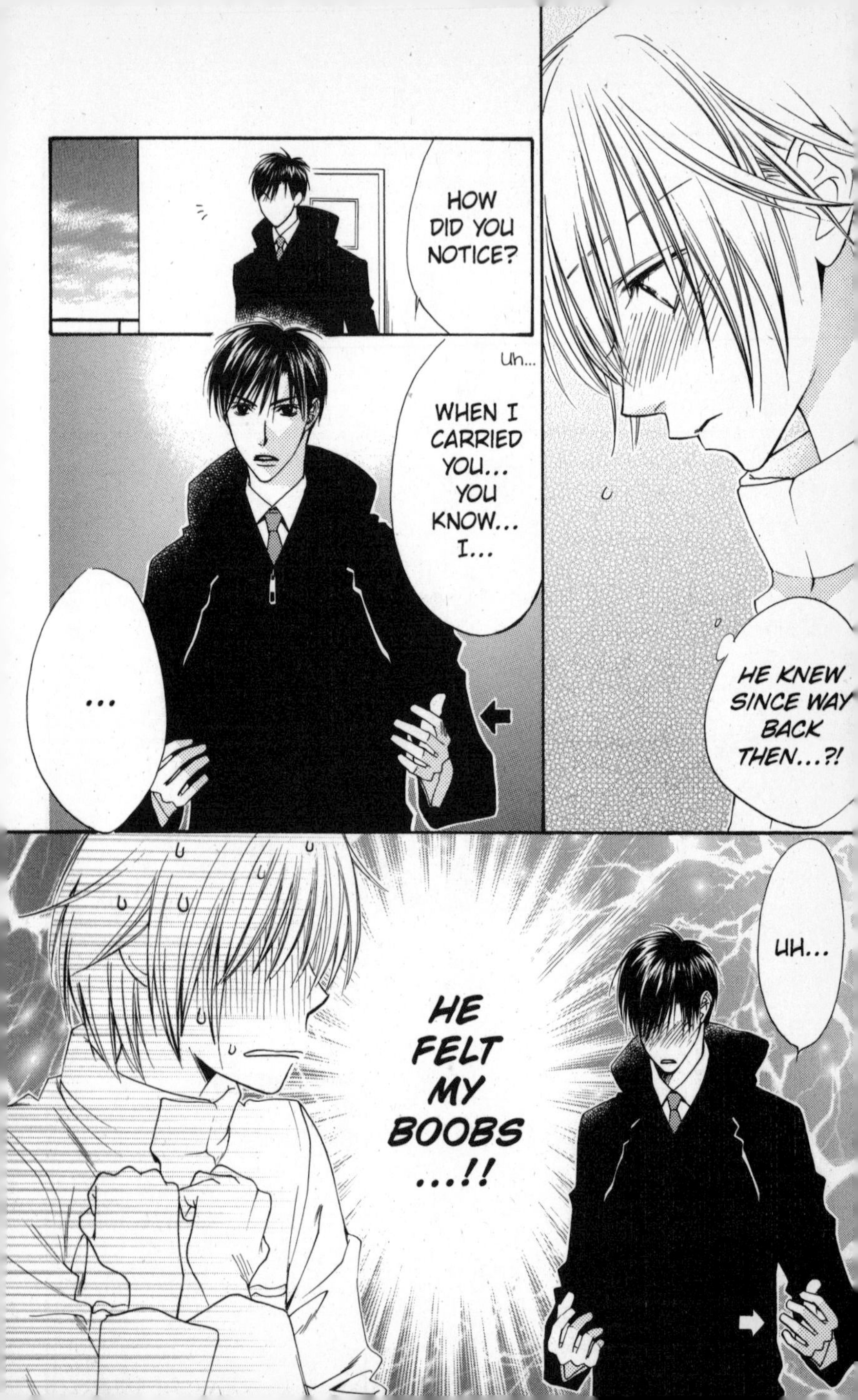
HOW DID YOU NOTICE?
Uh...
WHEN I CARRIED YOU... YOU KNOW... I...
...
HE KNEW SINCE WAY BACK THEN...?!
UH...
HE FELT MY BOOBS ...!!

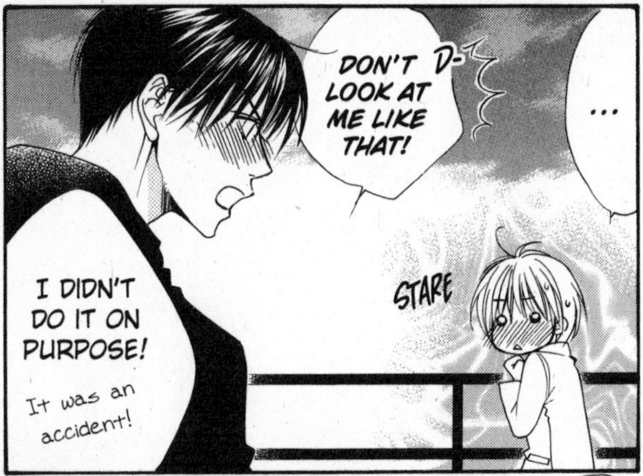
...
D-
DON'T LOOK AT ME LIKE THAT!
STARE
I DIDN'T DO IT ON PURPOSE!
It was an accident!

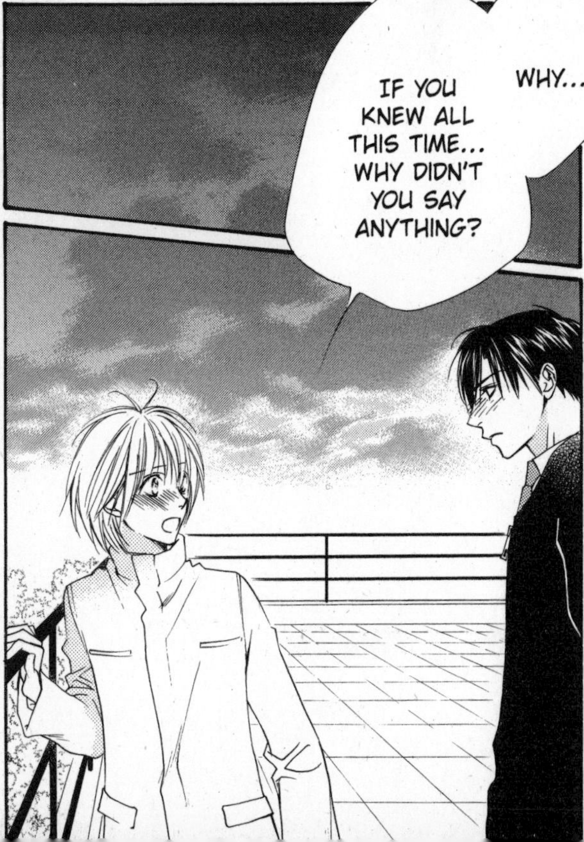
WHY...
IF YOU KNEW ALL THIS TIME... WHY DIDN'T YOU SAY ANYTHING?

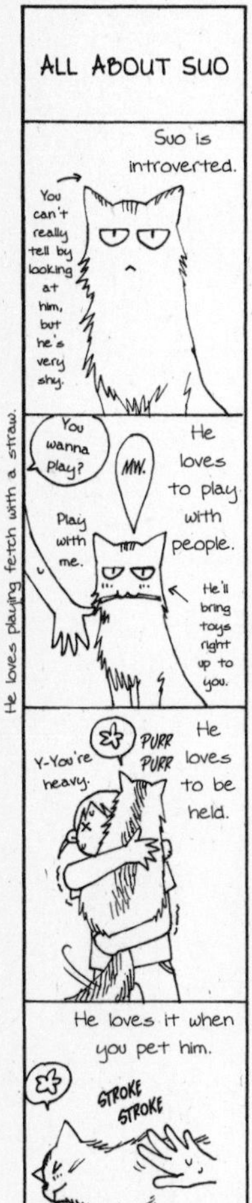
ALL ABOUT SUO
Suo is introverted.
You can't really tell by looking at him, but he's very shy.
He loves to play with people.
You wanna play?
MW.
Play with me.
He'll bring toys right up to you.
He loves playing fetch with a straw.
He loves to be held.
PURR PURR
Y-You're heavy.
He loves it when you pet him.
STROKE STROKE
PURR PURR
My hand's getting tired.
As soon as my hand stops he gets mad.
SMACK

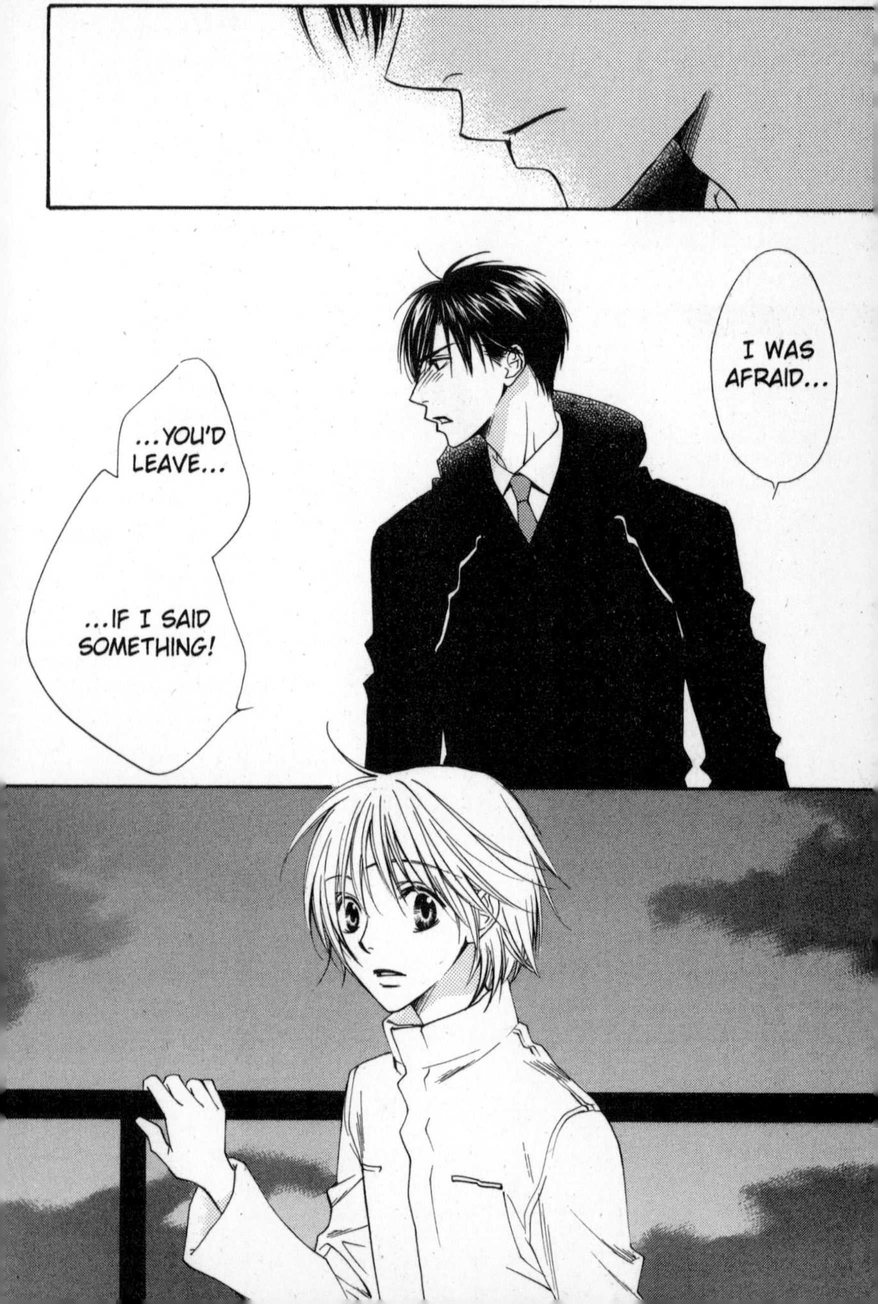
I WAS AFRAID...
...YOU'D LEAVE...
...IF I SAID SOMETHING!

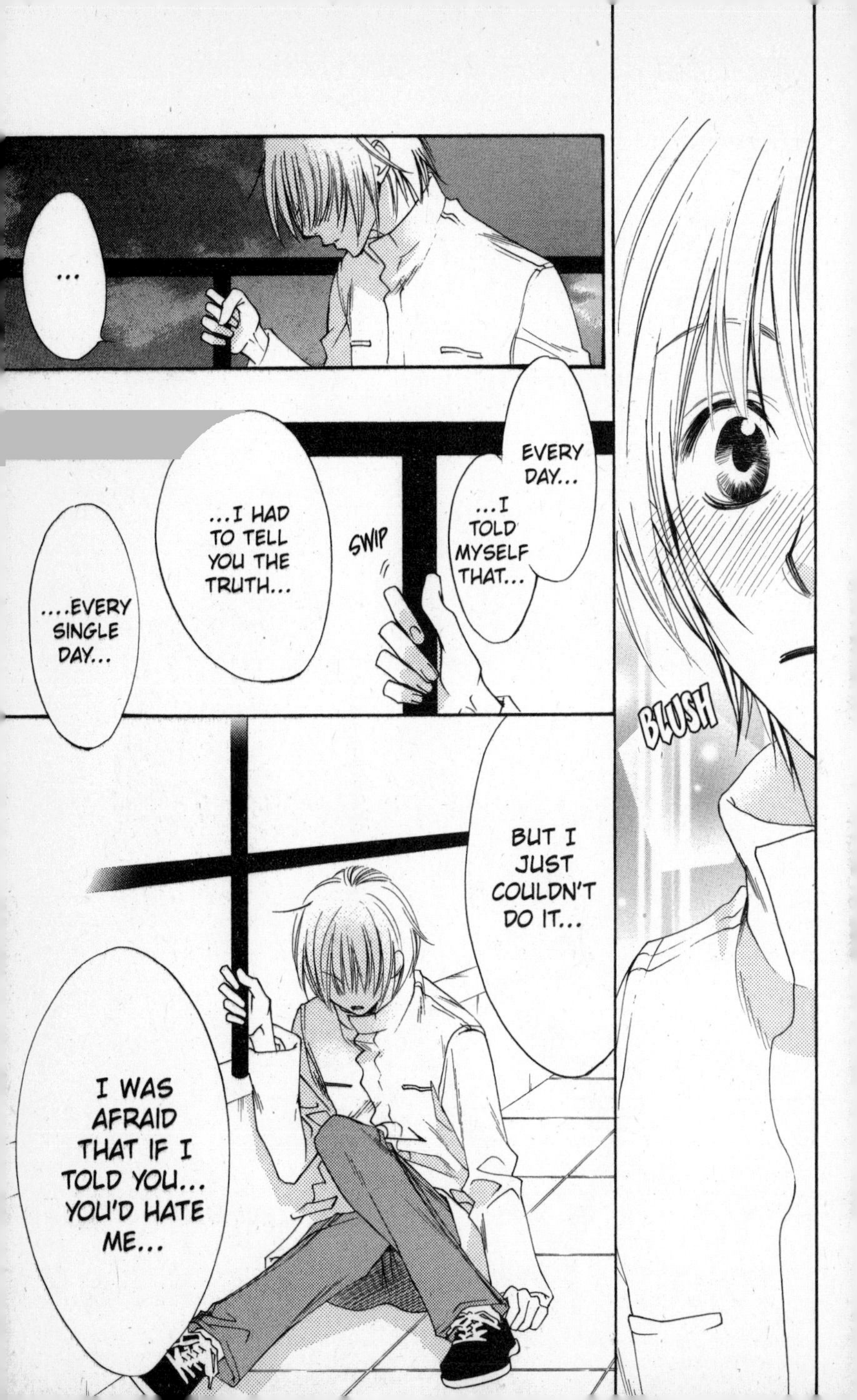
BLUSH
...
EVERY DAY...
...I TOLD MYSELF THAT...
...I HAD TO TELL YOU THE TRUTH...
SWIP
....EVERY SINGLE DAY...
BUT I JUST COULDN'T DO IT...
I WAS AFRAID THAT IF I TOLD YOU... YOU'D HATE ME...

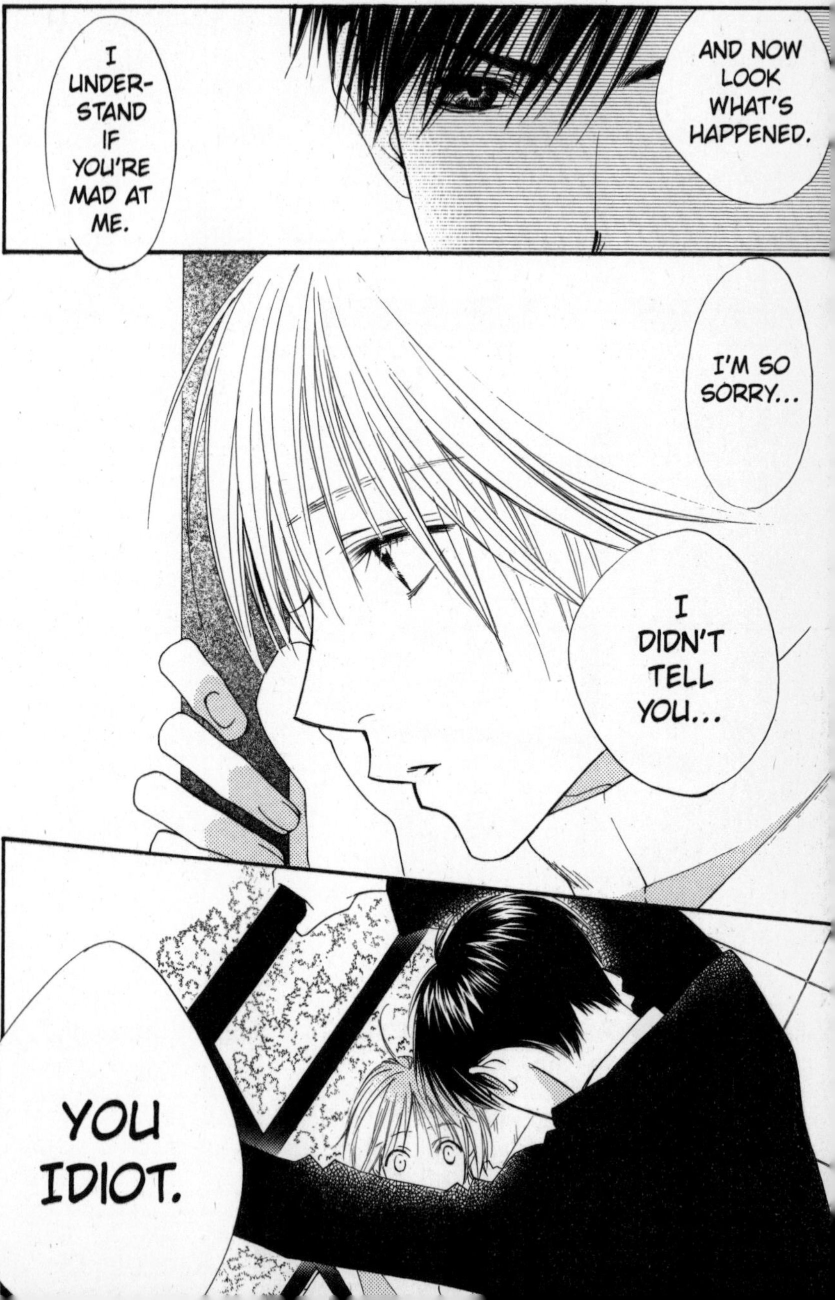
AND NOW LOOK WHAT'S HAPPENED.
I UNDER-STAND IF YOU'RE MAD AT ME.
I'M SO SORRY...
I DIDN'T TELL YOU...
YOU IDIOT.

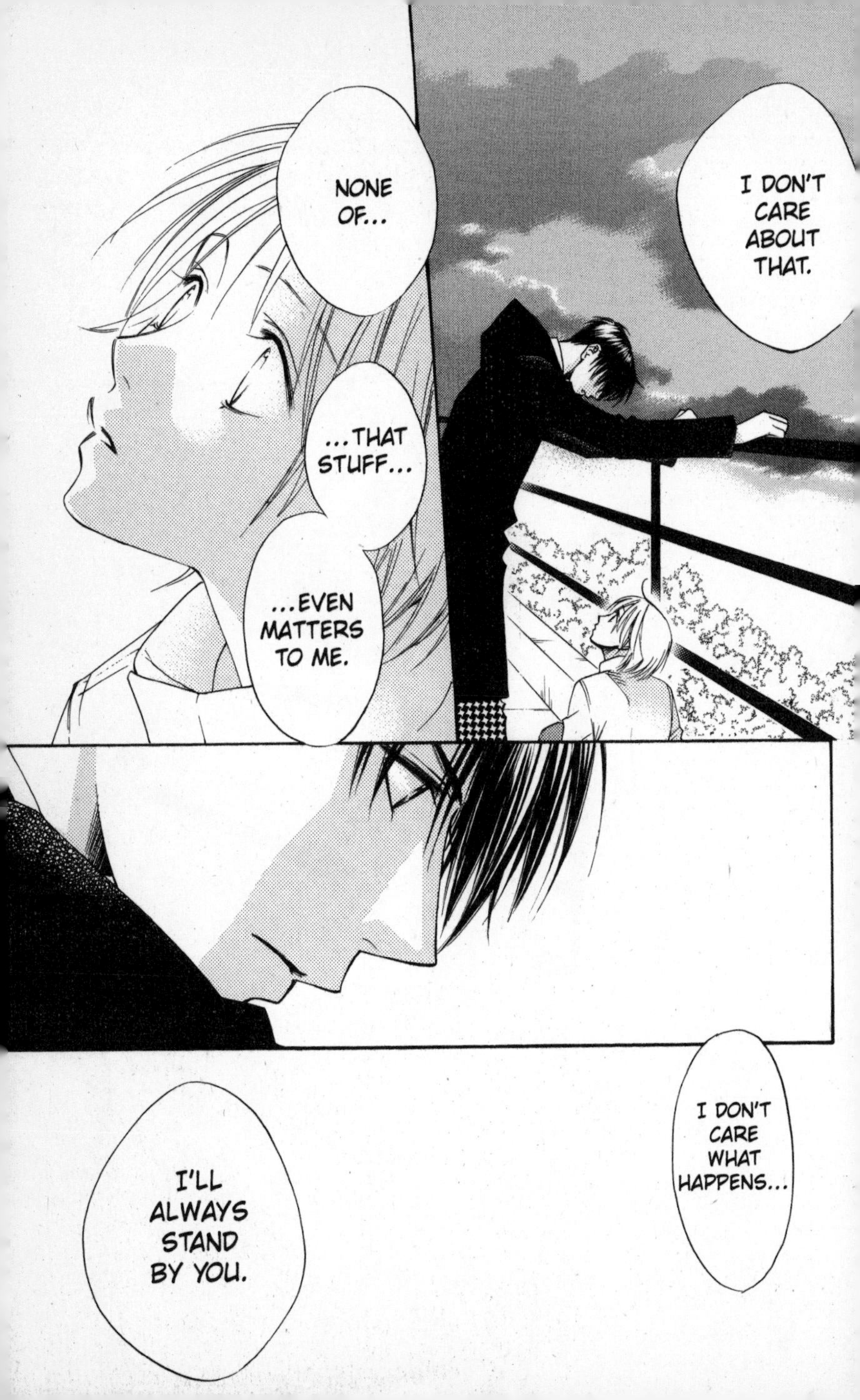
I DON'T CARE ABOUT THAT.
NONE OF...
...THAT STUFF...
...EVEN MATTERS TO ME.
I DON'T CARE WHAT HAPPENS...
I'LL ALWAYS STAND BY YOU.

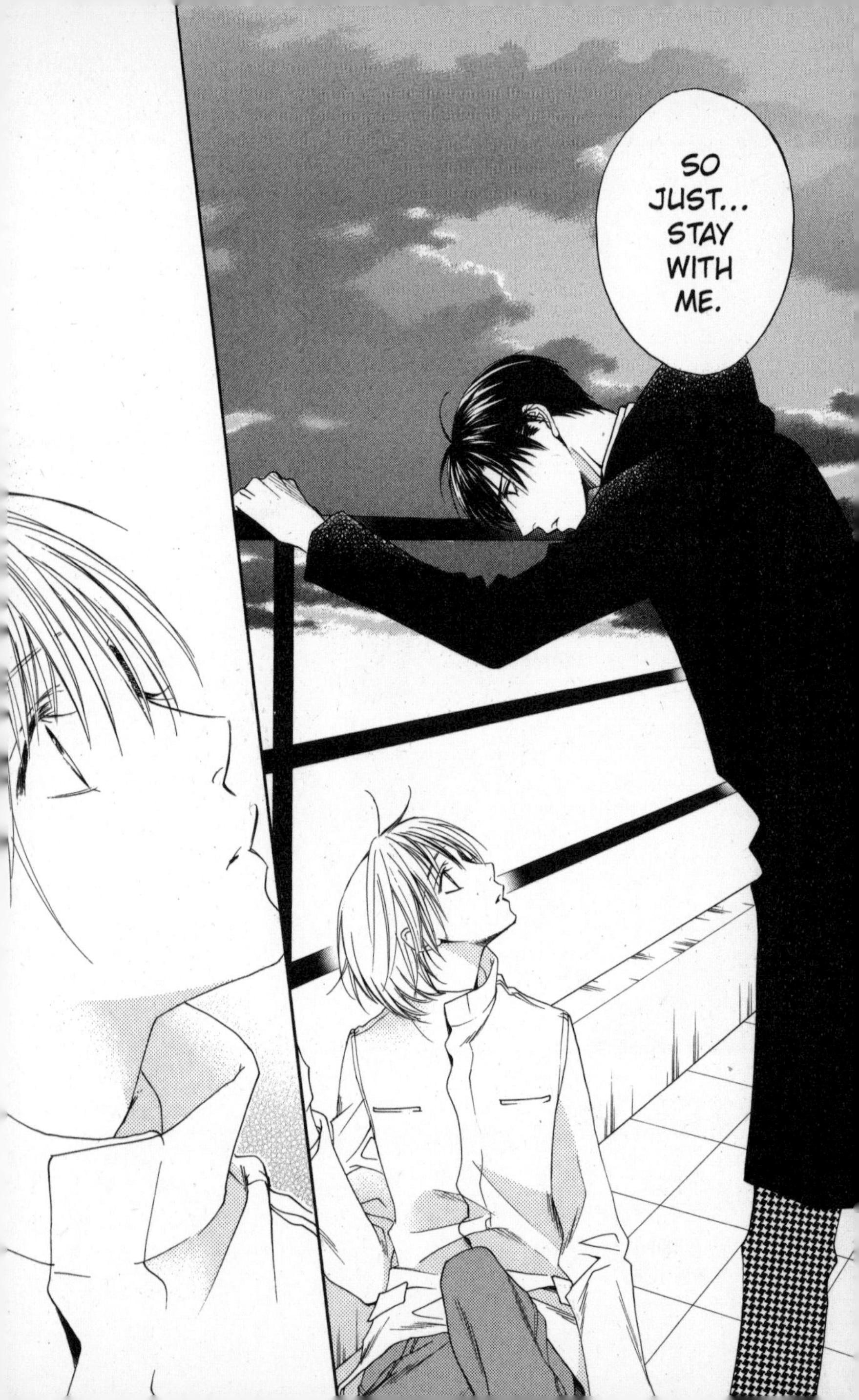
SO JUST... STAY WITH ME.

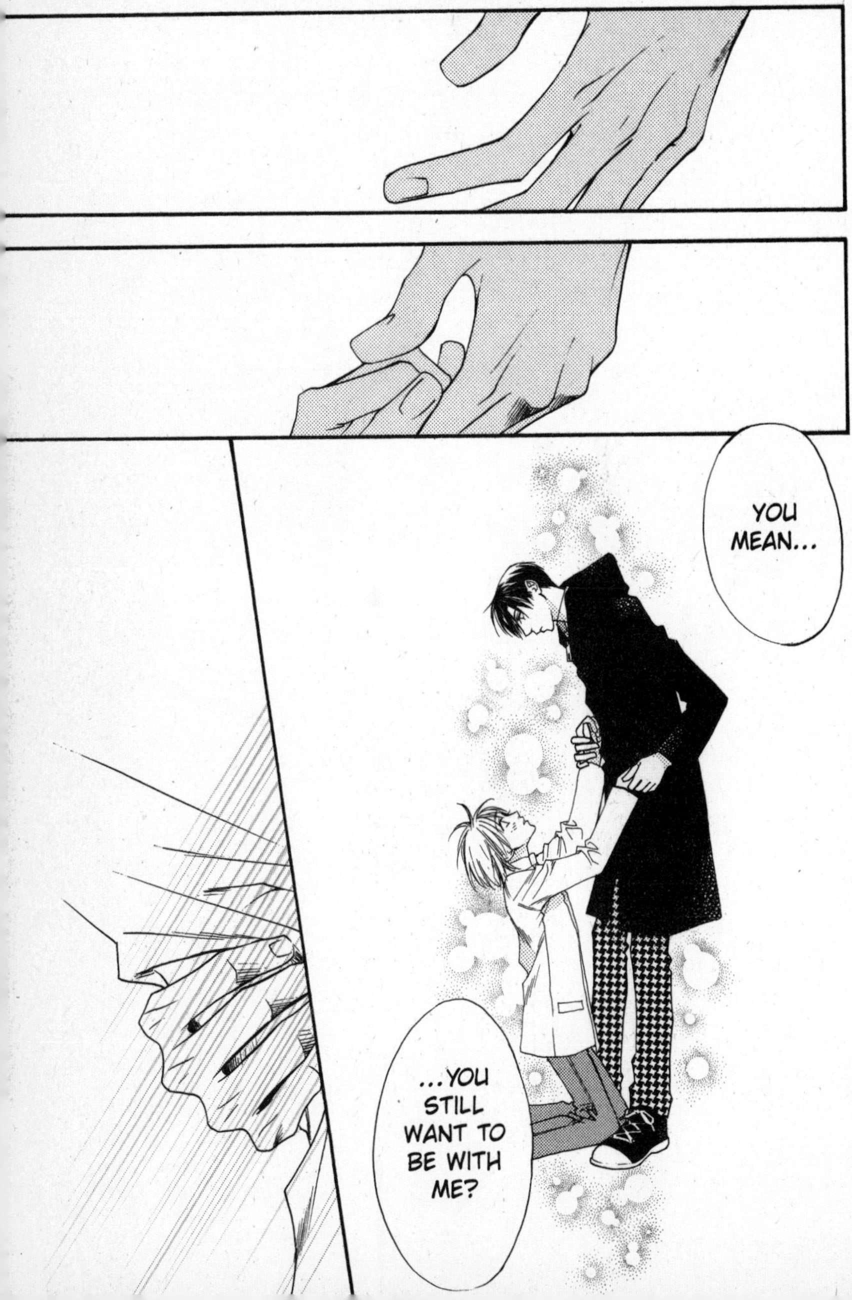
YOU MEAN...
...YOU STILL WANT TO BE WITH ME?

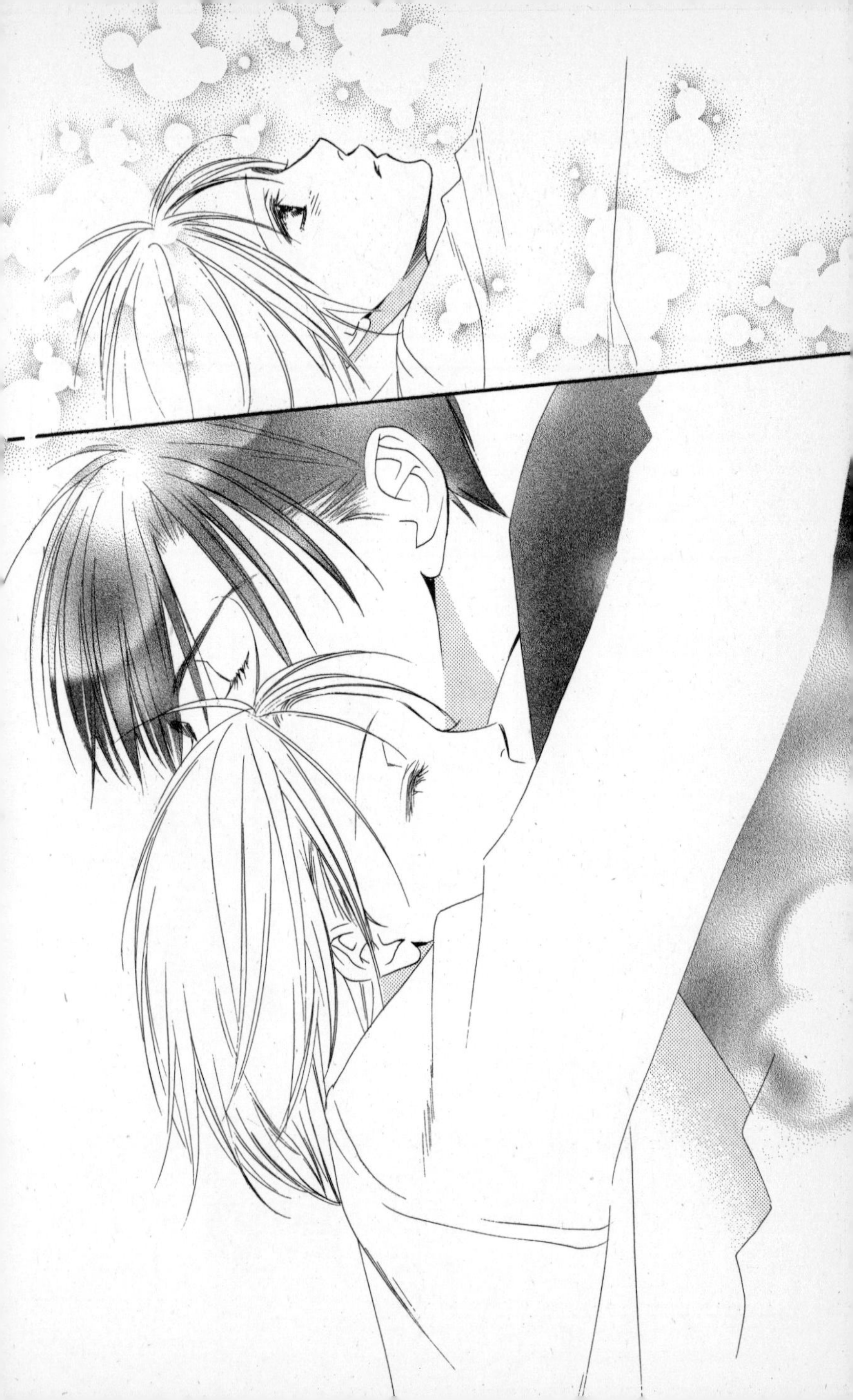

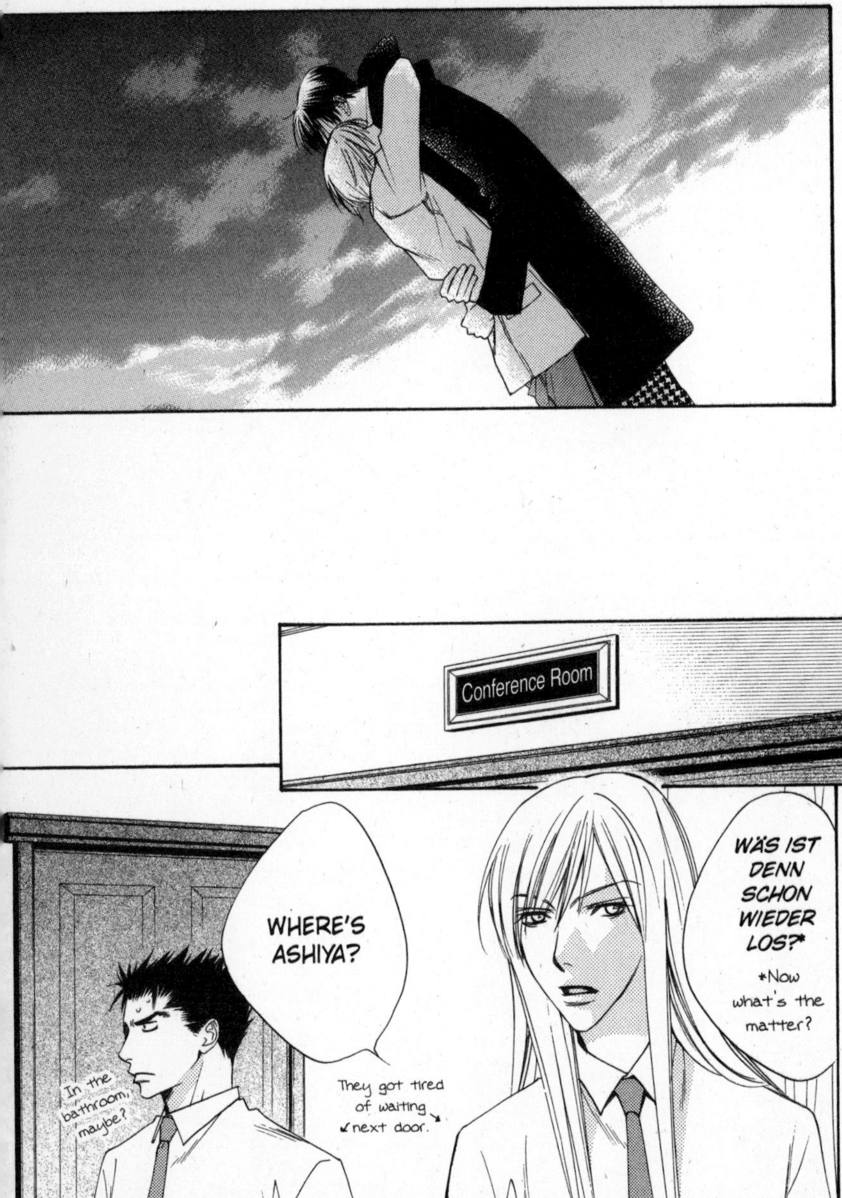
Conference Room
WÄS IST DENN SCHON WIEDER LOS?*
*Now what's the matter?
WHERE'S ASHIYA?
They got tired of waiting next door.
In the bathroom, maybe?

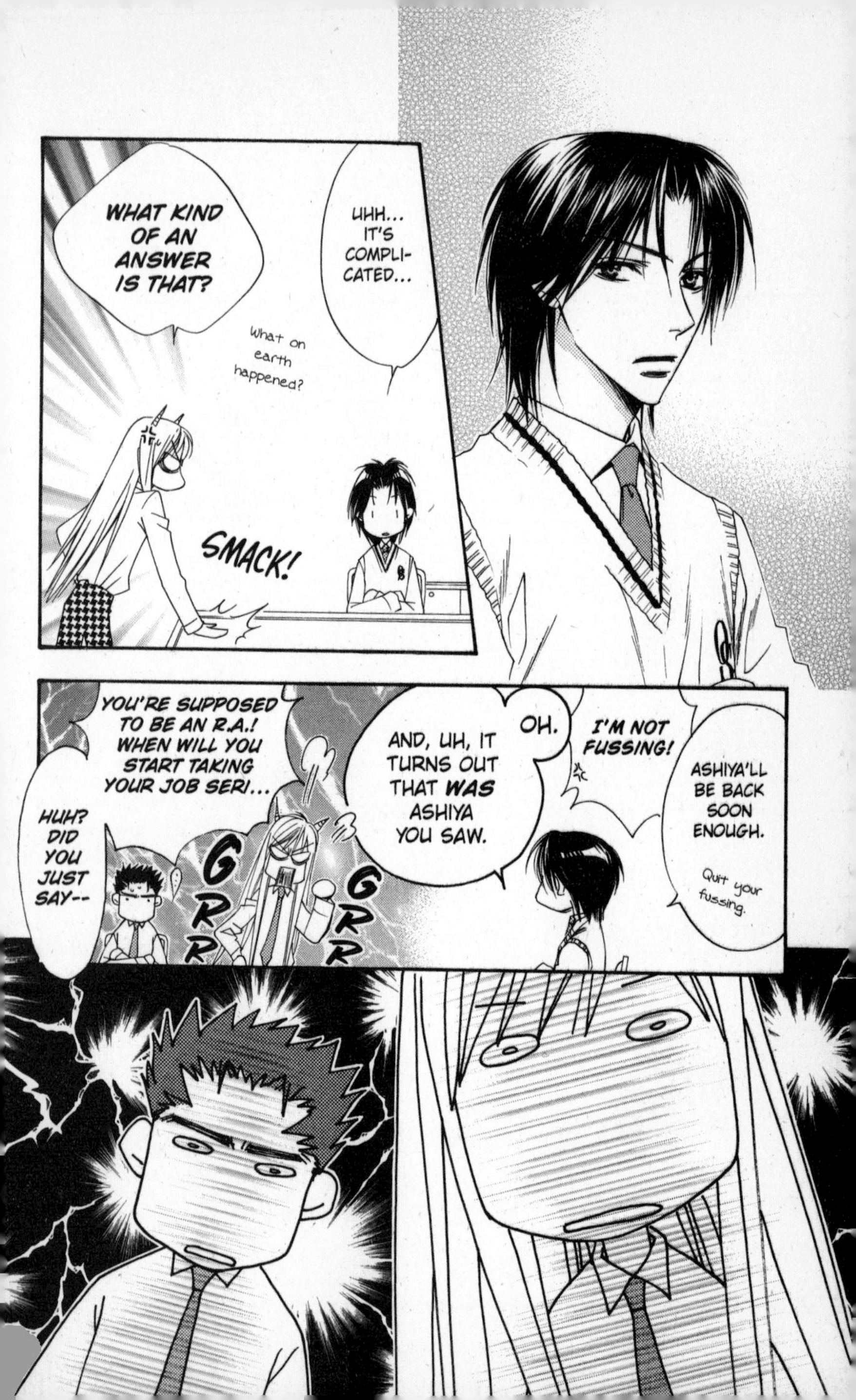
UHH... IT'S COMPLICATED...
What on earth happened?
WHAT KIND OF AN ANSWER IS THAT?
SMACK!
ASHIYA'LL BE BACK SOON ENOUGH.
Quit your fussing.
I'M NOT FUSSING!
OH.
AND, UH, IT TURNS OUT THAT WAS ASHIYA YOU SAW.
YOU'RE SUPPOSED TO BE AN R.A.! WHEN WILL YOU START TAKING YOUR JOB SERI...
GRRR
GRRR
HUH? DID YOU JUST SAY--

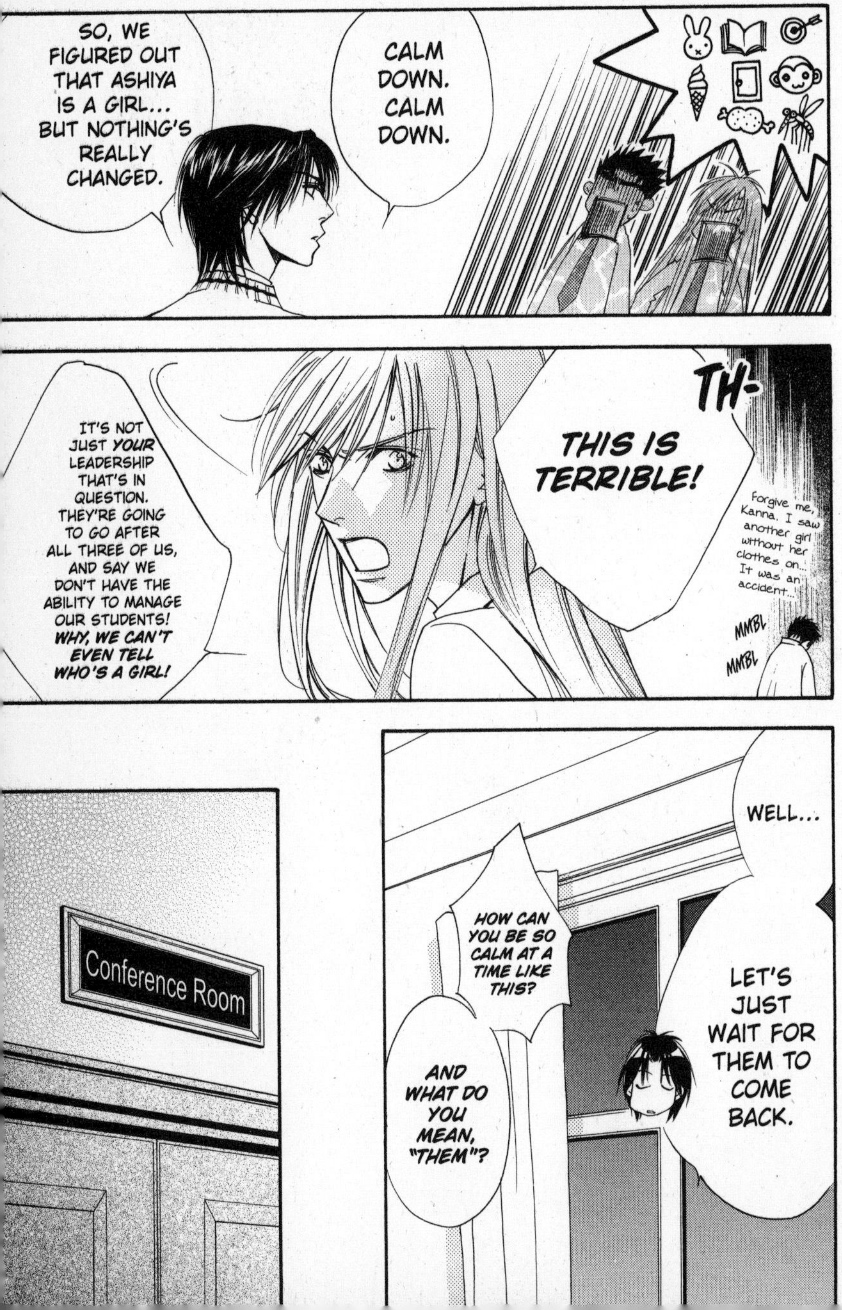
CALM DOWN. CALM DOWN.
SO, WE FIGURED OUT THAT ASHIYA IS A GIRL... BUT NOTHING'S REALLY CHANGED.
TH-
THIS IS TERRIBLE!
Forgive me, Kanna. I saw another girl without her clothes on... It was an accident...
MMBL
MMBL
IT'S NOT JUST *YOUR* LEADERSHIP THAT'S IN QUESTION. THEY'RE GOING TO GO AFTER ALL THREE OF US, AND SAY WE DON'T HAVE THE ABILITY TO MANAGE OUR STUDENTS! *WHY, WE CAN'T EVEN TELL WHO'S A GIRL!*
WELL...
LET'S JUST WAIT FOR THEM TO COME BACK.
HOW CAN YOU BE SO CALM AT A TIME LIKE THIS?
AND WHAT DO YOU MEAN, "THEM"?
Conference Room

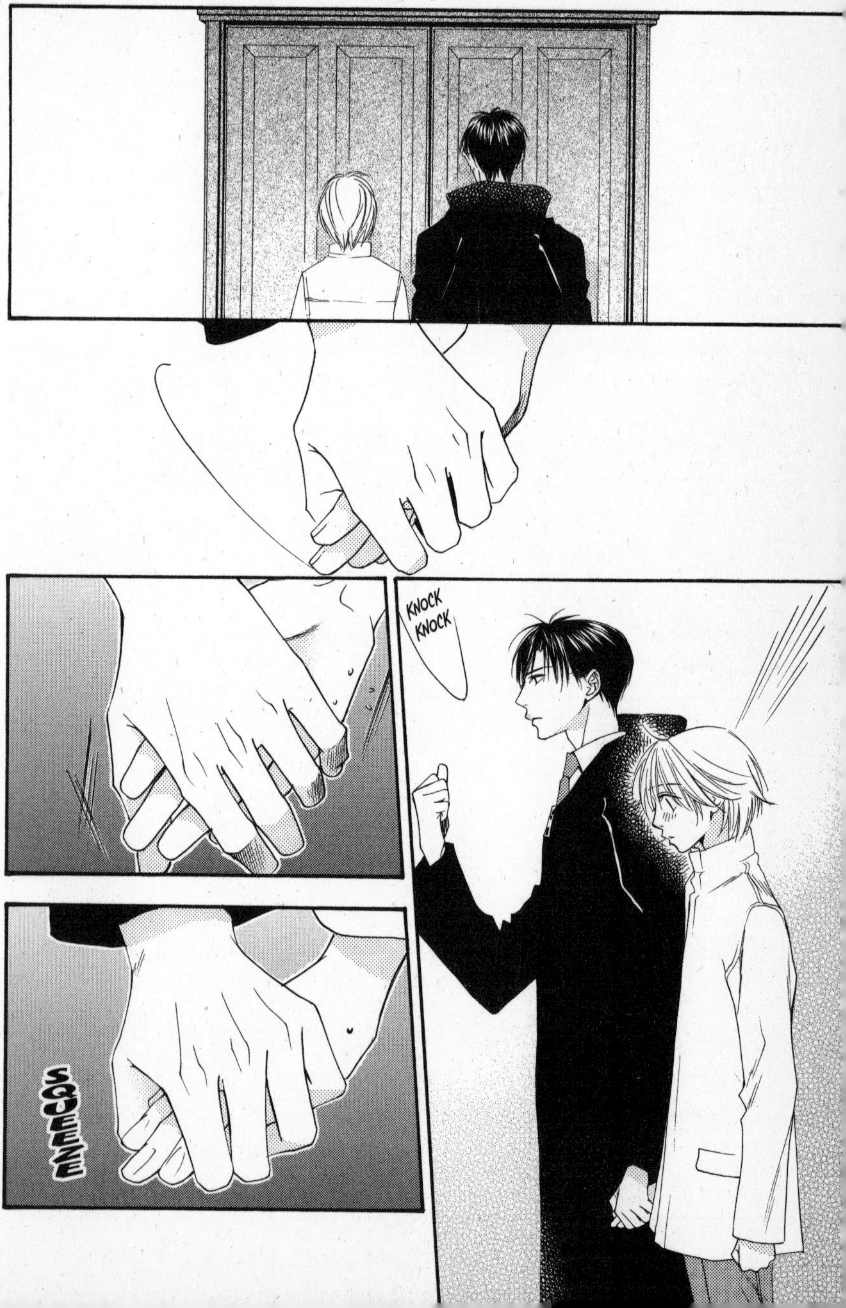
KNOCK KNOCK
SQUEEZE

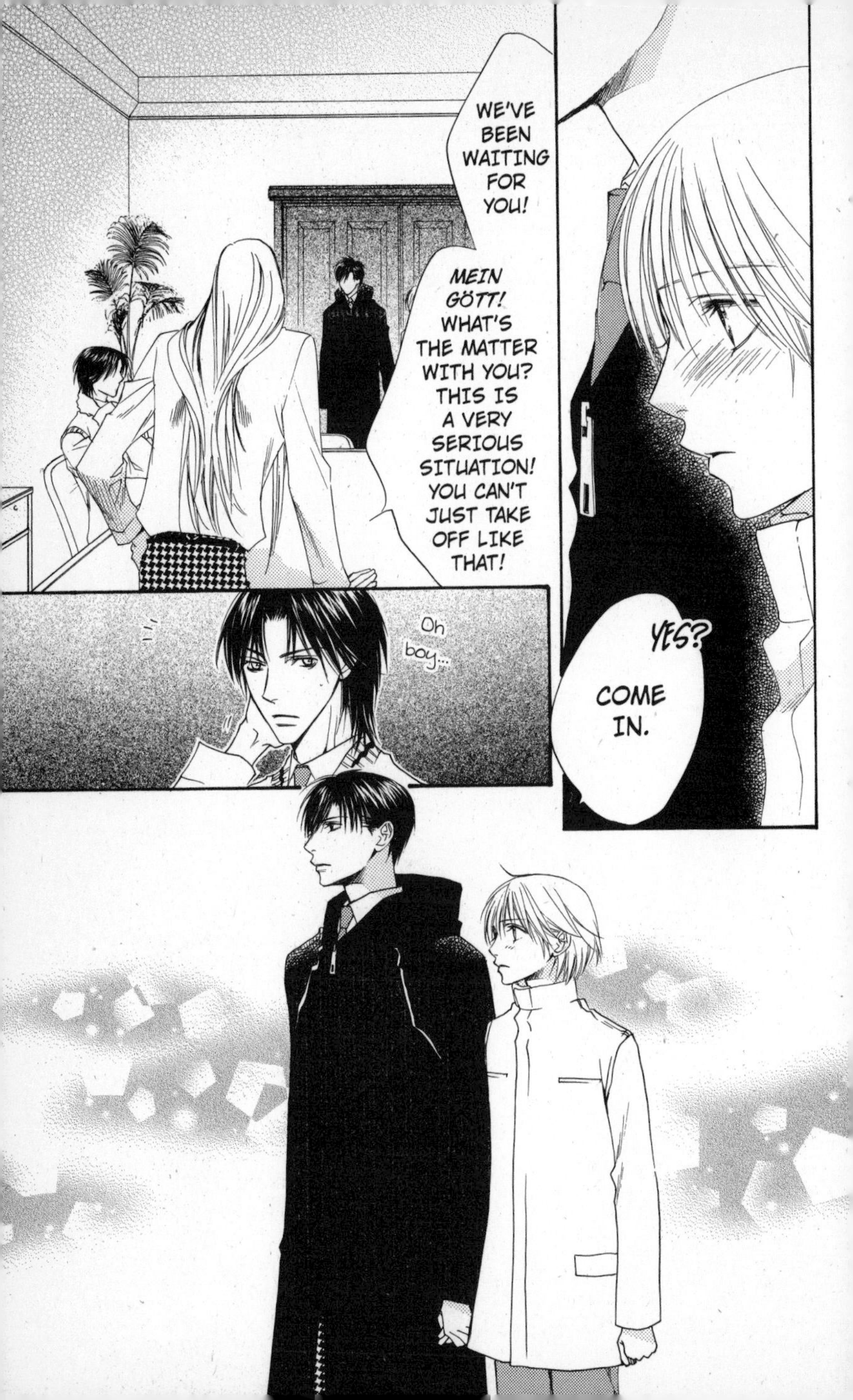
YES? COME IN.
WE'VE BEEN WAITING FOR YOU!
MEIN GÖTT! WHAT'S THE MATTER WITH YOU? THIS IS A VERY SERIOUS SITUATION! YOU CAN'T JUST TAKE OFF LIKE THAT!
Oh boy...

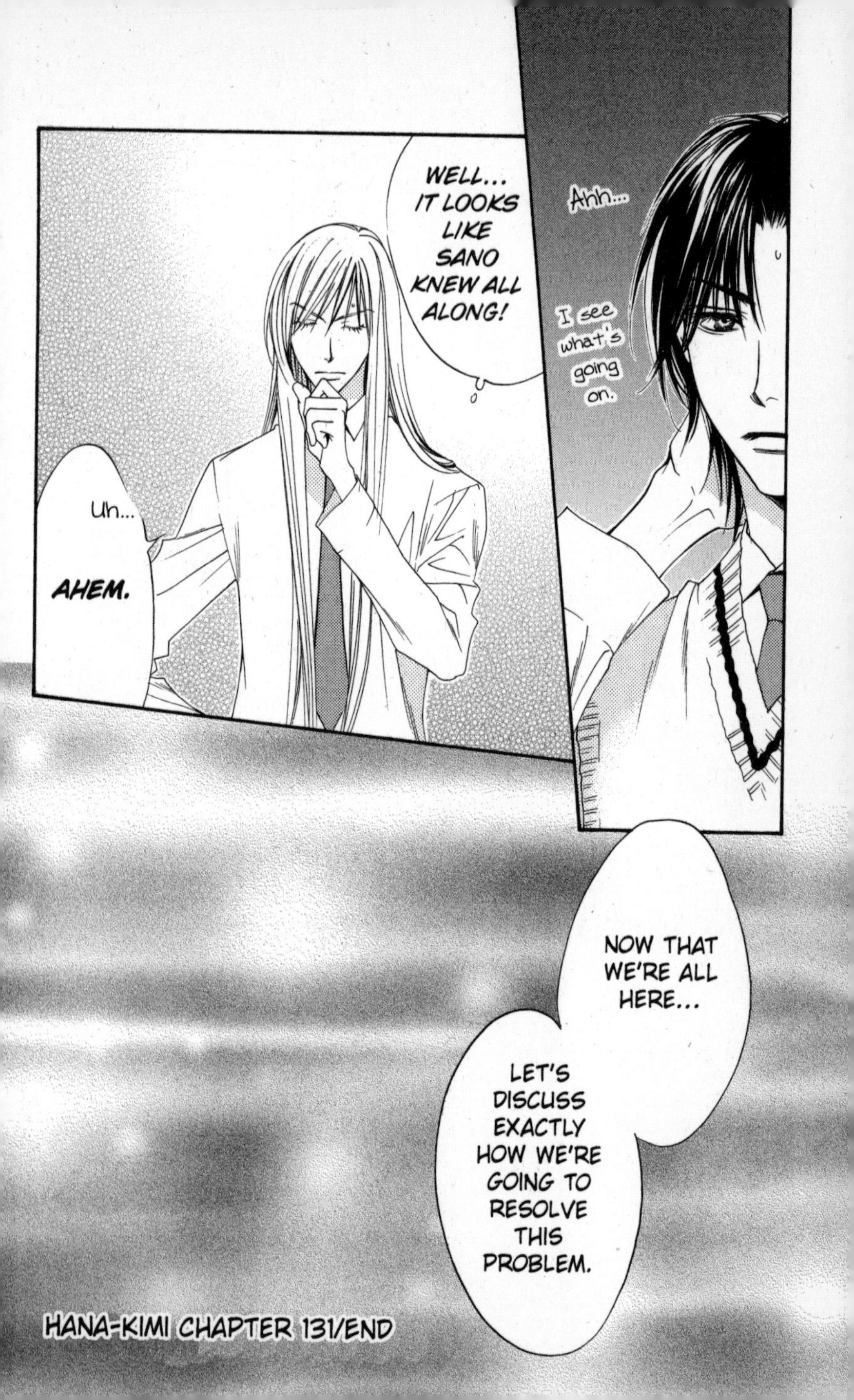
Ahhh...
I see what's going on.
WELL... IT LOOKS LIKE SANO KNEW ALL ALONG!
Uh...
AHEM.
NOW THAT WE'RE ALL HERE...
LET'S DISCUSS EXACTLY HOW WE'RE GOING TO RESOLVE THIS PROBLEM.
HANA-KIMI CHAPTER 131/END

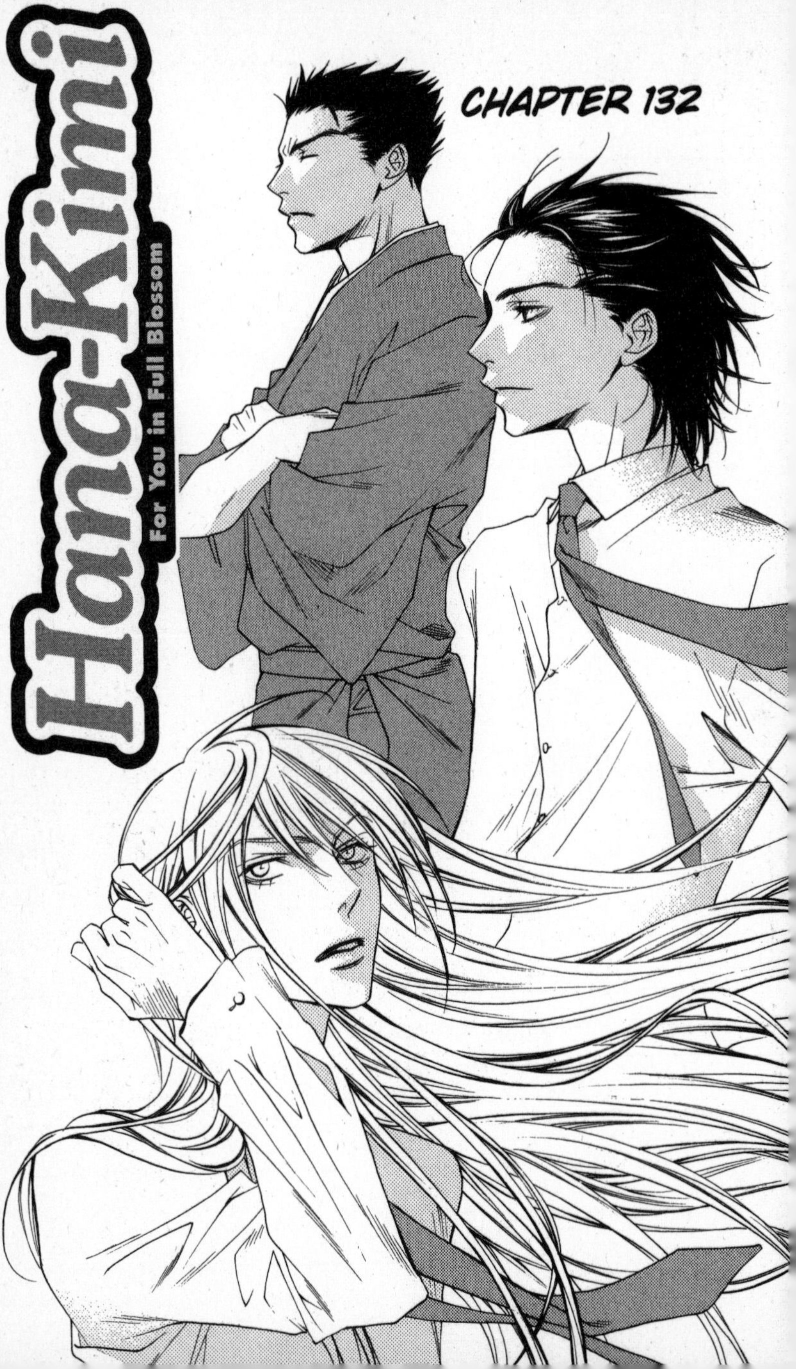
Hana-Kimi
For You in Full Blossom
CHAPTER 132

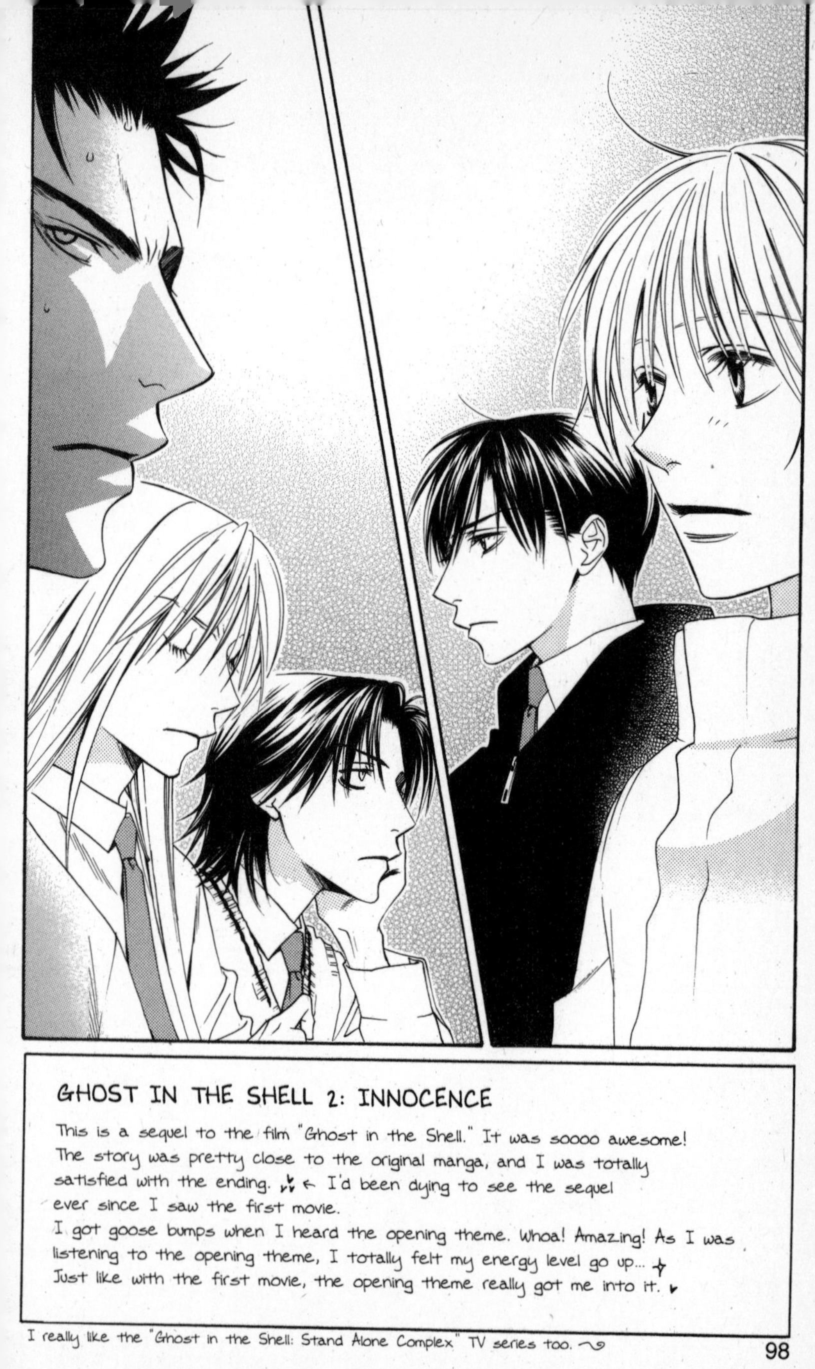

GHOST IN THE SHELL 2: INNOCENCE

This is a sequel to the film "Ghost in the Shell." It was soooo awesome! The story was pretty close to the original manga, and I was totally satisfied with the ending. ← I'd been dying to see the sequel ever since I saw the first movie.
I got goose bumps when I heard the opening theme. Whoa! Amazing! As I was listening to the opening theme, I totally felt my energy level go up... Just like with the first movie, the opening theme really got me into it.

I really like the "Ghost in the Shell: Stand Alone Complex" TV series too.

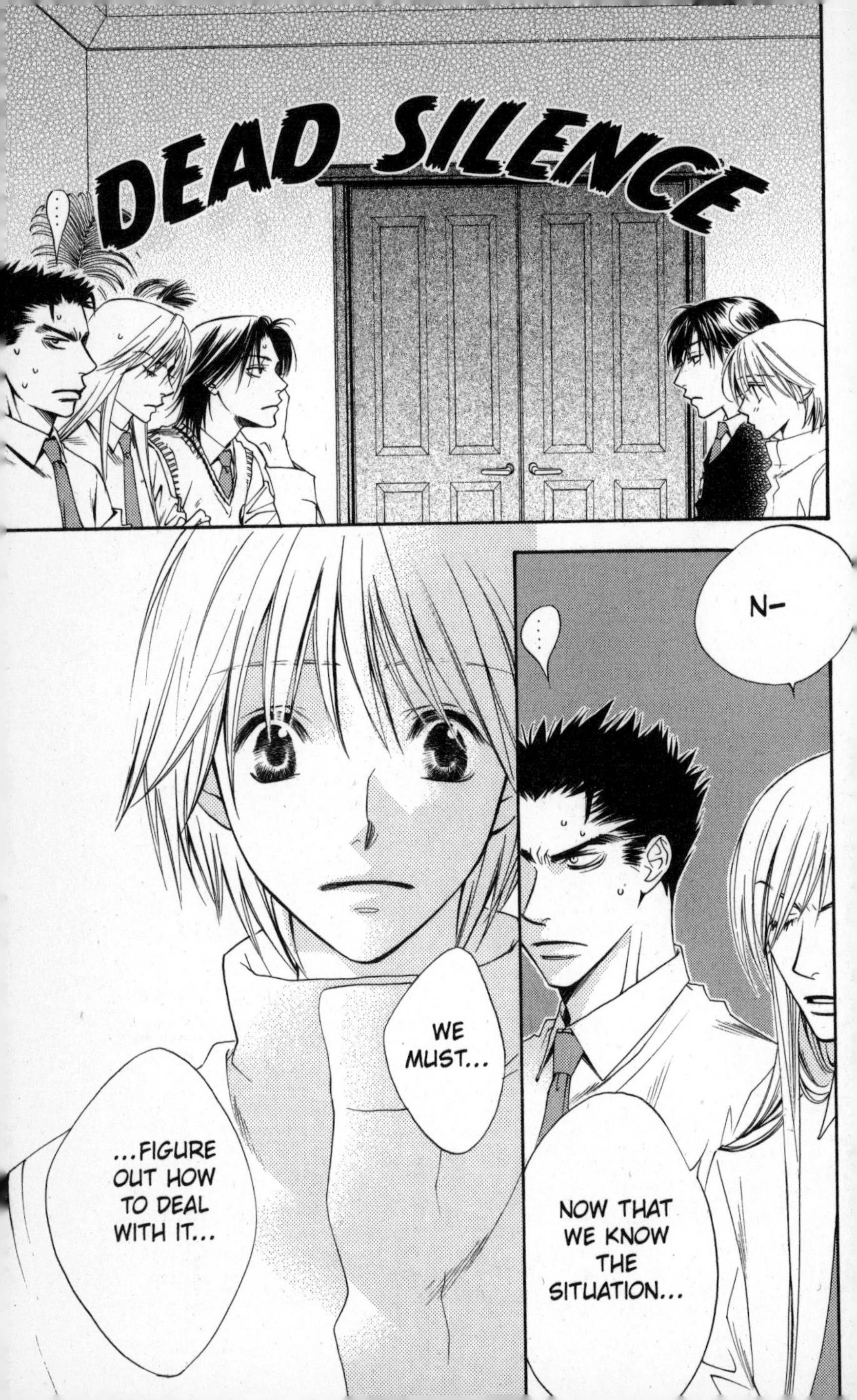

DEAD SILENCE
...
N-
...
NOW THAT WE KNOW THE SITUATION...
WE MUST...
...FIGURE OUT HOW TO DEAL WITH IT...

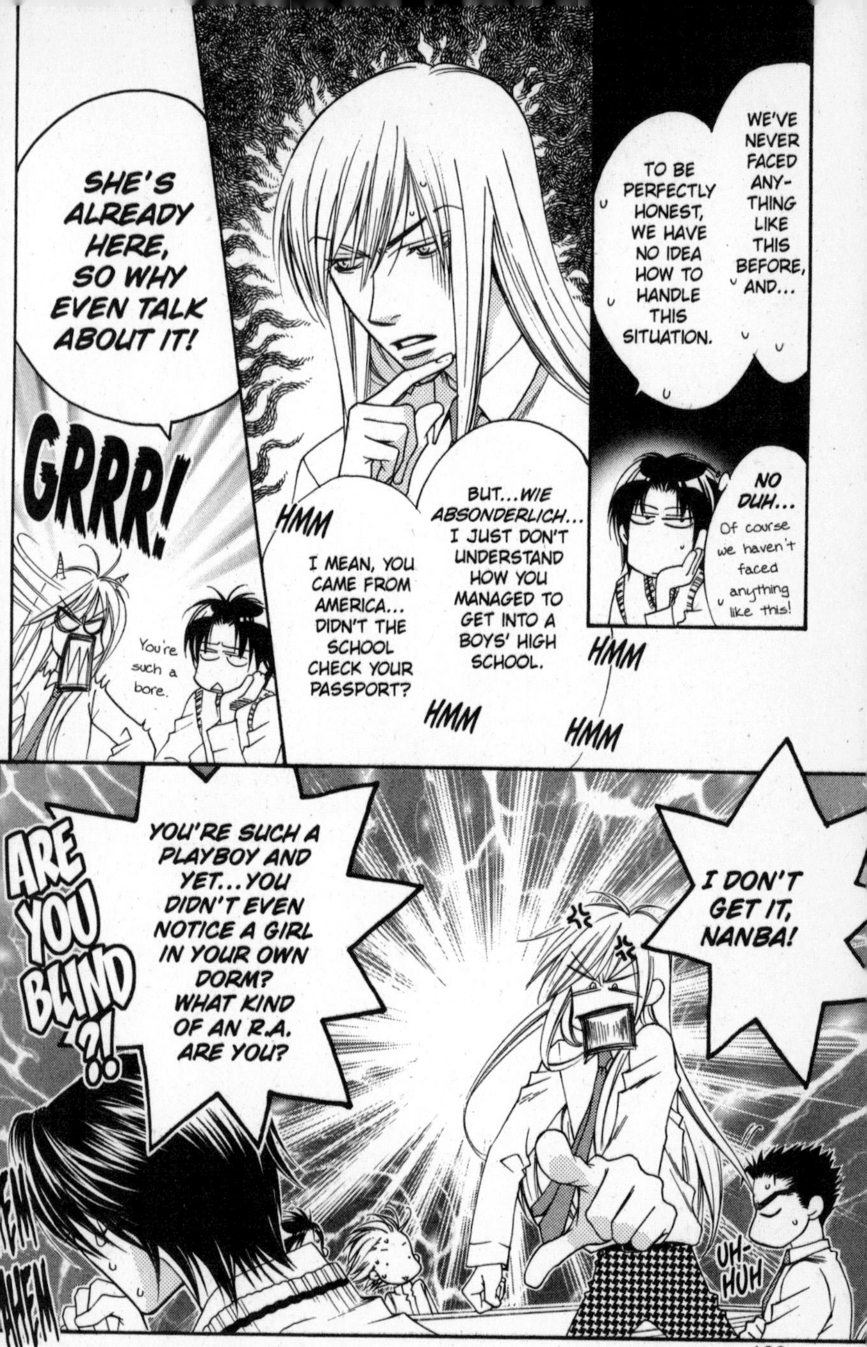
WE'VE NEVER FACED ANYTHING LIKE THIS BEFORE, AND...
TO BE PERFECTLY HONEST, WE HAVE NO IDEA HOW TO HANDLE THIS SITUATION.
NO DUH...
Of course we haven't faced anything like this!
BUT...WIE ABSONDERLICH... I JUST DON'T UNDERSTAND HOW YOU MANAGED TO GET INTO A BOYS' HIGH SCHOOL.
I MEAN, YOU CAME FROM AMERICA... DIDN'T THE SCHOOL CHECK YOUR PASSPORT?
HMM
HMM
HMM
HMM
SHE'S ALREADY HERE, SO WHY EVEN TALK ABOUT IT!
GRRR!
You're such a bore.
I DON'T GET IT, NANBA!
YOU'RE SUCH A PLAYBOY AND YET...YOU DIDN'T EVEN NOTICE A GIRL IN YOUR OWN DORM? WHAT KIND OF AN R.A. ARE YOU?
ARE YOU BLIND?!
UH-HUH
AHEM AHEM

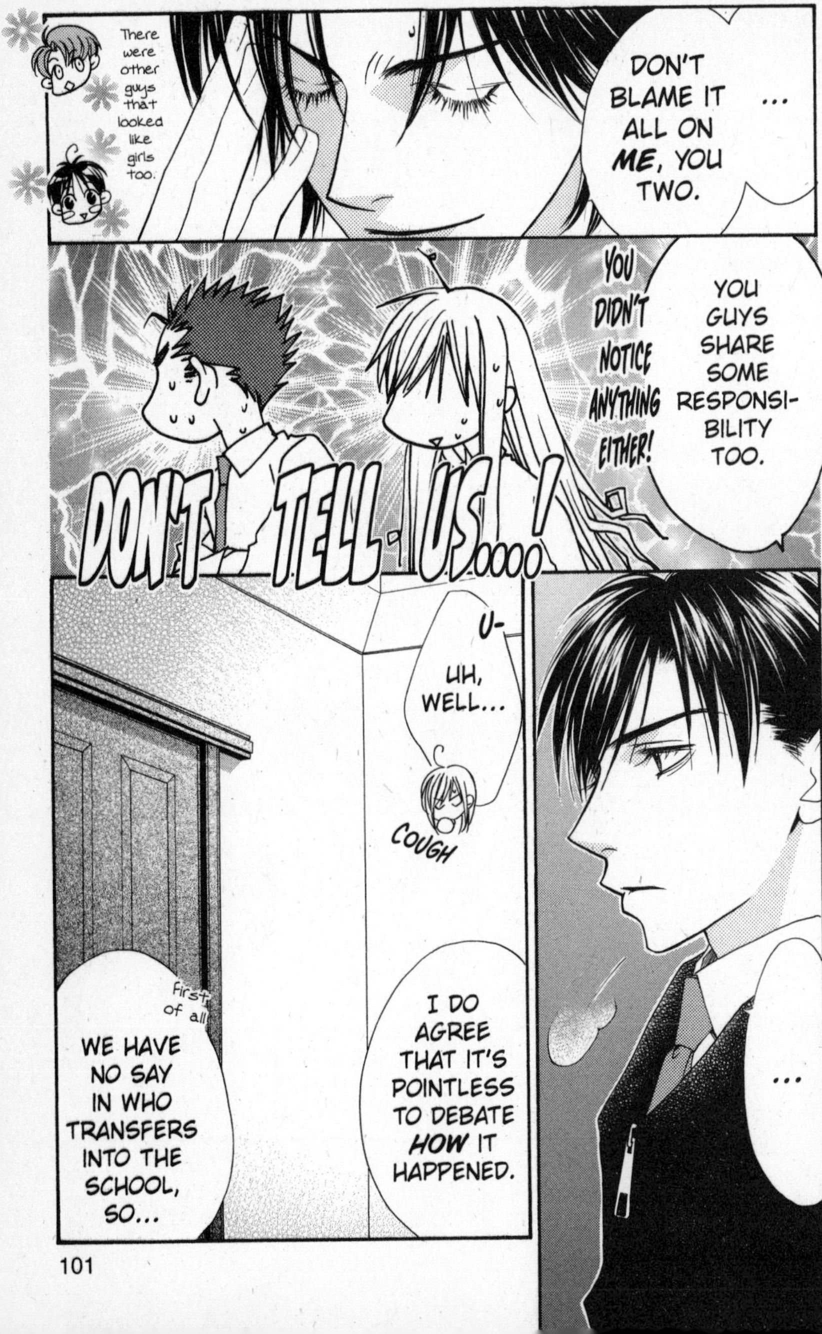
DON'T BLAME IT ALL ON ME, YOU TWO. ...
There were other guys that looked like girls too.
YOU GUYS SHARE SOME RESPONSI-BILITY TOO.
YOU DIDN'T NOTICE ANYTHING EITHER!
DON'T TELL US...!
...
U- UH, WELL...
COUGH
I DO AGREE THAT IT'S POINTLESS TO DEBATE HOW IT HAPPENED.
First of all
WE HAVE NO SAY IN WHO TRANSFERS INTO THE SCHOOL, SO...

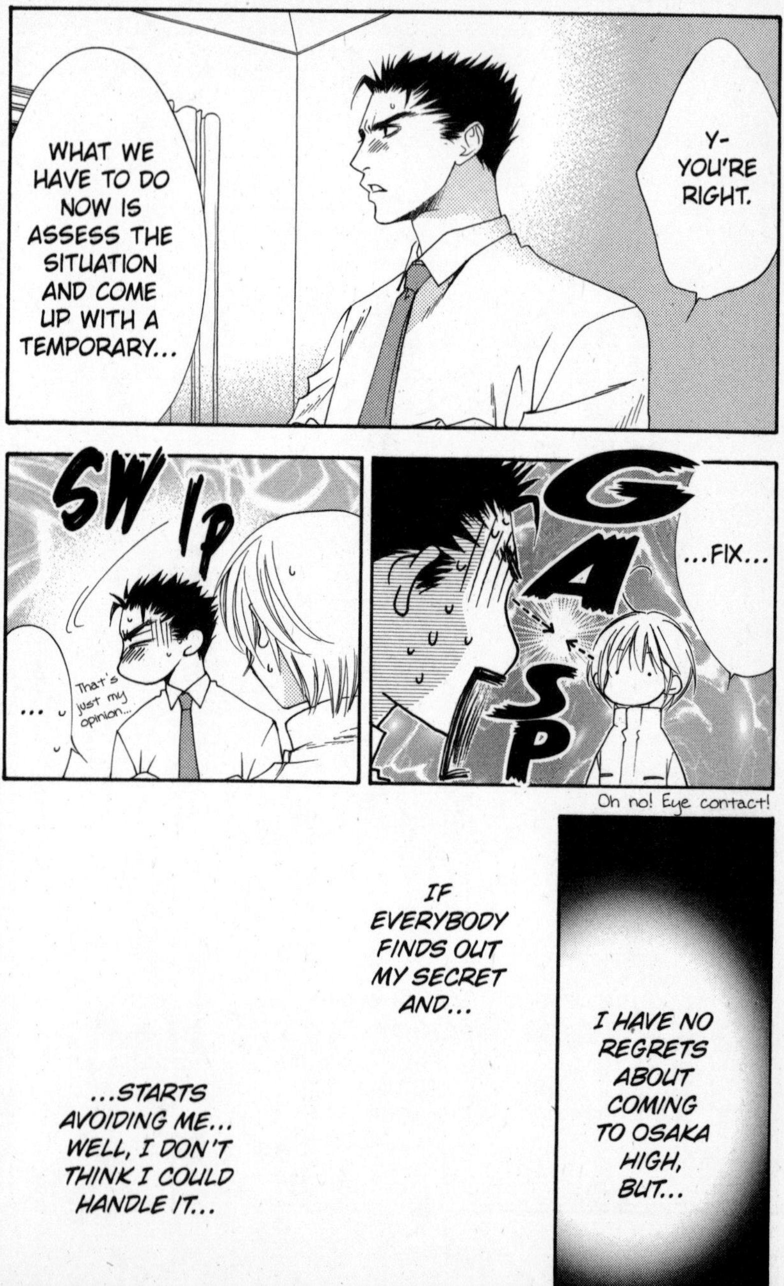
Y- YOU'RE RIGHT.
WHAT WE HAVE TO DO NOW IS ASSESS THE SITUATION AND COME UP WITH A TEMPORARY...
GASP
...FIX...
Oh no! Eye contact!
SWIP
...
That's just my opinion...
I HAVE NO REGRETS ABOUT COMING TO OSAKA HIGH, BUT...
IF EVERYBODY FINDS OUT MY SECRET AND...
...STARTS AVOIDING ME... WELL, I DON'T THINK I COULD HANDLE IT...

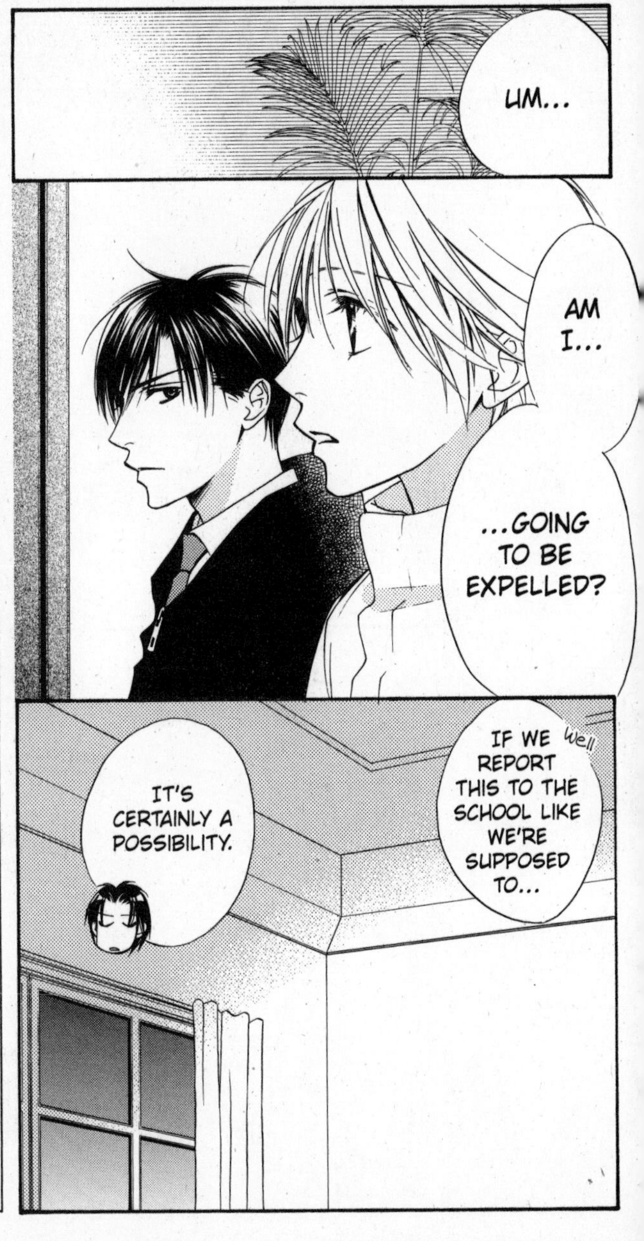
UM...
AM I...
...GOING TO BE EXPELLED?
Well
IF WE REPORT THIS TO THE SCHOOL LIKE WE'RE SUPPOSED TO...
IT'S CERTAINLY A POSSIBILITY.

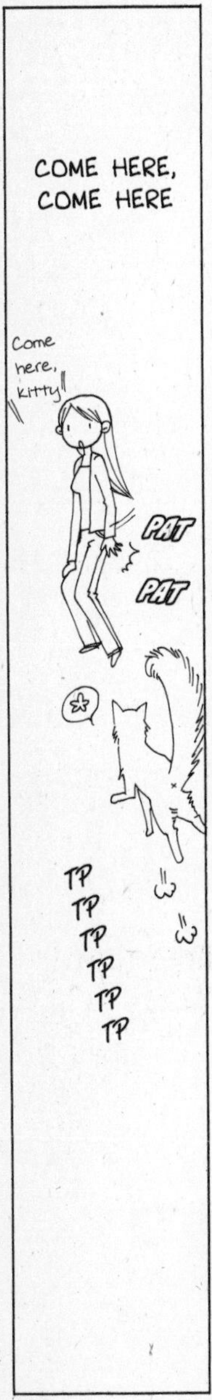
COME HERE, COME HERE
Come here, kitty
PAT
PAT
TP
TP
TP
TP
TP
TP

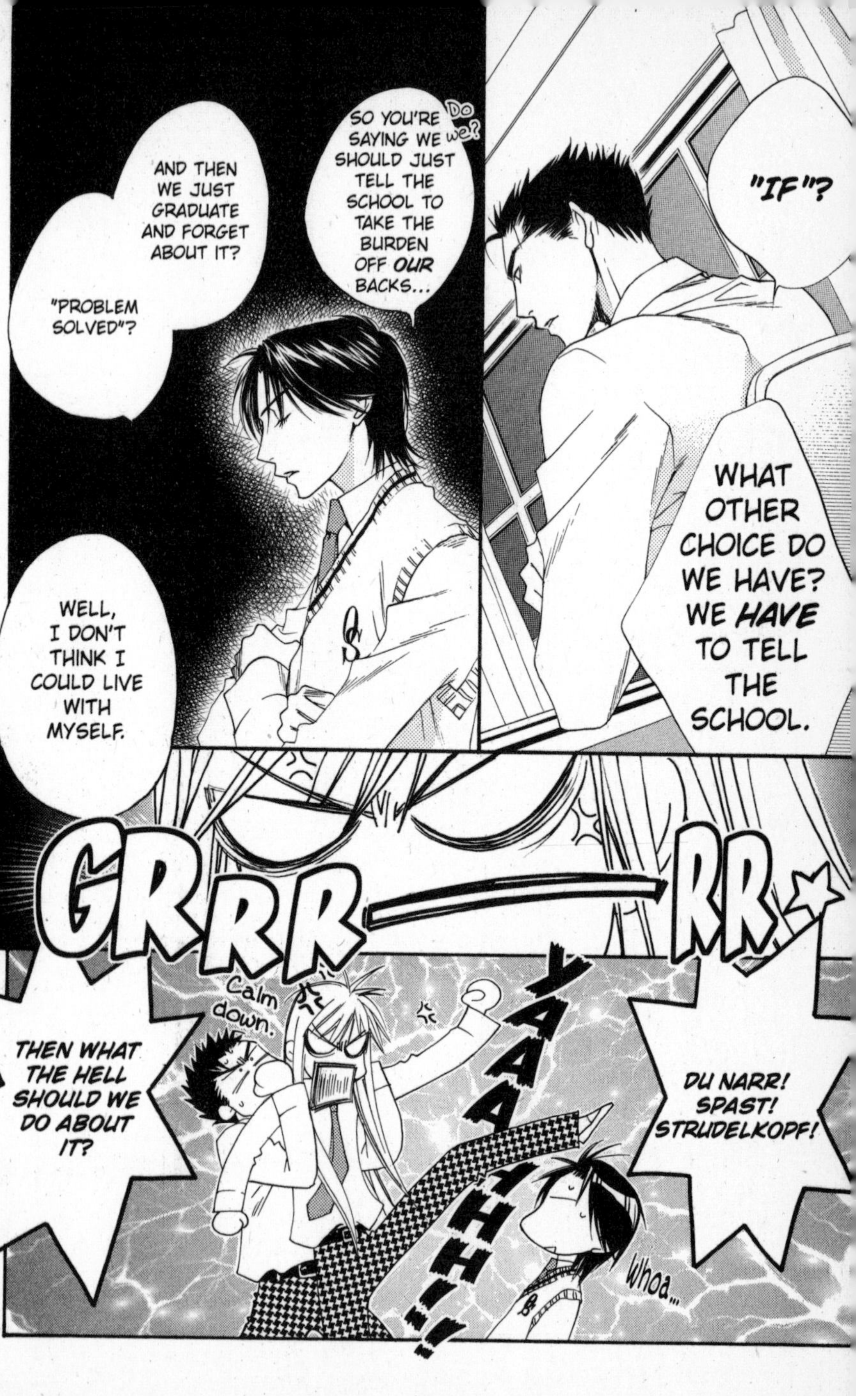
"IF"?
WHAT OTHER CHOICE DO WE HAVE? WE *HAVE* TO TELL THE SCHOOL.
SO YOU'RE SAYING WE SHOULD JUST TELL THE SCHOOL TO TAKE THE BURDEN OFF *OUR* BACKS...
Do we?
AND THEN WE JUST GRADUATE AND FORGET ABOUT IT?
"PROBLEM SOLVED"?
WELL, I DON'T THINK I COULD LIVE WITH MYSELF.
GRRRR—RR☆
DU NARR! SPAST! STRUDELKOPF!
YAAAAHHHH!!
Calm down.
THEN WHAT THE HELL SHOULD WE DO ABOUT IT?
Whoa...

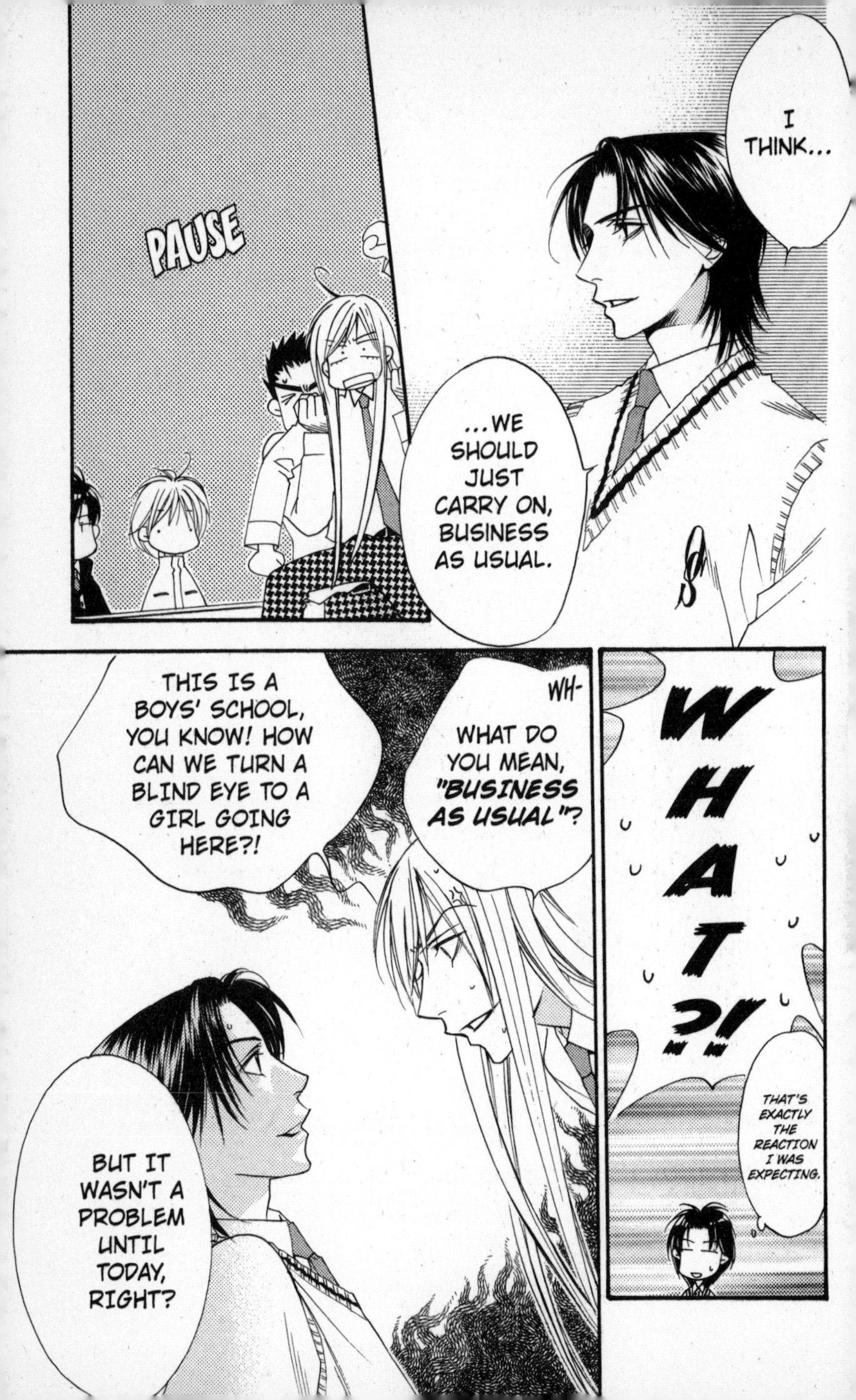
I THINK...
...WE SHOULD JUST CARRY ON, BUSINESS AS USUAL.
PAUSE
WHAT?!
THAT'S EXACTLY THE REACTION I WAS EXPECTING.
WH-
WHAT DO YOU MEAN, "BUSINESS AS USUAL"?
THIS IS A BOYS' SCHOOL, YOU KNOW! HOW CAN WE TURN A BLIND EYE TO A GIRL GOING HERE?!
BUT IT WASN'T A PROBLEM UNTIL TODAY, RIGHT?

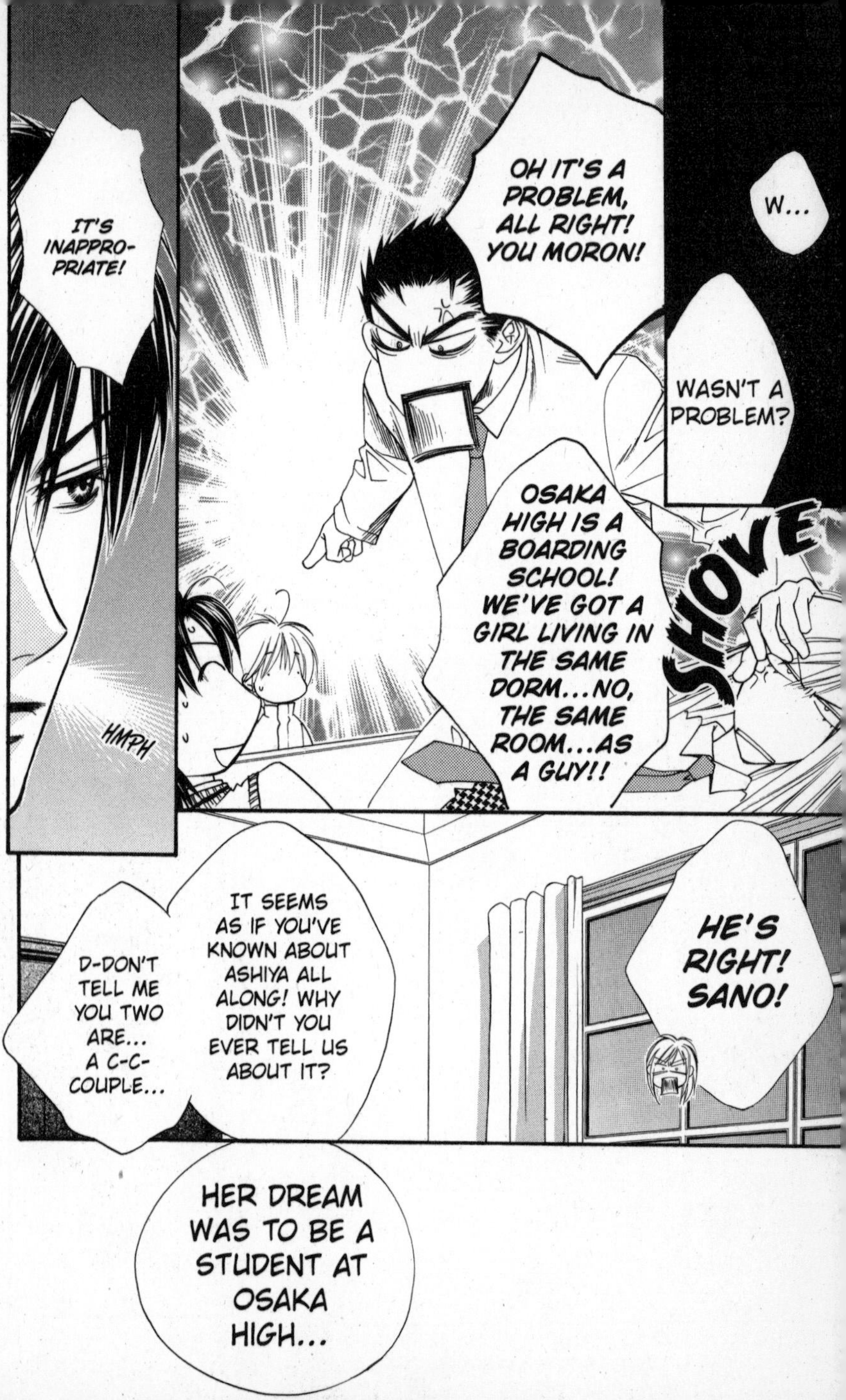
W...
WASN'T A PROBLEM?
OH IT'S A PROBLEM, ALL RIGHT! YOU MORON!
SHOVE
OSAKA HIGH IS A BOARDING SCHOOL! WE'VE GOT A GIRL LIVING IN THE SAME DORM...NO, THE SAME ROOM...AS A GUY!!
IT'S INAPPROPRIATE!
HMPH
HE'S RIGHT! SANO!
IT SEEMS AS IF YOU'VE KNOWN ABOUT ASHIYA ALL ALONG! WHY DIDN'T YOU EVER TELL US ABOUT IT?
D-DON'T TELL ME YOU TWO ARE... A C-C-COUPLE...
HER DREAM WAS TO BE A STUDENT AT OSAKA HIGH...

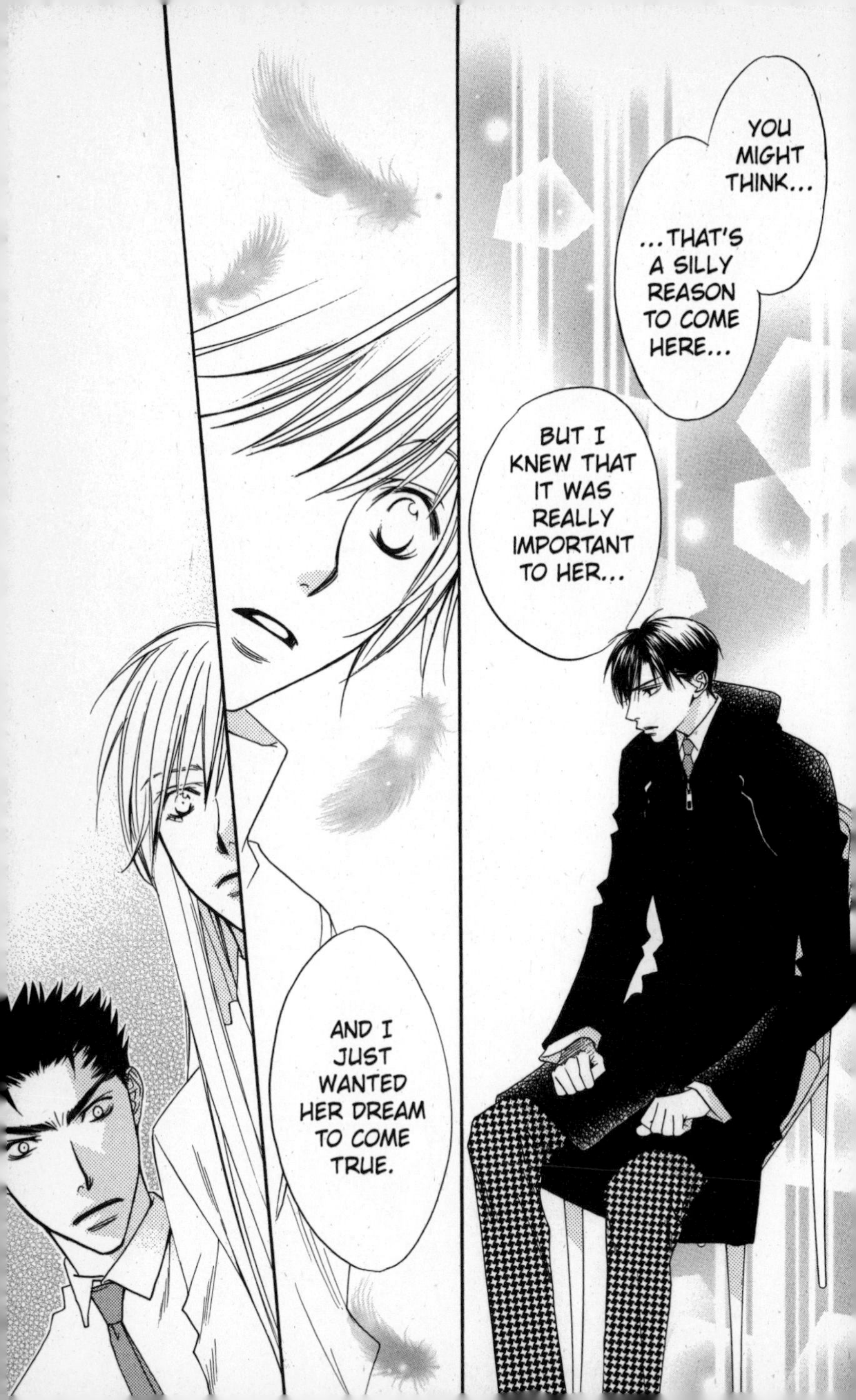
YOU MIGHT THINK...
...THAT'S A SILLY REASON TO COME HERE...
BUT I KNEW THAT IT WAS REALLY IMPORTANT TO HER...
AND I JUST WANTED HER DREAM TO COME TRUE.

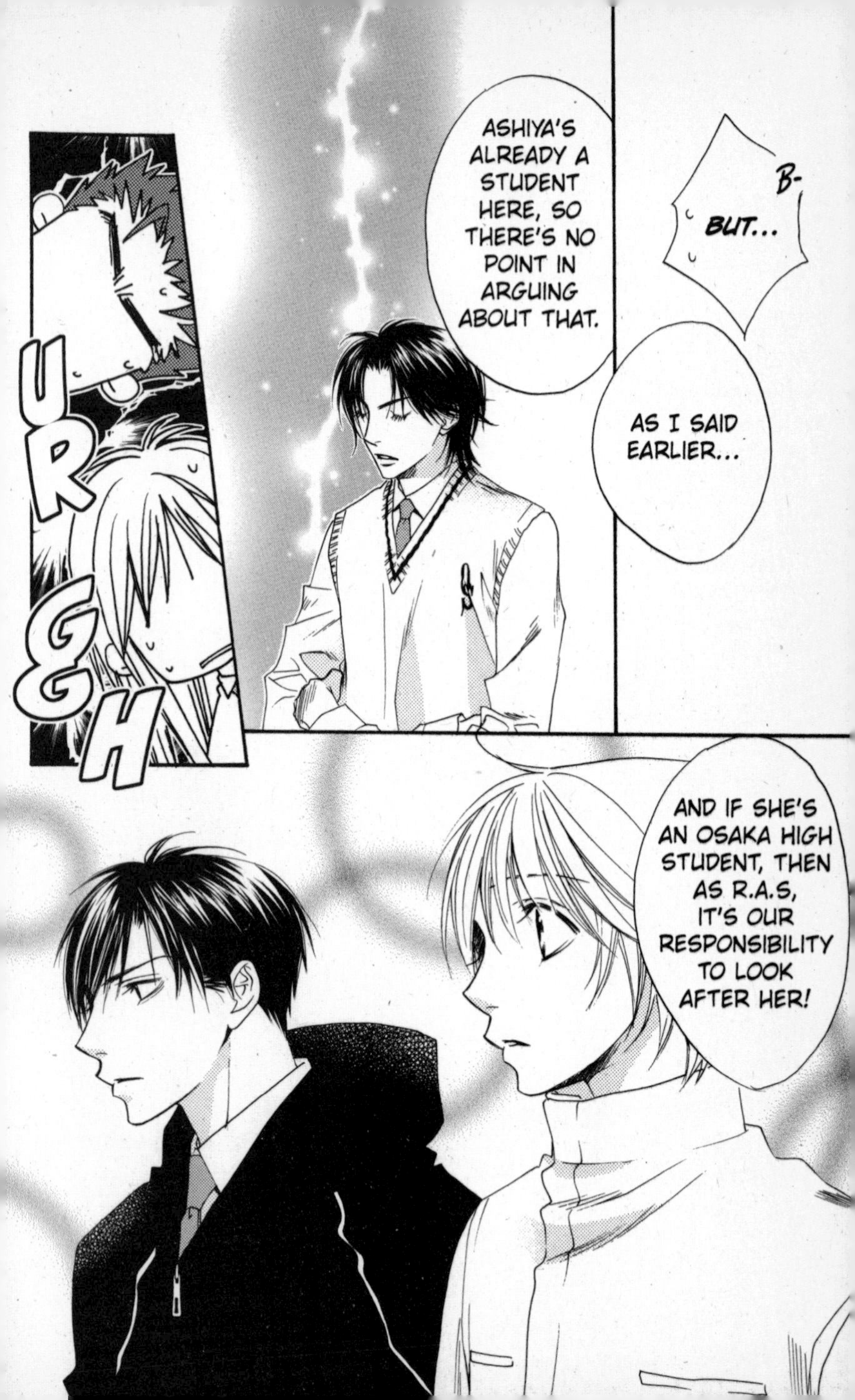
B-BUT...
AS I SAID EARLIER...
ASHIYA'S ALREADY A STUDENT HERE, SO THERE'S NO POINT IN ARGUING ABOUT THAT.
URGH
AND IF SHE'S AN OSAKA HIGH STUDENT, THEN AS R.A.S, IT'S OUR RESPONSIBILITY TO LOOK AFTER HER!

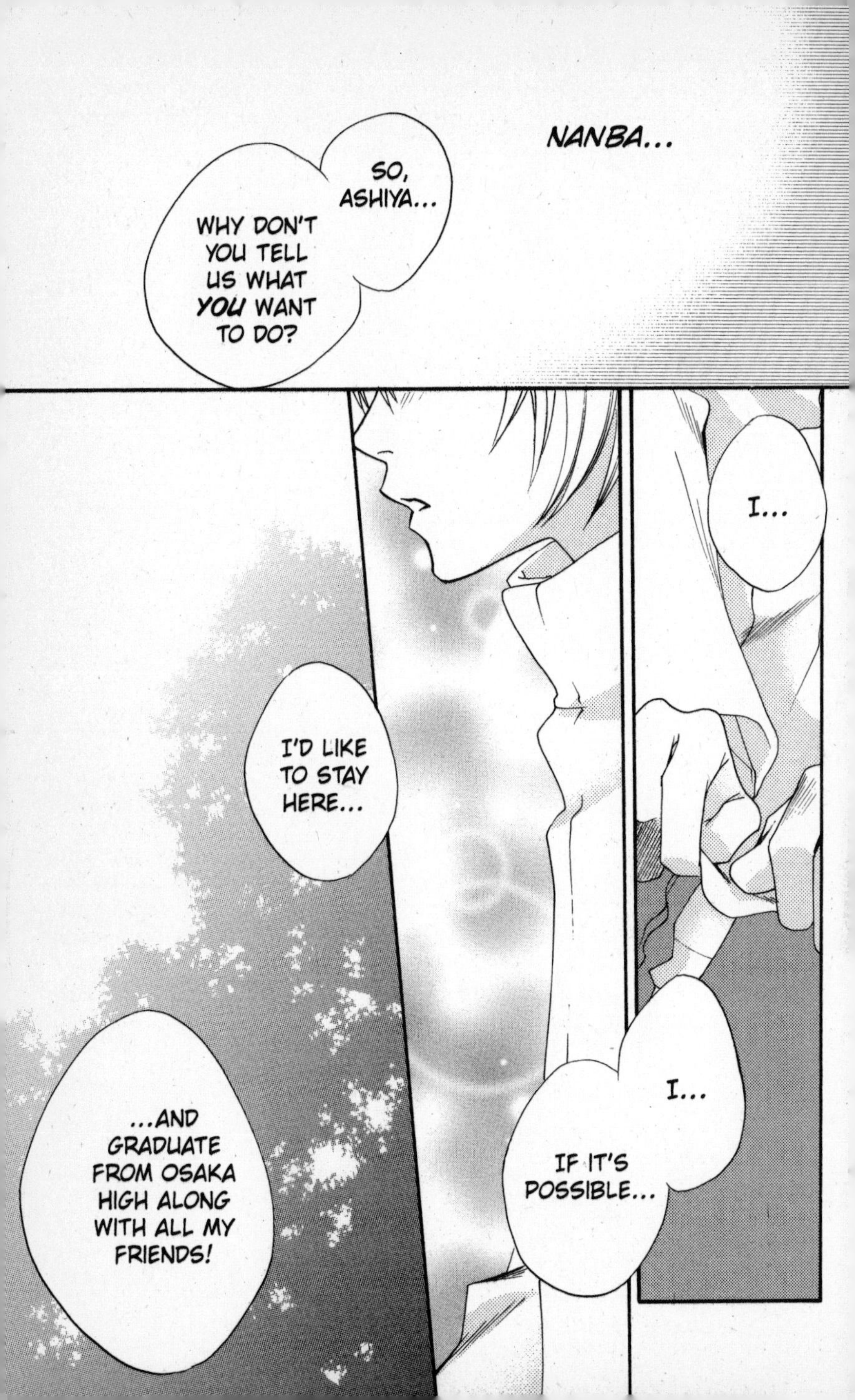
NANBA...
SO, ASHIYA... WHY DON'T YOU TELL US WHAT *YOU* WANT TO DO?
I...
I... IF IT'S POSSIBLE...
I'D LIKE TO STAY HERE...
...AND GRADUATE FROM OSAKA HIGH ALONG WITH ALL MY FRIENDS!

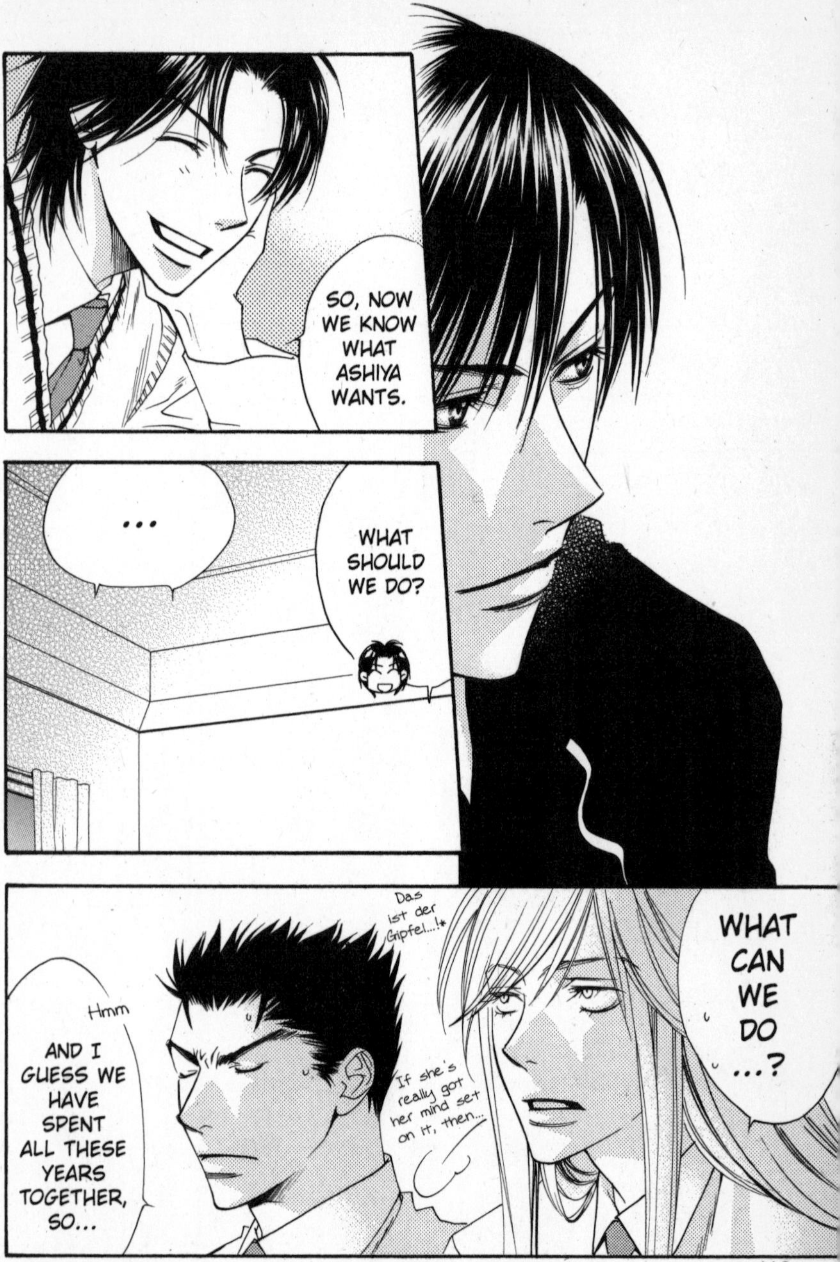
SO, NOW WE KNOW WHAT ASHIYA WANTS.
WHAT SHOULD WE DO?
...
WHAT CAN WE DO ...?
Das ist der Gipfel...!*
If she's really got her mind set on it, then...
Hmm
AND I GUESS WE HAVE SPENT ALL THESE YEARS TOGETHER, SO...

*That beats everything!

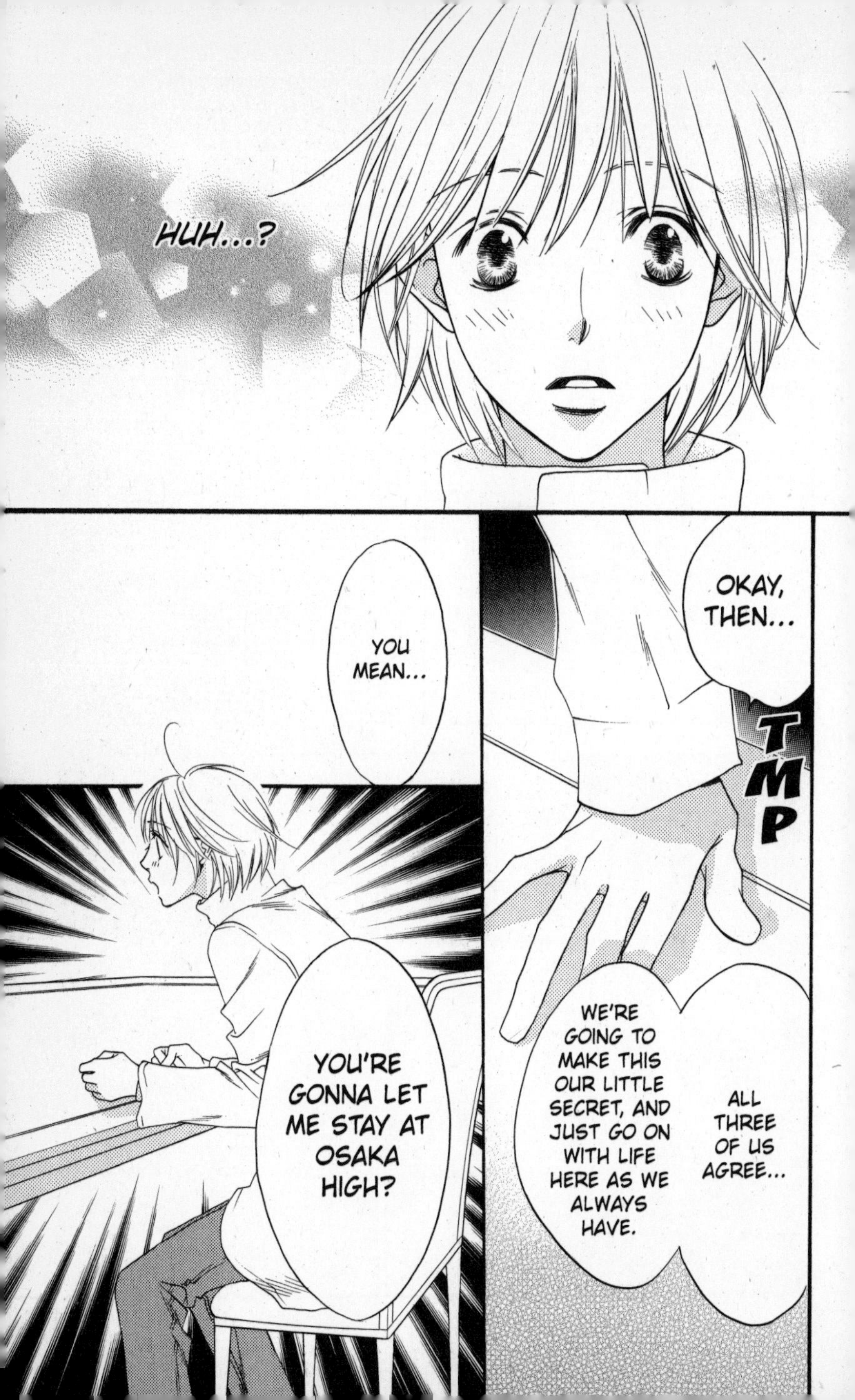
HUH...?
OKAY, THEN...
TMP
ALL THREE OF US AGREE...
WE'RE GOING TO MAKE THIS OUR LITTLE SECRET, AND JUST GO ON WITH LIFE HERE AS WE ALWAYS HAVE.
YOU MEAN...
YOU'RE GONNA LET ME STAY AT OSAKA HIGH?

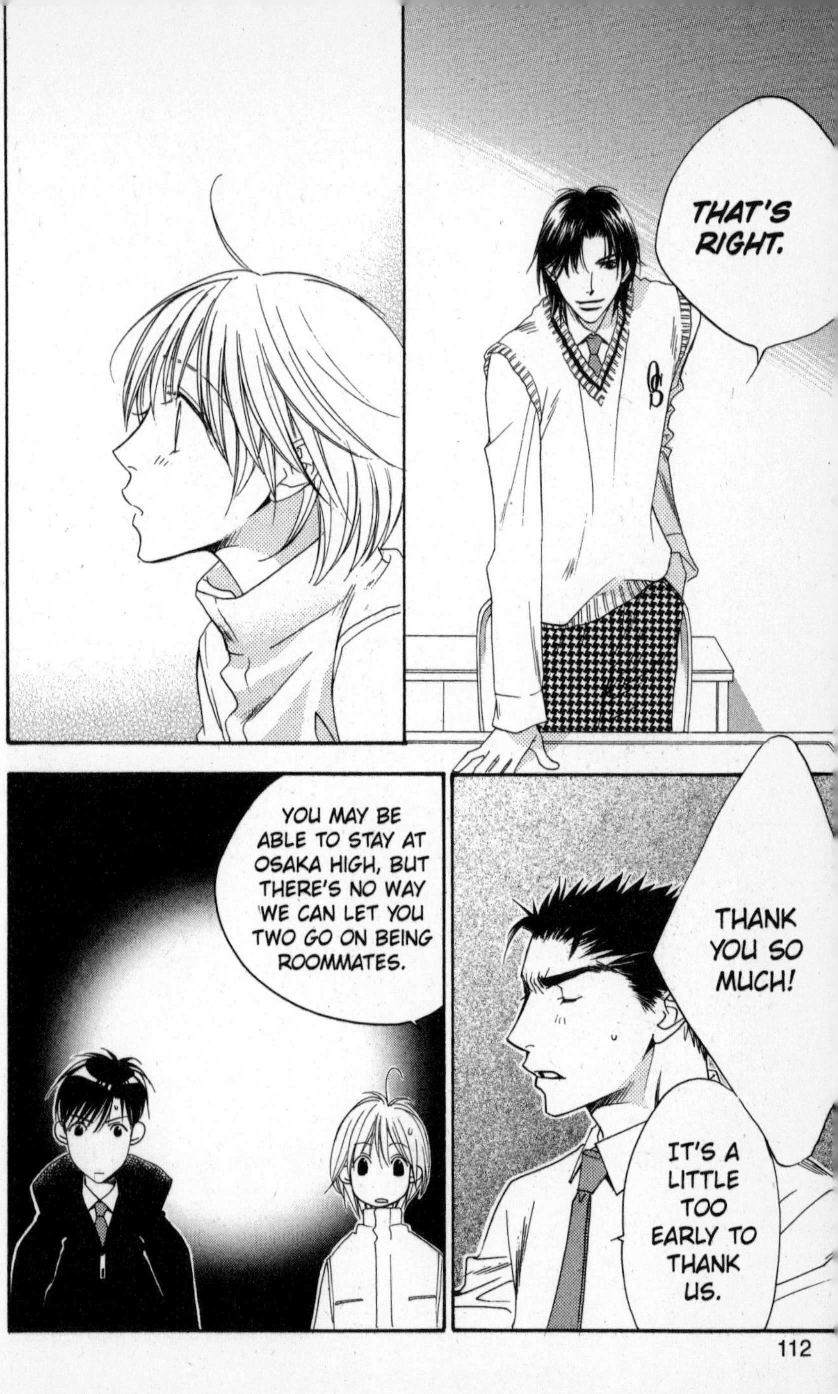
THAT'S RIGHT.
THANK YOU SO MUCH!
IT'S A LITTLE TOO EARLY TO THANK US.
YOU MAY BE ABLE TO STAY AT OSAKA HIGH, BUT THERE'S NO WAY WE CAN LET YOU TWO GO ON BEING ROOMMATES.

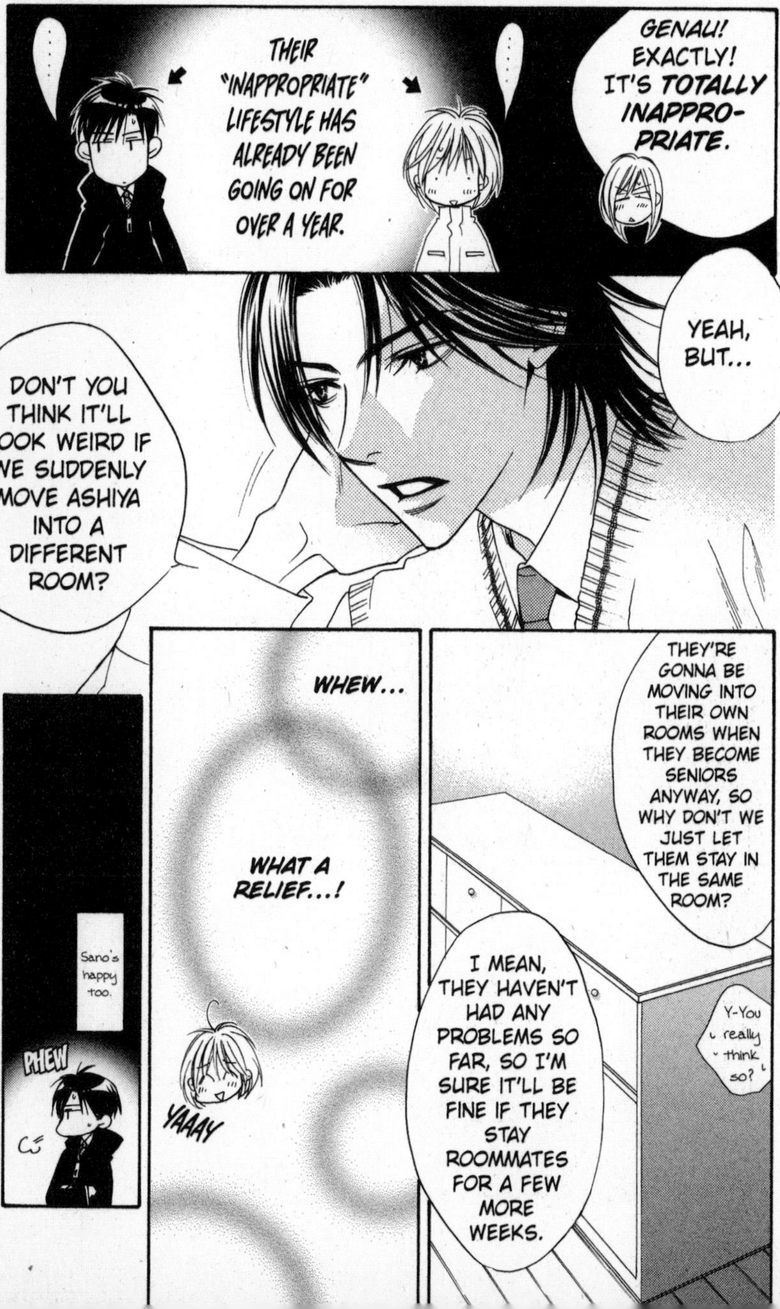
GENAU! EXACTLY! IT'S TOTALLY INAPPROPRIATE.
THEIR "INAPPROPRIATE" LIFESTYLE HAS ALREADY BEEN GOING ON FOR OVER A YEAR.
YEAH, BUT...
DON'T YOU THINK IT'LL LOOK WEIRD IF WE SUDDENLY MOVE ASHIYA INTO A DIFFERENT ROOM?
THEY'RE GONNA BE MOVING INTO THEIR OWN ROOMS WHEN THEY BECOME SENIORS ANYWAY, SO WHY DON'T WE JUST LET THEM STAY IN THE SAME ROOM?
I MEAN, THEY HAVEN'T HAD ANY PROBLEMS SO FAR, SO I'M SURE IT'LL BE FINE IF THEY STAY ROOMMATES FOR A FEW MORE WEEKS.
Y-You really think so?
WHEW...
WHAT A RELIEF...!
YAAAY
Sano's happy too.
PHEW

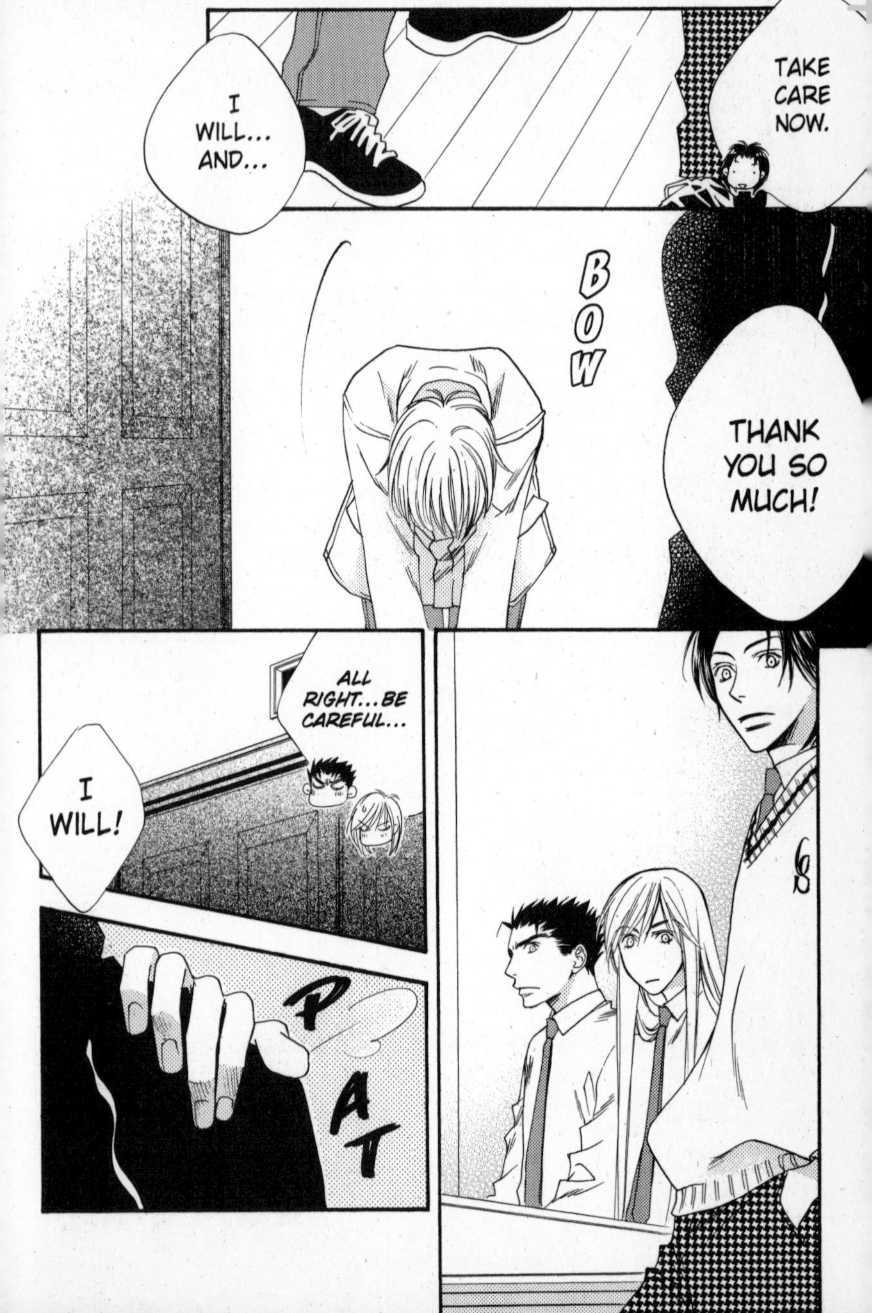
TAKE CARE NOW.
I WILL... AND...
THANK YOU SO MUCH!
BOW
ALL RIGHT...BE CAREFUL...
I WILL!
PAT

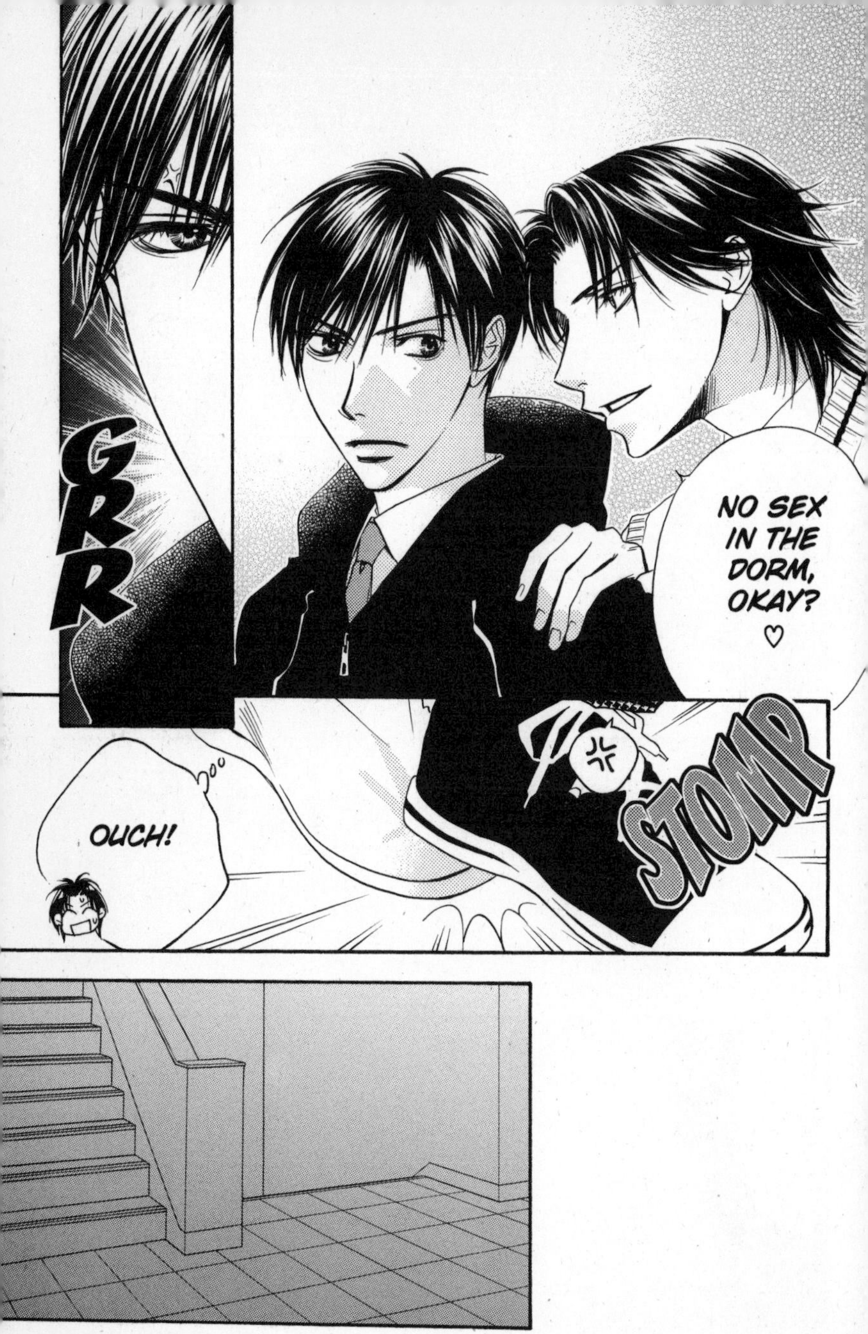
NO SEX IN THE DORM, OKAY? ♡
GRR
STOMP
OUCH!

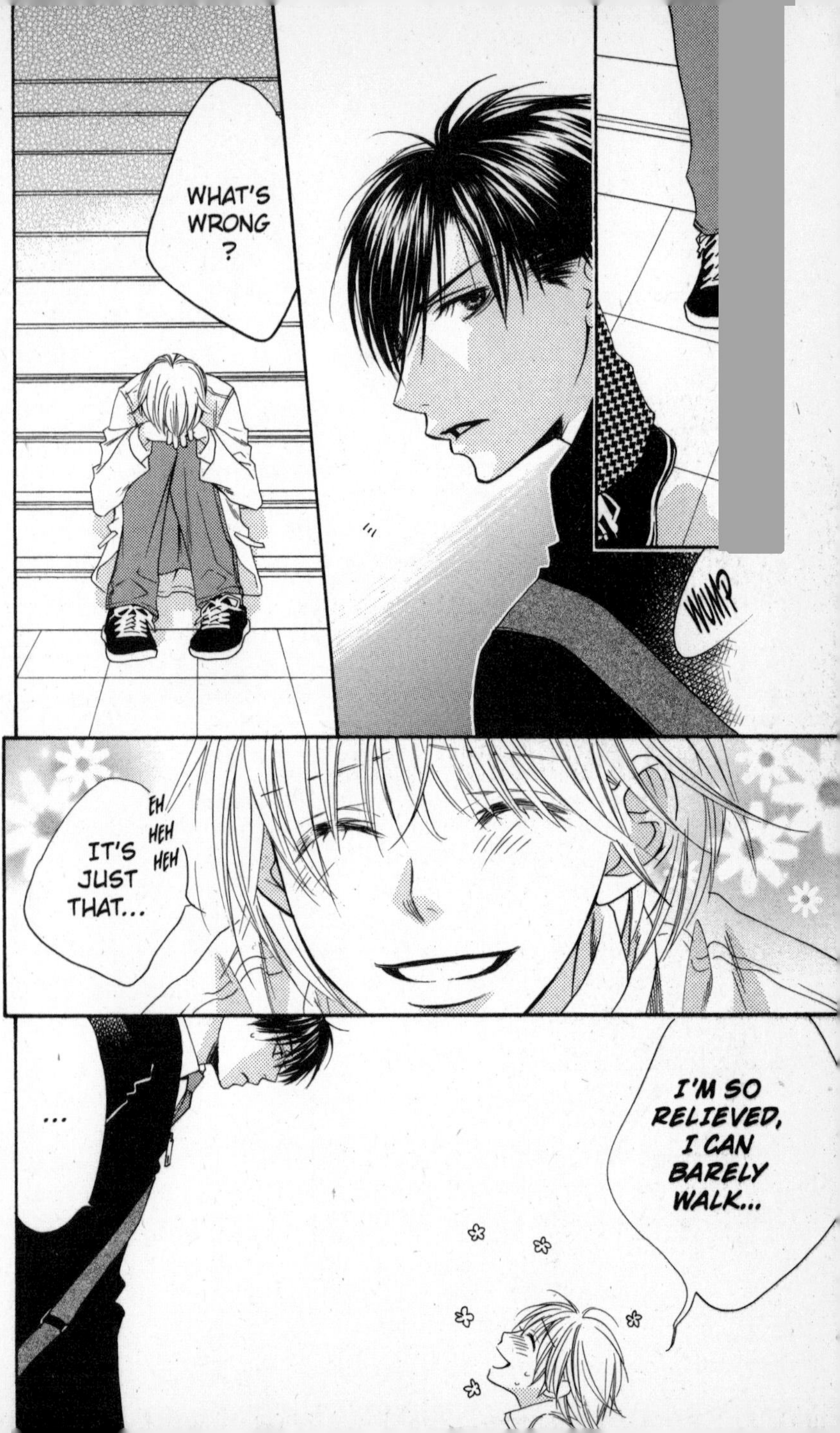
WUMP
WHAT'S WRONG?
EH HEH HEH
IT'S JUST THAT...
I'M SO RELIEVED, I CAN BARELY WALK...
...

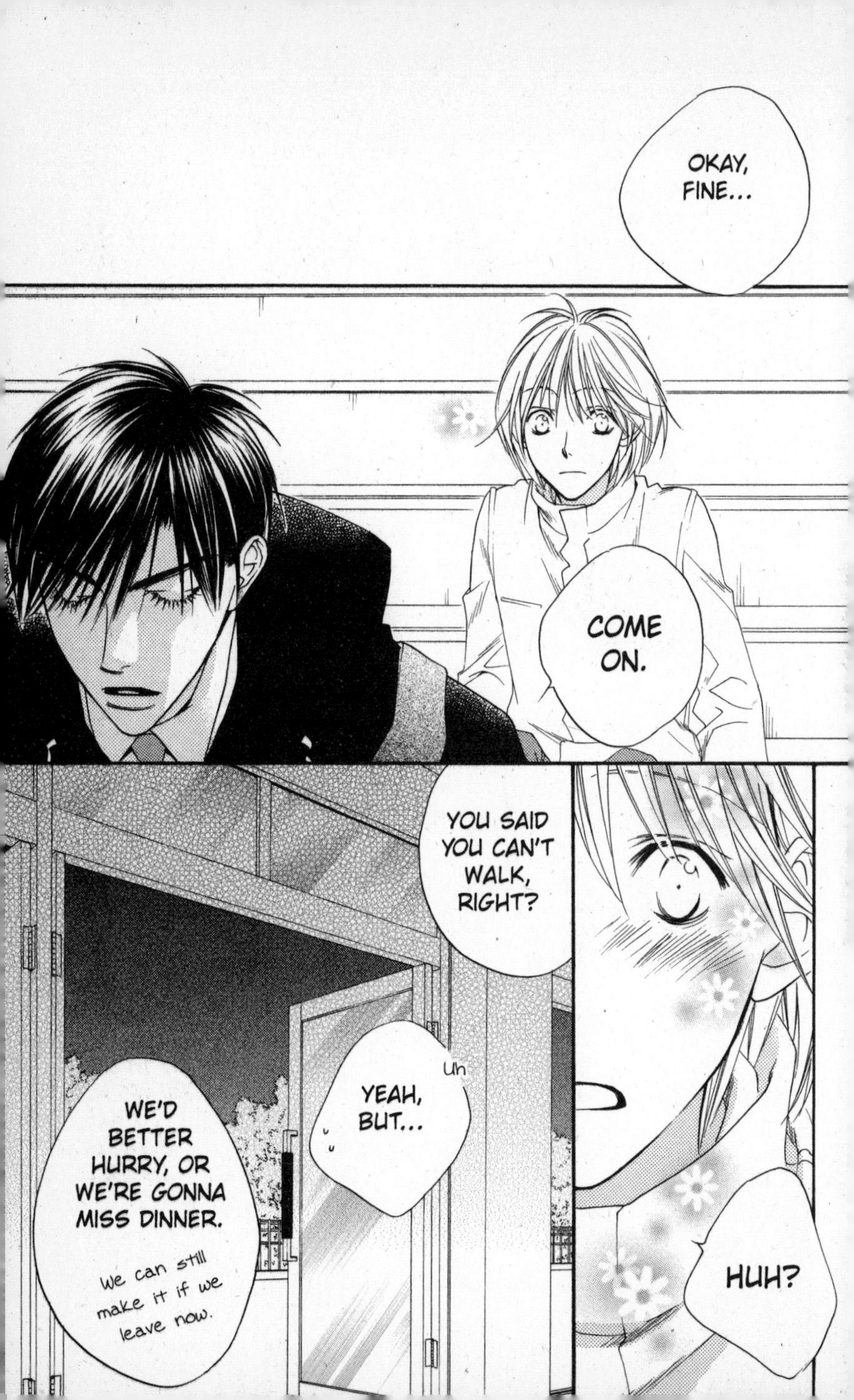
OKAY, FINE...
COME ON.
HUH?
YOU SAID YOU CAN'T WALK, RIGHT?
Uh
YEAH, BUT...
WE'D BETTER HURRY, OR WE'RE GONNA MISS DINNER.
We can still make it if we leave now.

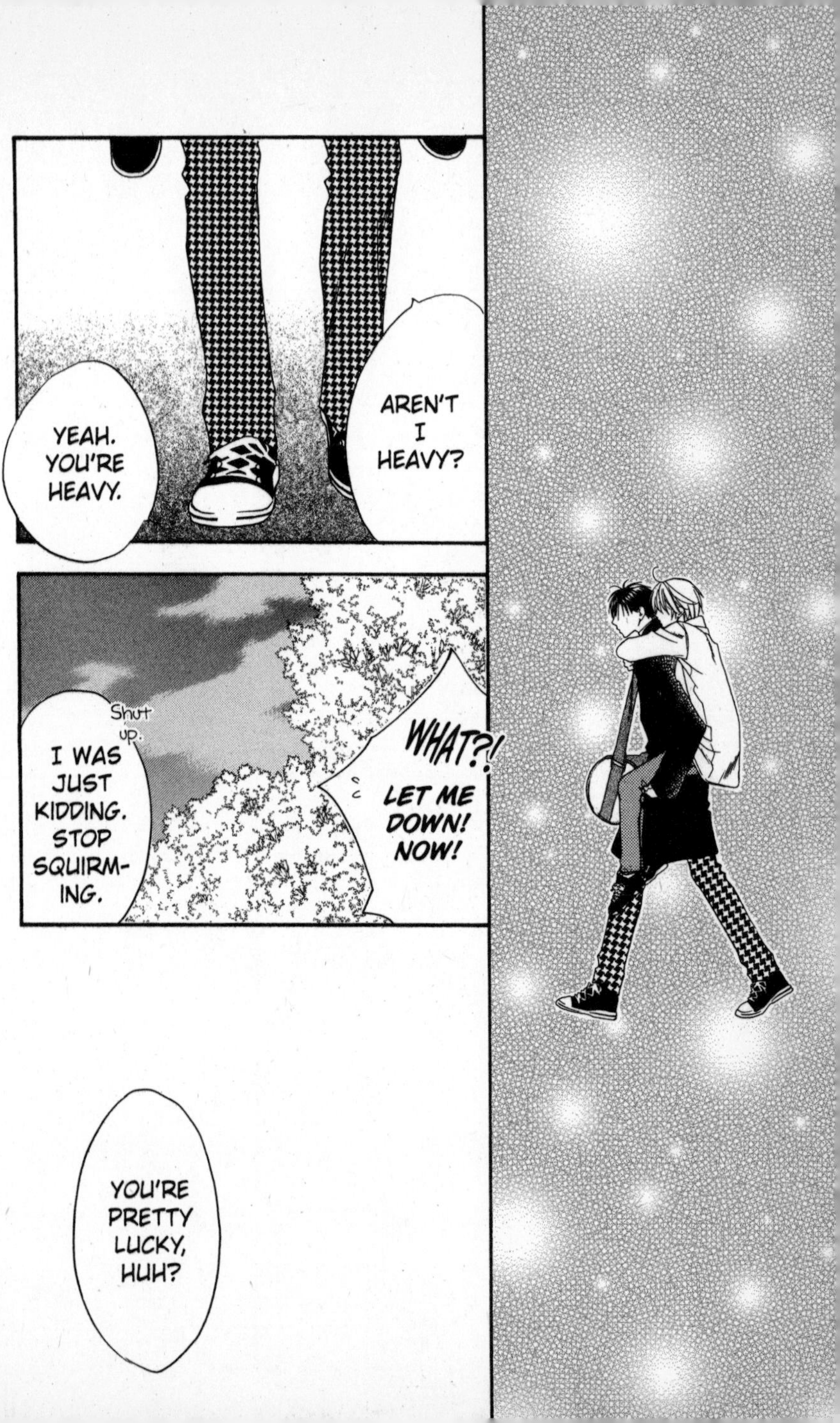
AREN'T I HEAVY?
YEAH. YOU'RE HEAVY.
WHAT?! LET ME DOWN! NOW!
Shut up.
I WAS JUST KIDDING. STOP SQUIRMING.
YOU'RE PRETTY LUCKY, HUH?

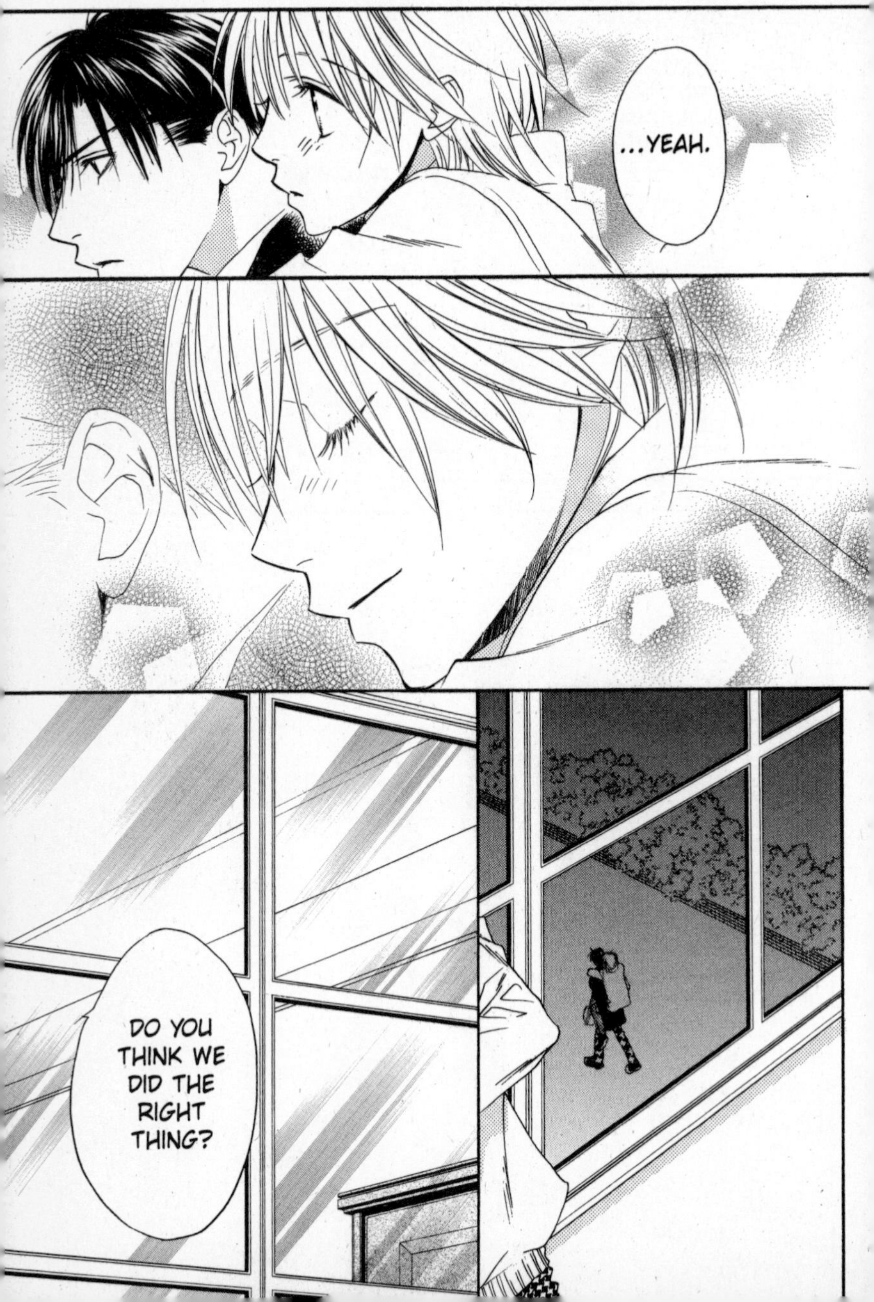
...YEAH.
DO YOU THINK WE DID THE RIGHT THING?

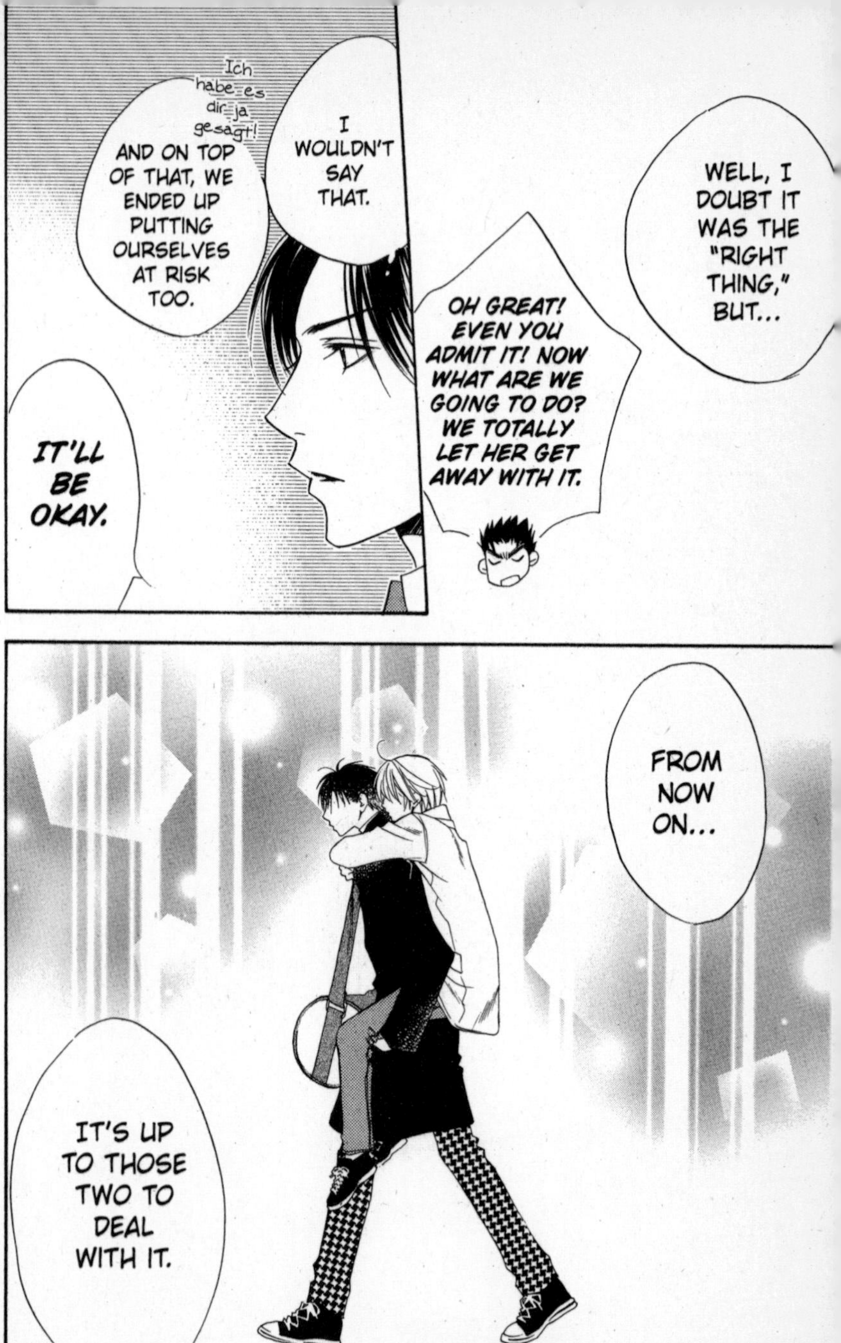
WELL, I DOUBT IT WAS THE "RIGHT THING," BUT...
OH GREAT! EVEN YOU ADMIT IT! NOW WHAT ARE WE GOING TO DO? WE TOTALLY LET HER GET AWAY WITH IT.
I WOULDN'T SAY THAT.
Ich habe es dir ja gesagt!
AND ON TOP OF THAT, WE ENDED UP PUTTING OURSELVES AT RISK TOO.
IT'LL BE OKAY.
FROM NOW ON...
IT'S UP TO THOSE TWO TO DEAL WITH IT.

HANA-KIMI CHAPTER 132/END

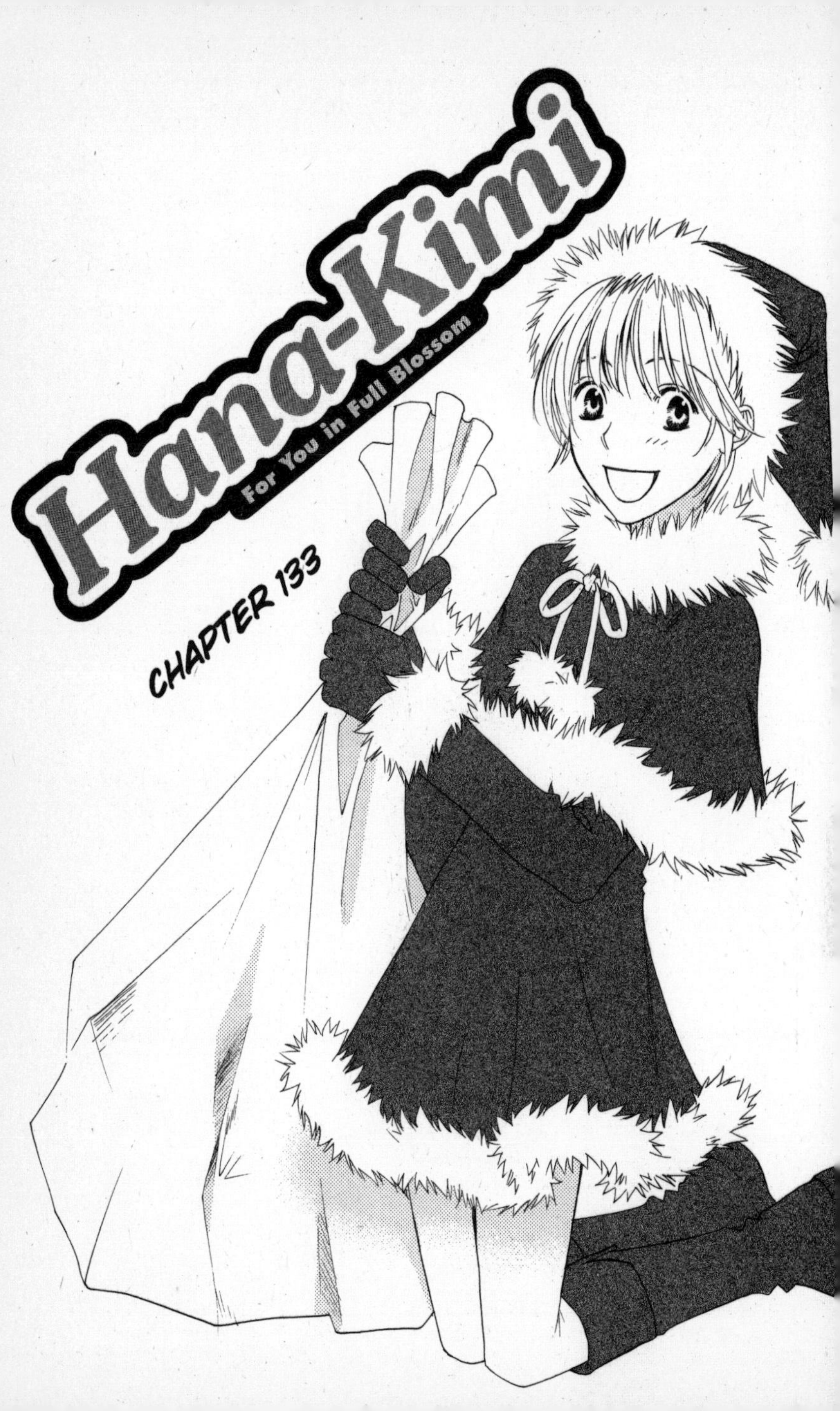
Hana-Kimi
For You in Full Blossom
CHAPTER 133

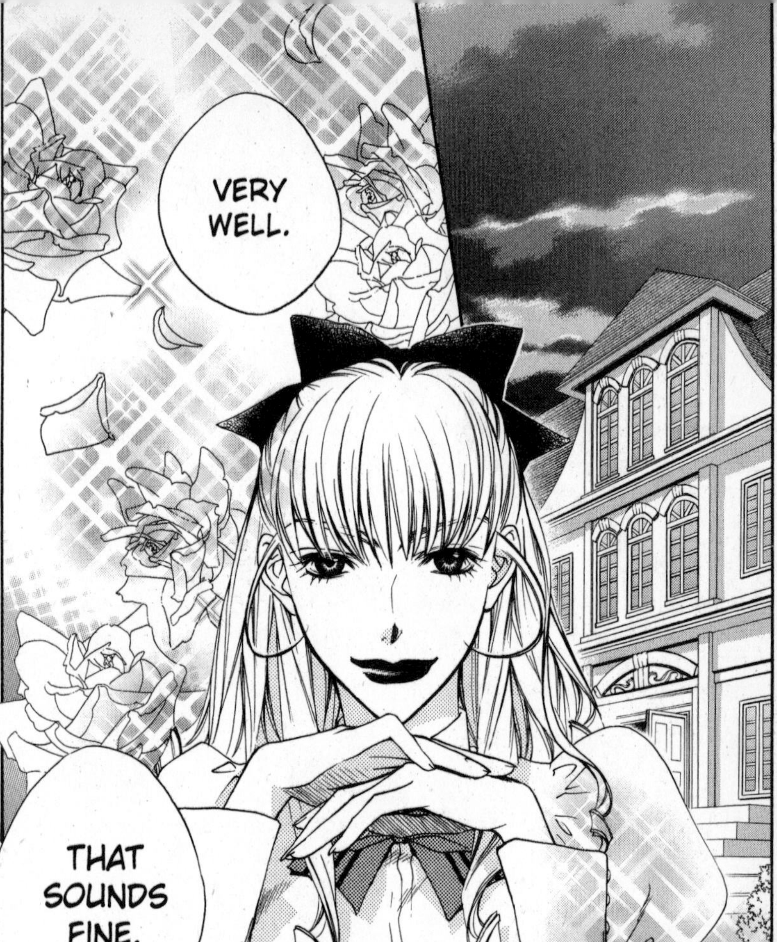
VERY WELL.
THAT SOUNDS FINE.

DOLL EXHIBITION

Recently I went to a doll exhibition. I saw some pictures of dolls made by Katan Amano and Ryo Yoshida in a magazine 15 years ago, and I finally got the chance to see the real thing! I was soooo moved! ✿

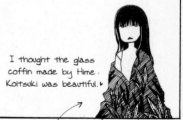

I thought the glass coffin made by Hime Koitsuki was beautiful.

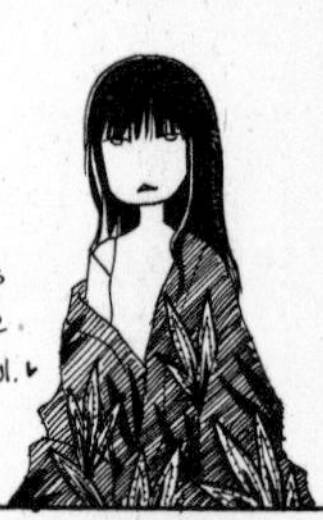

This one was my favorite. (Created by Ryo Yoshida)

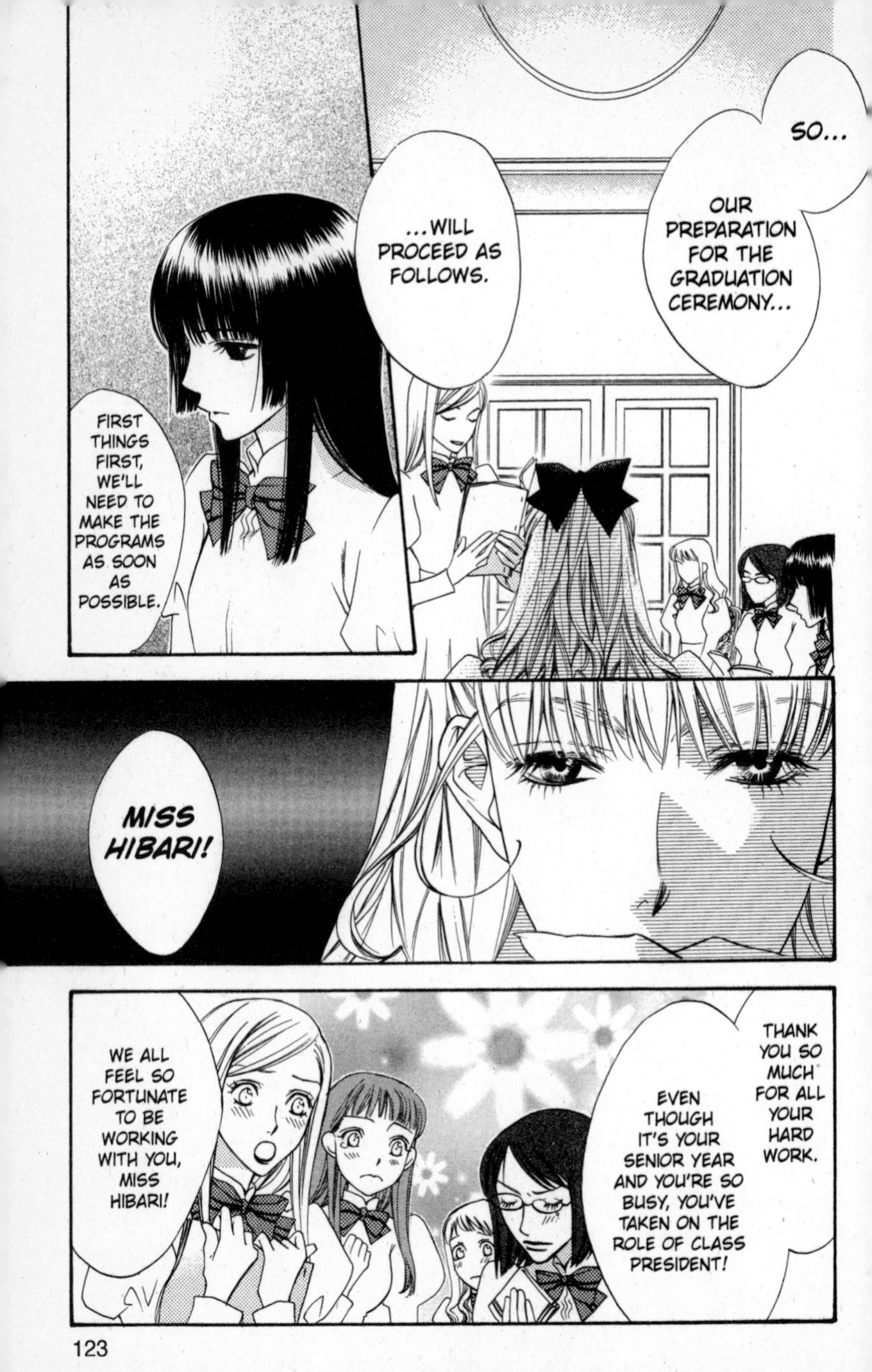
SO...
OUR PREPARATION FOR THE GRADUATION CEREMONY...
...WILL PROCEED AS FOLLOWS.
FIRST THINGS FIRST, WE'LL NEED TO MAKE THE PROGRAMS AS SOON AS POSSIBLE.
MISS HIBARI!
THANK YOU SO MUCH FOR ALL YOUR HARD WORK.
EVEN THOUGH IT'S YOUR SENIOR YEAR AND YOU'RE SO BUSY, YOU'VE TAKEN ON THE ROLE OF CLASS PRESIDENT!
WE ALL FEEL SO FORTUNATE TO BE WORKING WITH YOU, MISS HIBARI!

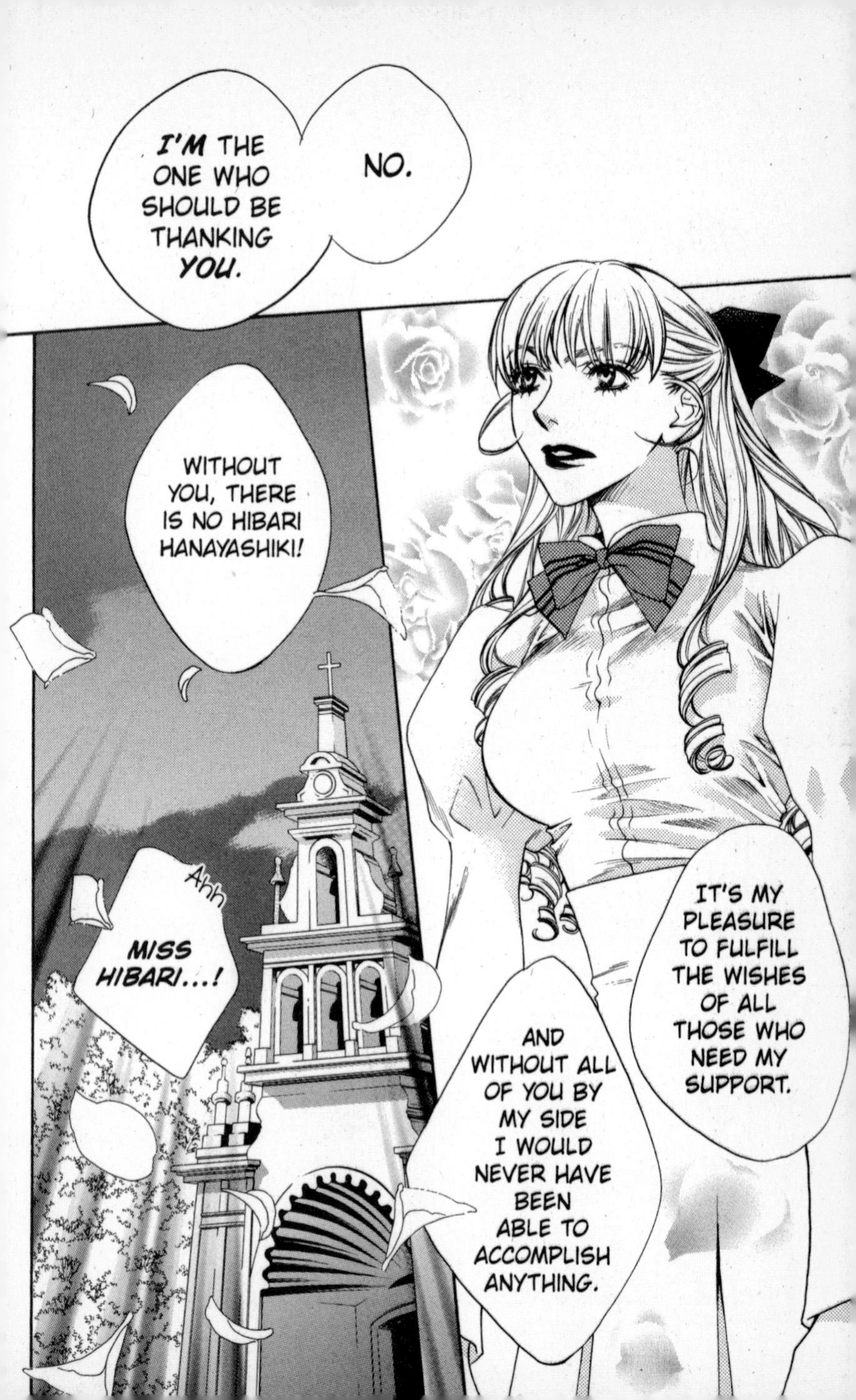
NO.
I'M THE ONE WHO SHOULD BE THANKING YOU.
IT'S MY PLEASURE TO FULFILL THE WISHES OF ALL THOSE WHO NEED MY SUPPORT.
AND WITHOUT ALL OF YOU BY MY SIDE I WOULD NEVER HAVE BEEN ABLE TO ACCOMPLISH ANYTHING.
WITHOUT YOU, THERE IS NO HIBARI HANAYASHIKI!
Ahh
MISS HIBARI...!

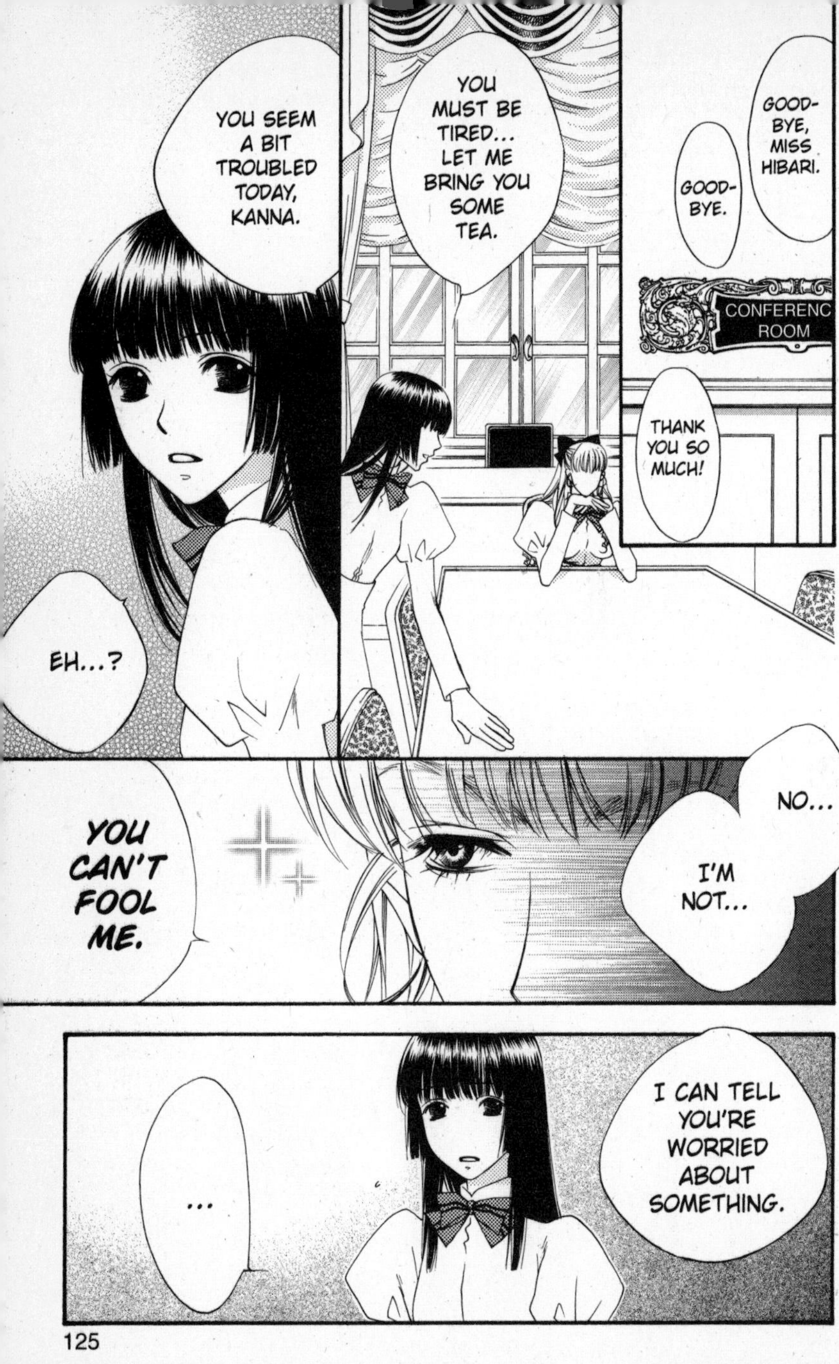
GOOD-BYE, MISS HIBARI.
GOOD-BYE.
CONFERENC ROOM
THANK YOU SO MUCH!
YOU MUST BE TIRED... LET ME BRING YOU SOME TEA.
YOU SEEM A BIT TROUBLED TODAY, KANNA.
EH...?
NO...
I'M NOT...
YOU CAN'T FOOL ME.
I CAN TELL YOU'RE WORRIED ABOUT SOMETHING.
...

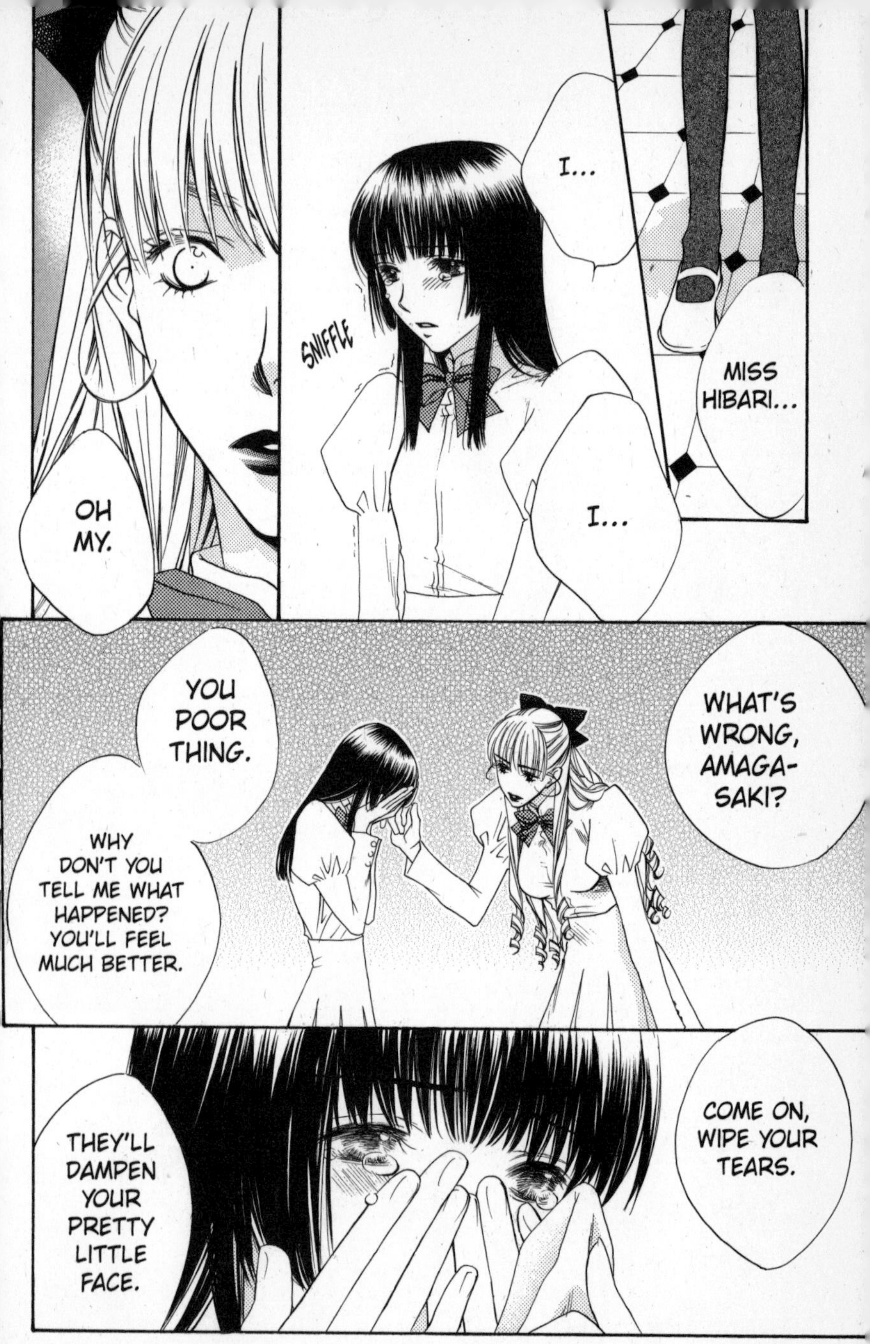
MISS HIBARI...
I...
SNIFFLE
I...
OH MY.
WHAT'S WRONG, AMAGA-SAKI?
YOU POOR THING.
WHY DON'T YOU TELL ME WHAT HAPPENED? YOU'LL FEEL MUCH BETTER.
COME ON, WIPE YOUR TEARS.
THEY'LL DAMPEN YOUR PRETTY LITTLE FACE.

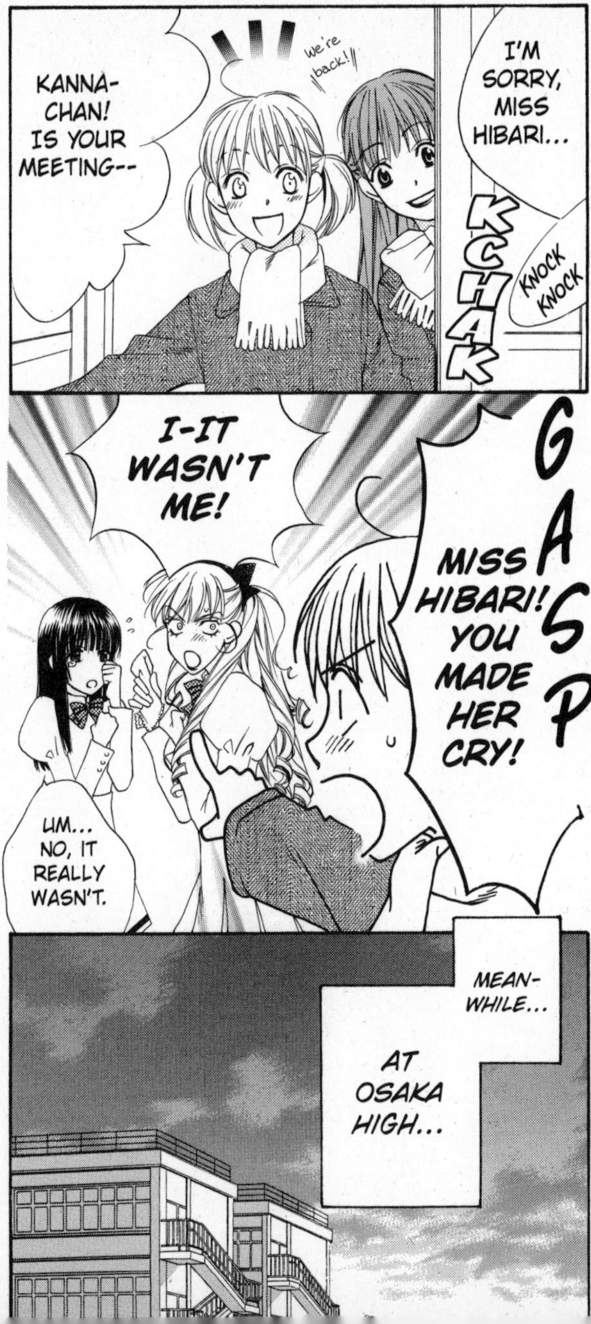
I'M SORRY, MISS HIBARI...
KNOCK KNOCK
KCHAK
We're back!
KANNA-CHAN! IS YOUR MEETING--
GASP
MISS HIBARI! YOU MADE HER CRY!
I-IT WASN'T ME!
UM... NO, IT REALLY WASN'T.
MEAN-WHILE...
AT OSAKA HIGH...

STUFFED MARTYRS

Both my cats loved this one.

Kisuke (Mascot)

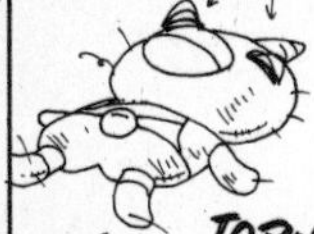
Eyes all chewed up
Covered with cat hair
TORN UP...

The Gurumii character that sits on top of my desk

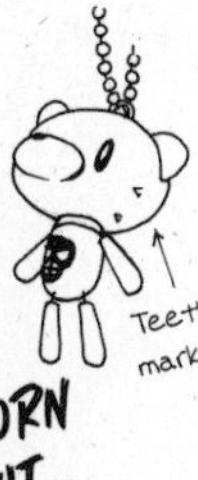
Teeth marks
WORN OUT...

Graduation rehearsal with the freshmen and sophomores

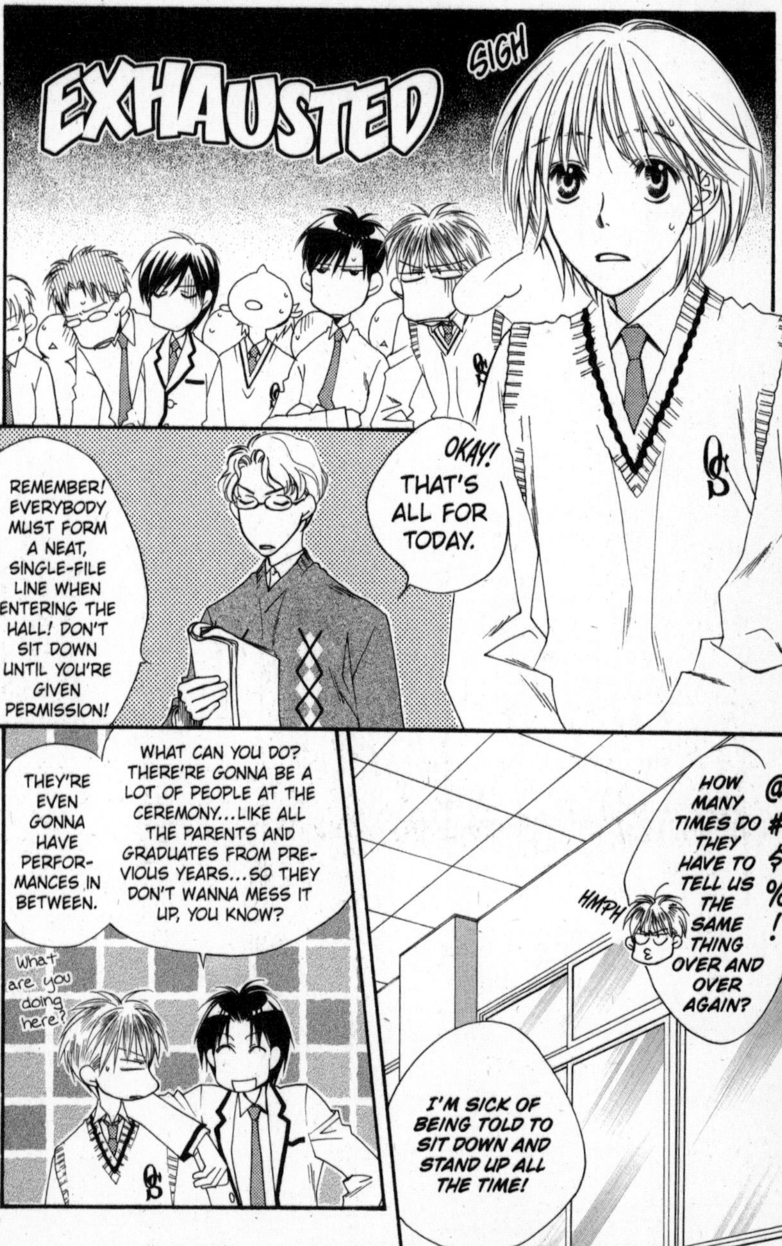
SIGH
EXHAUSTED
OKAY! THAT'S ALL FOR TODAY.
REMEMBER! EVERYBODY MUST FORM A NEAT, SINGLE-FILE LINE WHEN ENTERING THE HALL! DON'T SIT DOWN UNTIL YOU'RE GIVEN PERMISSION!
HOW MANY TIMES DO THEY HAVE TO TELL US THE SAME THING OVER AND OVER AGAIN?
@#$%!
HMPH
I'M SICK OF BEING TOLD TO SIT DOWN AND STAND UP ALL THE TIME!
WHAT CAN YOU DO? THERE'RE GONNA BE A LOT OF PEOPLE AT THE CEREMONY...LIKE ALL THE PARENTS AND GRADUATES FROM PREVIOUS YEARS...SO THEY DON'T WANNA MESS IT UP, YOU KNOW?
THEY'RE EVEN GONNA HAVE PERFORMANCES IN BETWEEN.
What are you doing here?

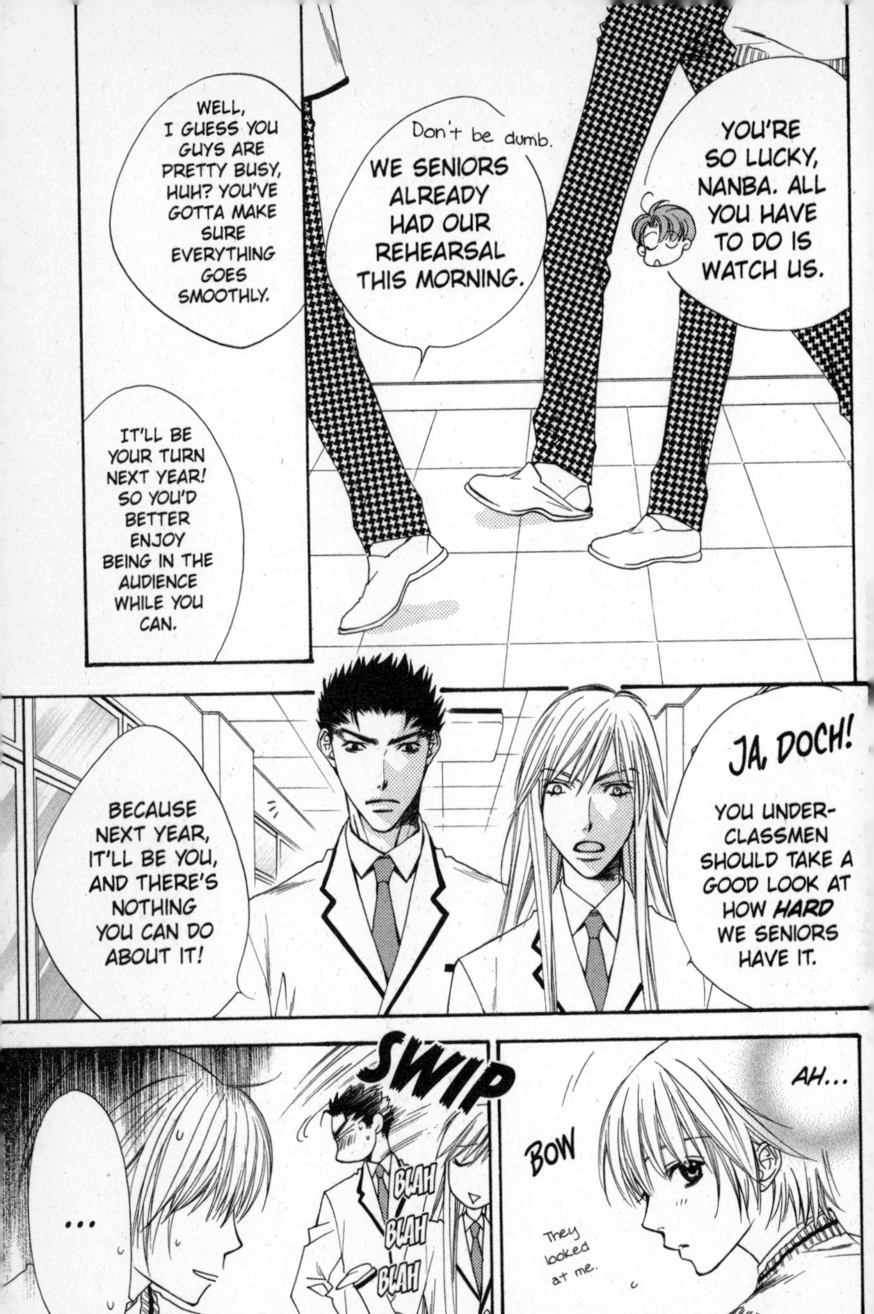
YOU'RE SO LUCKY, NANBA. ALL YOU HAVE TO DO IS WATCH US.
Don't be dumb.
WE SENIORS ALREADY HAD OUR REHEARSAL THIS MORNING.
WELL, I GUESS YOU GUYS ARE PRETTY BUSY, HUH? YOU'VE GOTTA MAKE SURE EVERYTHING GOES SMOOTHLY.
IT'LL BE YOUR TURN NEXT YEAR! SO YOU'D BETTER ENJOY BEING IN THE AUDIENCE WHILE YOU CAN.
JA, DOCH!
YOU UNDER-CLASSMEN SHOULD TAKE A GOOD LOOK AT HOW *HARD* WE SENIORS HAVE IT.
BECAUSE NEXT YEAR, IT'LL BE YOU, AND THERE'S NOTHING YOU CAN DO ABOUT IT!
AH...
BOW
They looked at me.
SWIP
BLAH
BLAH
BLAH
...

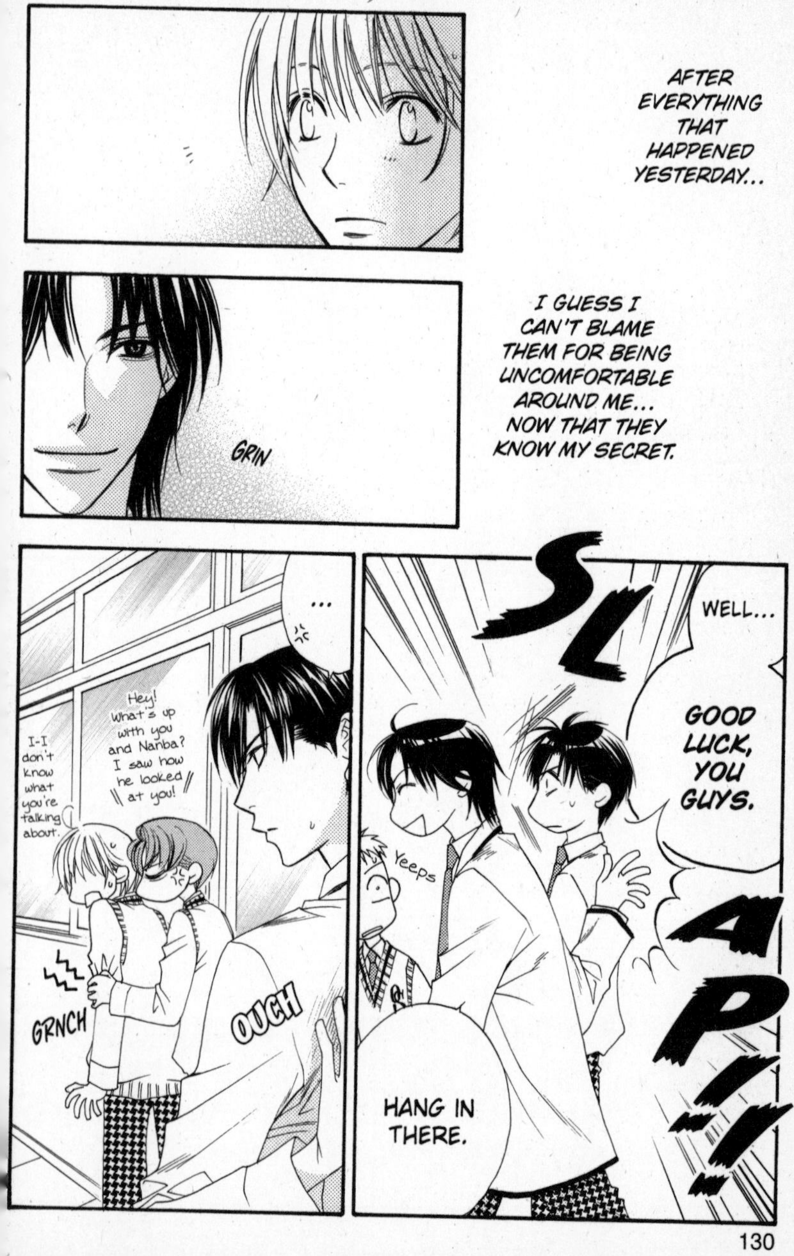
AFTER EVERYTHING THAT HAPPENED YESTERDAY...
I GUESS I CAN'T BLAME THEM FOR BEING UNCOMFORTABLE AROUND ME... NOW THAT THEY KNOW MY SECRET.
GRIN
SLAP!!
WELL...
GOOD LUCK, YOU GUYS.
Yeeps
HANG IN THERE.
...
Hey! What's up with you and Nanba? I saw how he looked at you!
I-I don't know what you're talking about.
GRNCH
OUCH

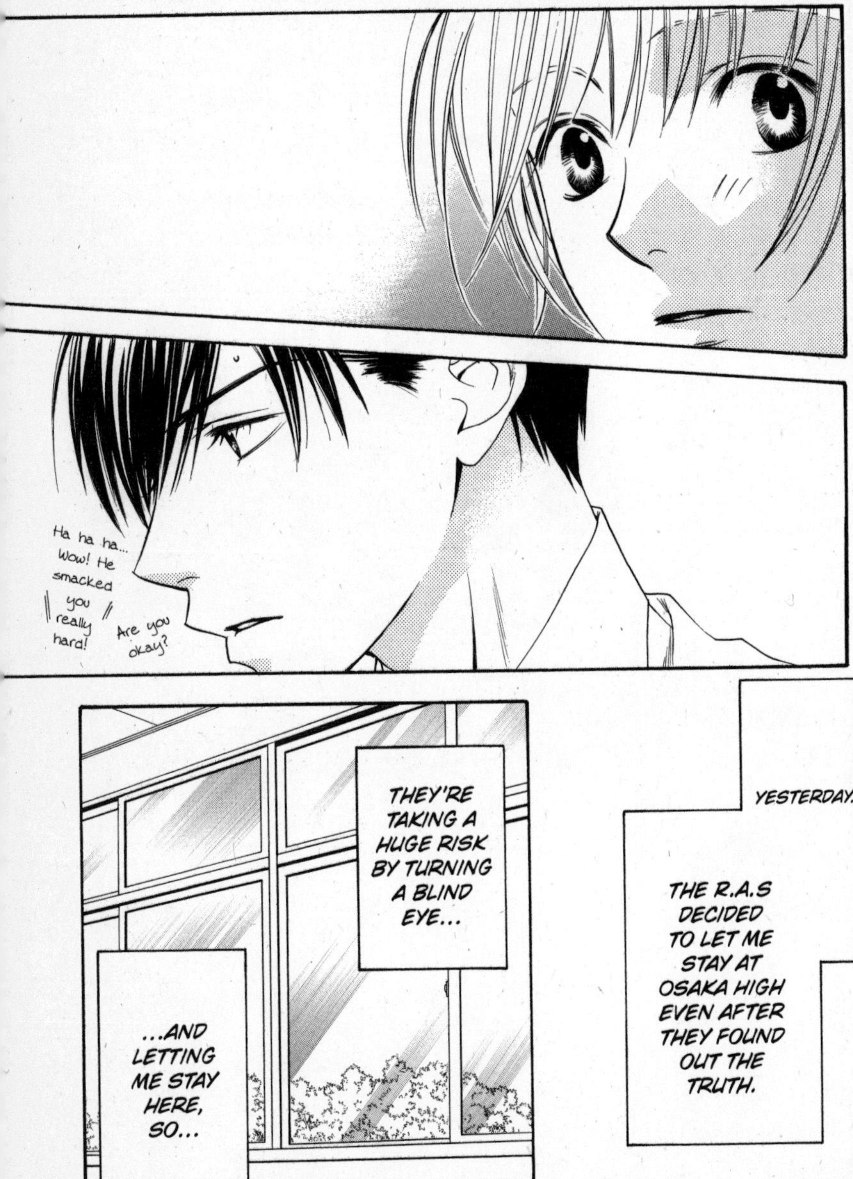
Ha ha ha... Wow! He smacked you really hard!
Are you okay?
YESTERDAY...
THE R.A.S DECIDED TO LET ME STAY AT OSAKA HIGH EVEN AFTER THEY FOUND OUT THE TRUTH.
THEY'RE TAKING A HUGE RISK BY TURNING A BLIND EYE...
...AND LETTING ME STAY HERE, SO...

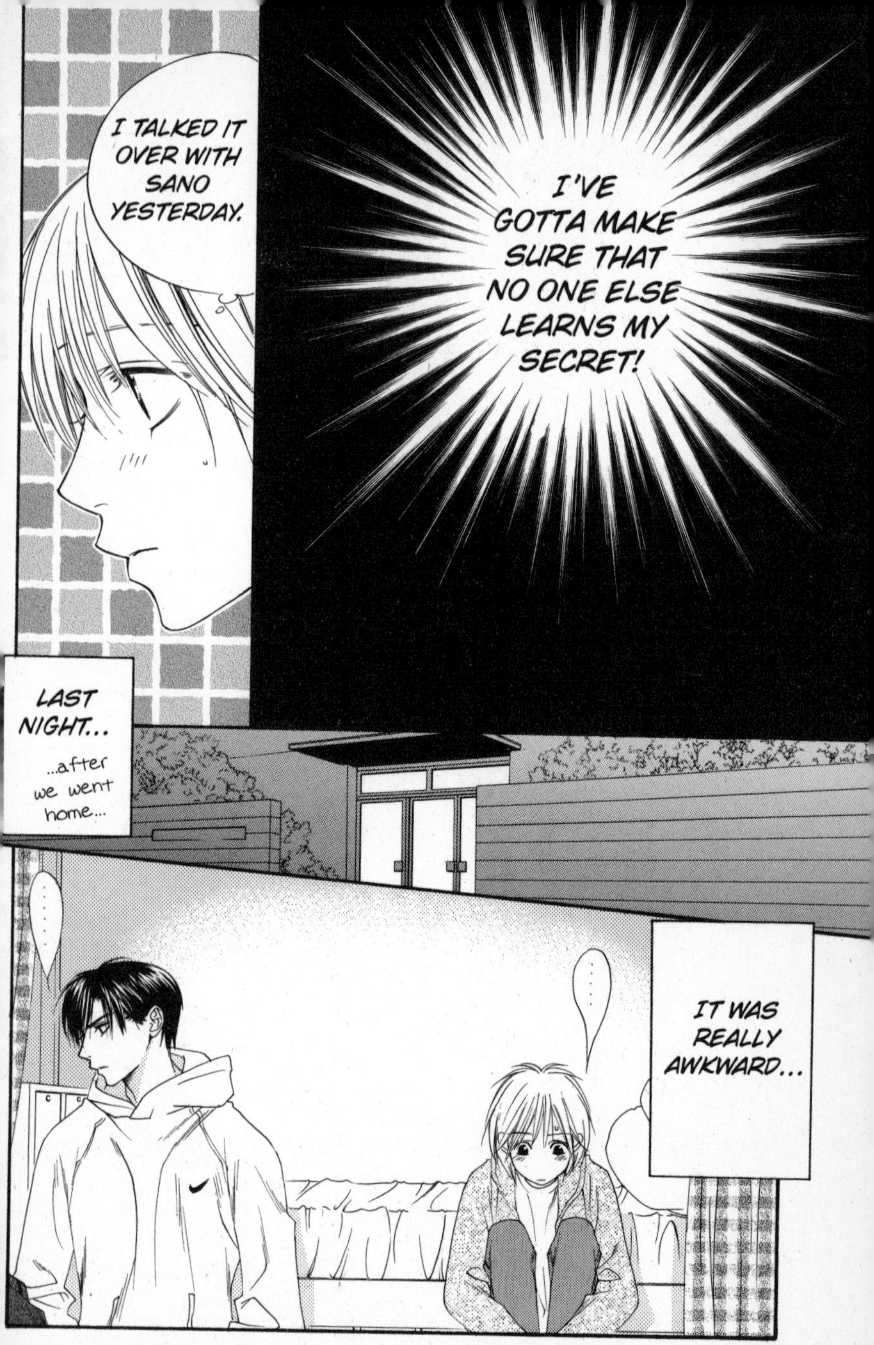
I'VE GOTTA MAKE SURE THAT NO ONE ELSE LEARNS MY SECRET!
I TALKED IT OVER WITH SANO YESTERDAY.
LAST NIGHT...
...after we went home...
IT WAS REALLY AWKWARD...
.....
.....

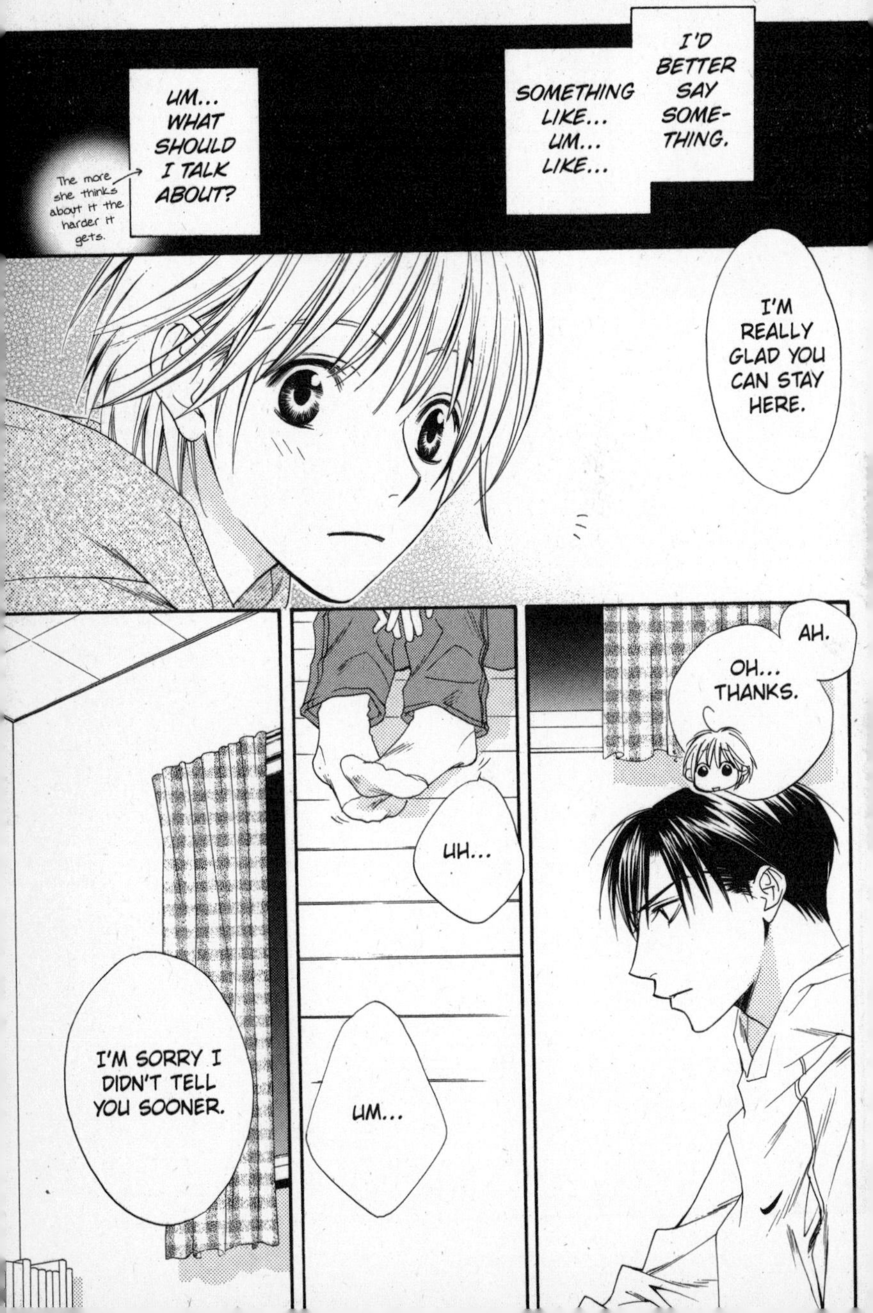
I'D BETTER SAY SOME-THING.
SOMETHING LIKE... UM... LIKE...
UM... WHAT SHOULD I TALK ABOUT?
The more she thinks about it the harder it gets.
I'M REALLY GLAD YOU CAN STAY HERE.
AH. OH... THANKS.
UH...
UM...
I'M SORRY I DIDN'T TELL YOU SOONER.

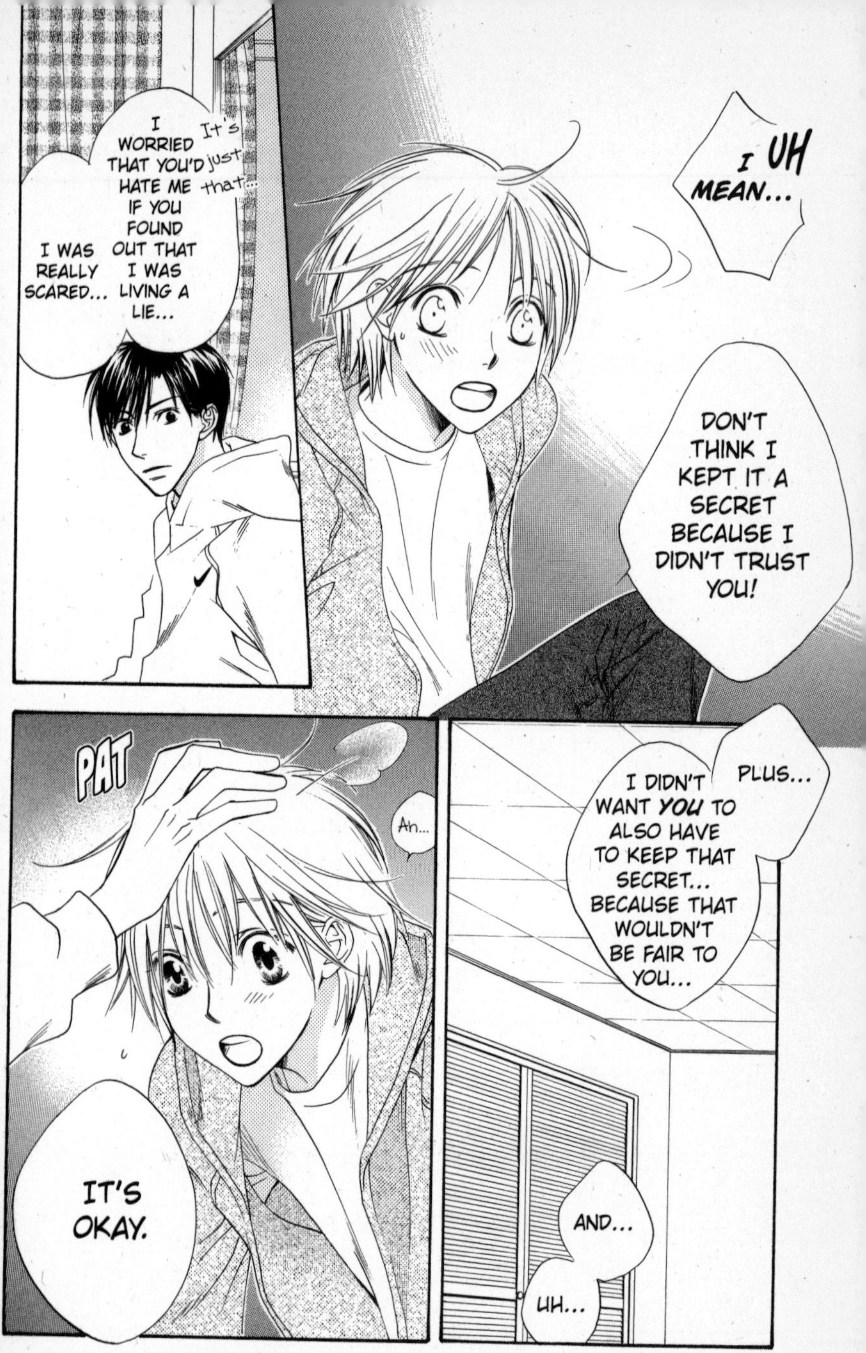
I UH MEAN...
DON'T THINK I KEPT IT A SECRET BECAUSE I DIDN'T TRUST YOU!
It's just that...
I WORRIED THAT YOU'D HATE ME IF YOU FOUND OUT THAT I WAS LIVING A LIE...
I WAS REALLY SCARED...
PLUS...
I DIDN'T WANT *YOU* TO ALSO HAVE TO KEEP THAT SECRET... BECAUSE THAT WOULDN'T BE FAIR TO YOU...
AND...
UH...
PAT
An...
IT'S OKAY.

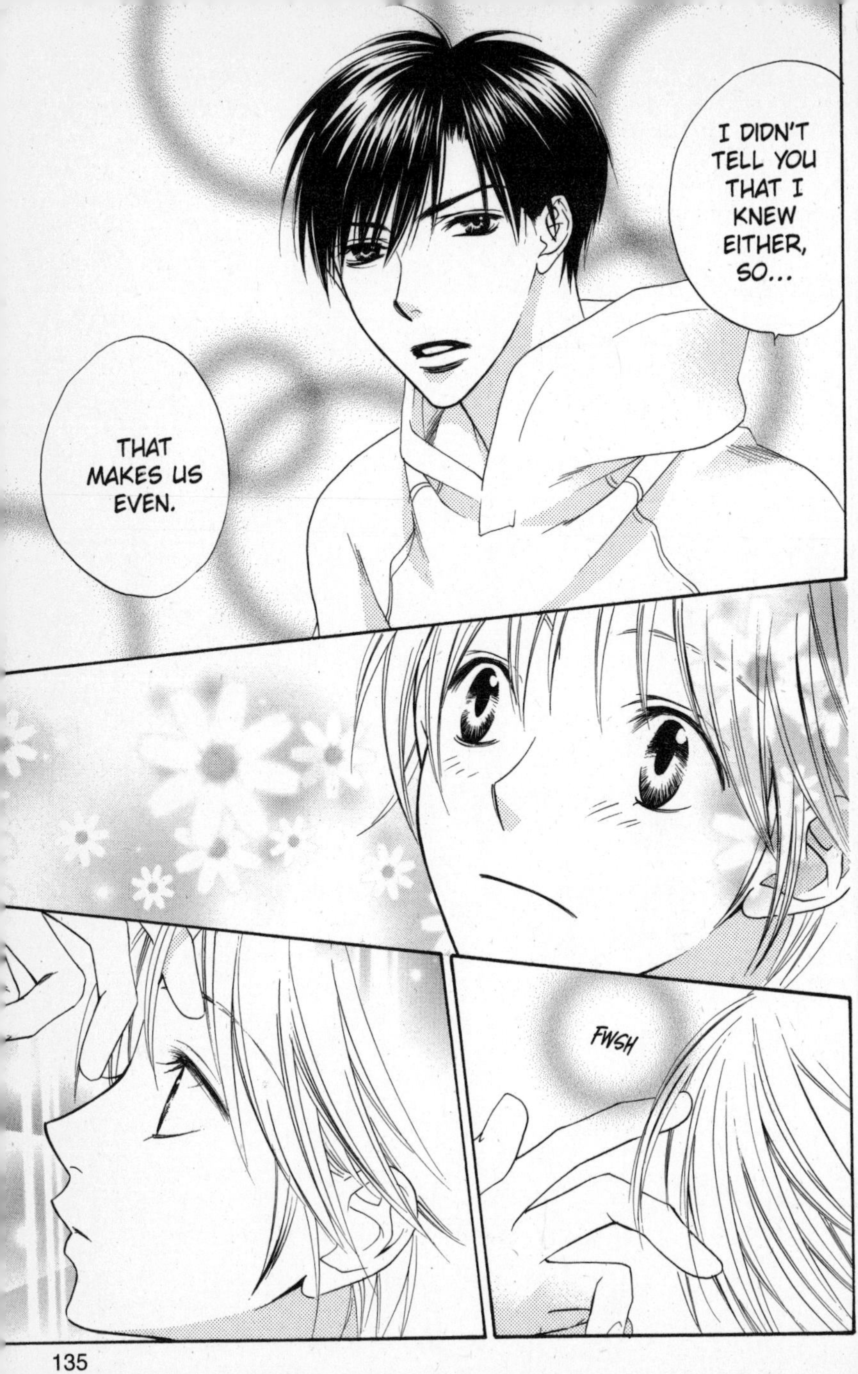
I DIDN'T TELL YOU THAT I KNEW EITHER, SO...
THAT MAKES US EVEN.
FWSH

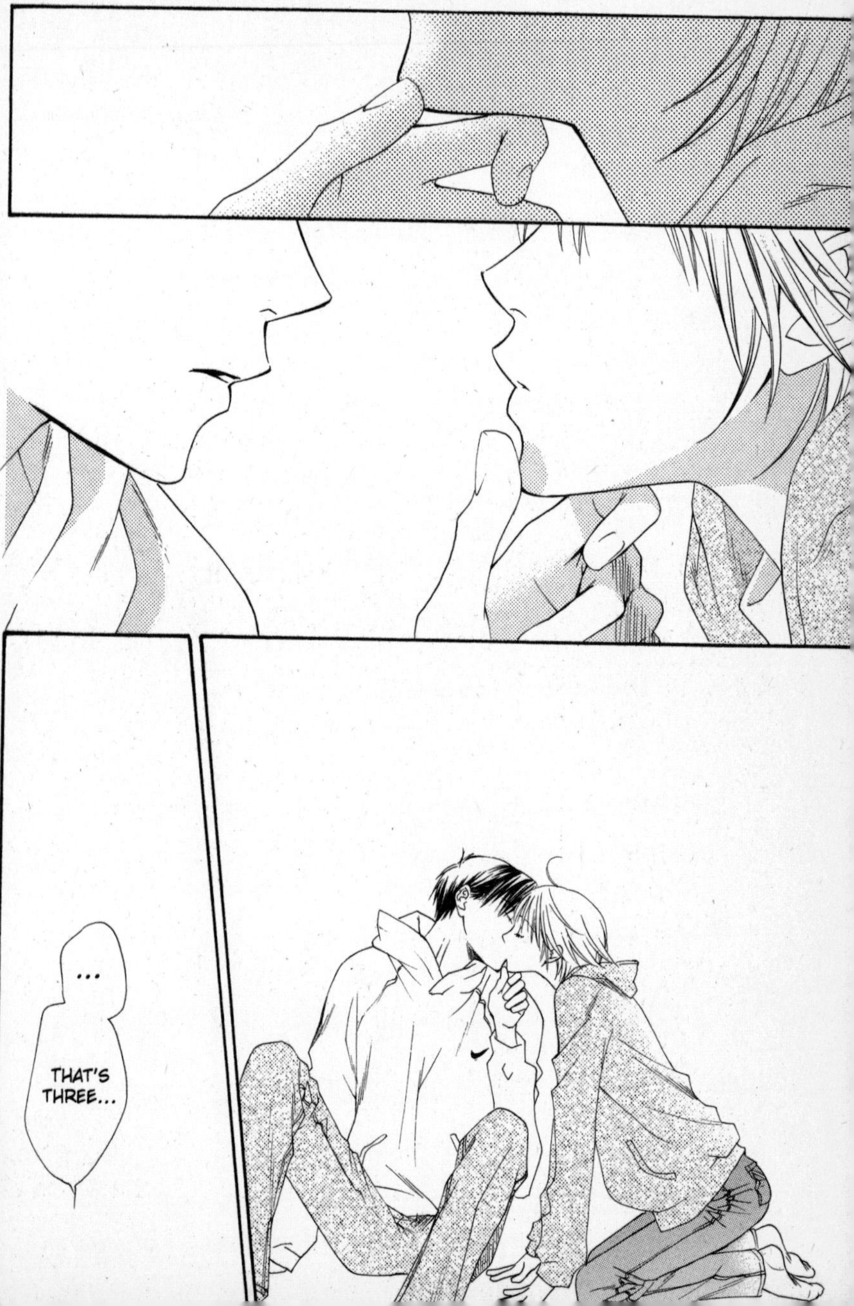
...
THAT'S THREE...

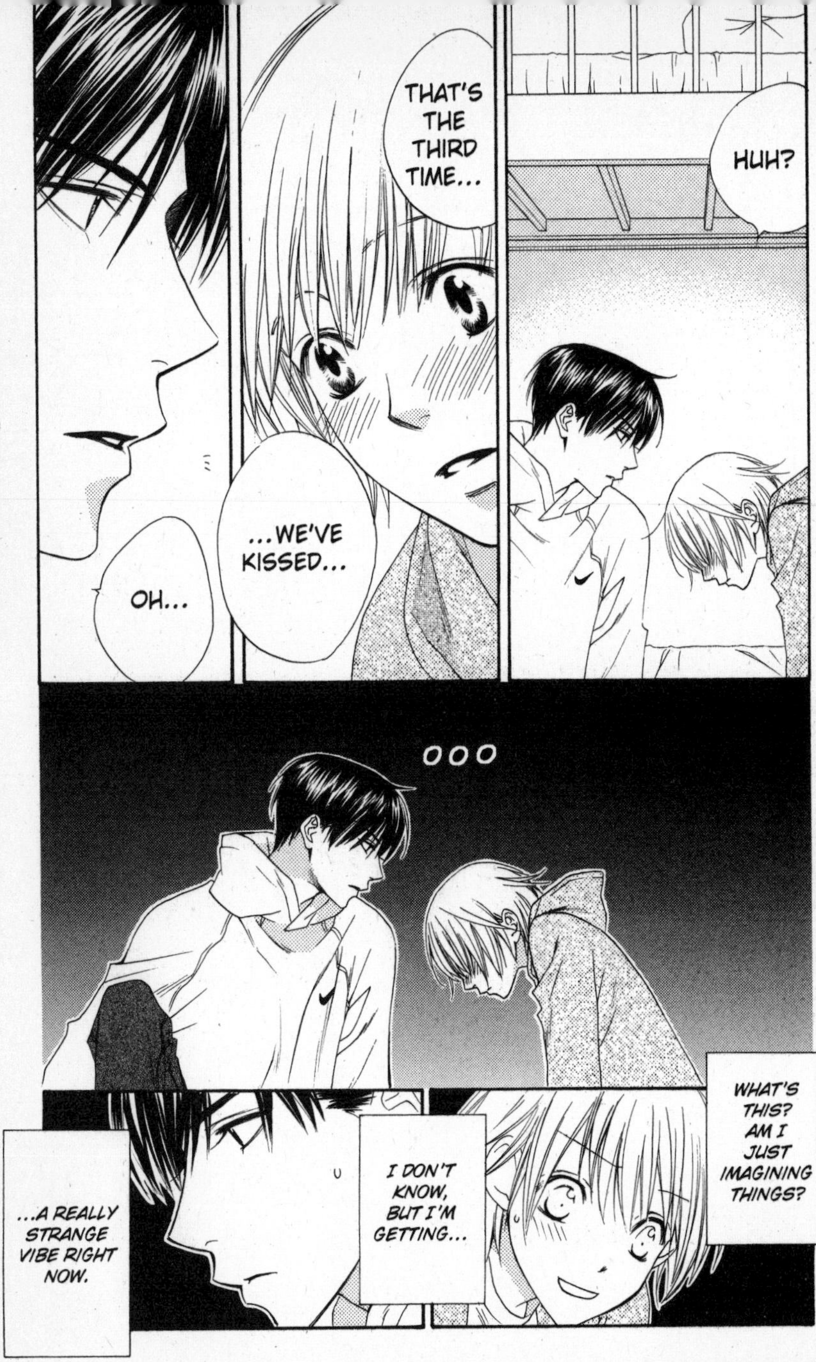
HUH?
THAT'S THE THIRD TIME...
...WE'VE KISSED...
OH...
OOO
WHAT'S THIS? AM I JUST IMAGINING THINGS?
I DON'T KNOW, BUT I'M GETTING...
...A REALLY STRANGE VIBE RIGHT NOW.

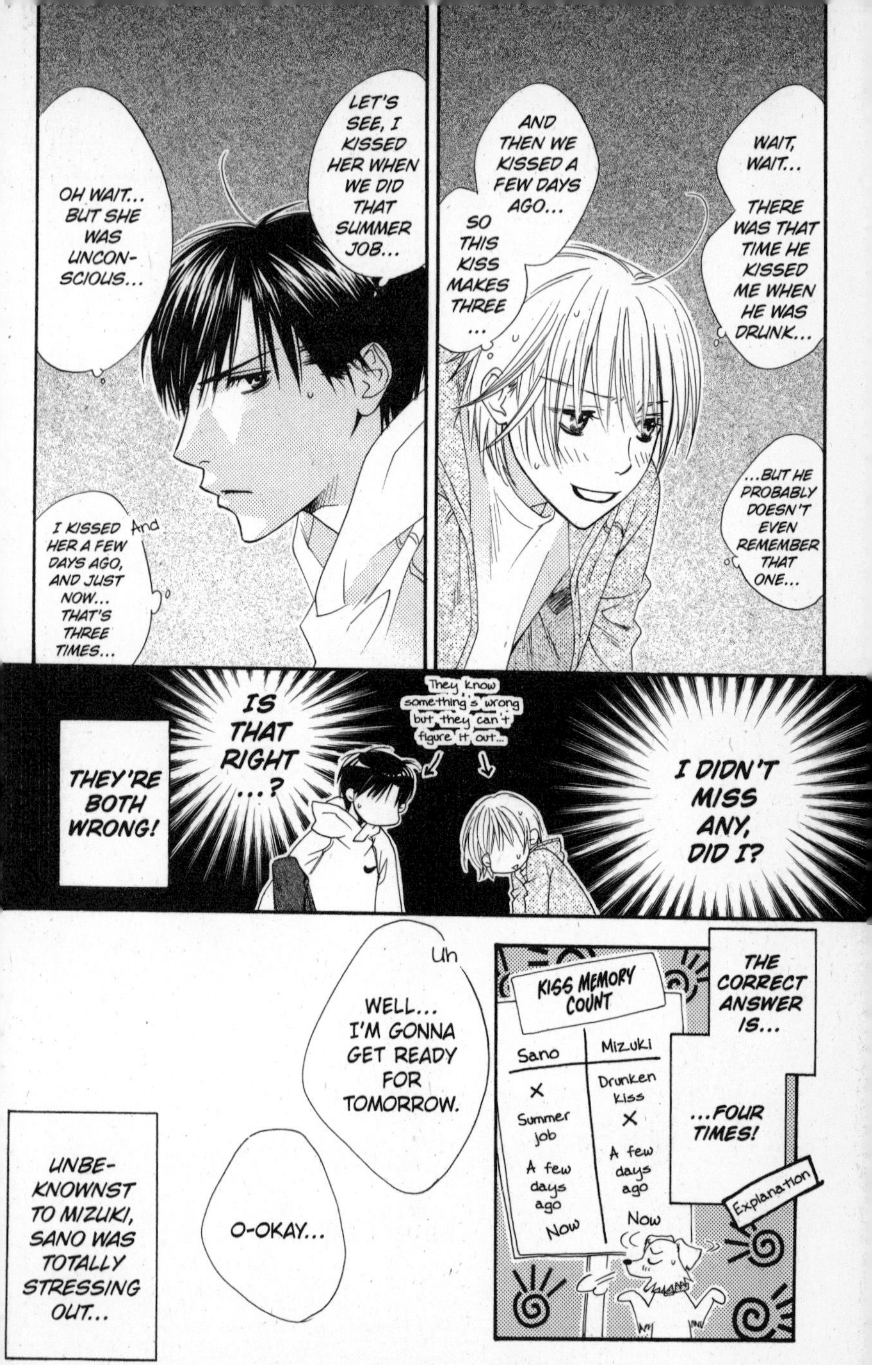
WAIT, WAIT... THERE WAS THAT TIME HE KISSED ME WHEN HE WAS DRUNK...
AND THEN WE KISSED A FEW DAYS AGO...
SO THIS KISS MAKES THREE...
...BUT HE PROBABLY DOESN'T EVEN REMEMBER THAT ONE...
LET'S SEE, I KISSED HER WHEN WE DID THAT SUMMER JOB...
OH WAIT... BUT SHE WAS UNCONSCIOUS...
And
I KISSED HER A FEW DAYS AGO, AND JUST NOW... THAT'S THREE TIMES...
I DIDN'T MISS ANY, DID I?
They know something's wrong but they can't figure it out...
IS THAT RIGHT...?
THEY'RE BOTH WRONG!
THE CORRECT ANSWER IS...
KISS MEMORY COUNT
Sano
Mizuki
Drunken kiss
×
Summer job
A few days ago
A few days ago
Now
Now
...FOUR TIMES!
Explanation
Uh
WELL... I'M GONNA GET READY FOR TOMORROW.
O-OKAY...
UNBE-KNOWNST TO MIZUKI, SANO WAS TOTALLY STRESSING OUT...

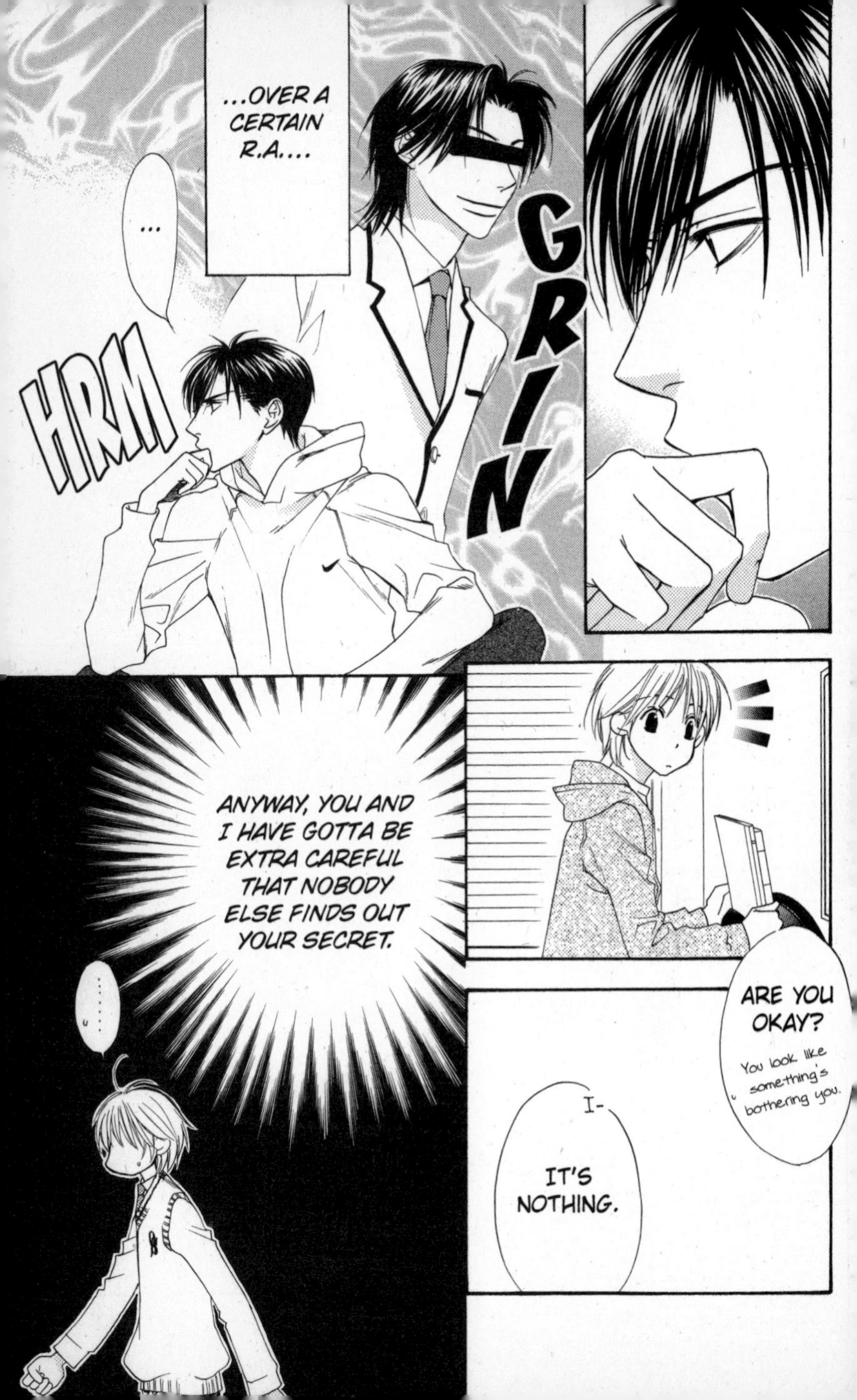
...OVER A CERTAIN R.A....
GRIN
...
HRM
ARE YOU OKAY?
You look like something's bothering you.
I-
IT'S NOTHING.
ANYWAY, YOU AND I HAVE GOTTA BE EXTRA CAREFUL THAT NOBODY ELSE FINDS OUT YOUR SECRET.
......

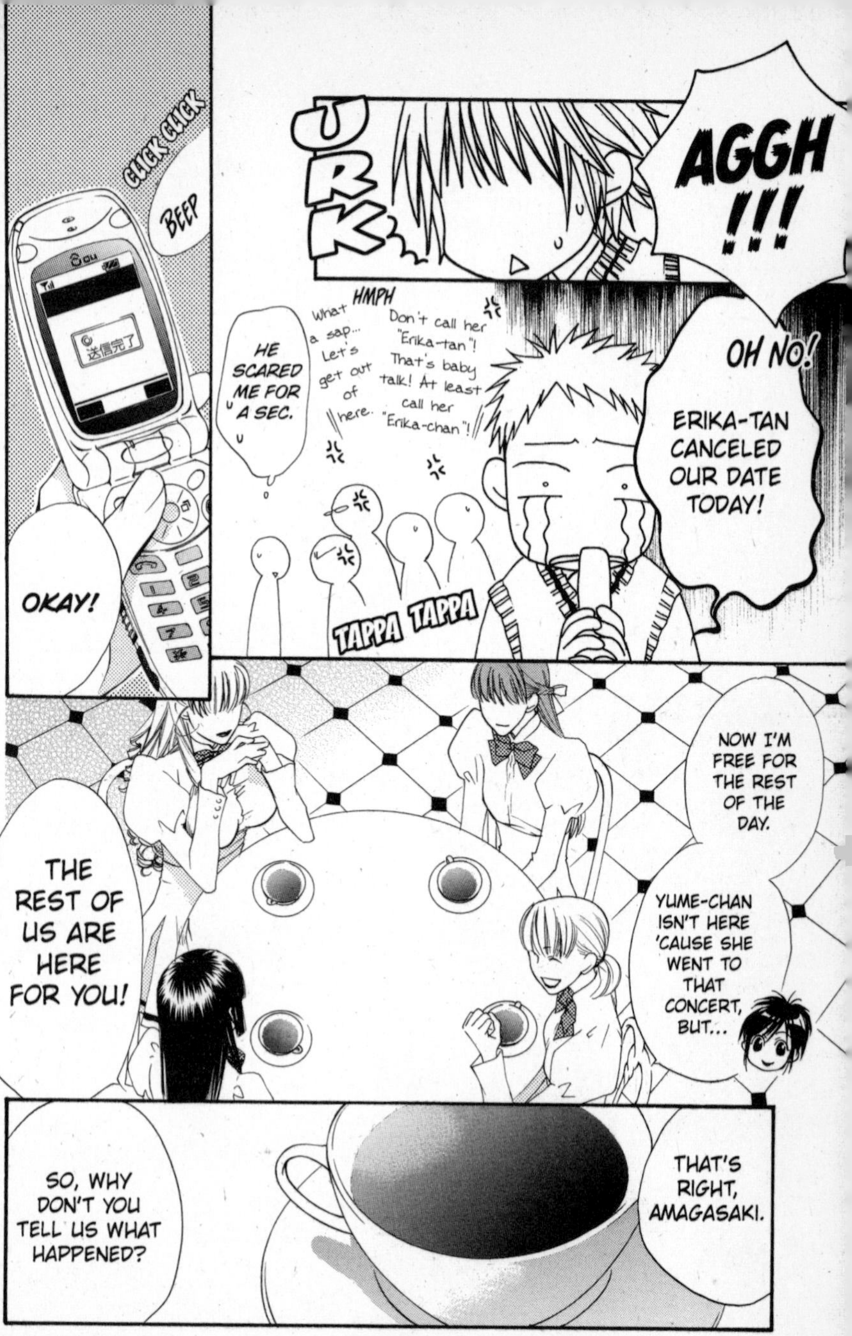
AGGH!!!
URK
OH NO!
ERIKA-TAN CANCELED OUR DATE TODAY!
Don't call her "Erika-tan"! That's baby talk! At least call her "Erika-chan"!
HMPH
What a sap... Let's get out of here.
HE SCARED ME FOR A SEC.
TAPPA TAPPA
CLICK CLICK
BEEP
送信完了
OKAY!
NOW I'M FREE FOR THE REST OF THE DAY.
YUME-CHAN ISN'T HERE 'CAUSE SHE WENT TO THAT CONCERT, BUT...
THE REST OF US ARE HERE FOR YOU!
THAT'S RIGHT, AMAGASAKI.
SO, WHY DON'T YOU TELL US WHAT HAPPENED?

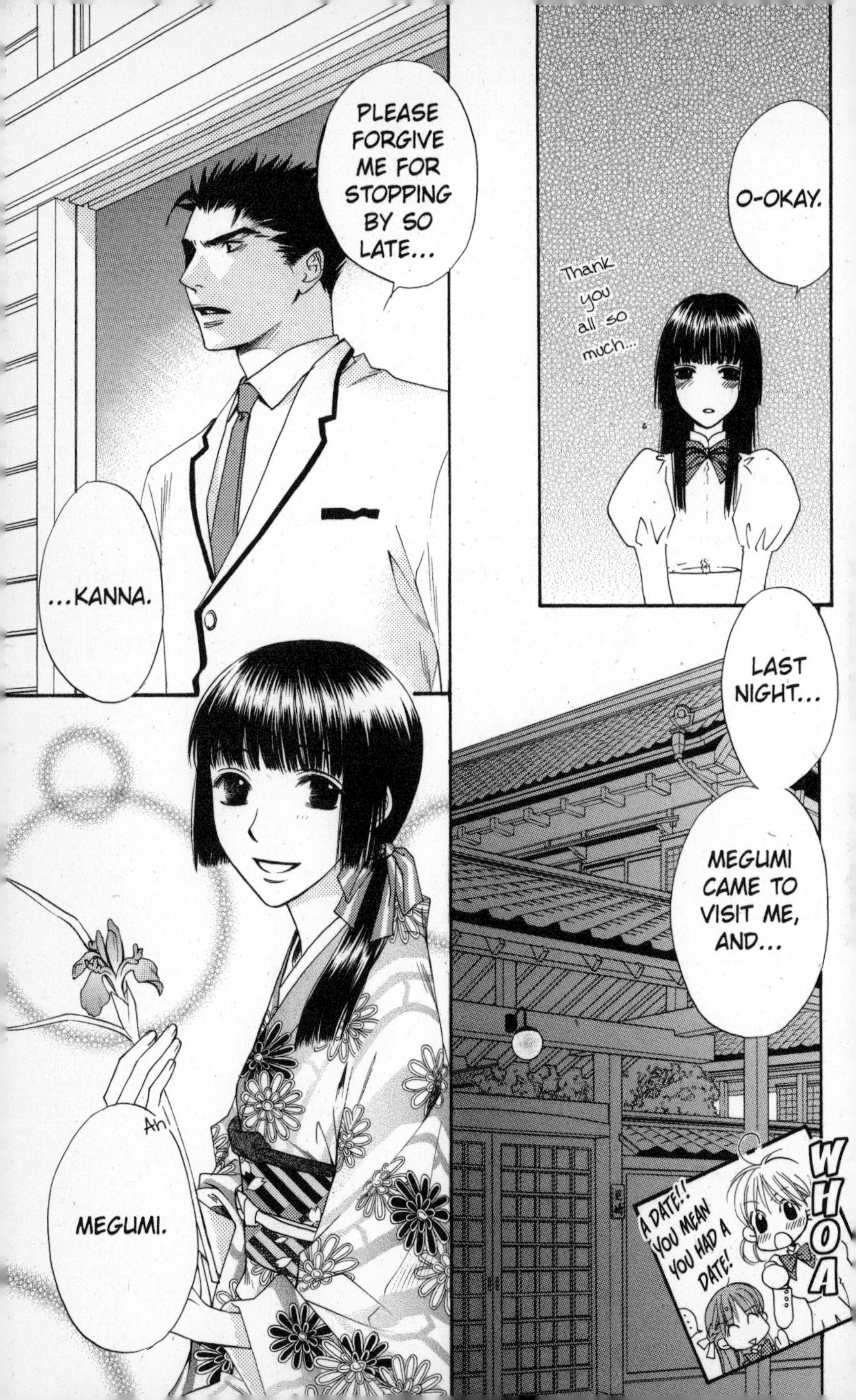
O-OKAY.
Thank you all so much...
PLEASE FORGIVE ME FOR STOPPING BY SO LATE...
...KANNA.
LAST NIGHT...
MEGUMI CAME TO VISIT ME, AND...
WHOA
A DATE!! YOU MEAN YOU HAD A DATE!
Ah!
MEGUMI.

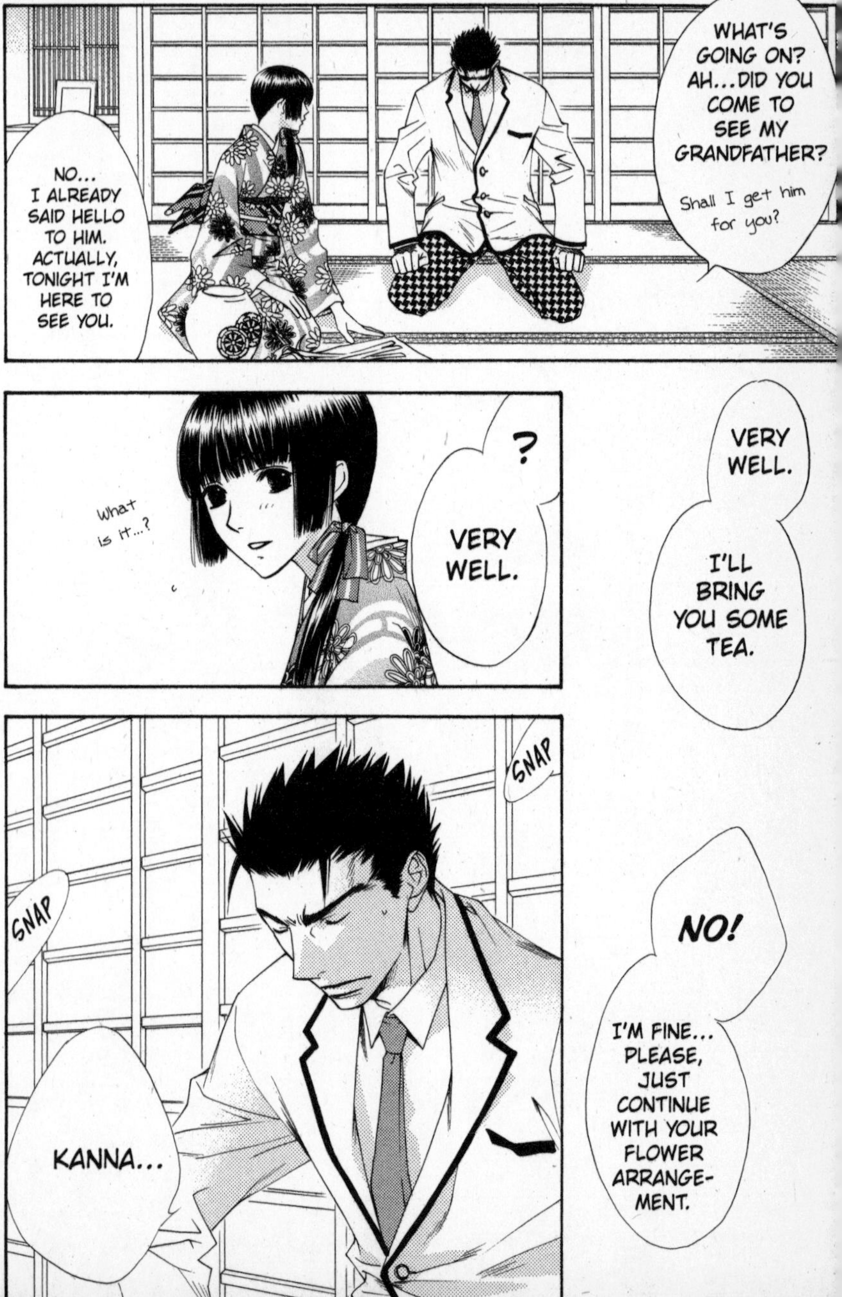
WHAT'S GOING ON? AH...DID YOU COME TO SEE MY GRANDFATHER?
Shall I get him for you?
NO... I ALREADY SAID HELLO TO HIM. ACTUALLY, TONIGHT I'M HERE TO SEE YOU.
VERY WELL.
I'LL BRING YOU SOME TEA.
NO!
I'M FINE... PLEASE, JUST CONTINUE WITH YOUR FLOWER ARRANGE-MENT.
?
VERY WELL.
What is it...?
SNAP
SNAP
KANNA...

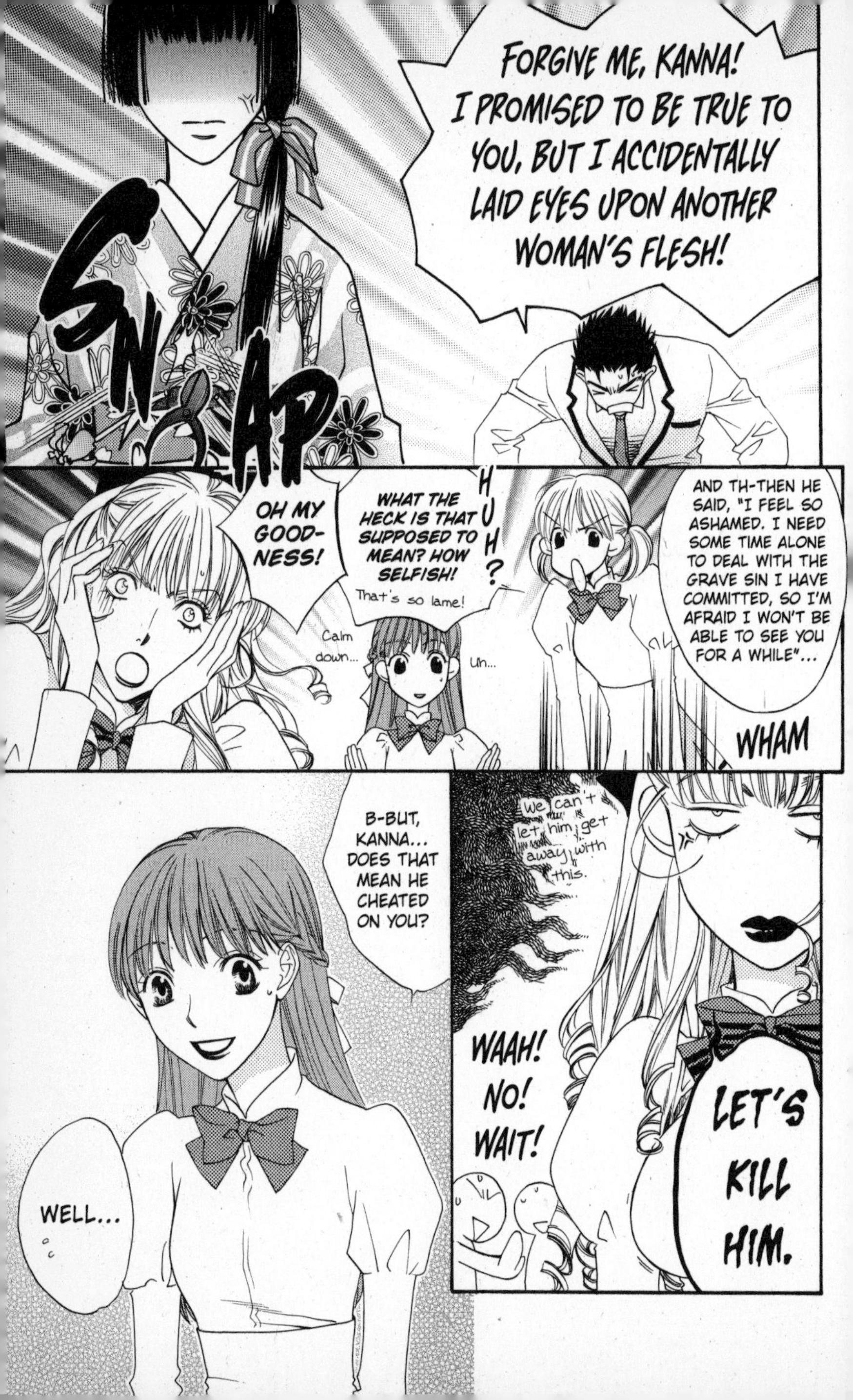
FORGIVE ME, KANNA! I PROMISED TO BE TRUE TO YOU, BUT I ACCIDENTALLY LAID EYES UPON ANOTHER WOMAN'S FLESH!
SNAP
AND TH-THEN HE SAID, "I FEEL SO ASHAMED. I NEED SOME TIME ALONE TO DEAL WITH THE GRAVE SIN I HAVE COMMITTED, SO I'M AFRAID I WON'T BE ABLE TO SEE YOU FOR A WHILE"...
WHAM
HUH?
Un...
WHAT THE HECK IS THAT SUPPOSED TO MEAN? HOW SELFISH!
That's so lame!
Calm down...
OH MY GOODNESS!
We can't let him get away with this.
LET'S KILL HIM.
WAAH! NO! WAIT!
B-BUT, KANNA... DOES THAT MEAN HE CHEATED ON YOU?
WELL...

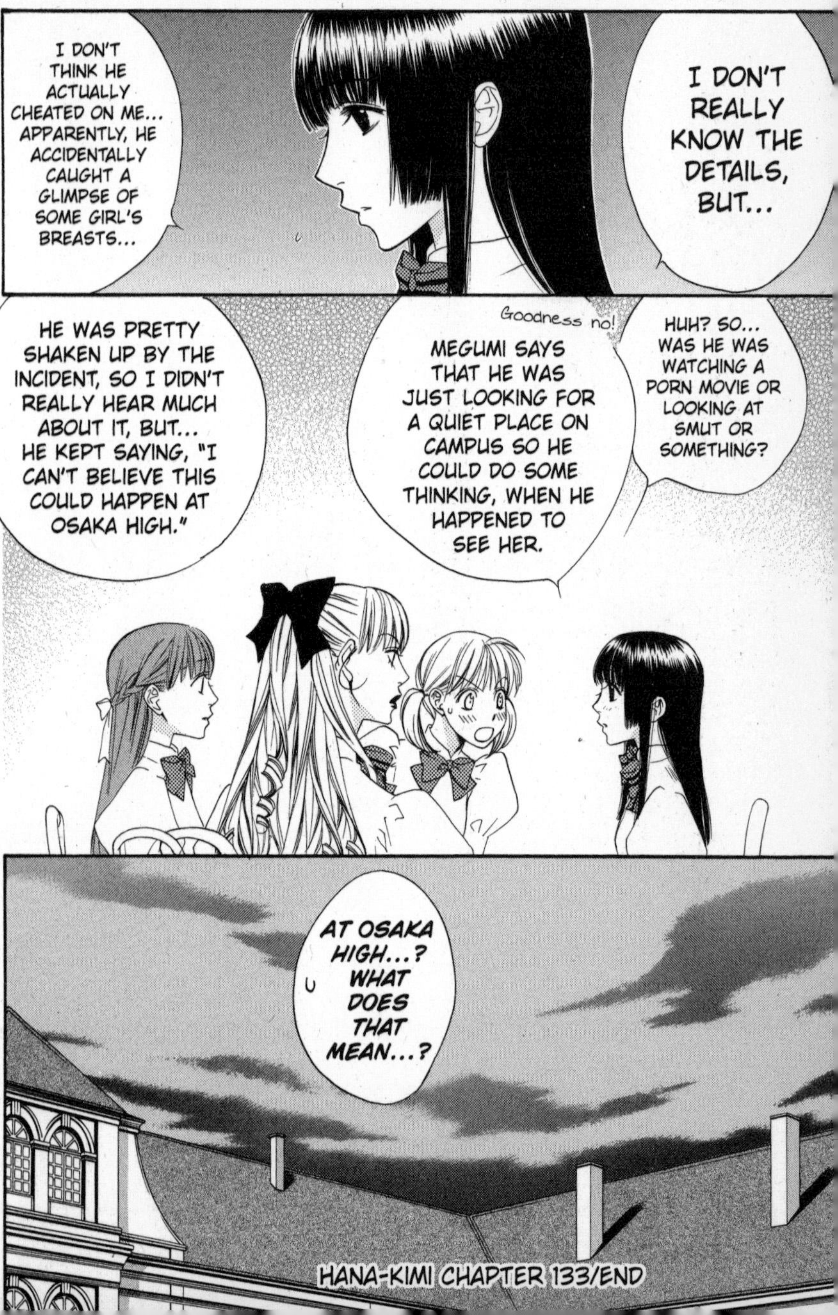
I DON'T REALLY KNOW THE DETAILS, BUT...
I DON'T THINK HE ACTUALLY CHEATED ON ME... APPARENTLY, HE ACCIDENTALLY CAUGHT A GLIMPSE OF SOME GIRL'S BREASTS...
HUH? SO... WAS HE WAS WATCHING A PORN MOVIE OR LOOKING AT SMUT OR SOMETHING?
Goodness no!
MEGUMI SAYS THAT HE WAS JUST LOOKING FOR A QUIET PLACE ON CAMPUS SO HE COULD DO SOME THINKING, WHEN HE HAPPENED TO SEE HER.
HE WAS PRETTY SHAKEN UP BY THE INCIDENT, SO I DIDN'T REALLY HEAR MUCH ABOUT IT, BUT... HE KEPT SAYING, "I CAN'T BELIEVE THIS COULD HAPPEN AT OSAKA HIGH."
AT OSAKA HIGH...? WHAT DOES THAT MEAN...?
HANA-KIMI CHAPTER 133/END

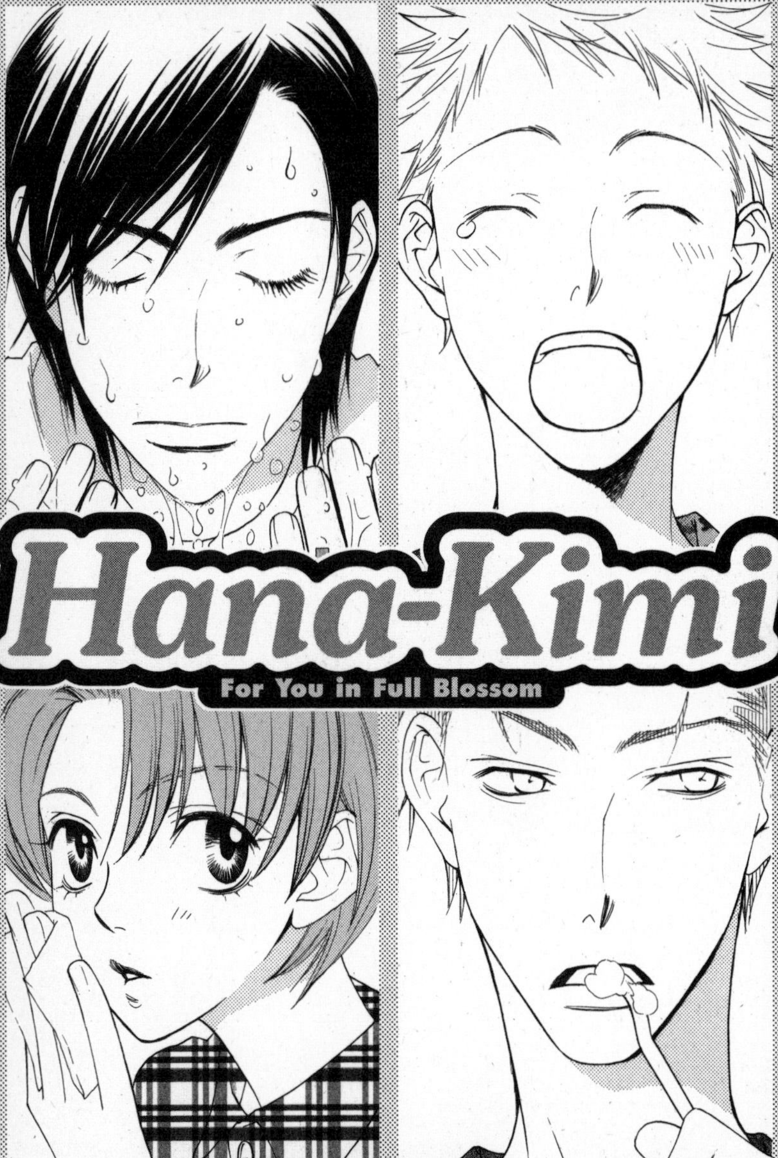
Hana-Kimi
For You in Full Blossom

CHAPTER 134

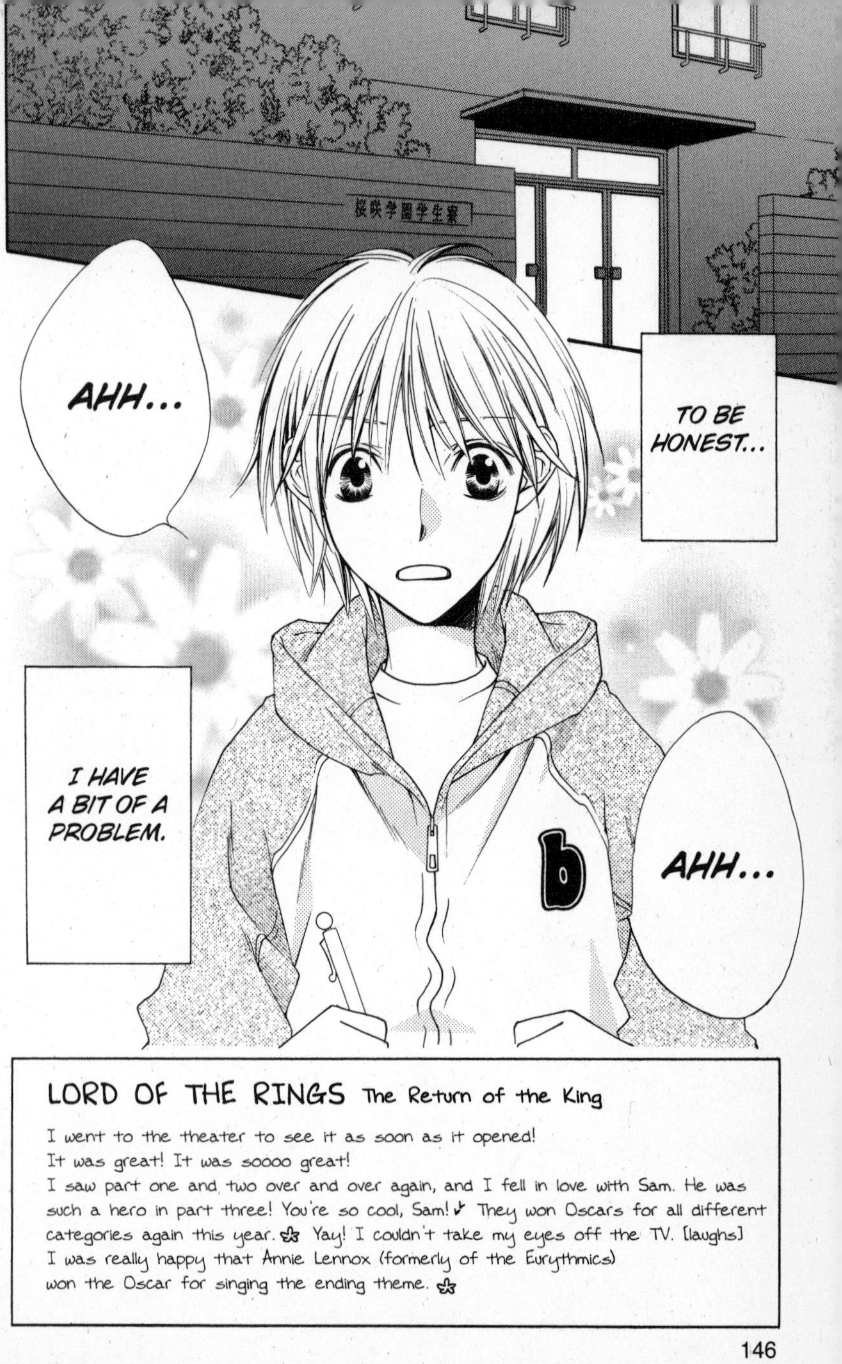
桜咲学園学生寮
TO BE HONEST...
AHH...
AHH...
I HAVE A BIT OF A PROBLEM.

LORD OF THE RINGS The Return of the King

I went to the theater to see it as soon as it opened!
It was great! It was soooo great!
I saw part one and two over and over again, and I fell in love with Sam. He was such a hero in part three! You're so cool, Sam! ♪ They won Oscars for all different categories again this year. ✿ Yay! I couldn't take my eyes off the TV. [laughs]
I was really happy that Annie Lennox (formerly of the Eurythmics) won the Oscar for singing the ending theme. ✿

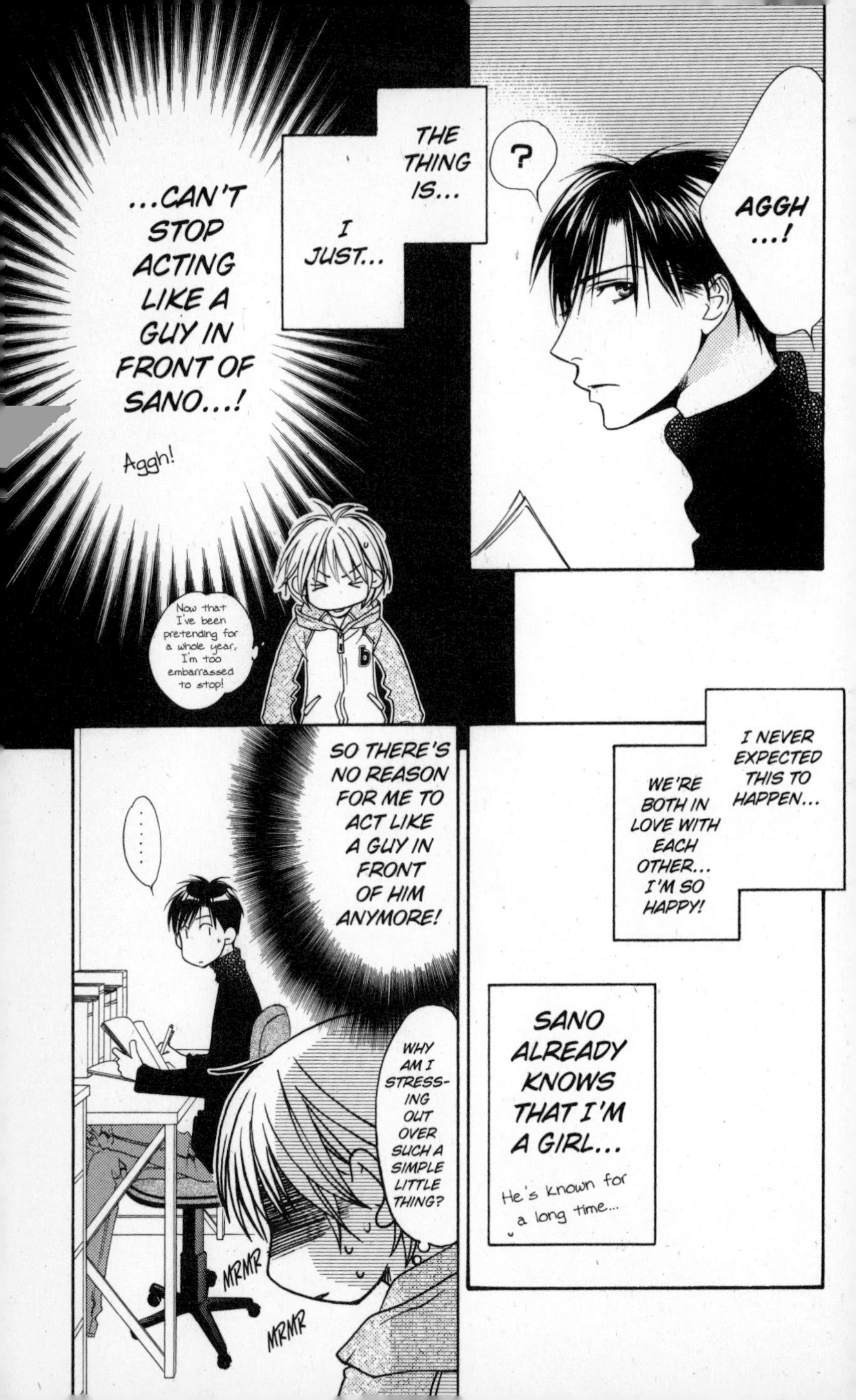
AGGH ...!
?
THE THING IS...
I JUST...
...CAN'T STOP ACTING LIKE A GUY IN FRONT OF SANO...!
Aggh!
Now that I've been pretending for a whole year, I'm too embarrassed to stop!
I NEVER EXPECTED THIS TO HAPPEN...
WE'RE BOTH IN LOVE WITH EACH OTHER... I'M SO HAPPY!
SANO ALREADY KNOWS THAT I'M A GIRL...
He's known for a long time...
SO THERE'S NO REASON FOR ME TO ACT LIKE A GUY IN FRONT OF HIM ANYMORE!
......
WHY AM I STRESSING OUT OVER SUCH A SIMPLE LITTLE THING?
MRMR
MRMR

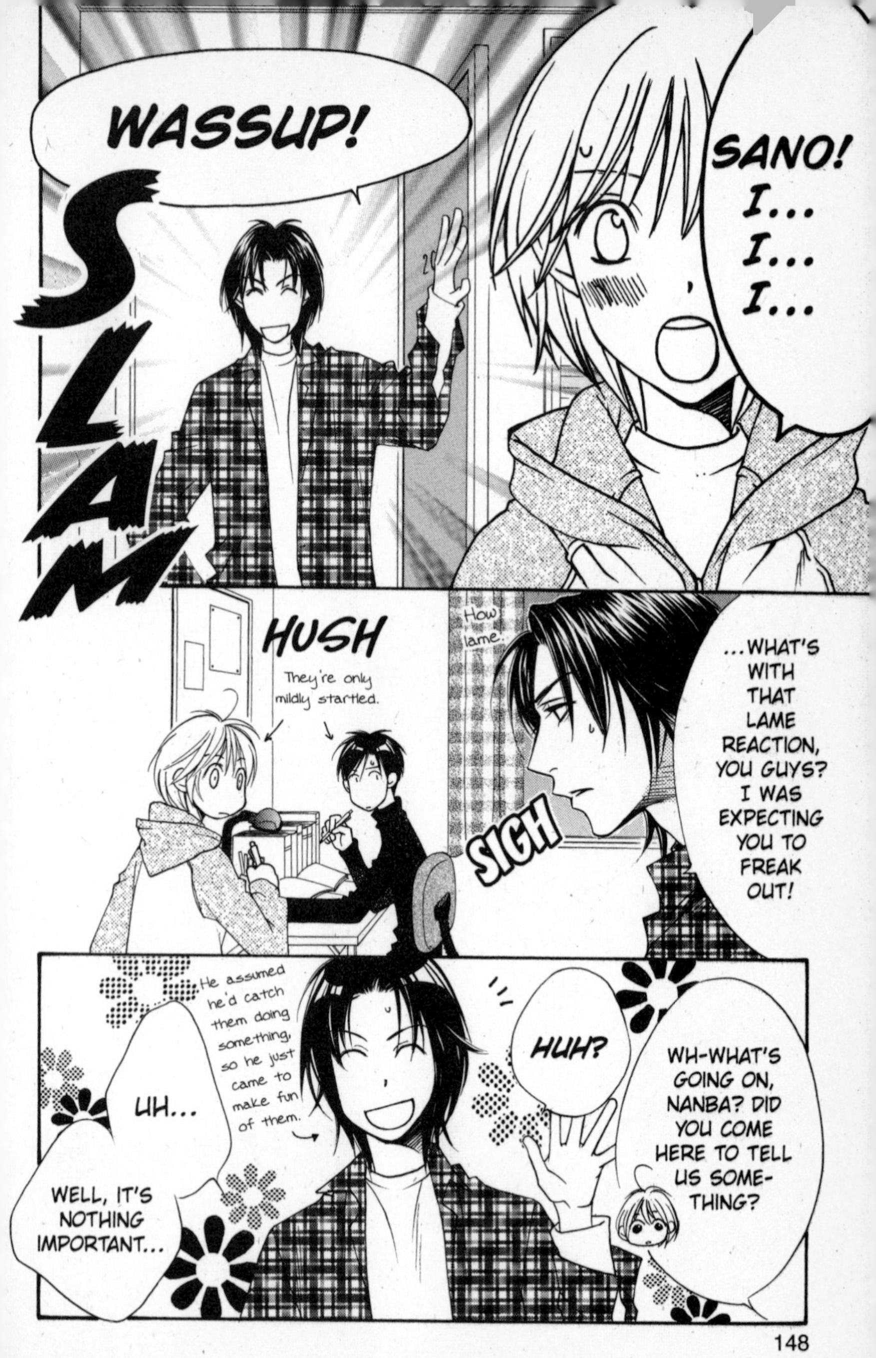
SANO! I... I... I...
WASSUP!
SLAM
How lame.
...WHAT'S WITH THAT LAME REACTION, YOU GUYS? I WAS EXPECTING YOU TO FREAK OUT!
SIGH
HUSH
They're only mildly startled.
WH-WHAT'S GOING ON, NANBA? DID YOU COME HERE TO TELL US SOME-THING?
HUH?
He assumed he'd catch them doing something, so he just came to make fun of them.
UH...
WELL, IT'S NOTHING IMPORTANT...

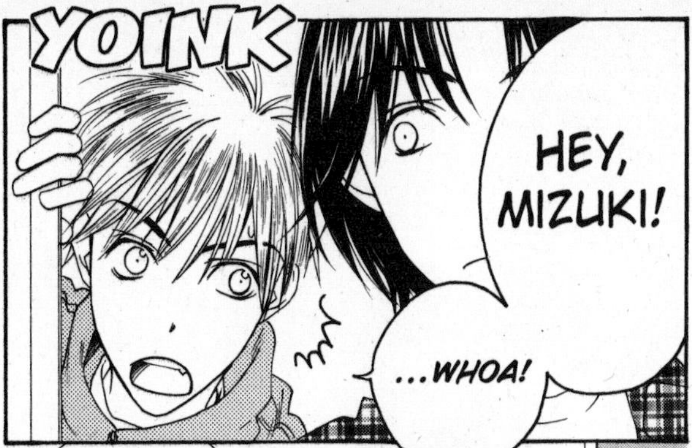
YOINK
HEY, MIZUKI!
...WHOA!

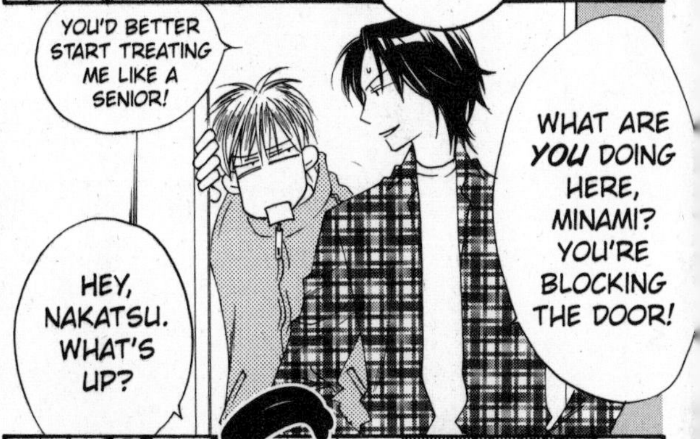
WHAT ARE *YOU* DOING HERE, MINAMI? YOU'RE BLOCKING THE DOOR!
HEY, NAKATSU. WHAT'S UP?
YOU'D BETTER START TREATING ME LIKE A SENIOR!

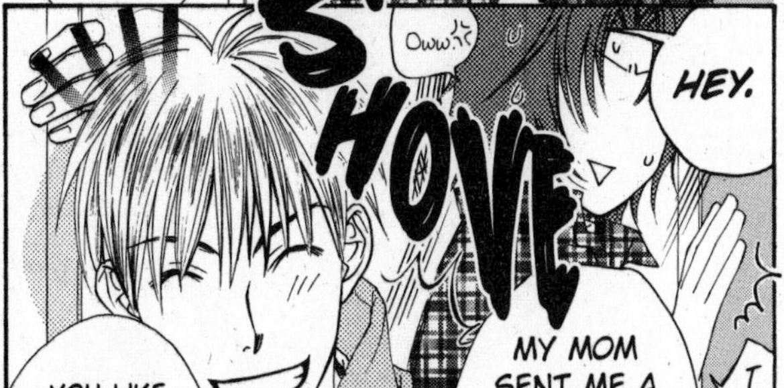
HEY.
Oww
SHOVE
TMP
MY MOM SENT ME A HUGE BOX OF CANDY, SO I'M SHARING WITH EVERYONE.
YOU LIKE SWEETS, RIGHT, MIZUKI? I THOUGHT YOU MIGHT WANT SOME.

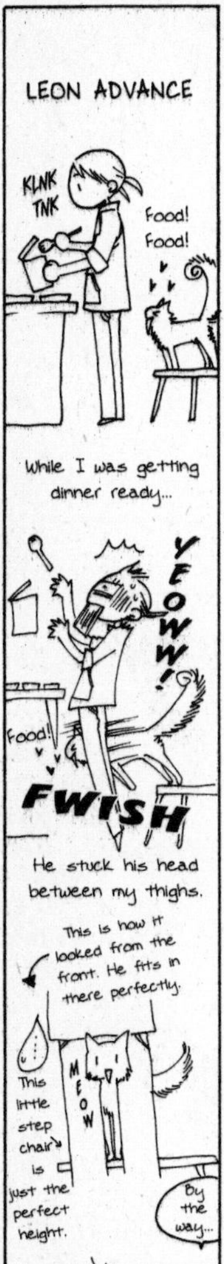
LEON ADVANCE
KLNK TNK
Food! Food!
While I was getting dinner ready...
YEOWW!
Food!
FWISH
He stuck his head between my thighs.
This is how it looked from the front. He fits in there perfectly.
MEOW
This little step chair is just the perfect height.
By the way...
Stay!
I taught my cats how to "stay."
I tried it out as a joke, but they actually listened...

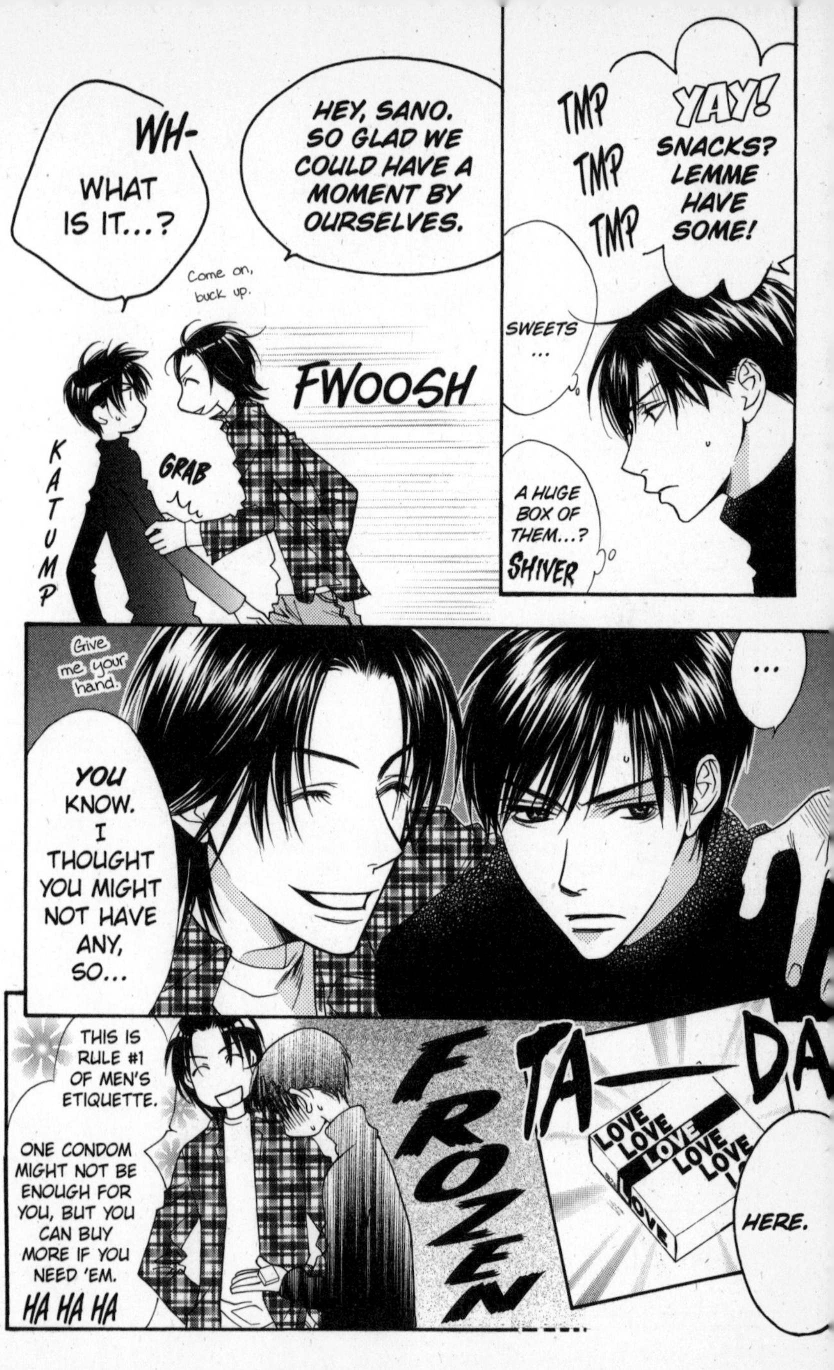
TMP TMP TMP
YAY!
SNACKS? LEMME HAVE SOME!
SWEETS ...
A HUGE BOX OF THEM...?
SHIVER
HEY, SANO. SO GLAD WE COULD HAVE A MOMENT BY OURSELVES.
WH-
WHAT IS IT...?
Come on, buck up.
FWOOSH
GRAB
KATUMP
...
Give me your hand.
YOU KNOW. I THOUGHT YOU MIGHT NOT HAVE ANY, SO...
TA—DA
LOVE LOVE LOVE LOVE LOVE
HERE.
FROZEN
THIS IS RULE #1 OF MEN'S ETIQUETTE.
ONE CONDOM MIGHT NOT BE ENOUGH FOR YOU, BUT YOU CAN BUY MORE IF YOU NEED 'EM.
HA HA HA

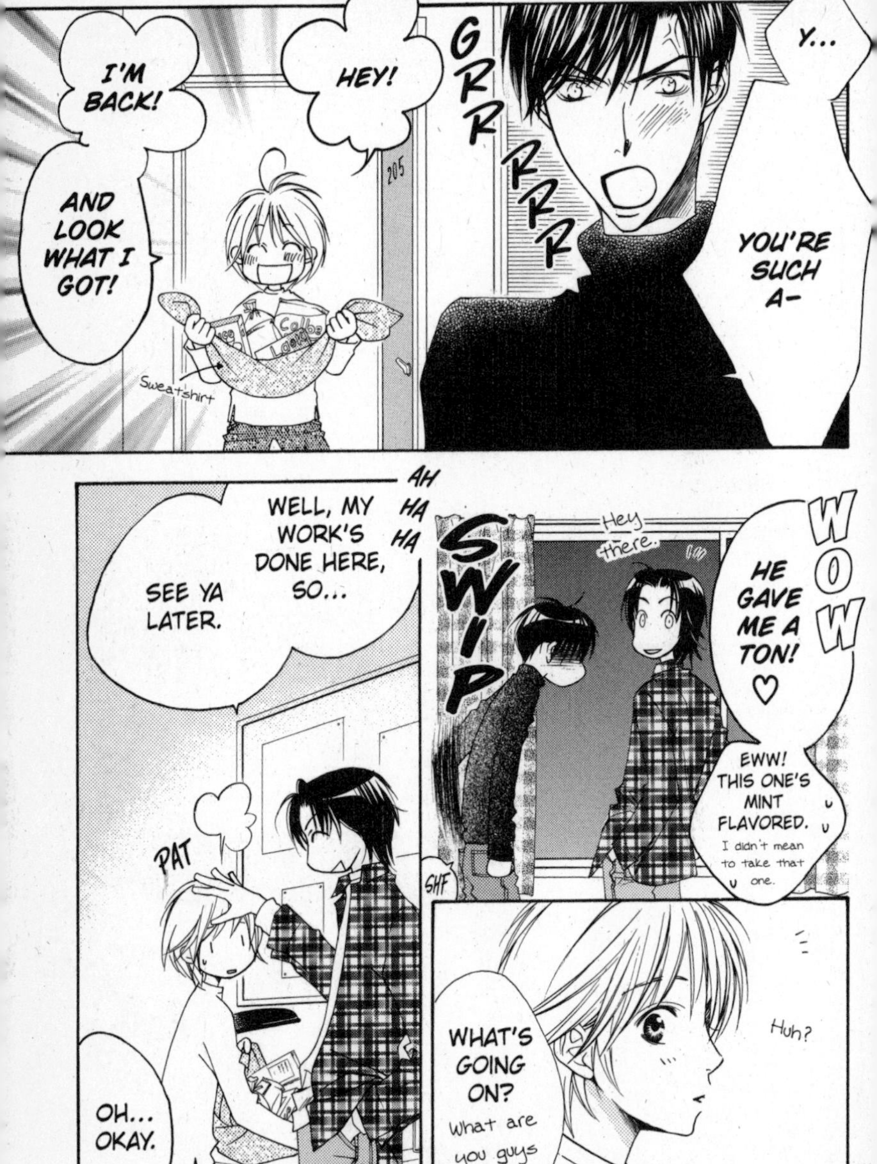
Y...
GRRRRR
YOU'RE SUCH A-
HEY!
I'M BACK!
AND LOOK WHAT I GOT!
Sweatshirt
WOW
HE GAVE ME A TON! ♡
EWW! THIS ONE'S MINT FLAVORED.
I didn't mean to take that one.
Hey there.
SWIP
SHF
Huh?
WHAT'S GOING ON?
What are you guys doing?
AH HA HA
WELL, MY WORK'S DONE HERE, SO...
SEE YA LATER.
PAT
OH... OKAY.

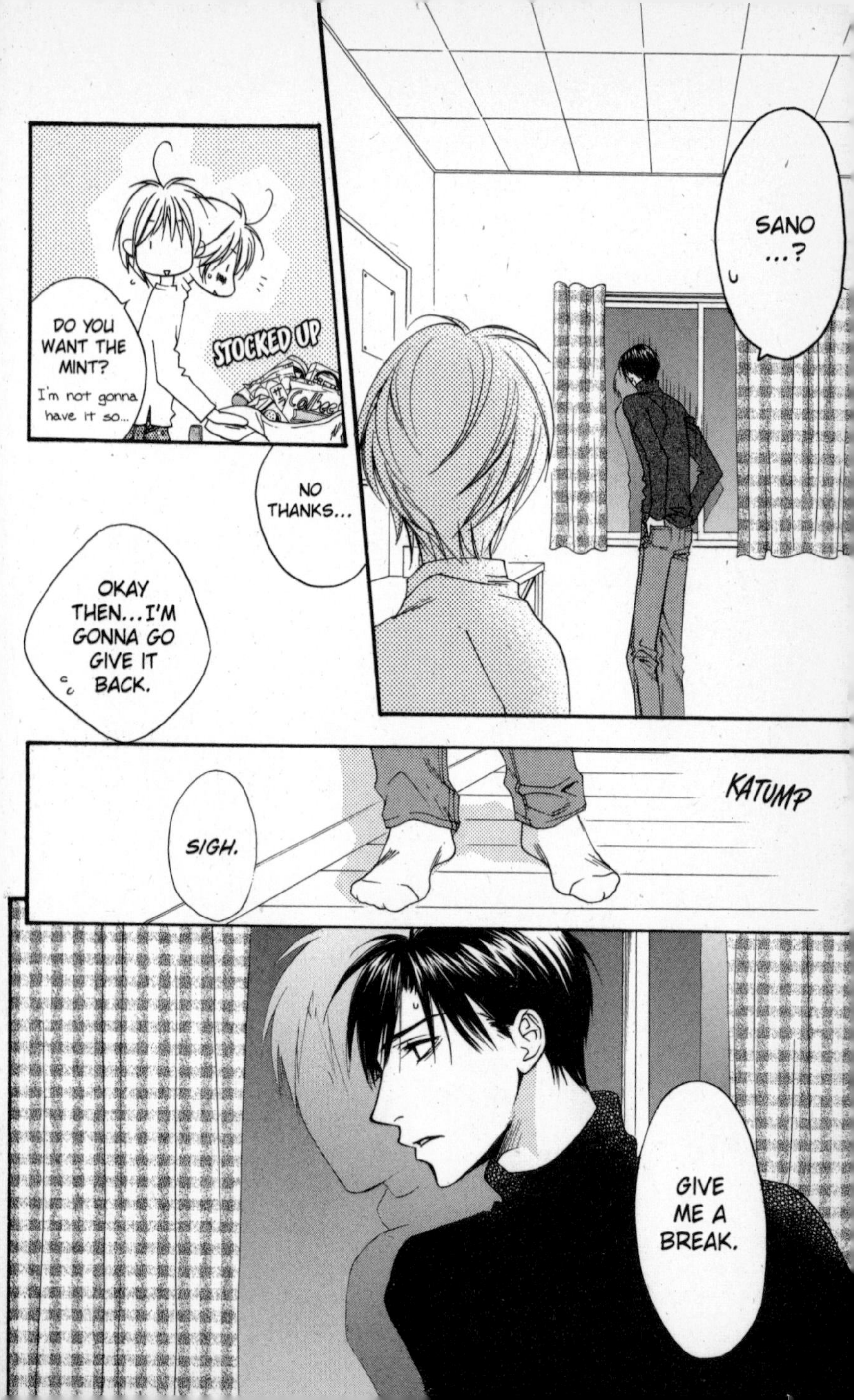
SANO ...?
DO YOU WANT THE MINT?
I'm not gonna have it so...
STOCKED UP
NO THANKS...
OKAY THEN... I'M GONNA GO GIVE IT BACK.
KATUMP
SIGH.
GIVE ME A BREAK.

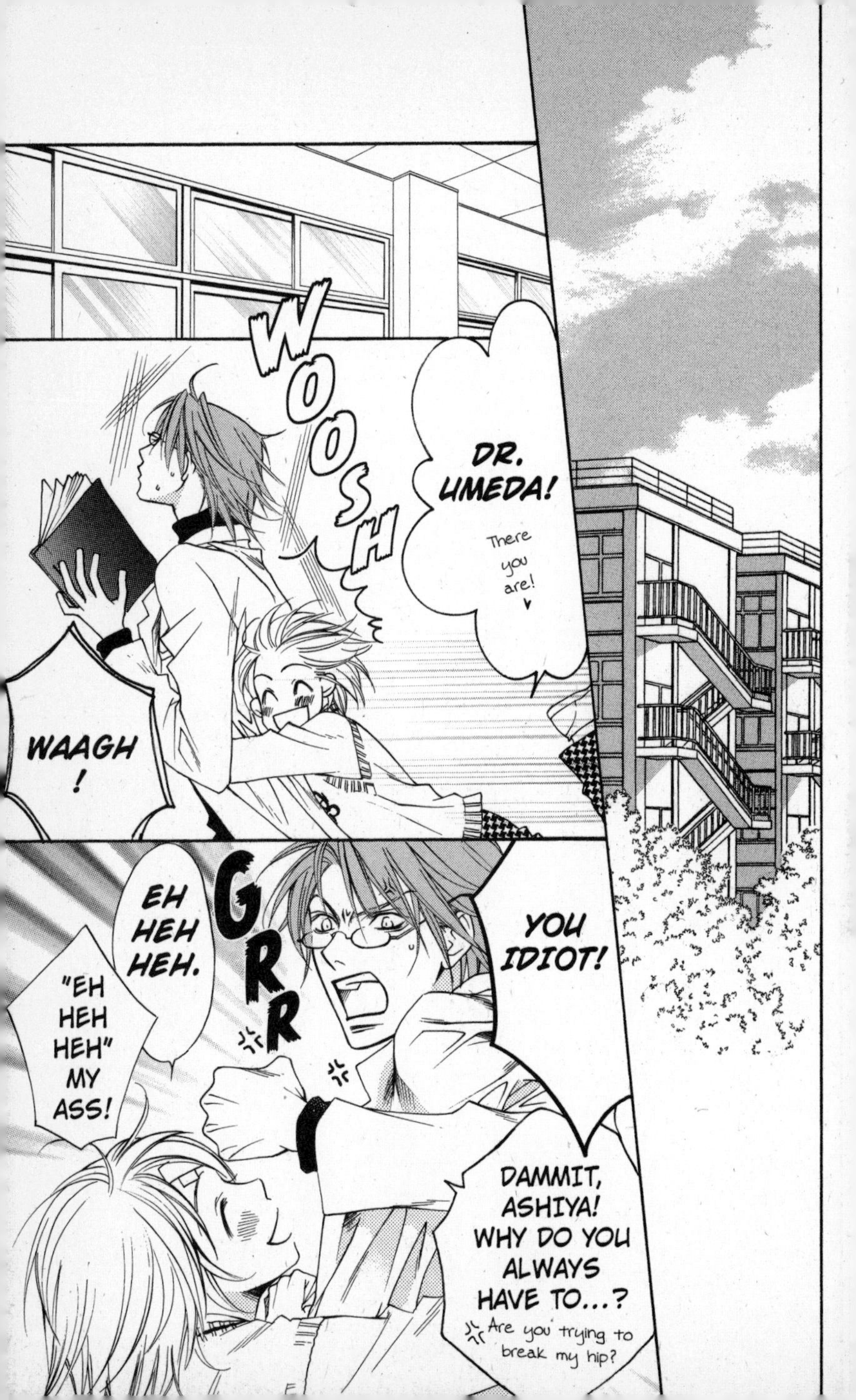
DR. UMEDA!
There you are!
WOOSH
WAAGH!
YOU IDIOT!
GRR
EH HEH HEH.
"EH HEH HEH" MY ASS!
DAMMIT, ASHIYA! WHY DO YOU ALWAYS HAVE TO...?
Are you trying to break my hip?

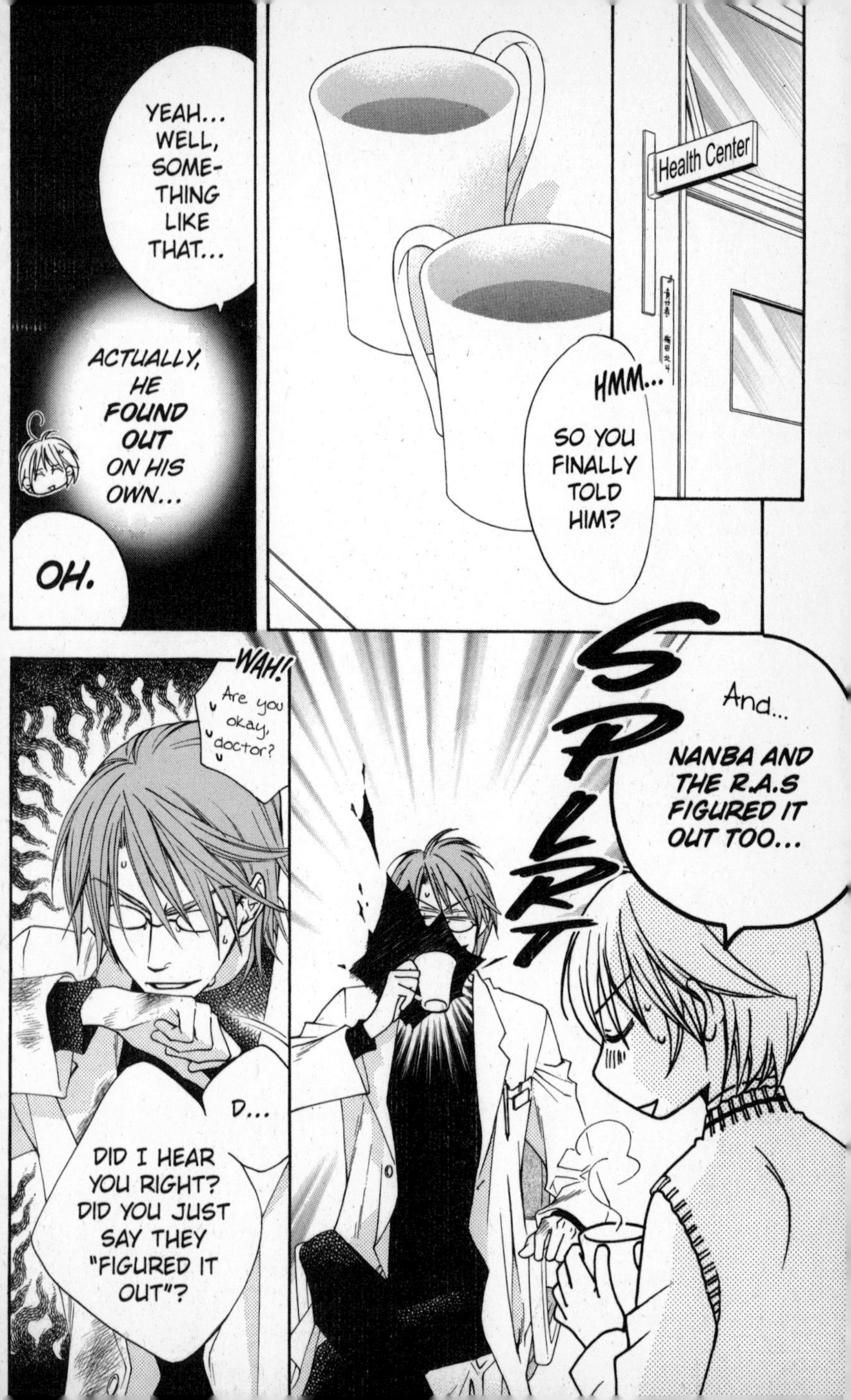
Health Center
HMM...
SO YOU FINALLY TOLD HIM?
YEAH... WELL, SOME-THING LIKE THAT...
ACTUALLY, HE FOUND OUT ON HIS OWN...
OH.
And...
NANBA AND THE R.A.S FIGURED IT OUT TOO...
SPLRT
WAH!
Are you okay, doctor?
D...
DID I HEAR YOU RIGHT? DID YOU JUST SAY THEY "FIGURED IT OUT"?

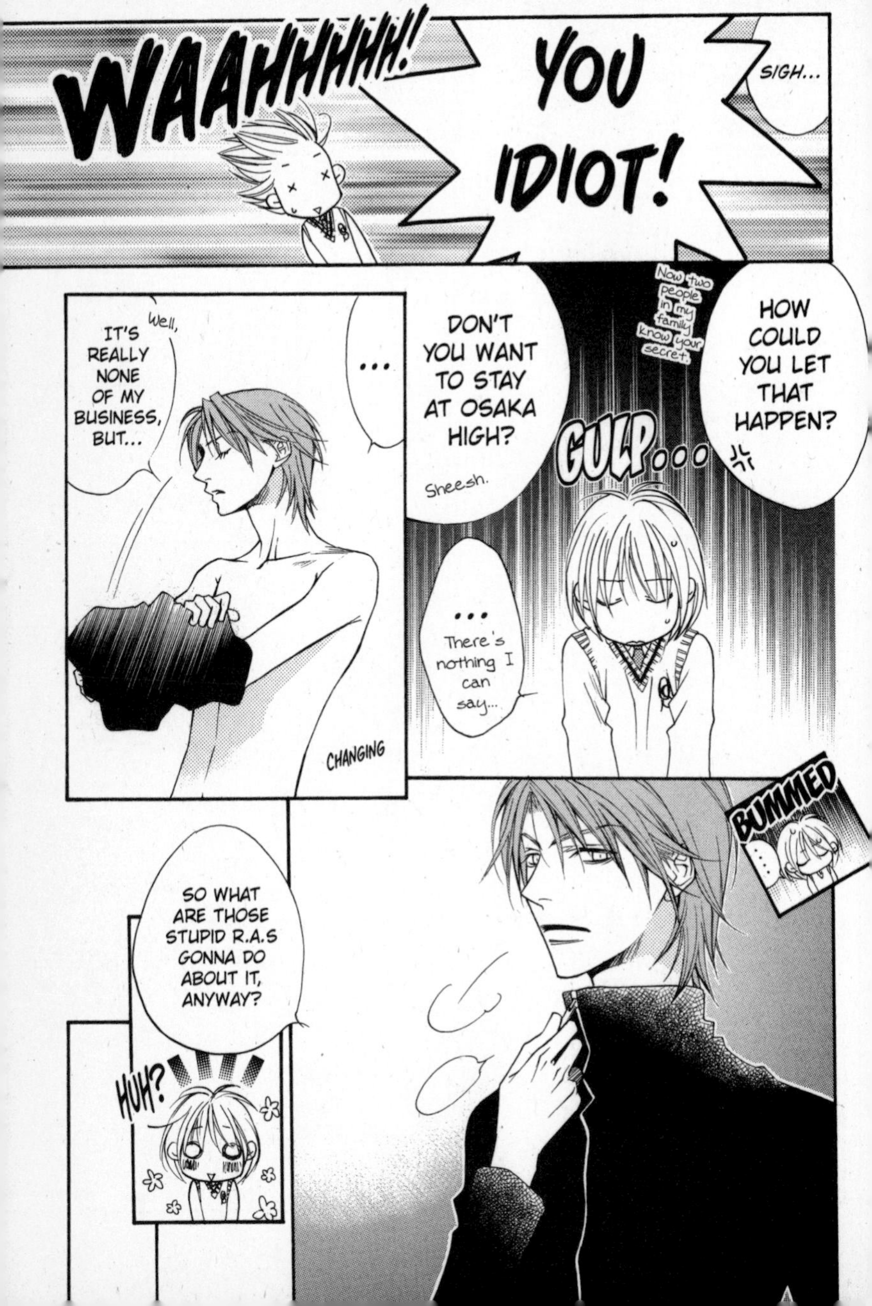
SIGH...
YOU IDIOT!
WAAHHHHHH!
HOW COULD YOU LET THAT HAPPEN?
Now two people in my family know your secret.
GULP...
DON'T YOU WANT TO STAY AT OSAKA HIGH?
Sheesh.
...
There's nothing I can say...
...
Well,
IT'S REALLY NONE OF MY BUSINESS, BUT...
CHANGING
BUMMED
...
SO WHAT ARE THOSE STUPID R.A.S GONNA DO ABOUT IT, ANYWAY?
HUH?

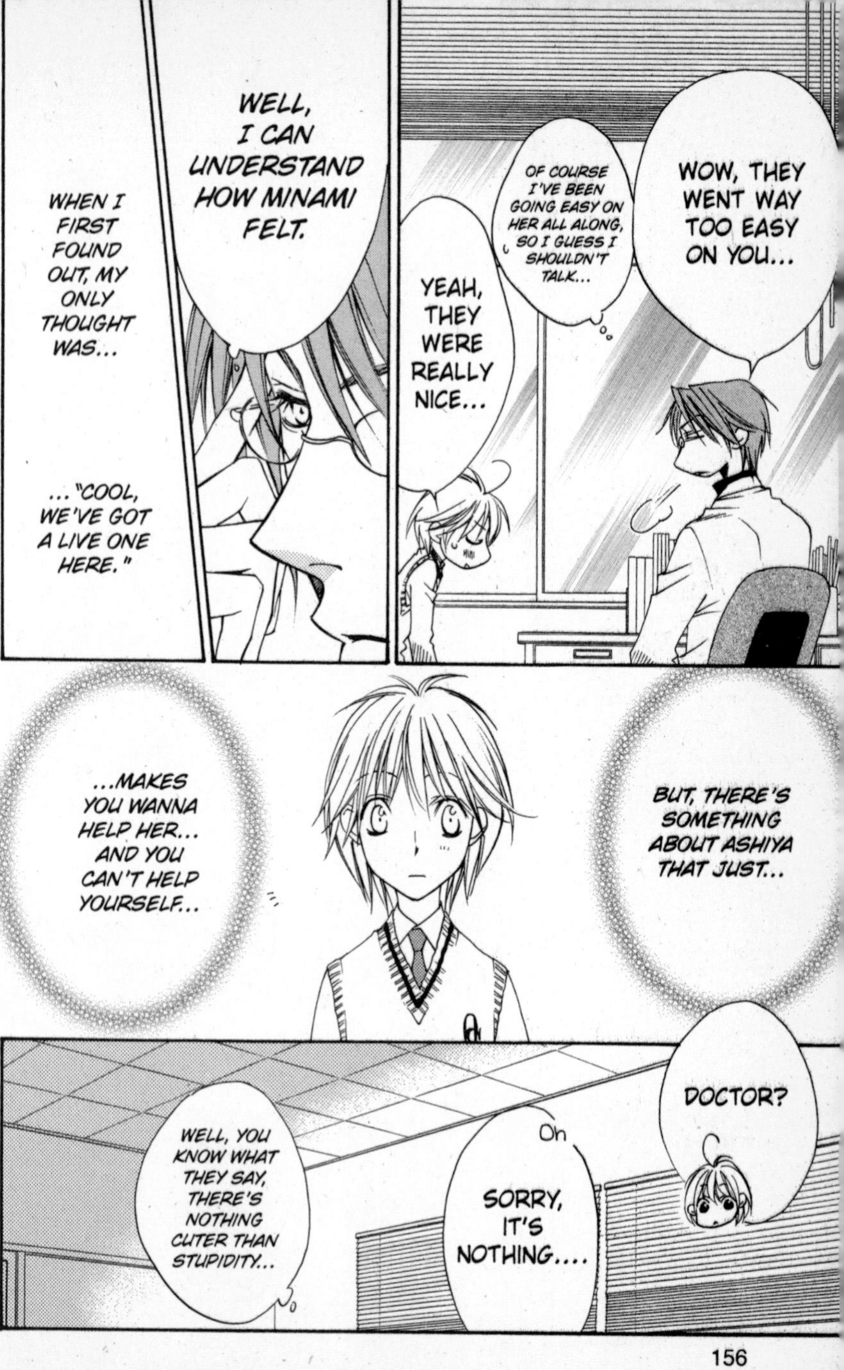

WOW, THEY WENT WAY TOO EASY ON YOU...
OF COURSE I'VE BEEN GOING EASY ON HER ALL ALONG, SO I GUESS I SHOULDN'T TALK...
YEAH, THEY WERE REALLY NICE...
WELL, I CAN UNDERSTAND HOW MINAMI FELT.
WHEN I FIRST FOUND OUT, MY ONLY THOUGHT WAS...
..."COOL, WE'VE GOT A LIVE ONE HERE."
BUT, THERE'S SOMETHING ABOUT ASHIYA THAT JUST...
...MAKES YOU WANNA HELP HER... AND YOU CAN'T HELP YOURSELF...
DOCTOR?
Oh
SORRY, IT'S NOTHING....
WELL, YOU KNOW WHAT THEY SAY, THERE'S NOTHING CUTER THAN STUPIDITY...

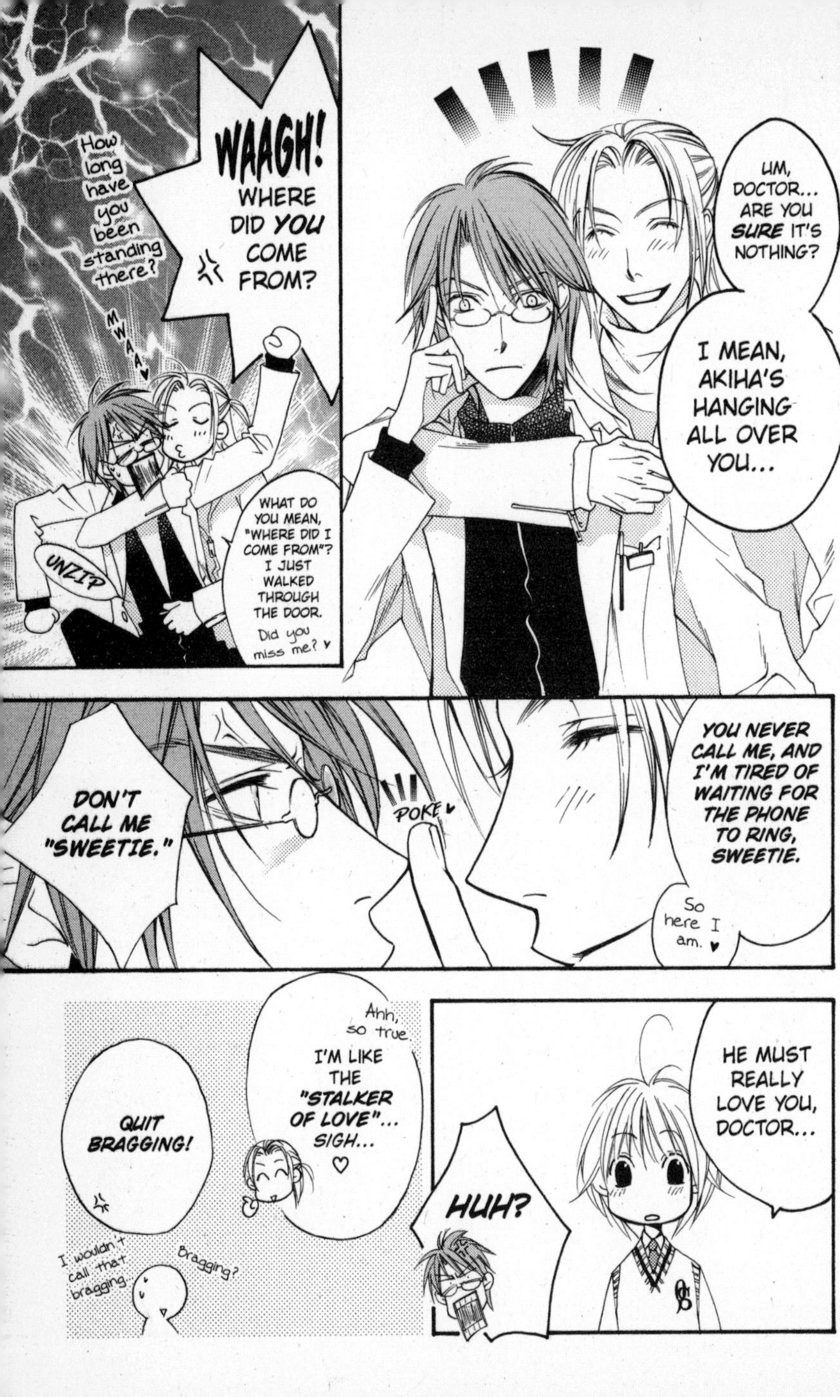
UM, DOCTOR... ARE YOU SURE IT'S NOTHING?
I MEAN, AKIHA'S HANGING ALL OVER YOU...
WAAGH! WHERE DID YOU COME FROM?
How long have you been standing there?
MWAA ♥
UNZIP
WHAT DO YOU MEAN, "WHERE DID I COME FROM"? I JUST WALKED THROUGH THE DOOR.
Did you miss me? ♥
YOU NEVER CALL ME, AND I'M TIRED OF WAITING FOR THE PHONE TO RING, SWEETIE.
So here I am. ♥
POKE ♥
DON'T CALL ME "SWEETIE."
HE MUST REALLY LOVE YOU, DOCTOR...
HUH?
Ahh, so true.
I'M LIKE THE "STALKER OF LOVE"... SIGH... ♡
QUIT BRAGGING!
Bragging?
I wouldn't call that bragging.

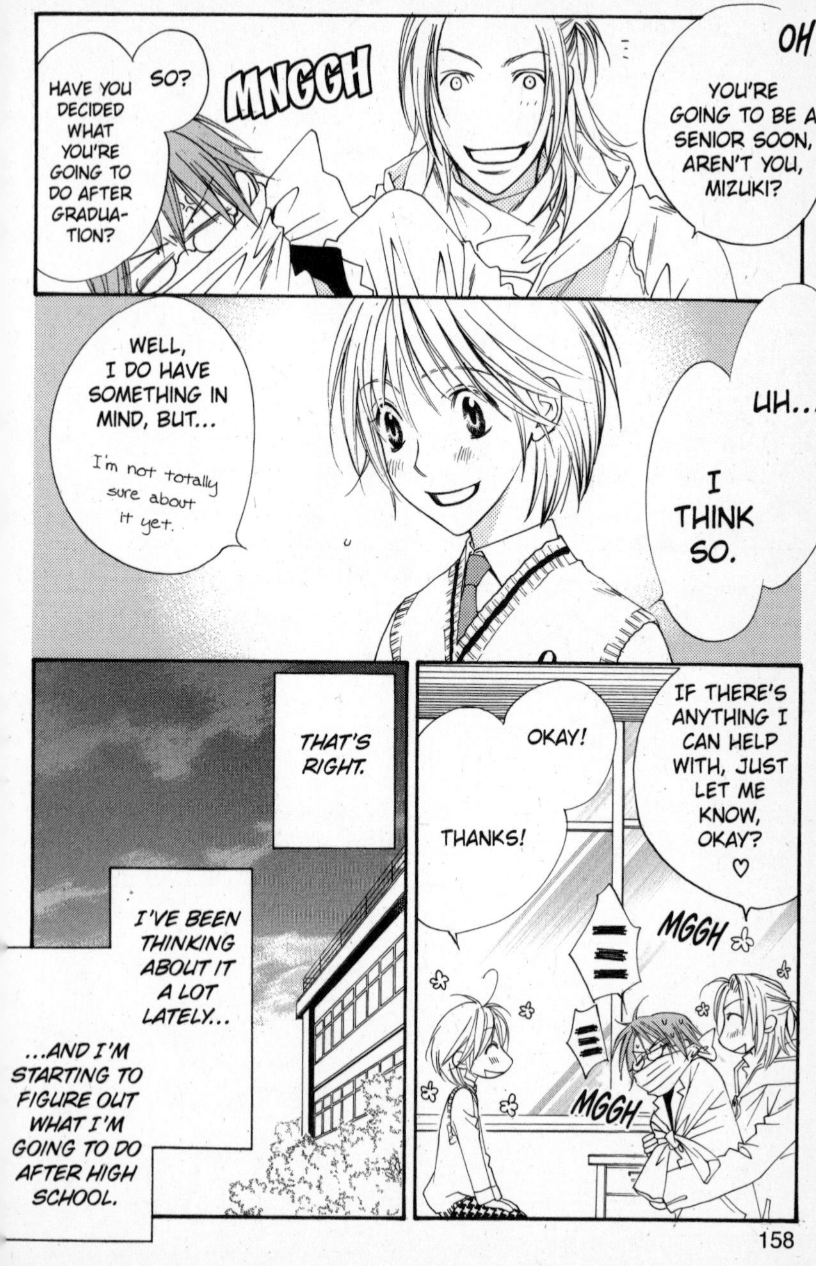
OH
YOU'RE GOING TO BE A SENIOR SOON, AREN'T YOU, MIZUKI?
MNGGH
SO?
HAVE YOU DECIDED WHAT YOU'RE GOING TO DO AFTER GRADUATION?
UH...
I THINK SO.
WELL, I DO HAVE SOMETHING IN MIND, BUT...
I'm not totally sure about it yet.
IF THERE'S ANYTHING I CAN HELP WITH, JUST LET ME KNOW, OKAY? ♡
OKAY!
THANKS!
MGGH
MGGH
THAT'S RIGHT.
I'VE BEEN THINKING ABOUT IT A LOT LATELY...
...AND I'M STARTING TO FIGURE OUT WHAT I'M GOING TO DO AFTER HIGH SCHOOL.

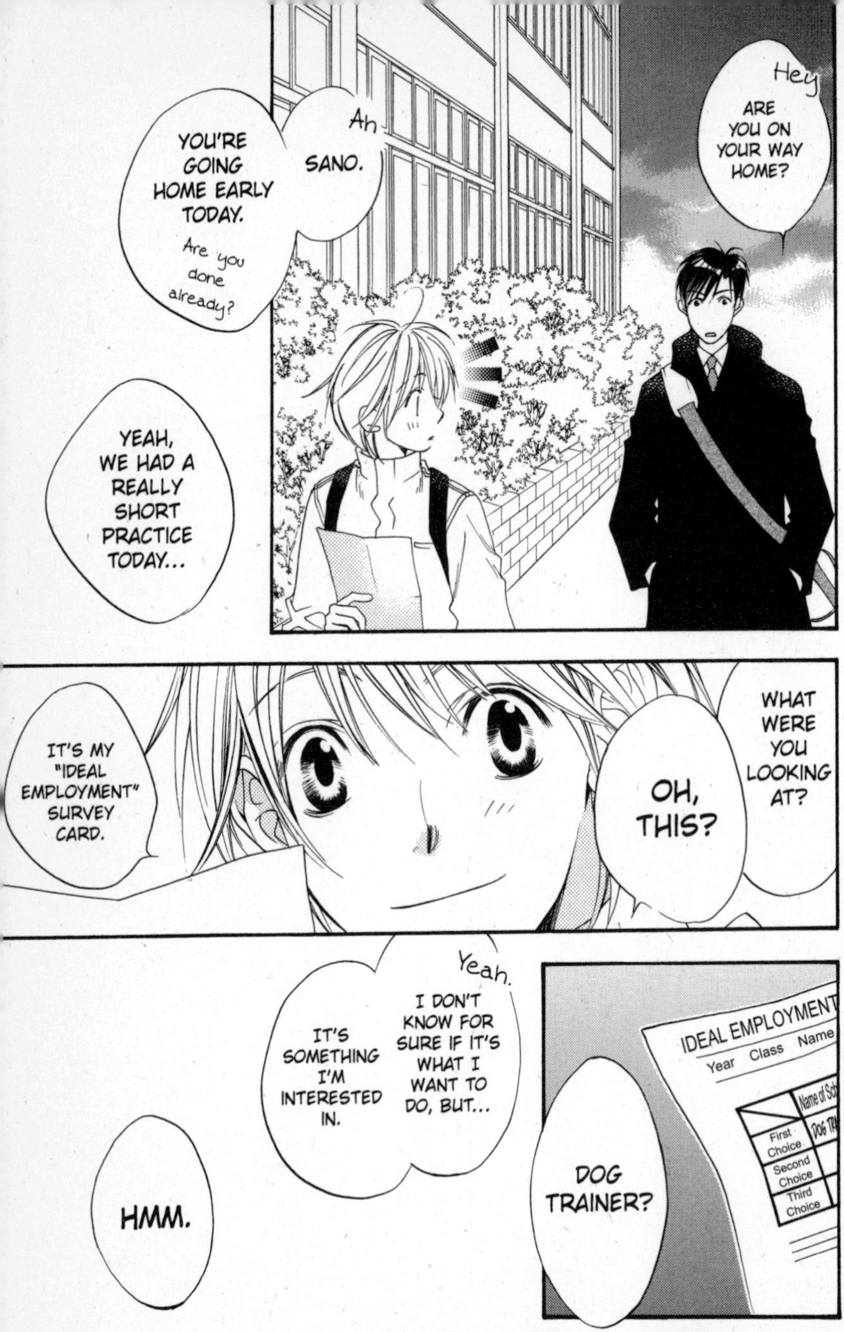

Hey
ARE YOU ON YOUR WAY HOME?
Ah
SANO.
YOU'RE GOING HOME EARLY TODAY.
Are you done already?
YEAH, WE HAD A REALLY SHORT PRACTICE TODAY...
WHAT WERE YOU LOOKING AT?
OH, THIS?
IT'S MY "IDEAL EMPLOYMENT" SURVEY CARD.
IDEAL EMPLOYMENT
Year Class Name
First Choice
Second Choice
Third Choice
DOG TRAINER?
Yeah.
I DON'T KNOW FOR SURE IF IT'S WHAT I WANT TO DO, BUT...
IT'S SOMETHING I'M INTERESTED IN.
HMM.

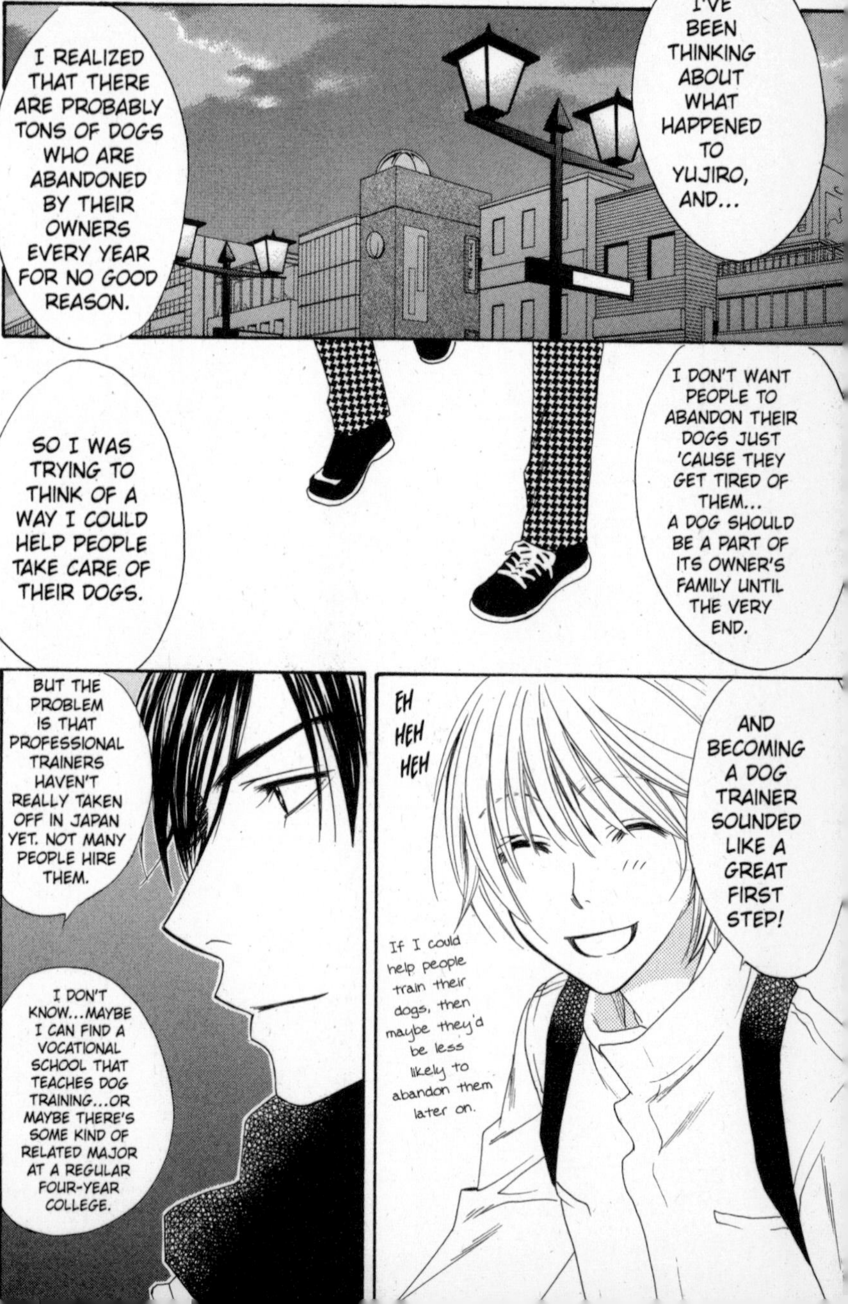
I'VE BEEN THINKING ABOUT WHAT HAPPENED TO YUJIRO, AND...
I REALIZED THAT THERE ARE PROBABLY TONS OF DOGS WHO ARE ABANDONED BY THEIR OWNERS EVERY YEAR FOR NO GOOD REASON.
I DON'T WANT PEOPLE TO ABANDON THEIR DOGS JUST 'CAUSE THEY GET TIRED OF THEM... A DOG SHOULD BE A PART OF ITS OWNER'S FAMILY UNTIL THE VERY END.
SO I WAS TRYING TO THINK OF A WAY I COULD HELP PEOPLE TAKE CARE OF THEIR DOGS.
AND BECOMING A DOG TRAINER SOUNDED LIKE A GREAT FIRST STEP!
EH HEH HEH
If I could help people train their dogs, then maybe they'd be less likely to abandon them later on.
BUT THE PROBLEM IS THAT PROFESSIONAL TRAINERS HAVEN'T REALLY TAKEN OFF IN JAPAN YET. NOT MANY PEOPLE HIRE THEM.
I DON'T KNOW...MAYBE I CAN FIND A VOCATIONAL SCHOOL THAT TEACHES DOG TRAINING...OR MAYBE THERE'S SOME KIND OF RELATED MAJOR AT A REGULAR FOUR-YEAR COLLEGE.

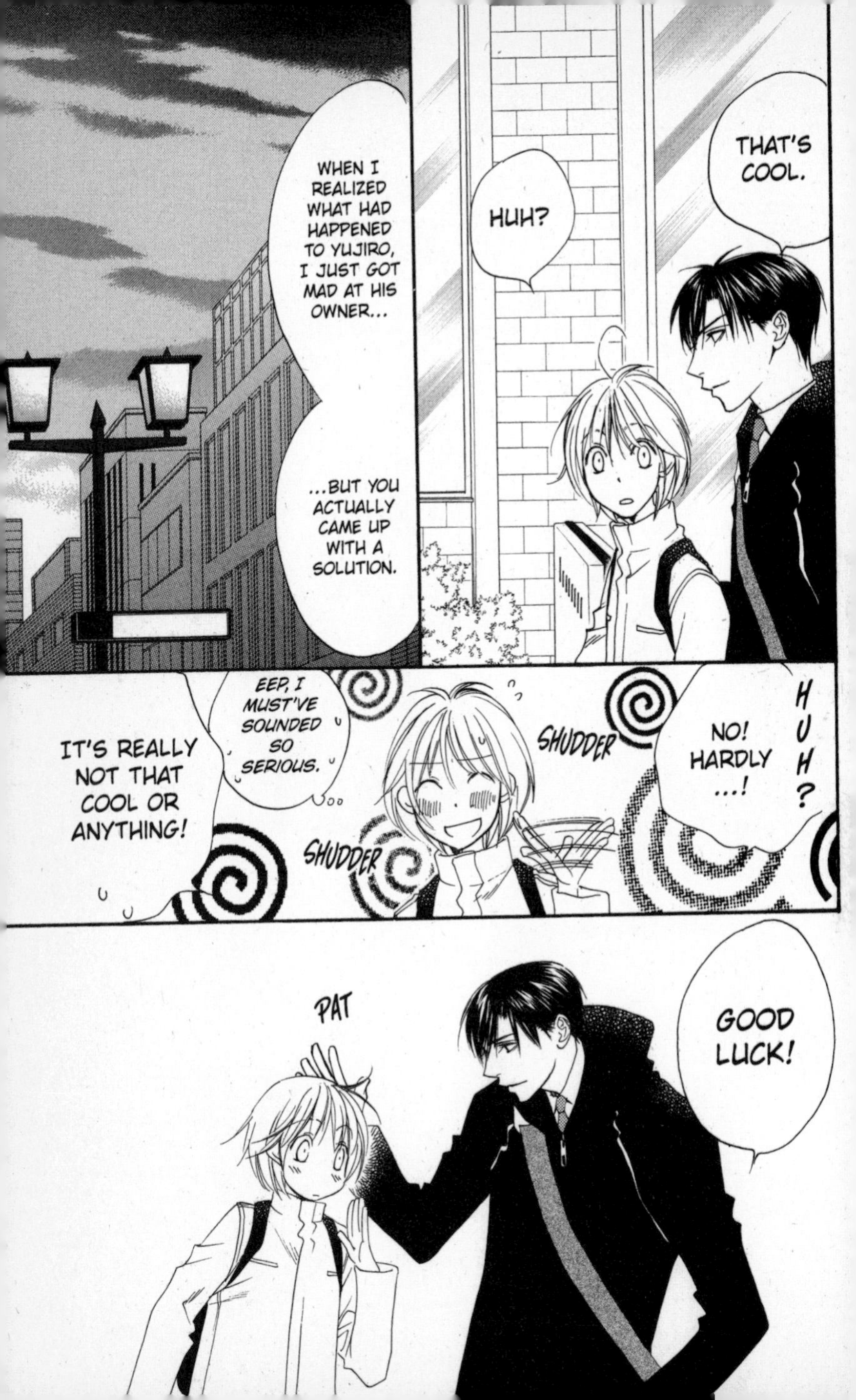
THAT'S COOL.
HUH?
WHEN I REALIZED WHAT HAD HAPPENED TO YUJIRO, I JUST GOT MAD AT HIS OWNER...
...BUT YOU ACTUALLY CAME UP WITH A SOLUTION.
HUH?
NO! HARDLY ...!
SHUDDER
EEP, I MUST'VE SOUNDED SO SERIOUS.
SHUDDER
IT'S REALLY NOT THAT COOL OR ANYTHING!
GOOD LUCK!
PAT

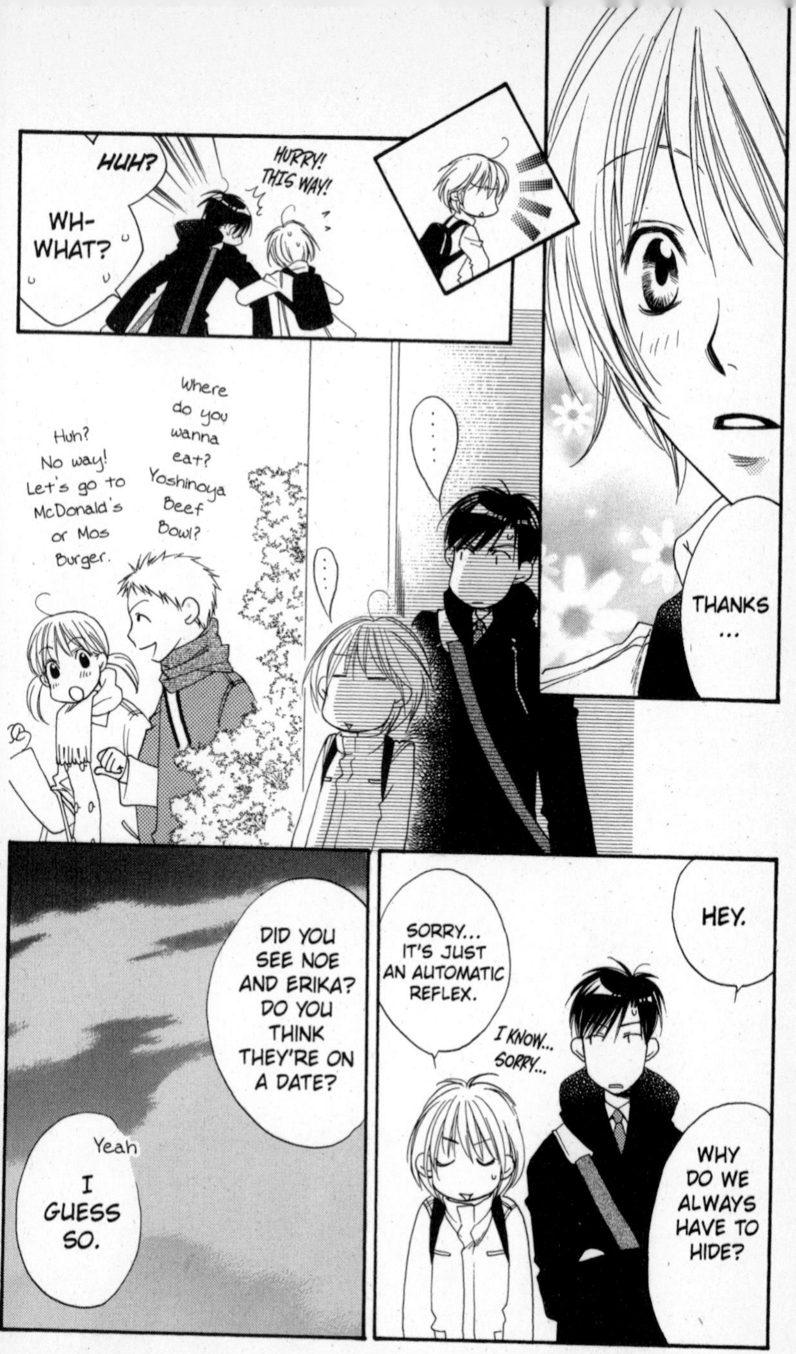
THANKS ...
HURRY! THIS WAY!
HUH?
WH- WHAT?
...
...
Where do you wanna eat? Yoshinoya Beef Bowl?
Huh? No way! Let's go to McDonald's or Mos Burger.
HEY.
SORRY... IT'S JUST AN AUTOMATIC REFLEX.
I KNOW... SORRY...
WHY DO WE ALWAYS HAVE TO HIDE?
DID YOU SEE NOE AND ERIKA? DO YOU THINK THEY'RE ON A DATE?
Yeah
I GUESS SO.

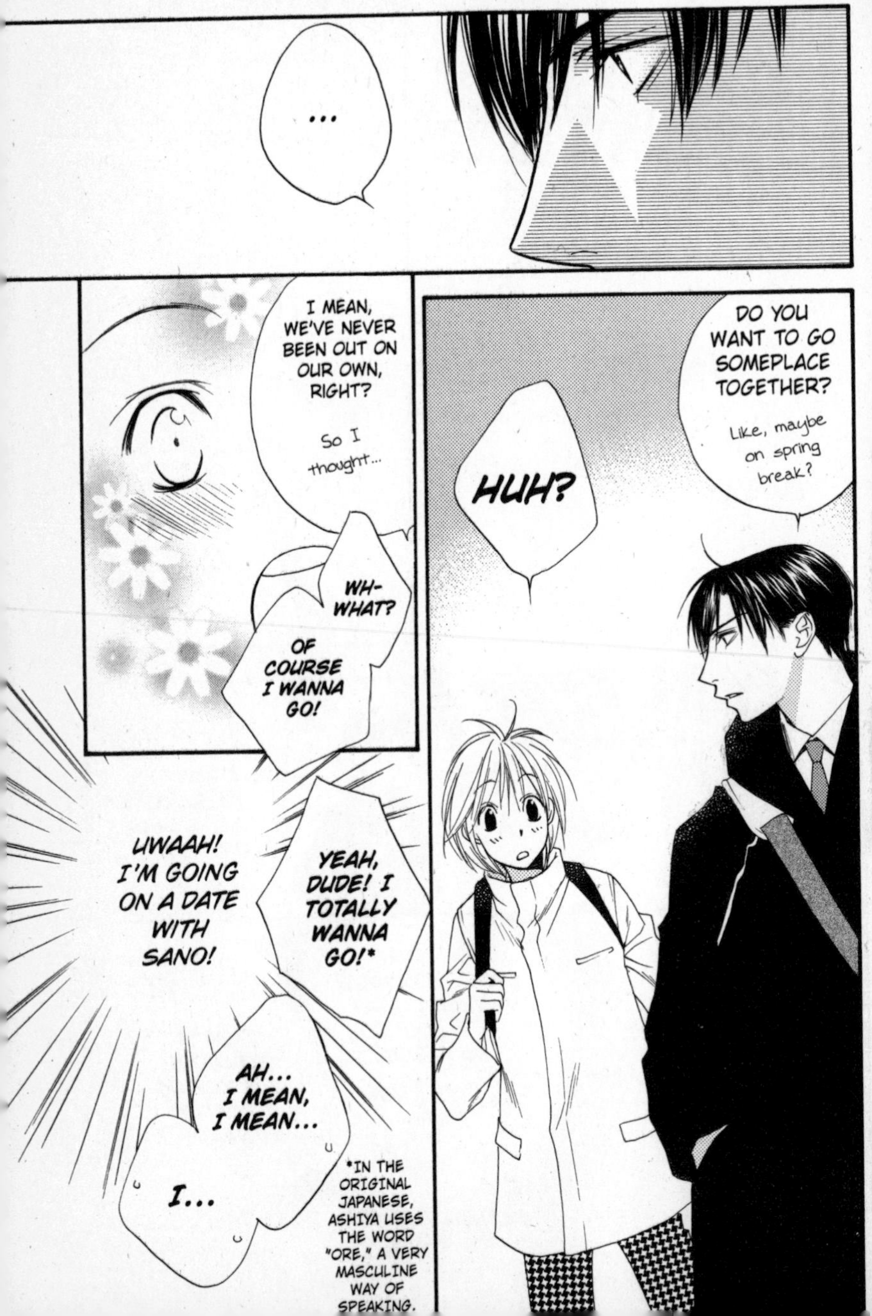
...
DO YOU WANT TO GO SOMEPLACE TOGETHER?
Like, maybe on spring break?
HUH?
I MEAN, WE'VE NEVER BEEN OUT ON OUR OWN, RIGHT?
So I thought...
WH- WHAT?
OF COURSE I WANNA GO!
YEAH, DUDE! I TOTALLY WANNA GO!*
UWAAH! I'M GOING ON A DATE WITH SANO!
AH... I MEAN, I MEAN...
I...
*IN THE ORIGINAL JAPANESE, ASHIYA USES THE WORD "ORE," A VERY MASCULINE WAY OF SPEAKING.

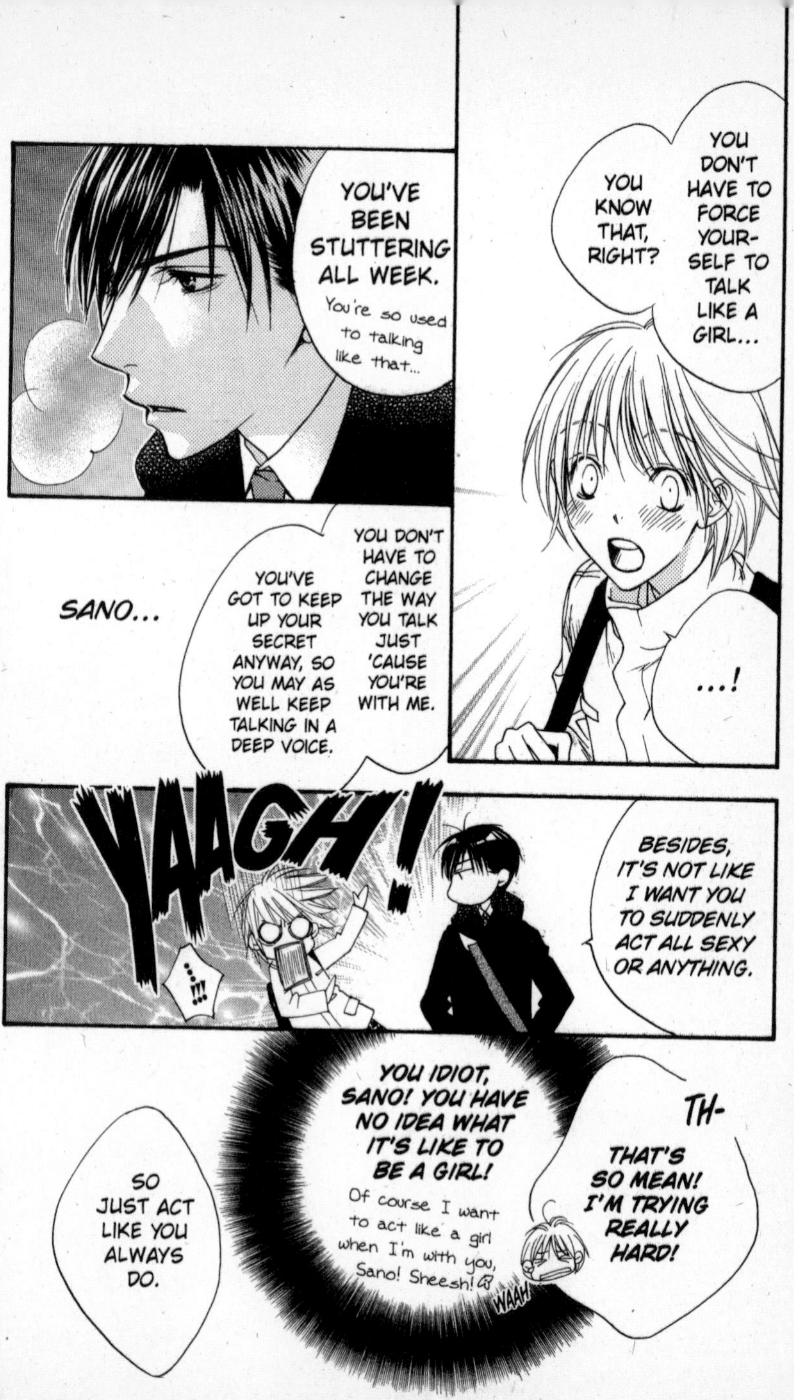

YOU DON'T HAVE TO FORCE YOURSELF TO TALK LIKE A GIRL...
YOU KNOW THAT, RIGHT?
...!
YOU'VE BEEN STUTTERING ALL WEEK.
You're so used to talking like that...
YOU DON'T HAVE TO CHANGE THE WAY YOU TALK JUST 'CAUSE YOU'RE WITH ME.
YOU'VE GOT TO KEEP UP YOUR SECRET ANYWAY, SO YOU MAY AS WELL KEEP TALKING IN A DEEP VOICE.
SANO...
BESIDES, IT'S NOT LIKE I WANT YOU TO SUDDENLY ACT ALL SEXY OR ANYTHING.
YAAGH!
...!!!
TH-
THAT'S SO MEAN! I'M TRYING REALLY HARD!
WAAH
YOU IDIOT, SANO! YOU HAVE NO IDEA WHAT IT'S LIKE TO BE A GIRL!
Of course I want to act like a girl when I'm with you, Sano! Sheesh!
SO JUST ACT LIKE YOU ALWAYS DO.

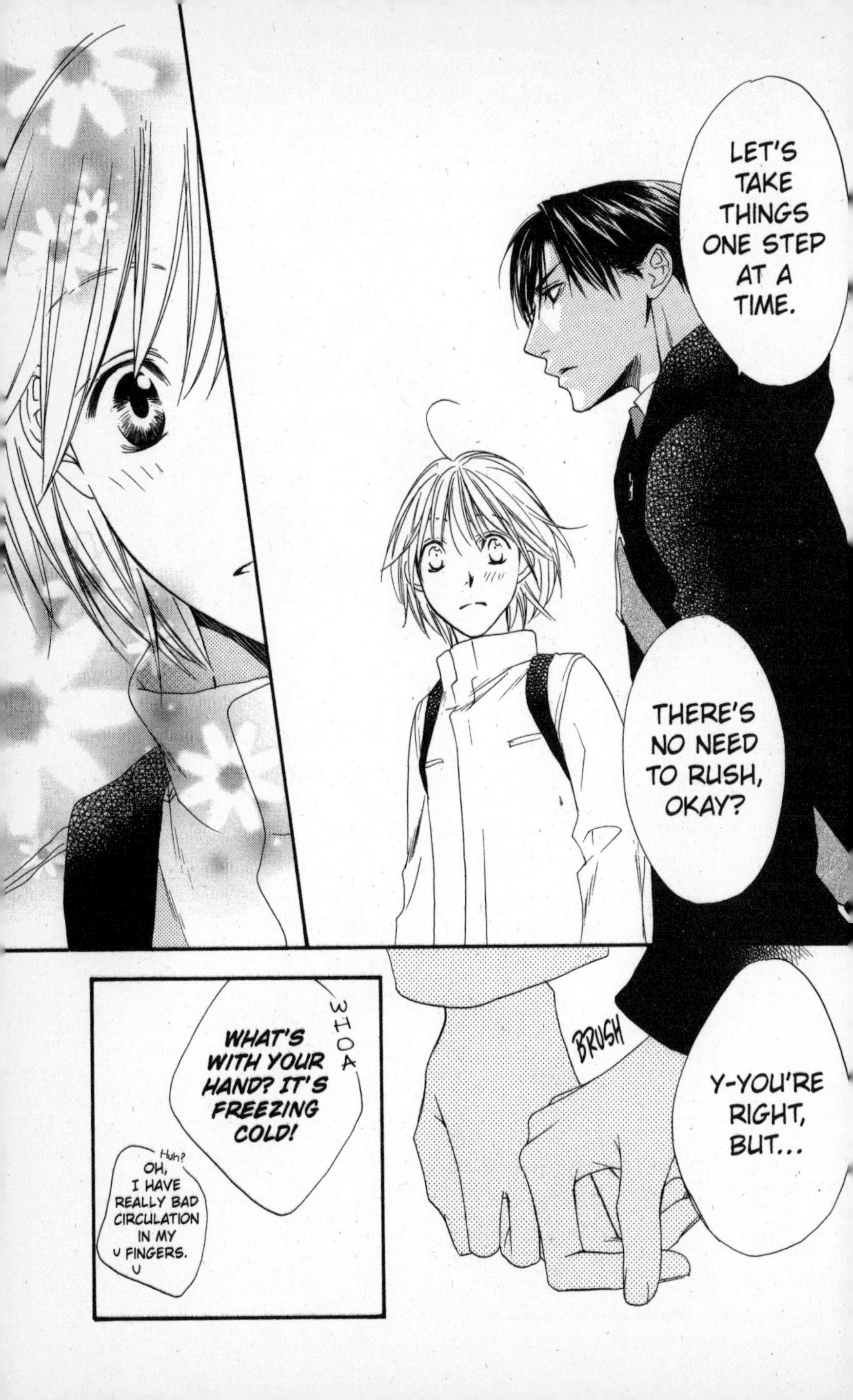
LET'S TAKE THINGS ONE STEP AT A TIME.
THERE'S NO NEED TO RUSH, OKAY?
BRUSH
Y-YOU'RE RIGHT, BUT...
WHOA
WHAT'S WITH YOUR HAND? IT'S FREEZING COLD!
Huh?
OH, I HAVE REALLY BAD CIRCULATION IN MY FINGERS.

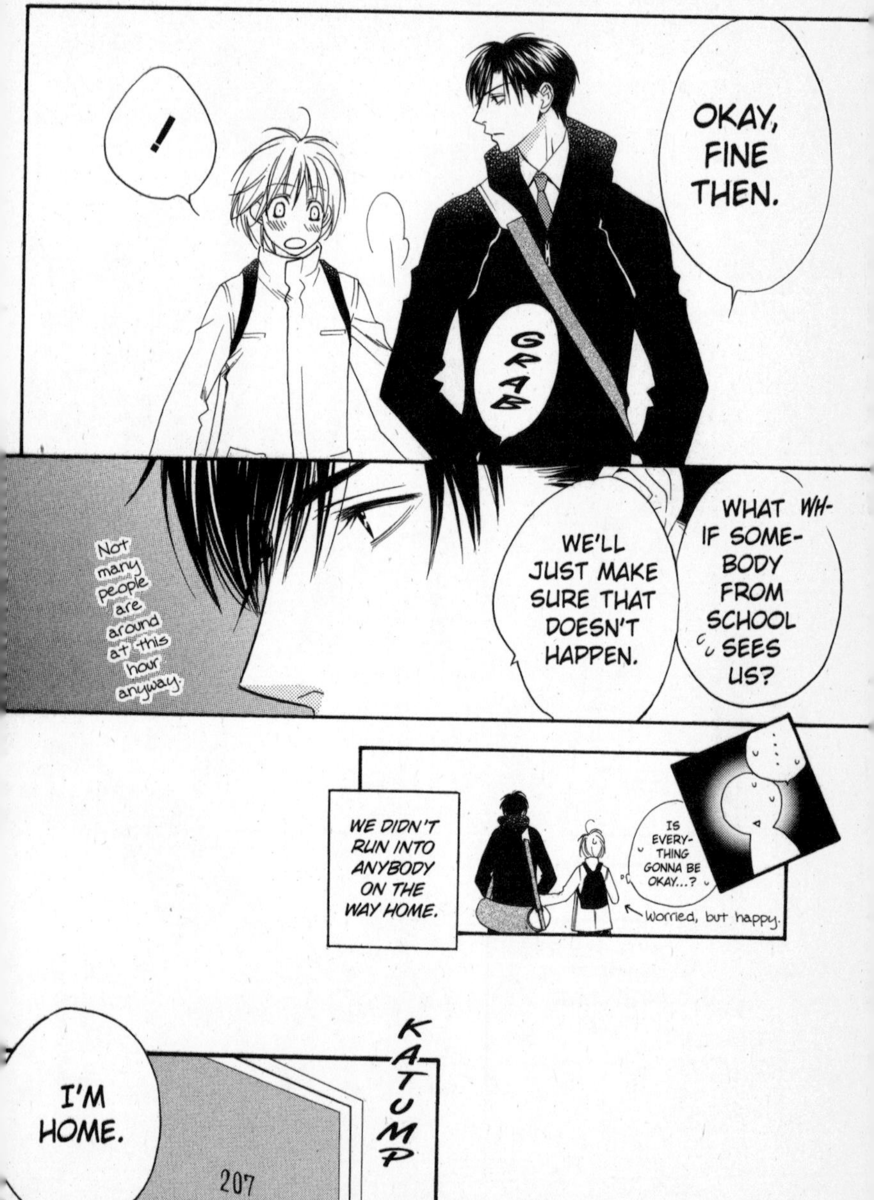

OKAY, FINE THEN.
!
GRAB
WHAT IF SOMEBODY FROM SCHOOL SEES US?
WH-
WE'LL JUST MAKE SURE THAT DOESN'T HAPPEN.
Not many people are around at this hour anyway.
....
IS EVERYTHING GONNA BE OKAY...?
Worried, but happy.
WE DIDN'T RUN INTO ANYBODY ON THE WAY HOME.
KATUMP
I'M HOME.

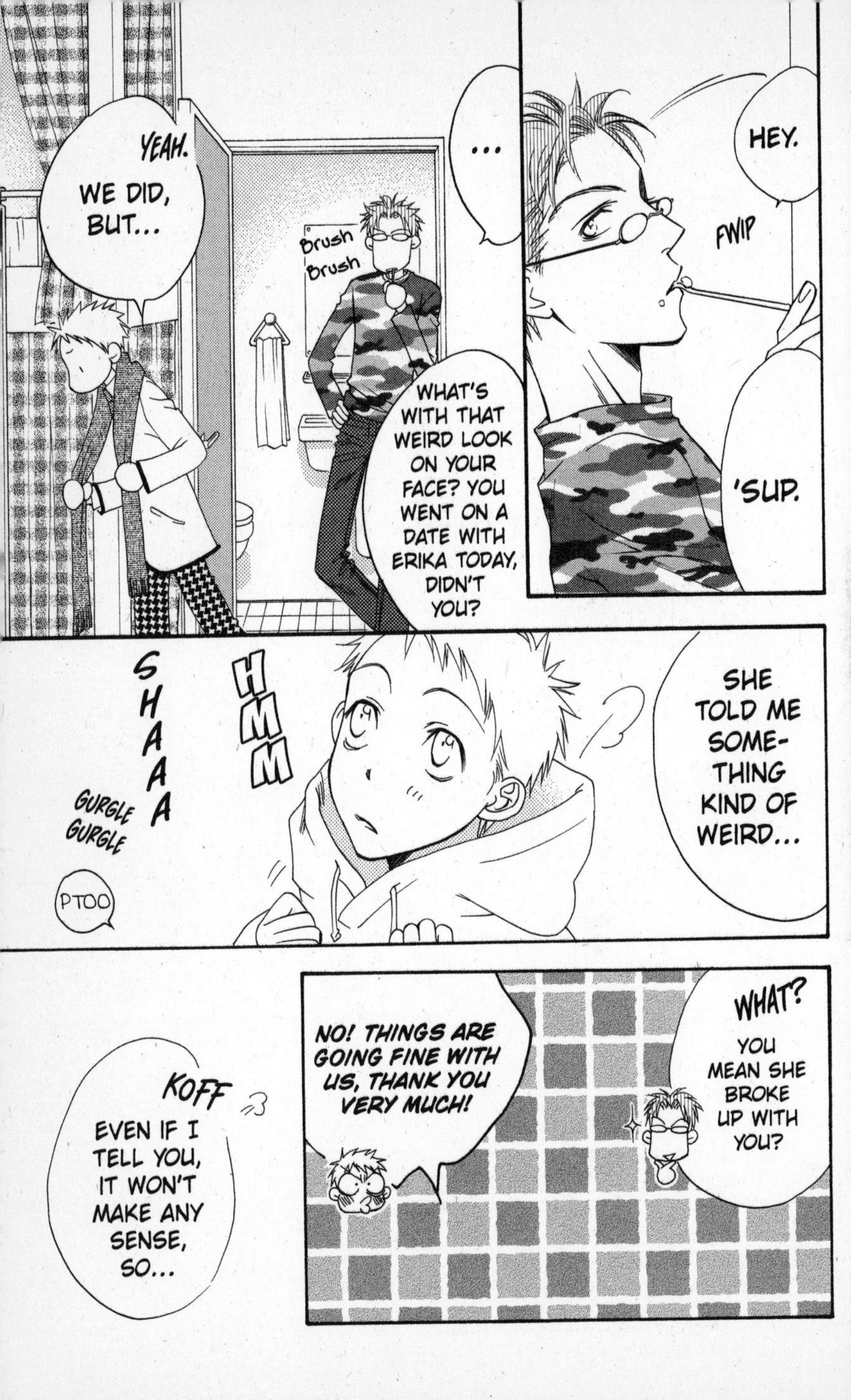
HEY.
FWIP
'SUP.
...
WHAT'S WITH THAT WEIRD LOOK ON YOUR FACE? YOU WENT ON A DATE WITH ERIKA TODAY, DIDN'T YOU?
Brush Brush
YEAH.
WE DID, BUT...
SHE TOLD ME SOME-THING KIND OF WEIRD...
HMM
SHAAAA
GURGLE GURGLE
PTOO
WHAT?
YOU MEAN SHE BROKE UP WITH YOU?
NO! THINGS ARE GOING FINE WITH US, THANK YOU VERY MUCH!
KOFF
EVEN IF I TELL YOU, IT WON'T MAKE ANY SENSE, SO...

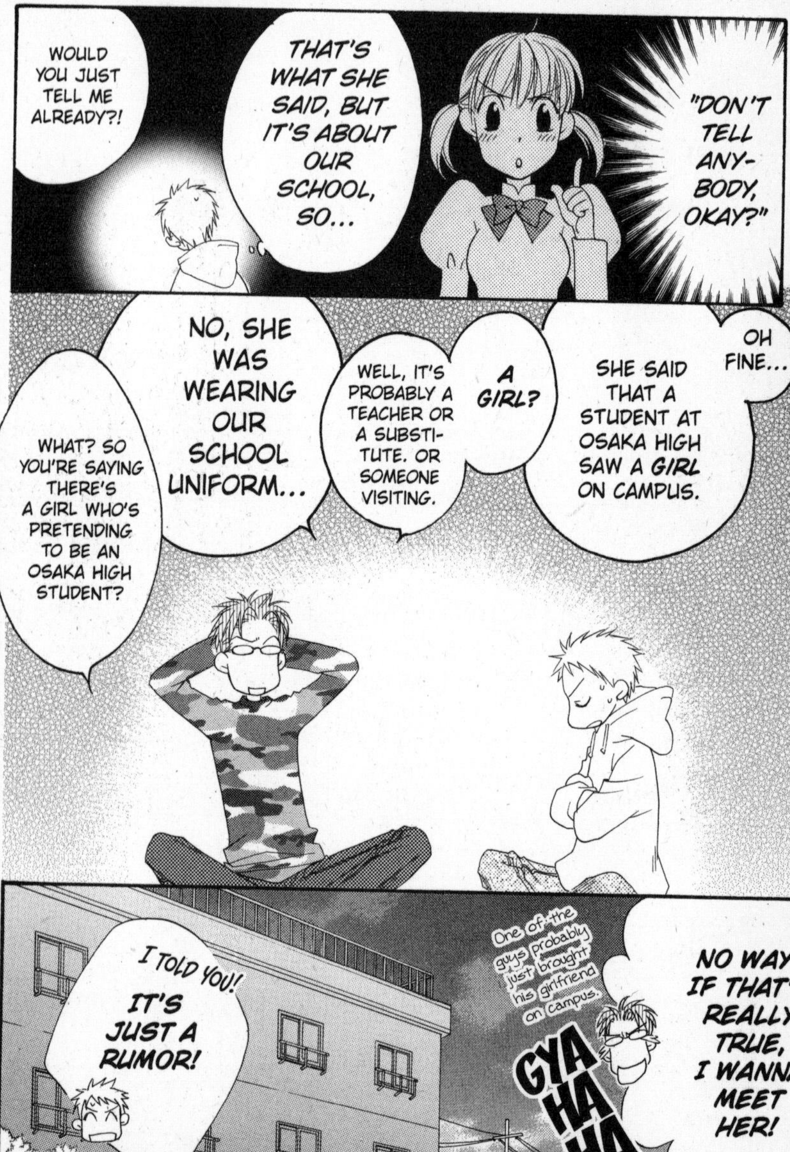
"DON'T TELL ANY-BODY, OKAY?"
THAT'S WHAT SHE SAID, BUT IT'S ABOUT OUR SCHOOL, SO...
WOULD YOU JUST TELL ME ALREADY?!
OH FINE...
SHE SAID THAT A STUDENT AT OSAKA HIGH SAW A GIRL ON CAMPUS.
A GIRL?
WELL, IT'S PROBABLY A TEACHER OR A SUBSTI-TUTE. OR SOMEONE VISITING.
NO, SHE WAS WEARING OUR SCHOOL UNIFORM...
WHAT? SO YOU'RE SAYING THERE'S A GIRL WHO'S PRETENDING TO BE AN OSAKA HIGH STUDENT?
NO WAY! IF THAT'S REALLY TRUE, I WANNA MEET HER!
GYAHAHAHA
One of the guys probably just brought his girlfriend on campus.
I TOLD YOU! IT'S JUST A RUMOR!

HANA-KIMI CHAPTER 134/END

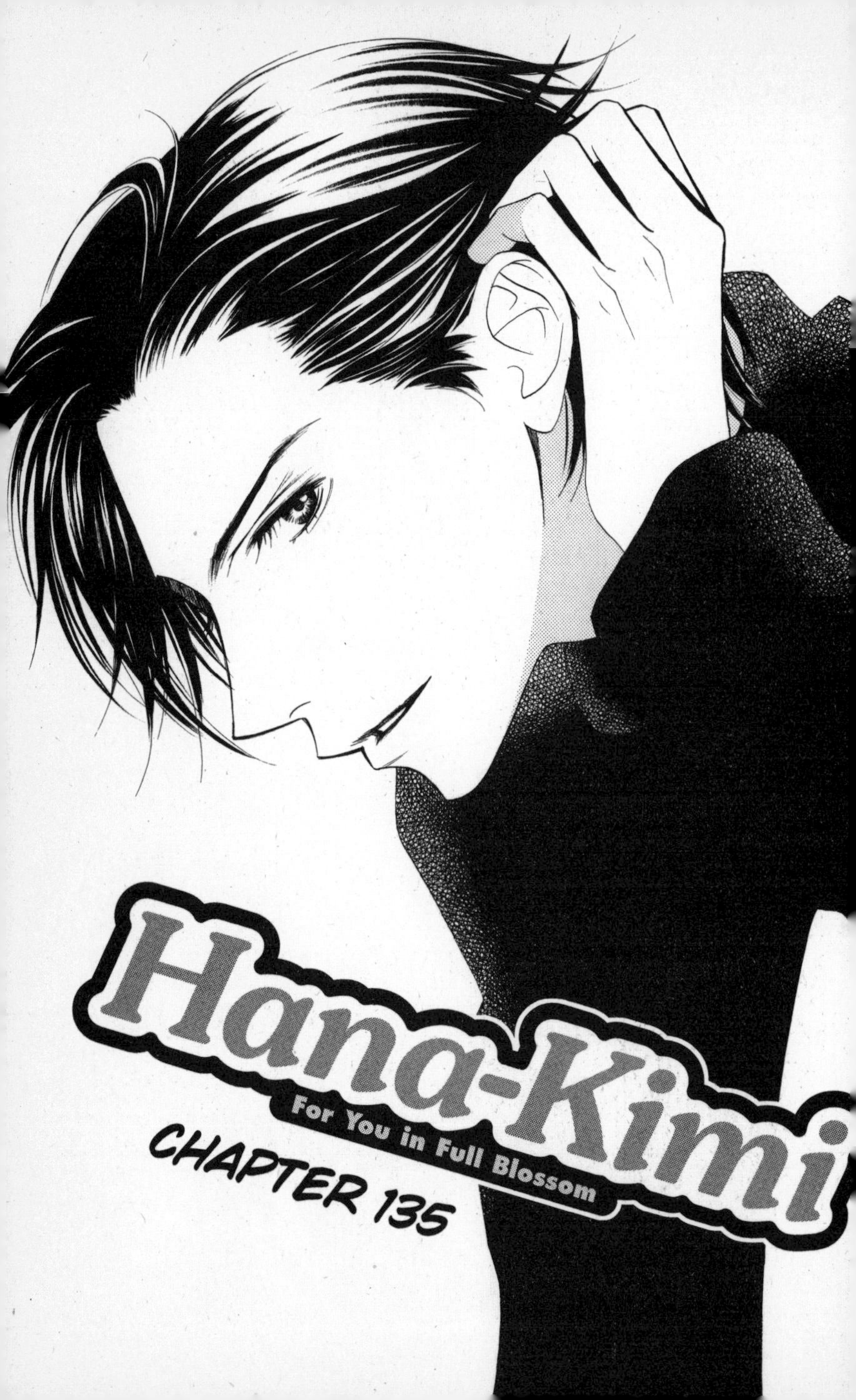
Hana-Kimi
For You in Full Blossom
CHAPTER 135

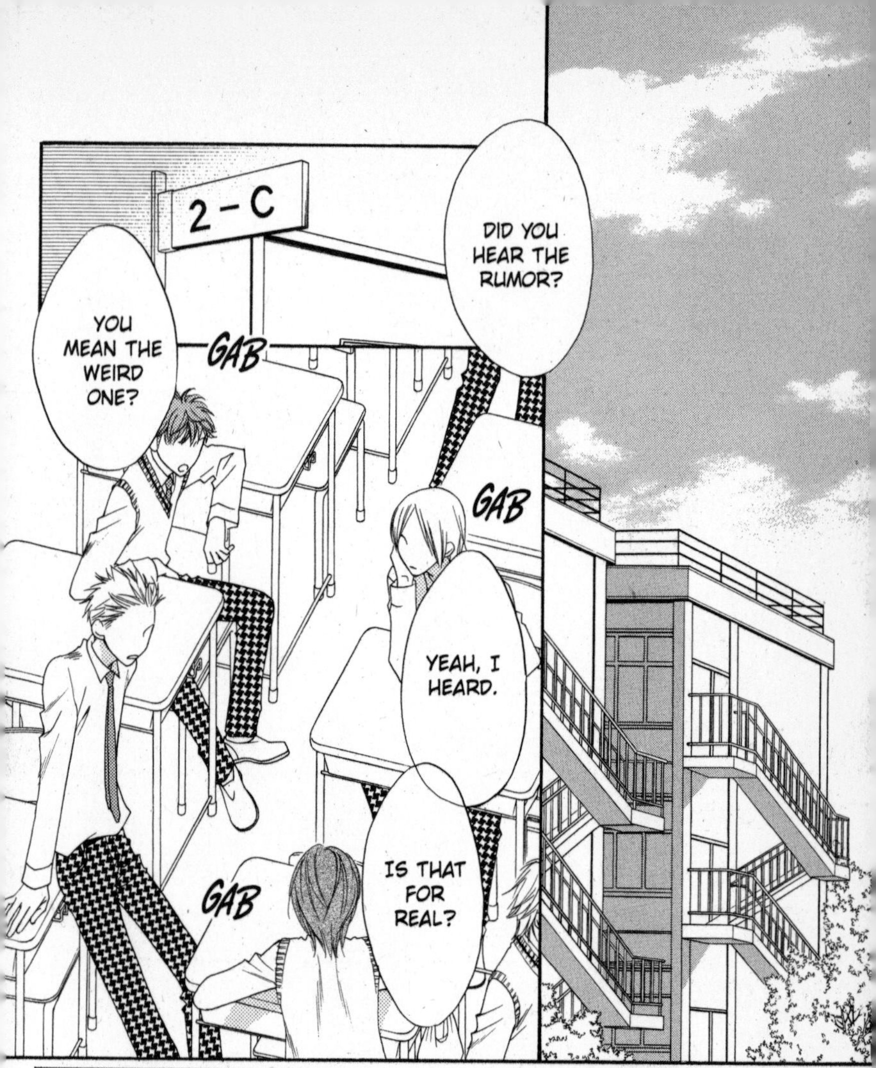
DID YOU HEAR THE RUMOR?
2 – C
YOU MEAN THE WEIRD ONE?
GAB
GAB
YEAH, I HEARD.
IS THAT FOR REAL?
GAB

*Please enjoy the silhouettes.

GAMES I'M INTO

The "Phoenix Wright: Ace Attorney" Series

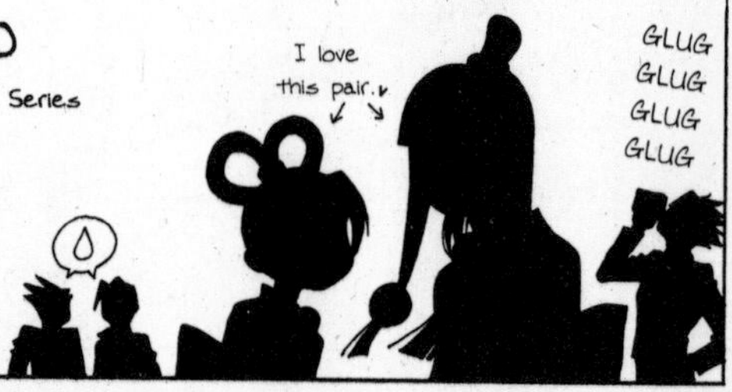
GLUG
GLUG
GLUG
GLUG
I love this pair.

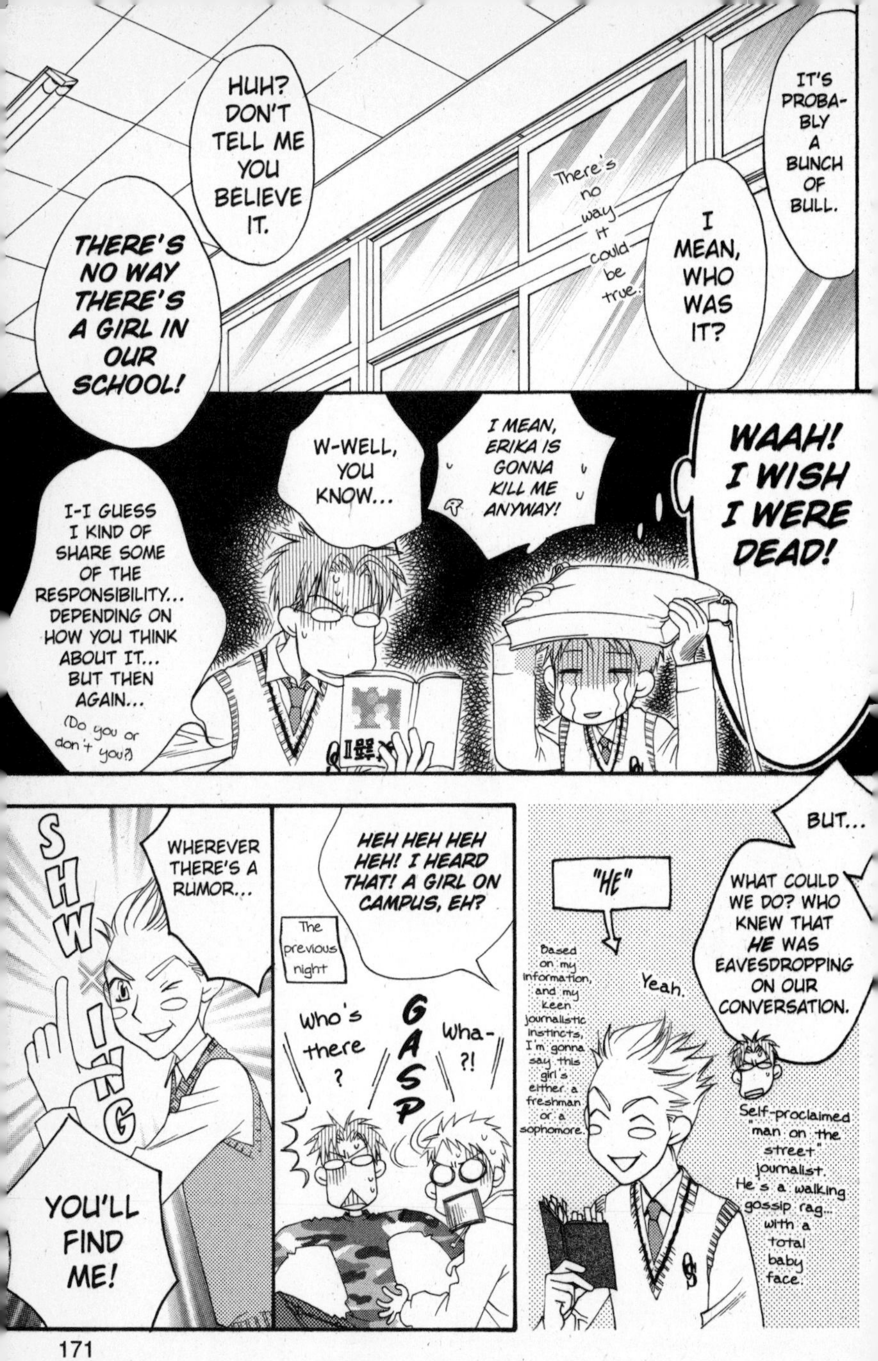

IT'S PROBABLY A BUNCH OF BULL.
I MEAN, WHO WAS IT?
There's no way it could be true.
HUH? DON'T TELL ME YOU BELIEVE IT.
THERE'S NO WAY THERE'S A GIRL IN OUR SCHOOL!
WAAH! I WISH I WERE DEAD!
I MEAN, ERIKA IS GONNA KILL ME ANYWAY!
W-WELL, YOU KNOW...
I-I GUESS I KIND OF SHARE SOME OF THE RESPONSIBILITY... DEPENDING ON HOW YOU THINK ABOUT IT... BUT THEN AGAIN...
(Do you or don't you?)
BUT...
WHAT COULD WE DO? WHO KNEW THAT HE WAS EAVESDROPPING ON OUR CONVERSATION.
"HE"
Yeah.
Based on my information, and my keen journalistic instincts, I'm gonna say this girl's either a freshman or a sophomore.
Self-proclaimed "man on the street" journalist. He's a walking gossip rag... with a total baby face.
HEH HEH HEH HEH! I HEARD THAT! A GIRL ON CAMPUS, EH?
The previous night
Wha-?!
GASP
Who's there?
WHEREVER THERE'S A RUMOR...
SHWING
YOU'LL FIND ME!

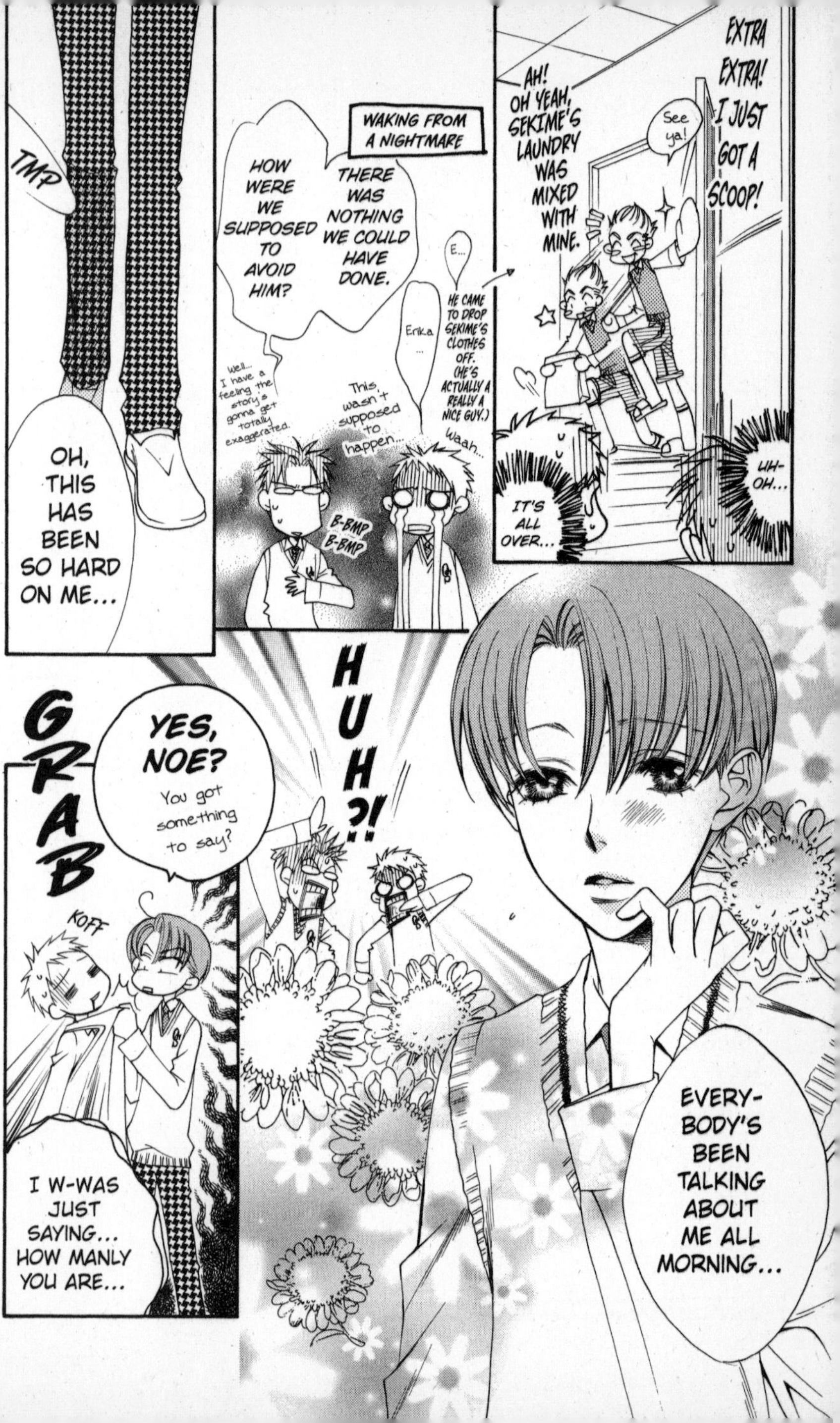
EXTRA EXTRA! I JUST GOT A SCOOP!
See ya!
AH! OH YEAH, SEKIME'S LAUNDRY WAS MIXED WITH MINE.
UH-OH...
IT'S ALL OVER...
WAKING FROM A NIGHTMARE
THERE WAS NOTHING WE COULD HAVE DONE.
HOW WERE WE SUPPOSED TO AVOID HIM?
E...
HE CAME TO DROP SEKIME'S CLOTHES OFF. (HE'S ACTUALLY A REALLY A NICE GUY.)
Erika ...
This wasn't supposed to happen...
Waah...
Well... I have a feeling the story's gonna get totally exaggerated.
B-BMP B-BMP
TMP
OH, THIS HAS BEEN SO HARD ON ME...
HUH?!
EVERY-BODY'S BEEN TALKING ABOUT ME ALL MORNING...
GRAB
YES, NOE?
You got something to say?
KOFF
I W-WAS JUST SAYING... HOW MANLY YOU ARE...

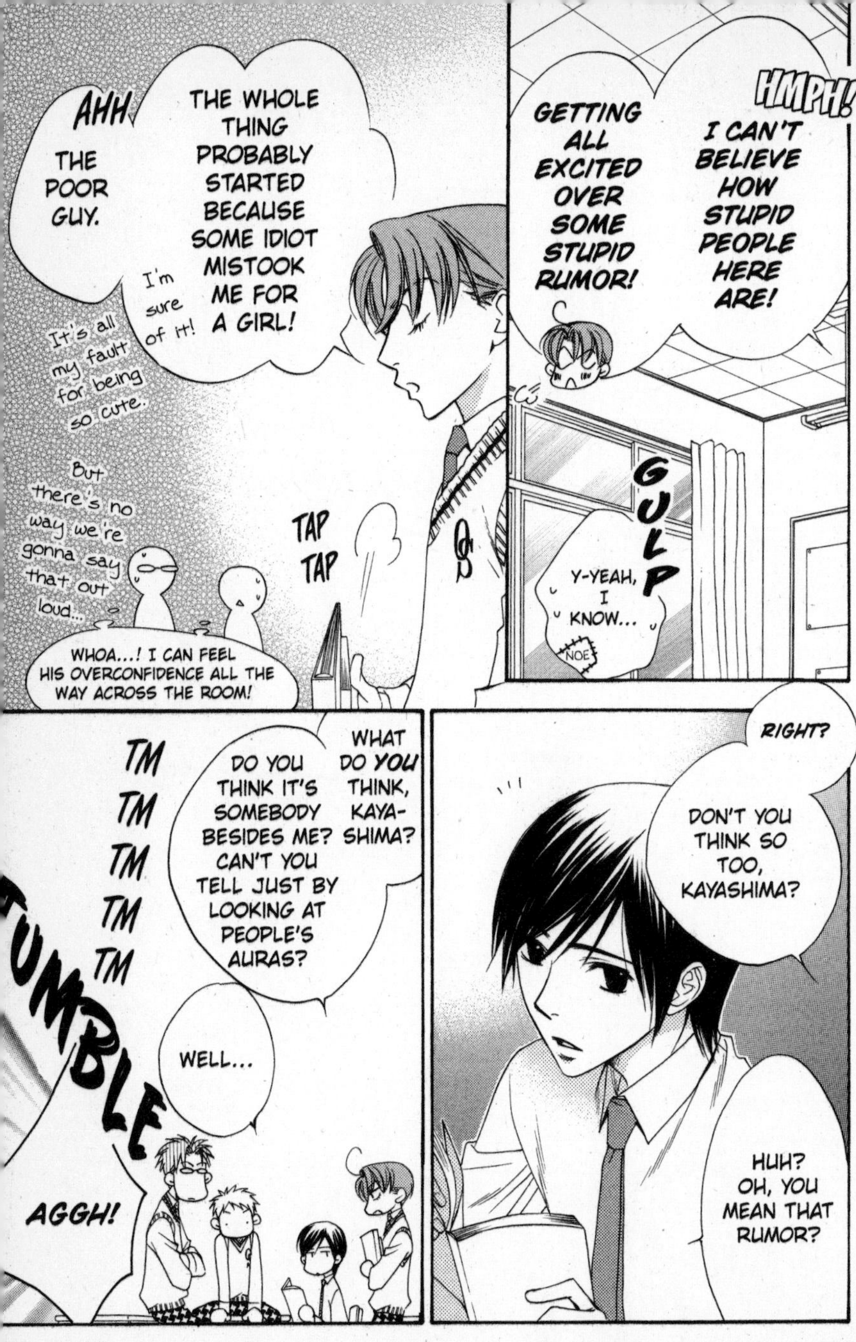
HMPH!
I CAN'T BELIEVE HOW STUPID PEOPLE HERE ARE!
GETTING ALL EXCITED OVER SOME STUPID RUMOR!
GULP
Y-YEAH, I KNOW...
NOE
THE WHOLE THING PROBABLY STARTED BECAUSE SOME IDIOT MISTOOK ME FOR A GIRL!
I'm sure of it!
AHH
THE POOR GUY.
It's all my fault for being so cute.
TAP TAP
But there's no way we're gonna say that out loud...
WHOA...! I CAN FEEL HIS OVERCONFIDENCE ALL THE WAY ACROSS THE ROOM!
RIGHT?
DON'T YOU THINK SO TOO, KAYASHIMA?
HUH? OH, YOU MEAN THAT RUMOR?
WHAT DO YOU THINK, KAYA-SHIMA?
DO YOU THINK IT'S SOMEBODY BESIDES ME? CAN'T YOU TELL JUST BY LOOKING AT PEOPLE'S AURAS?
TM TM TM TM TM
WELL...
UMBLE
AGGH!

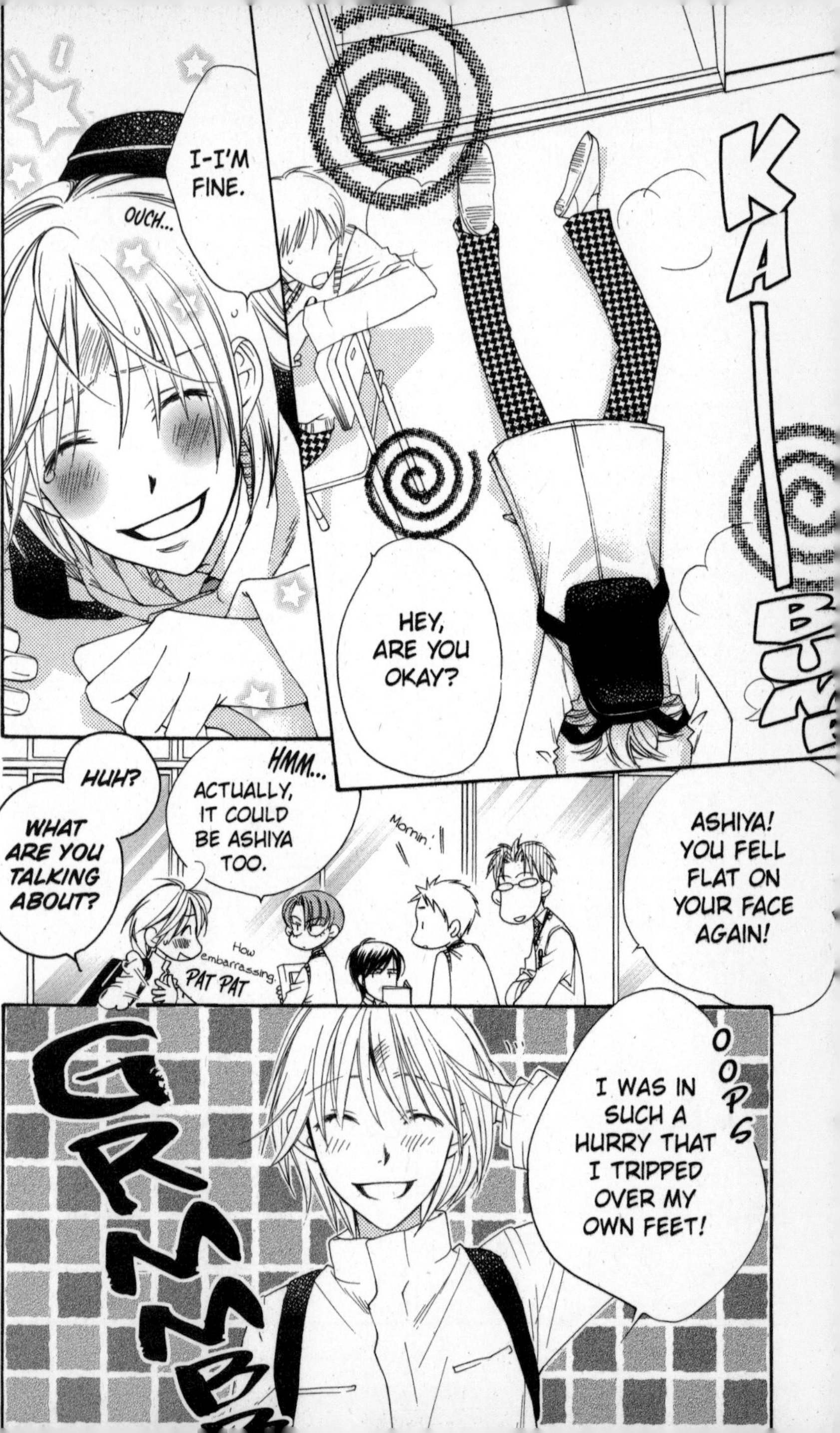
KA-BUN
HEY, ARE YOU OKAY?
OUCH...
I-I'M FINE.
ASHIYA! YOU FELL FLAT ON YOUR FACE AGAIN!
Mornin'
HMM...
ACTUALLY, IT COULD BE ASHIYA TOO.
HUH?
WHAT ARE YOU TALKING ABOUT?
How embarrassing.
PAT PAT
OOPS
I WAS IN SUCH A HURRY THAT I TRIPPED OVER MY OWN FEET!
GRMMB

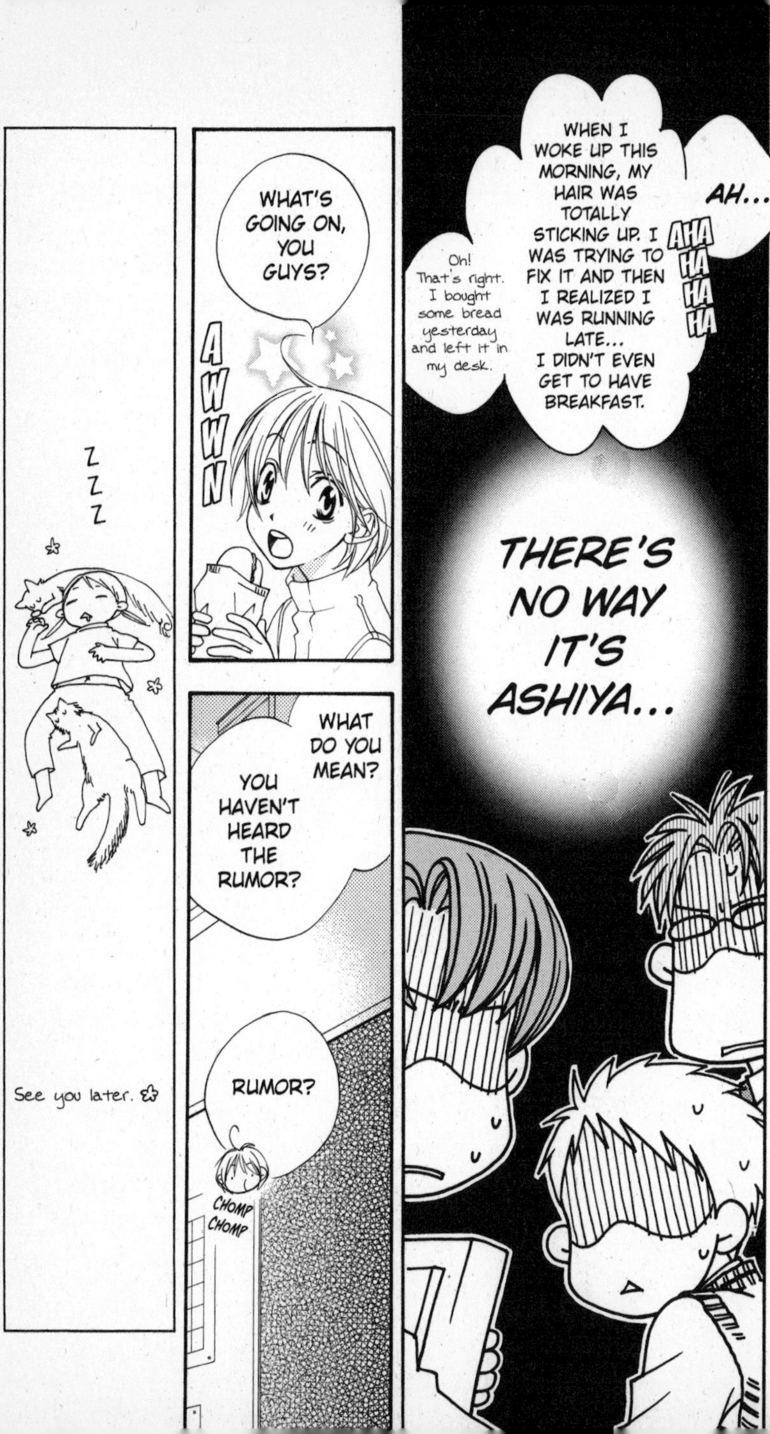
AH...
AHA HA HA HA
WHEN I WOKE UP THIS MORNING, MY HAIR WAS TOTALLY STICKING UP. I WAS TRYING TO FIX IT AND THEN I REALIZED I WAS RUNNING LATE... I DIDN'T EVEN GET TO HAVE BREAKFAST.
Oh! That's right. I bought some bread yesterday and left it in my desk.
THERE'S NO WAY IT'S ASHIYA...
WHAT'S GOING ON, YOU GUYS?
AWWWN
WHAT DO YOU MEAN?
YOU HAVEN'T HEARD THE RUMOR?
RUMOR?
CHOMP CHOMP
Z Z Z
See you later.

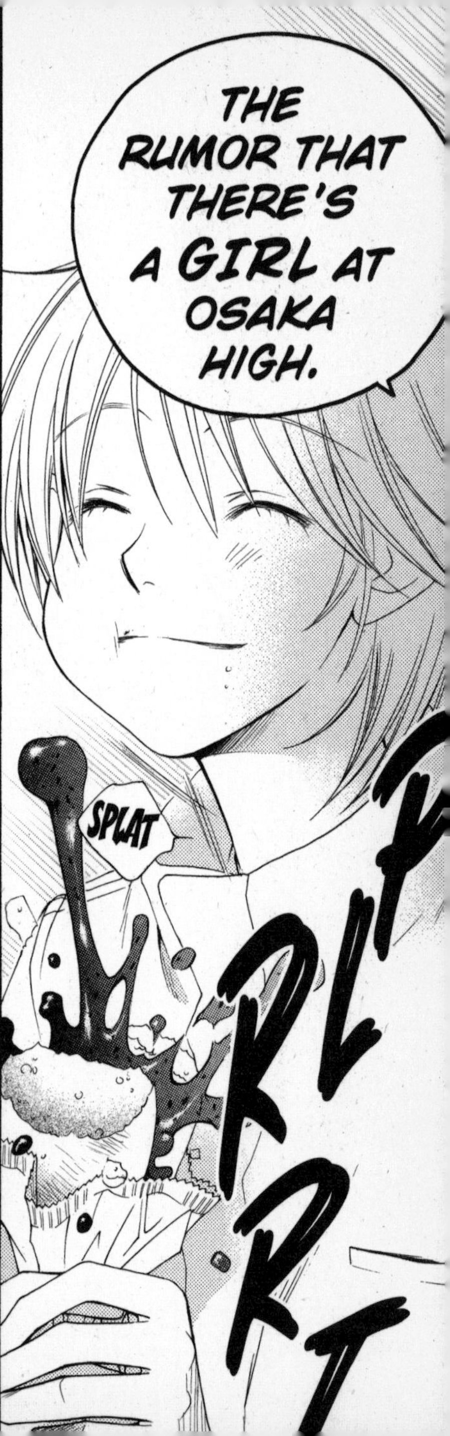
THE RUMOR THAT THERE'S A GIRL AT OSAKA HIGH.
SPLAT
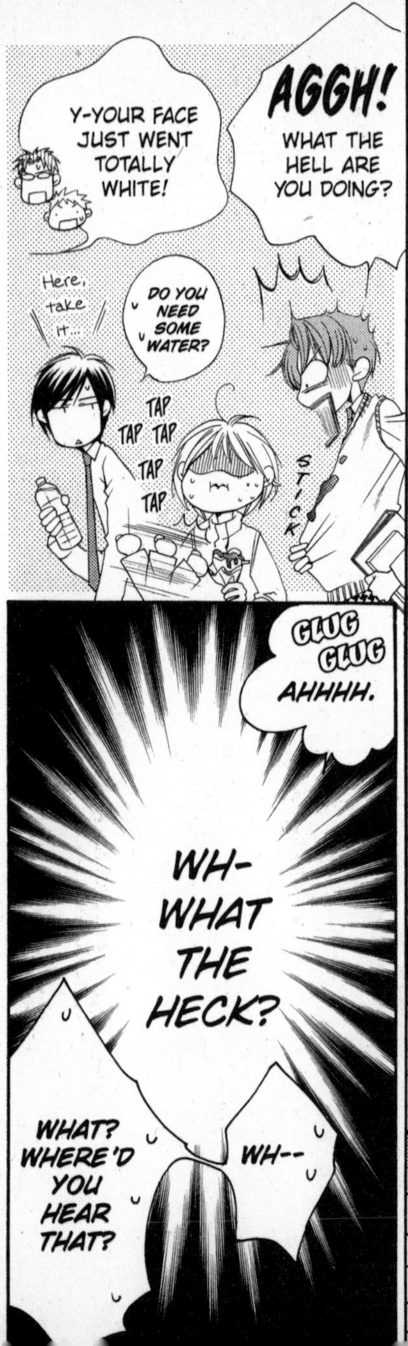
AGGH! WHAT THE HELL ARE YOU DOING?
STICK
Y-YOUR FACE JUST WENT TOTALLY WHITE!
DO YOU NEED SOME WATER?
Here, take it...
TAP TAP TAP TAP TAP
GLUG GLUG AHHHH.
WH-WHAT THE HECK?
WH--
WHAT? WHERE'D YOU HEAR THAT?

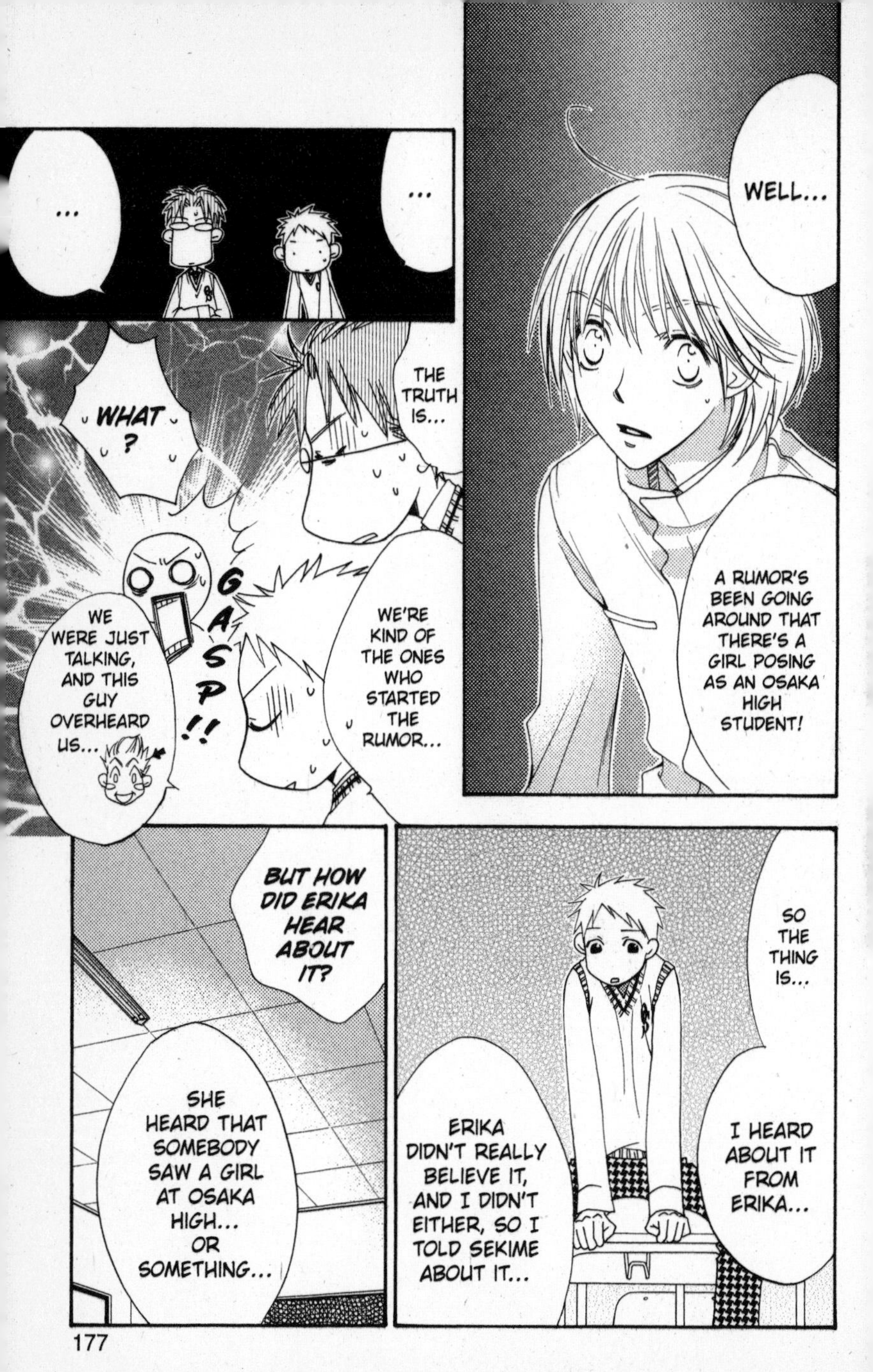
WELL...
A RUMOR'S BEEN GOING AROUND THAT THERE'S A GIRL POSING AS AN OSAKA HIGH STUDENT!
...
...
THE TRUTH IS...
WHAT?
GASP!!
WE'RE KIND OF THE ONES WHO STARTED THE RUMOR...
WE WERE JUST TALKING, AND THIS GUY OVERHEARD US...
SO THE THING IS...
I HEARD ABOUT IT FROM ERIKA...
ERIKA DIDN'T REALLY BELIEVE IT, AND I DIDN'T EITHER, SO I TOLD SEKIME ABOUT IT...
BUT HOW DID ERIKA HEAR ABOUT IT?
SHE HEARD THAT SOMEBODY SAW A GIRL AT OSAKA HIGH... OR SOMETHING...

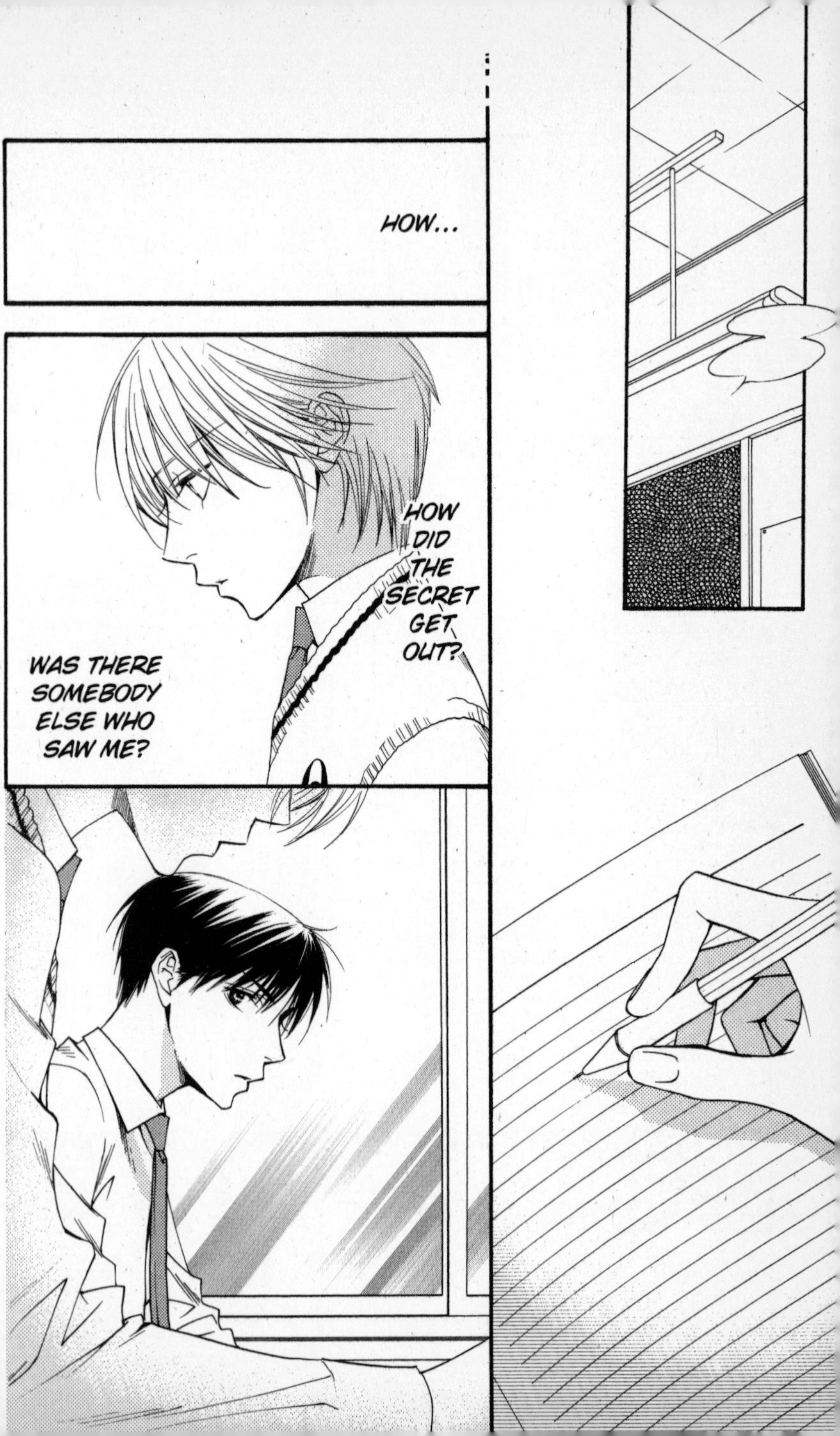
HOW...
HOW DID THE SECRET GET OUT?
WAS THERE SOMEBODY ELSE WHO SAW ME?

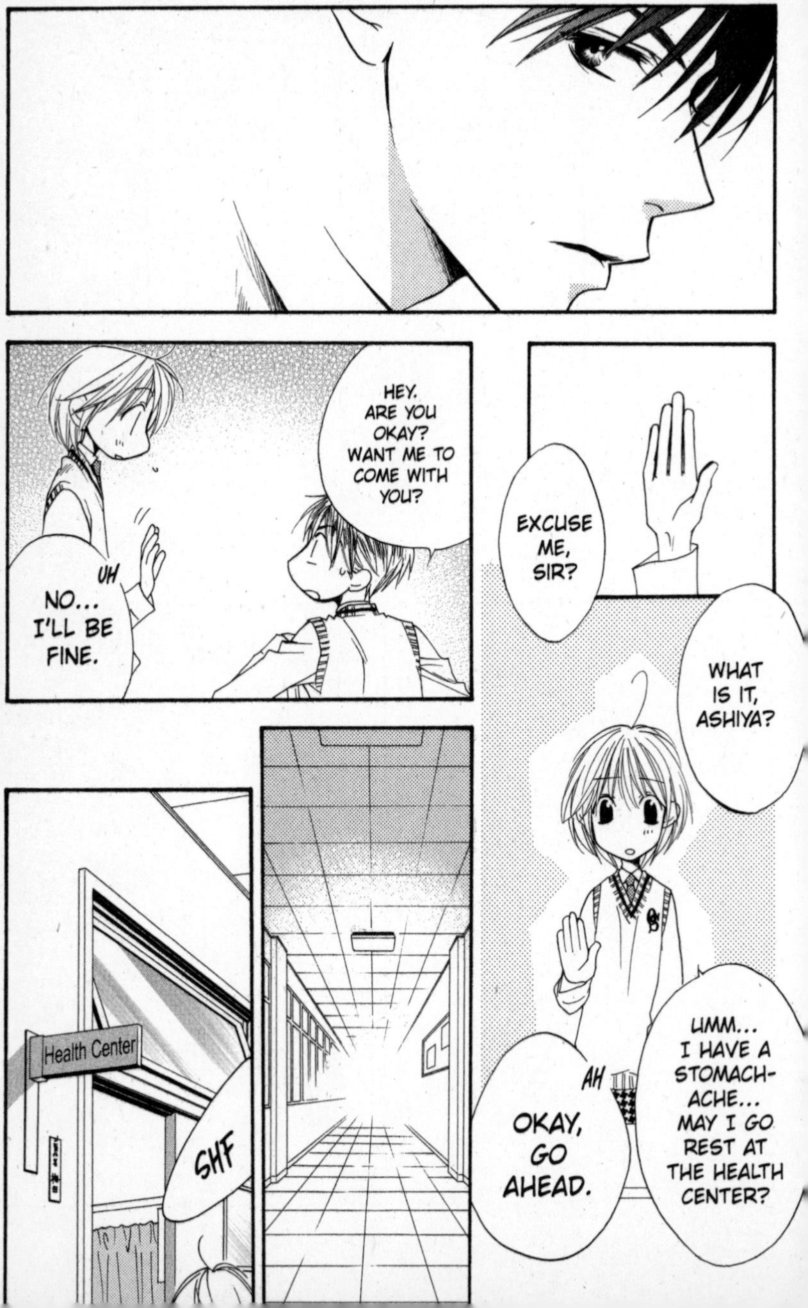
EXCUSE ME, SIR?
WHAT IS IT, ASHIYA?
UMM... I HAVE A STOMACH-ACHE... MAY I GO REST AT THE HEALTH CENTER?
AH
OKAY, GO AHEAD.
HEY. ARE YOU OKAY? WANT ME TO COME WITH YOU?
UH
NO... I'LL BE FINE.
Health Center
SHF

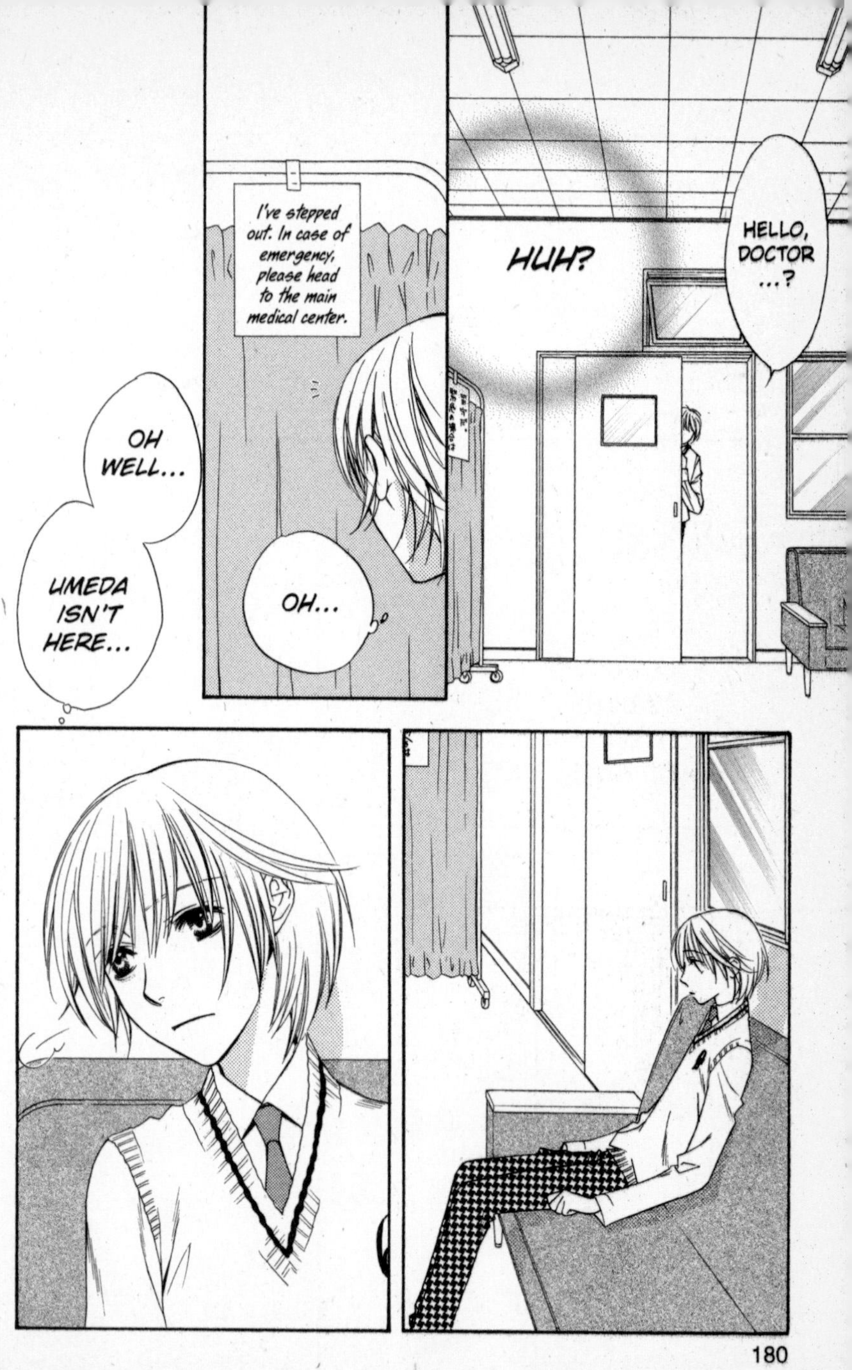
HELLO, DOCTOR ...?
HUH?
I've stepped out. In case of emergency, please head to the main medical center.
OH...
OH WELL...
UMEDA ISN'T HERE...

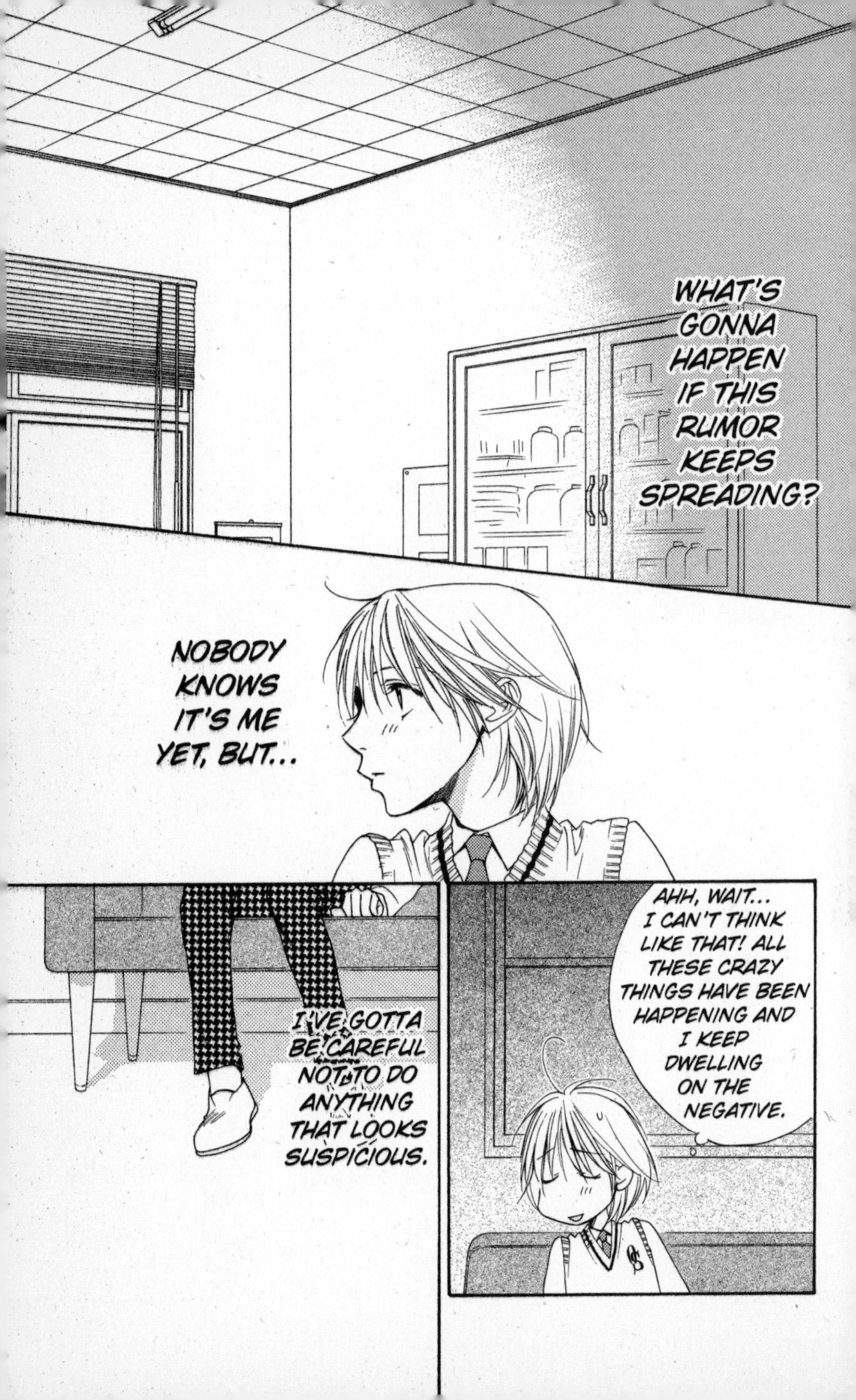
WHAT'S GONNA HAPPEN IF THIS RUMOR KEEPS SPREADING?
NOBODY KNOWS IT'S ME YET, BUT...
I'VE GOTTA BE CAREFUL NOT TO DO ANYTHING THAT LOOKS SUSPICIOUS.
AHH, WAIT... I CAN'T THINK LIKE THAT! ALL THESE CRAZY THINGS HAVE BEEN HAPPENING AND I KEEP DWELLING ON THE NEGATIVE.

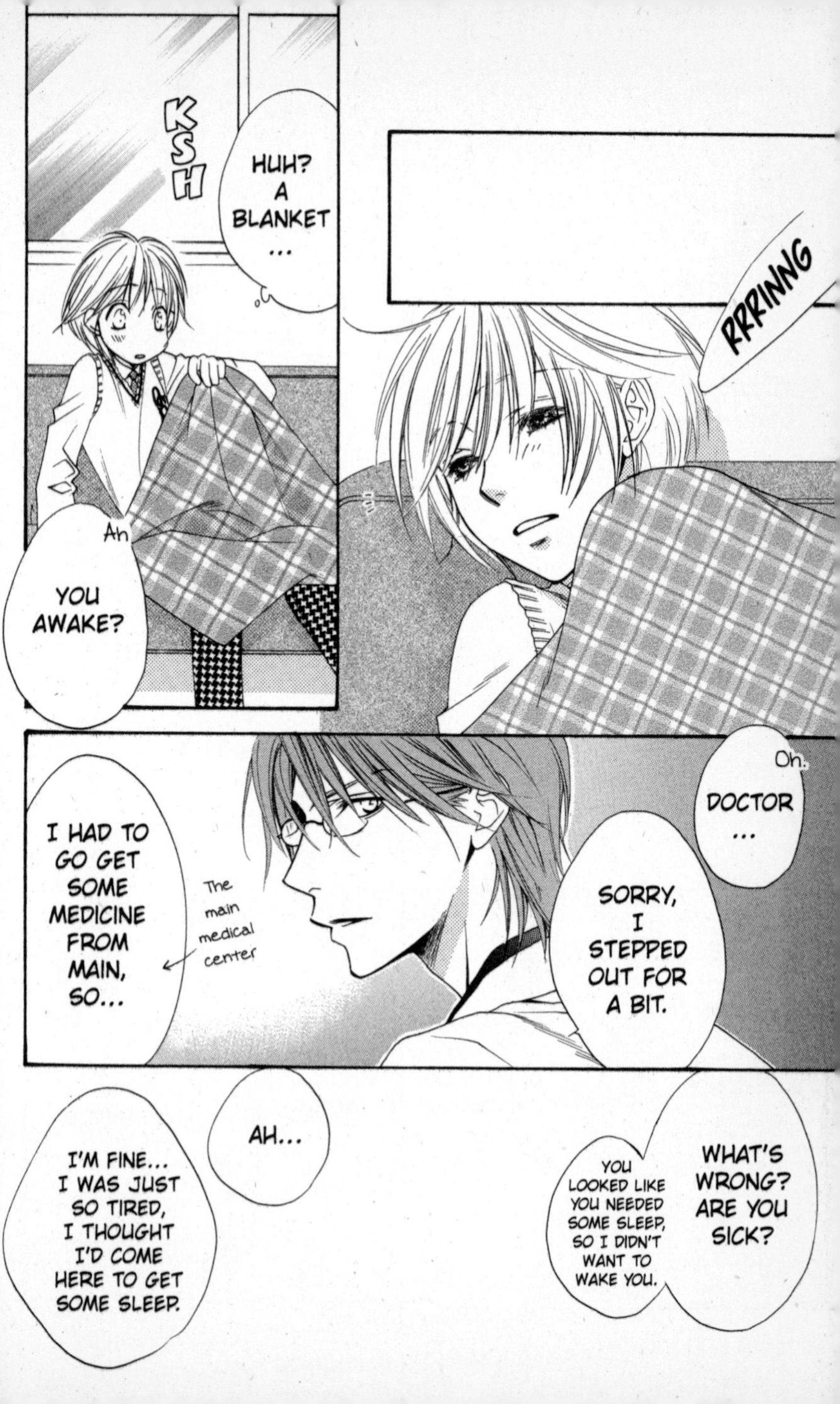
RRRINNG
KSH
HUH? A BLANKET...
Ah
YOU AWAKE?
Oh. DOCTOR...
SORRY, I STEPPED OUT FOR A BIT.
I HAD TO GO GET SOME MEDICINE FROM MAIN, SO...
The main medical center
WHAT'S WRONG? ARE YOU SICK?
YOU LOOKED LIKE YOU NEEDED SOME SLEEP, SO I DIDN'T WANT TO WAKE YOU.
AH...
I'M FINE... I WAS JUST SO TIRED, I THOUGHT I'D COME HERE TO GET SOME SLEEP.

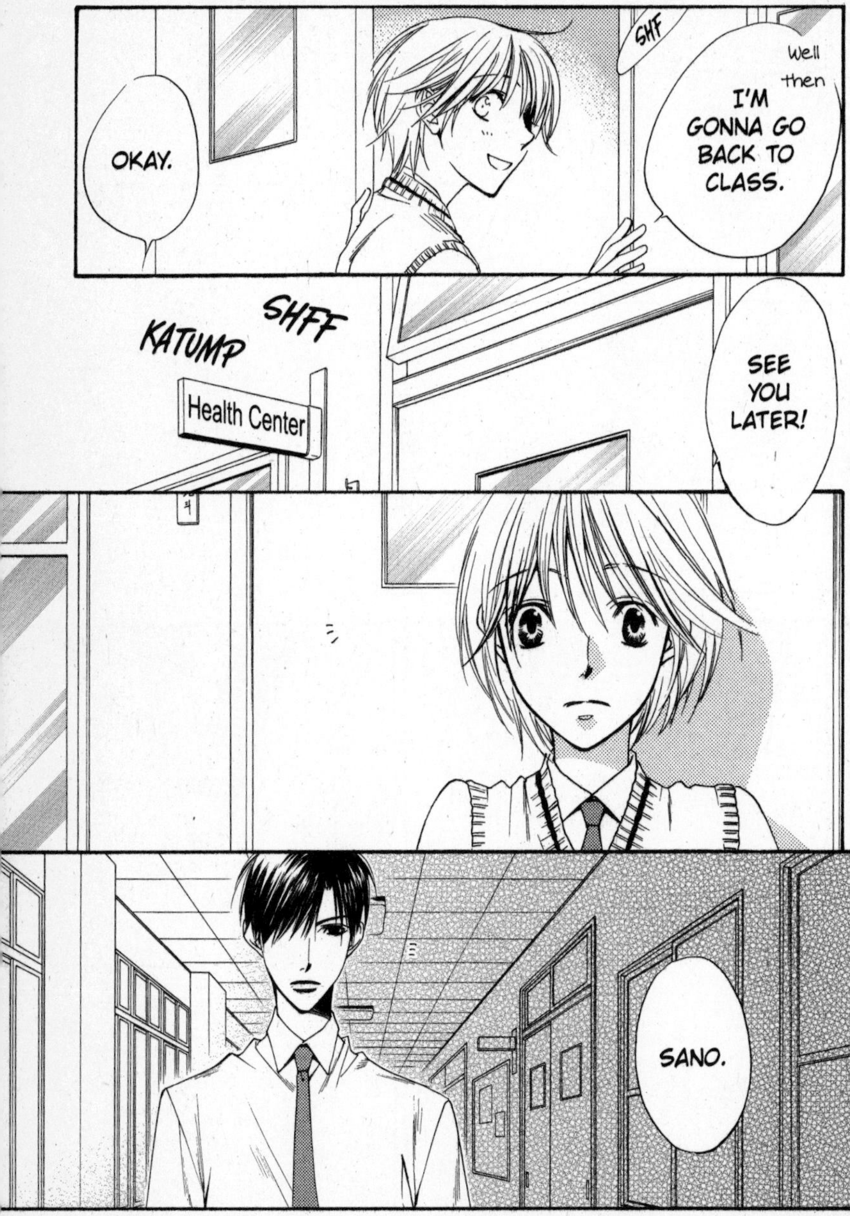
SHF
Well then I'M GONNA GO BACK TO CLASS.
OKAY.
SEE YOU LATER!
SHFF
KATUMP
Health Center
SANO.

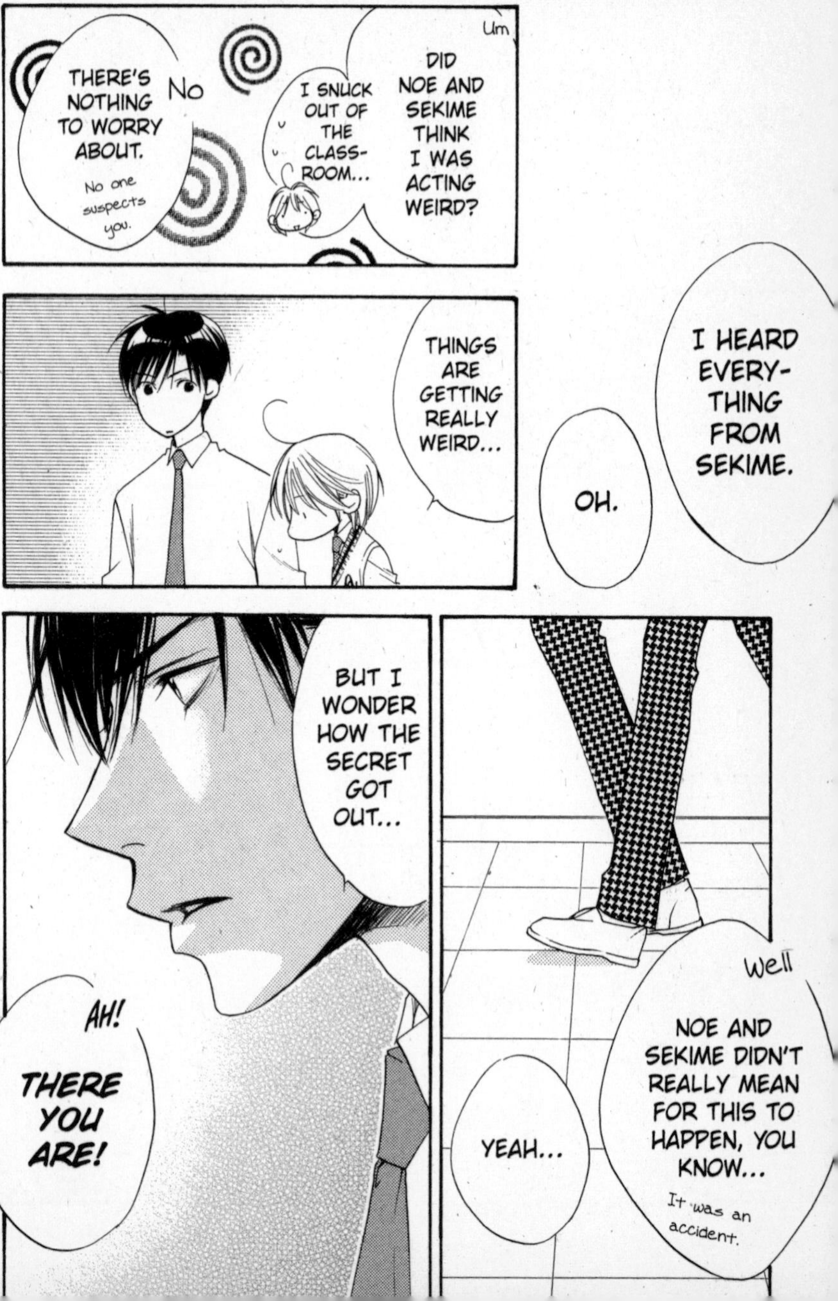
Um
DID NOE AND SEKIME THINK I WAS ACTING WEIRD?
I SNUCK OUT OF THE CLASS-ROOM...
No
THERE'S NOTHING TO WORRY ABOUT.
No one suspects you.
I HEARD EVERY-THING FROM SEKIME.
OH.
THINGS ARE GETTING REALLY WEIRD...
Well
NOE AND SEKIME DIDN'T REALLY MEAN FOR THIS TO HAPPEN, YOU KNOW...
It was an accident.
YEAH...
BUT I WONDER HOW THE SECRET GOT OUT...
AH!
THERE YOU ARE!

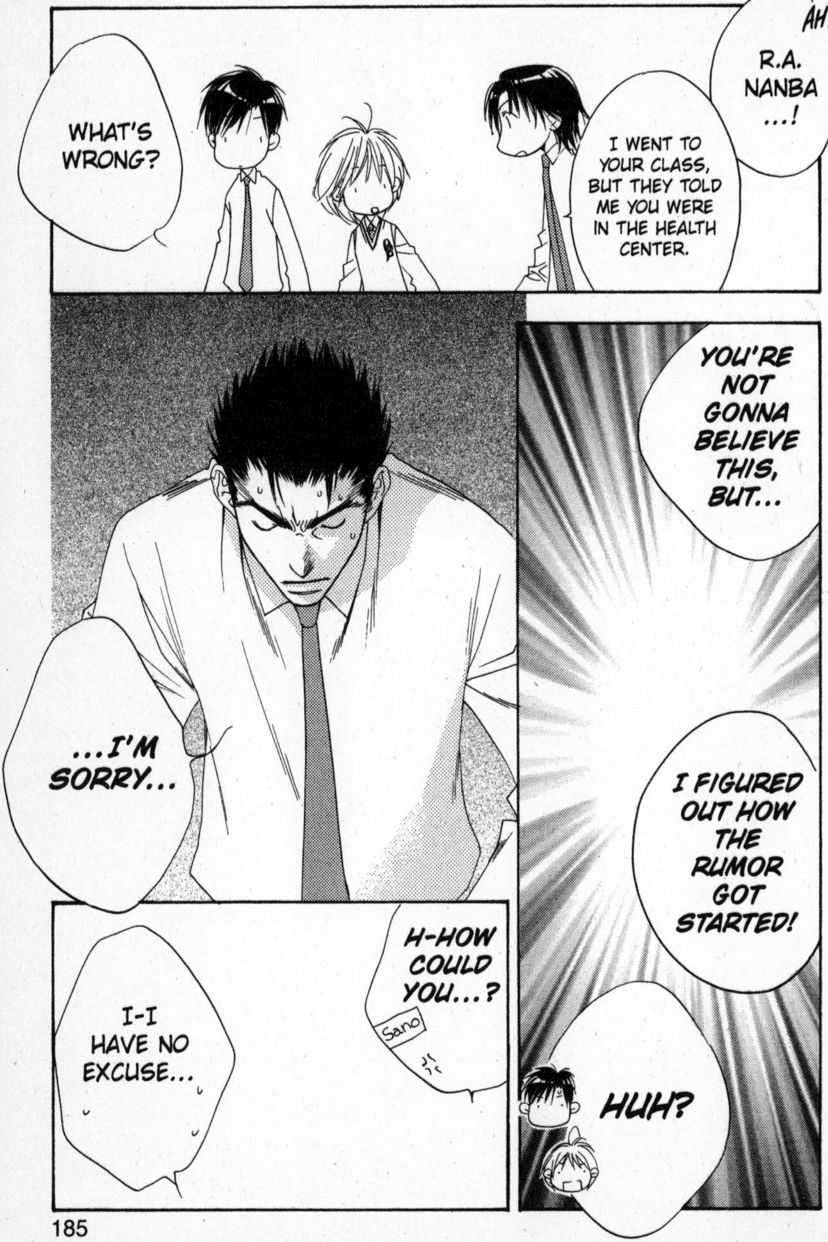
AH
R.A. NANBA...!
I WENT TO YOUR CLASS, BUT THEY TOLD ME YOU WERE IN THE HEALTH CENTER.
WHAT'S WRONG?
YOU'RE NOT GONNA BELIEVE THIS, BUT...
I FIGURED OUT HOW THE RUMOR GOT STARTED!
HUH?
...I'M SORRY...
H-HOW COULD YOU...?
Sano
I-I HAVE NO EXCUSE...

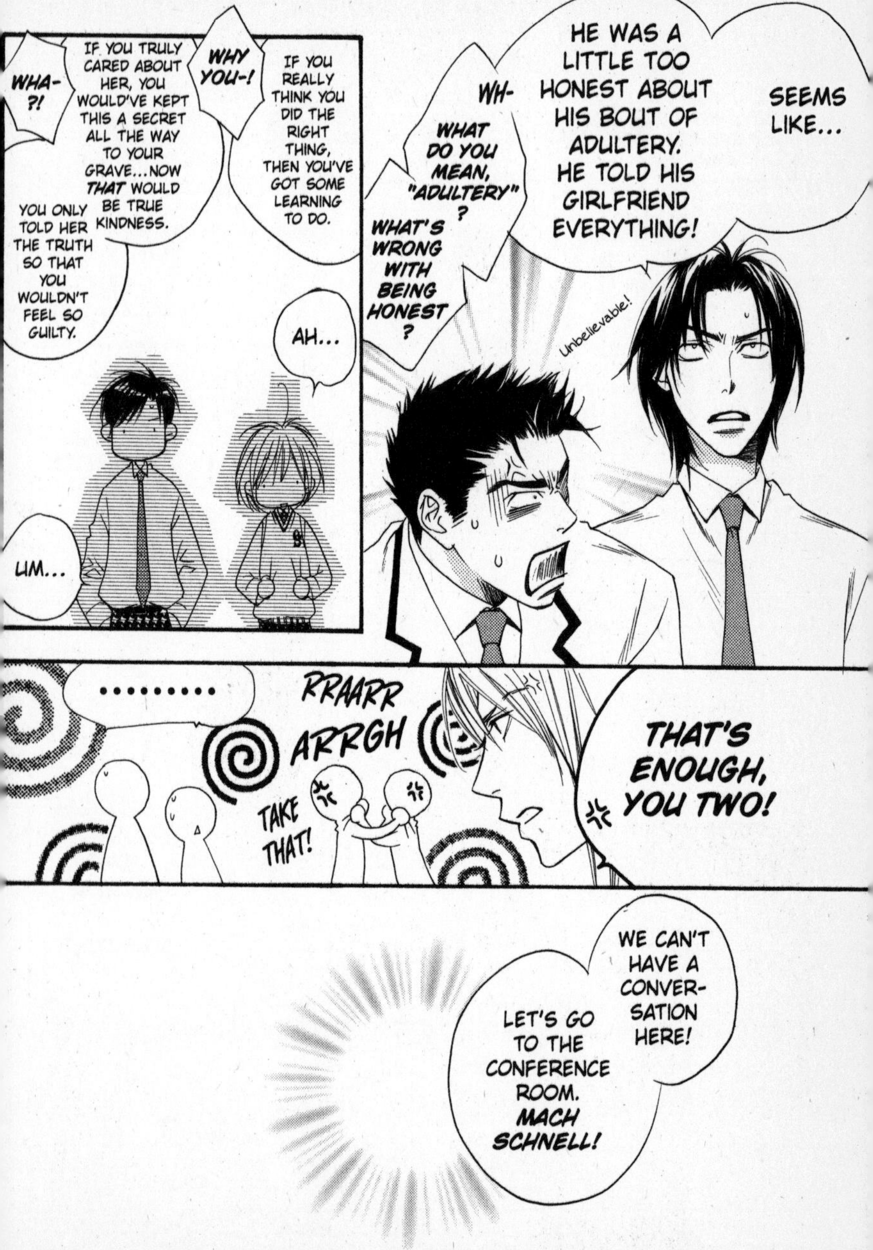
SEEMS LIKE...
HE WAS A LITTLE TOO HONEST ABOUT HIS BOUT OF ADULTERY. HE TOLD HIS GIRLFRIEND EVERYTHING!
WH- WHAT DO YOU MEAN, "ADULTERY"?
WHAT'S WRONG WITH BEING HONEST?
Unbelievable!
IF YOU REALLY THINK YOU DID THE RIGHT THING, THEN YOU'VE GOT SOME LEARNING TO DO.
WHY YOU-!
IF YOU TRULY CARED ABOUT HER, YOU WOULD'VE KEPT THIS A SECRET ALL THE WAY TO YOUR GRAVE...NOW THAT WOULD BE TRUE KINDNESS.
WHA-?!
YOU ONLY TOLD HER THE TRUTH SO THAT YOU WOULDN'T FEEL SO GUILTY.
AH...
UM...
THAT'S ENOUGH, YOU TWO!
RRAARR ARRGH
TAKE THAT!
....
WE CAN'T HAVE A CONVERSATION HERE!
LET'S GO TO THE CONFERENCE ROOM. MACH SCHNELL!

HANA-KIMI CHAPTER 135/END

TRUE TALES OF HORROR

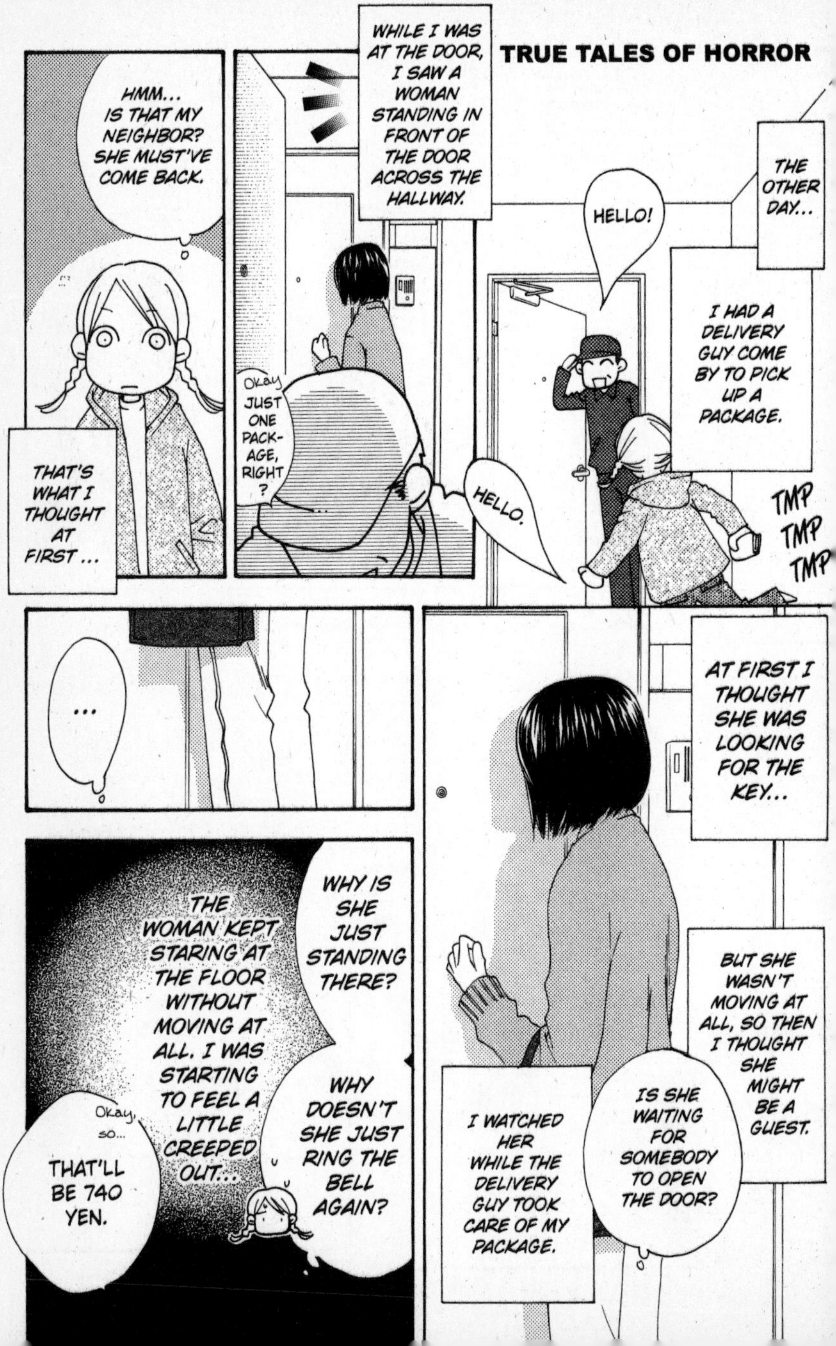
THE OTHER DAY...
I HAD A DELIVERY GUY COME BY TO PICK UP A PACKAGE.
HELLO!
HELLO.
TMP TMP TMP
WHILE I WAS AT THE DOOR, I SAW A WOMAN STANDING IN FRONT OF THE DOOR ACROSS THE HALLWAY.
Okay JUST ONE PACK-AGE, RIGHT?
HMM... IS THAT MY NEIGHBOR? SHE MUST'VE COME BACK.
THAT'S WHAT I THOUGHT AT FIRST...
AT FIRST I THOUGHT SHE WAS LOOKING FOR THE KEY...
BUT SHE WASN'T MOVING AT ALL, SO THEN I THOUGHT SHE MIGHT BE A GUEST.
IS SHE WAITING FOR SOMEBODY TO OPEN THE DOOR?
I WATCHED HER WHILE THE DELIVERY GUY TOOK CARE OF MY PACKAGE.
...
WHY IS SHE JUST STANDING THERE?
WHY DOESN'T SHE JUST RING THE BELL AGAIN?
THE WOMAN KEPT STARING AT THE FLOOR WITHOUT MOVING AT ALL. I WAS STARTING TO FEEL A LITTLE CREEPED OUT...
Okay, so...
THAT'LL BE 740 YEN.

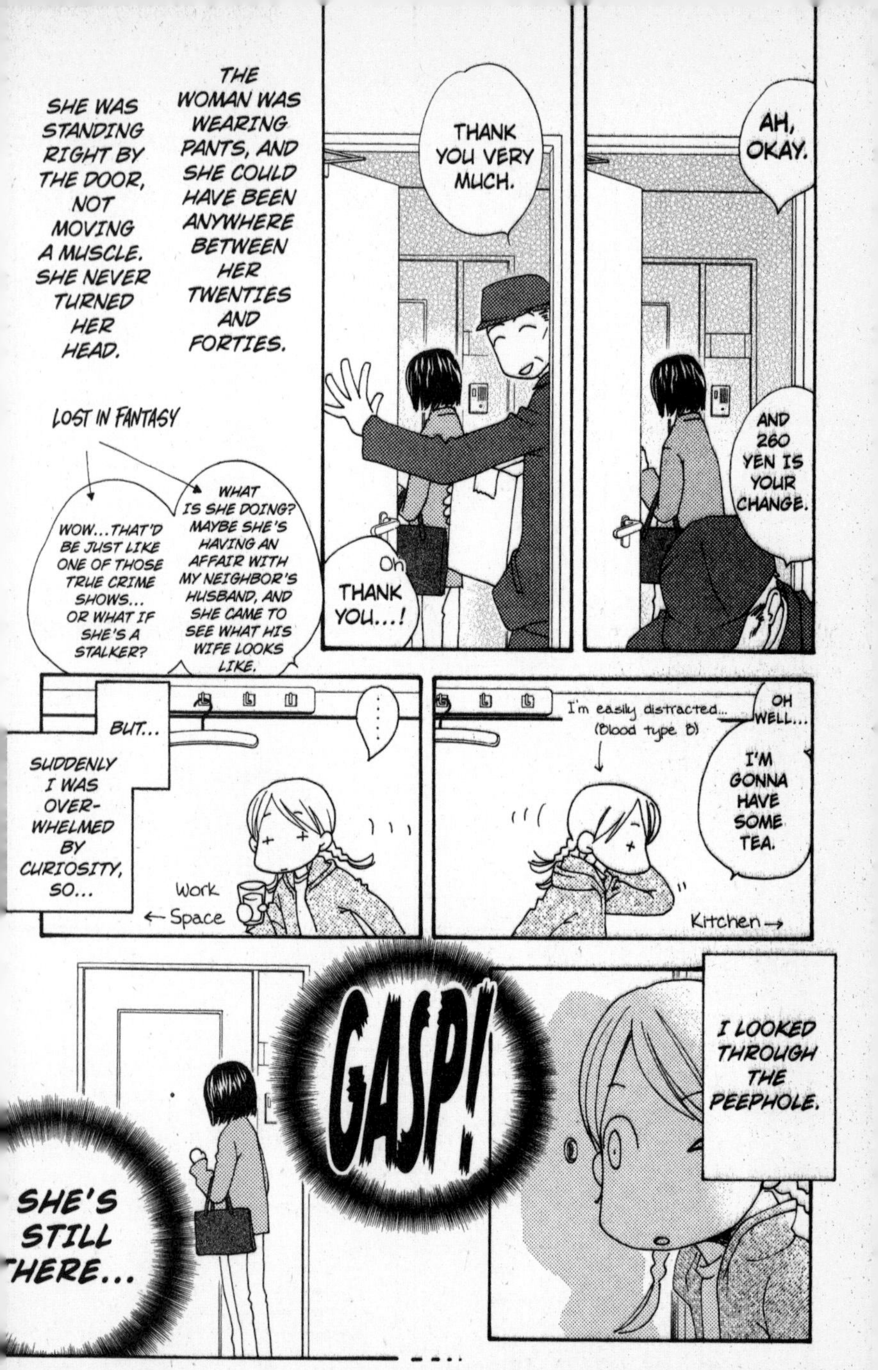
AH, OKAY.
AND 260 YEN IS YOUR CHANGE.
THANK YOU VERY MUCH.
Oh THANK YOU...!
THE WOMAN WAS WEARING PANTS, AND SHE COULD HAVE BEEN ANYWHERE BETWEEN HER TWENTIES AND FORTIES.
SHE WAS STANDING RIGHT BY THE DOOR, NOT MOVING A MUSCLE. SHE NEVER TURNED HER HEAD.
LOST IN FANTASY
WHAT IS SHE DOING? MAYBE SHE'S HAVING AN AFFAIR WITH MY NEIGHBOR'S HUSBAND, AND SHE CAME TO SEE WHAT HIS WIFE LOOKS LIKE.
WOW...THAT'D BE JUST LIKE ONE OF THOSE TRUE CRIME SHOWS... OR WHAT IF SHE'S A STALKER?
OH WELL...
I'M GONNA HAVE SOME TEA.
I'm easily distracted... (Blood type B)
Kitchen→
......
BUT...
SUDDENLY I WAS OVER-WHELMED BY CURIOSITY, SO...
←Work Space
I LOOKED THROUGH THE PEEPHOLE.
GASP!
SHE'S STILL THERE...

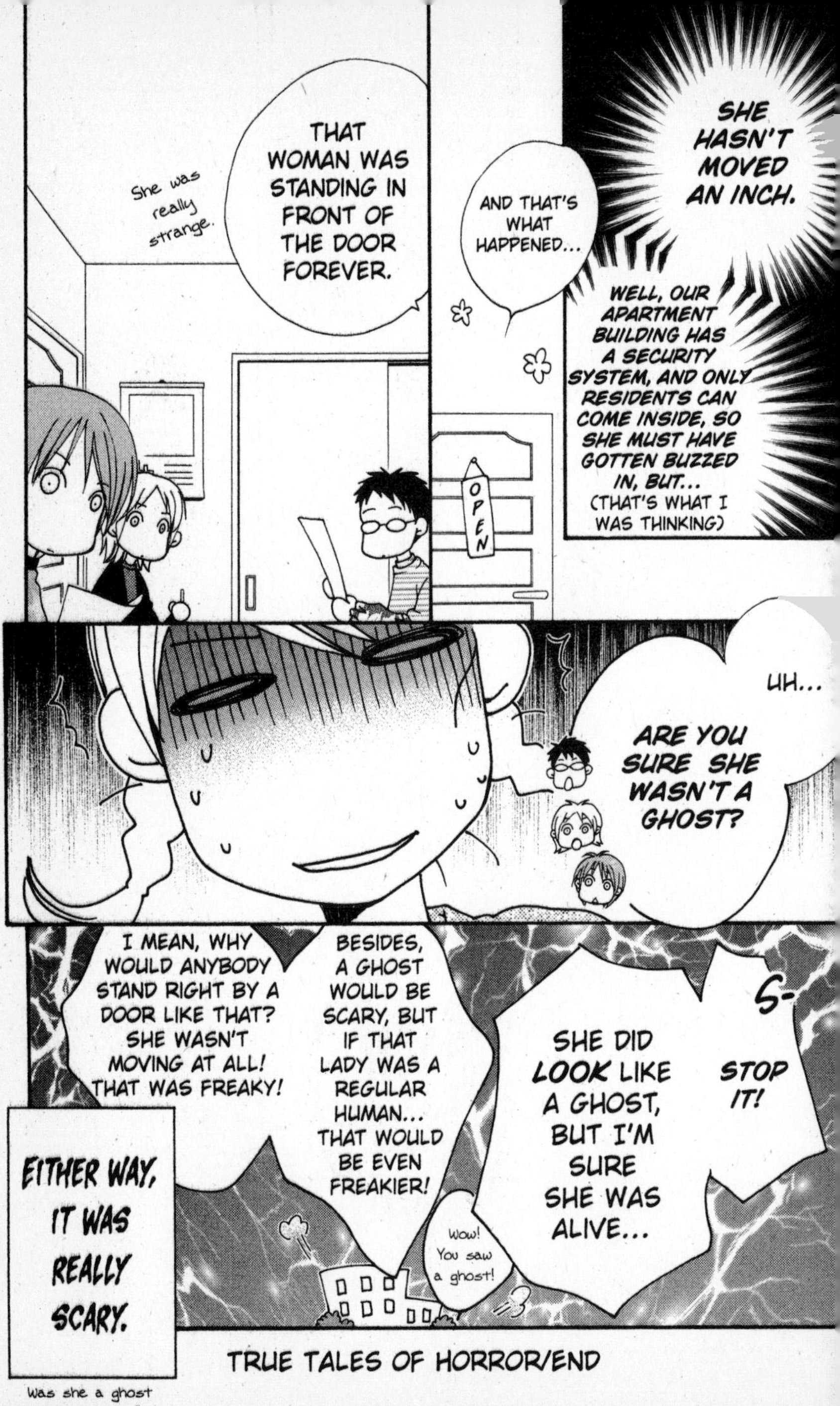
SHE HASN'T MOVED AN INCH.
WELL, OUR APARTMENT BUILDING HAS A SECURITY SYSTEM, AND ONLY RESIDENTS CAN COME INSIDE, SO SHE MUST HAVE GOTTEN BUZZED IN, BUT... (THAT'S WHAT I WAS THINKING)
AND THAT'S WHAT HAPPENED...
OPEN
THAT WOMAN WAS STANDING IN FRONT OF THE DOOR FOREVER.
She was really strange.
UH...
ARE YOU SURE SHE WASN'T A GHOST?
S-
STOP IT!
SHE DID LOOK LIKE A GHOST, BUT I'M SURE SHE WAS ALIVE...
BESIDES, A GHOST WOULD BE SCARY, BUT IF THAT LADY WAS A REGULAR HUMAN... THAT WOULD BE EVEN FREAKIER!
I MEAN, WHY WOULD ANYBODY STAND RIGHT BY A DOOR LIKE THAT? SHE WASN'T MOVING AT ALL! THAT WAS FREAKY!
Wow! You saw a ghost!
EITHER WAY, IT WAS REALLY SCARY.

TRUE TALES OF HORROR/END

Was she a ghost or a person...?

ABOUT THE AUTHOR

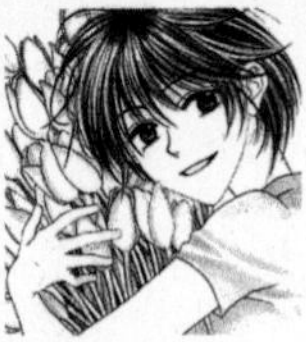

Hisaya Nakajo's manga series **Hanazakari no Kimitachi he** (For You in Full Blossom, casually known as **Hana-Kimi**) has been a hit since it first appeared in 1997 in the shôjo manga magazine **Hana to Yume** (Flowers and Dreams). In Japan, two **Hana-Kimi** art books and several "drama CDs" have been released. Her other manga series include **Missing Piece** (2 volumes), **Yumemiru Happa** (The Dreaming Leaf, 1 volume) and **Sugar Princess**.

Hisaya Nakajo's website:
www.wild-vanilla.com

IN THE NEXT VOLUME...

Has Mizuki been outed? Can she stay at Osaka High School? And when her relationship with Sano changes, will she gain a boyfriend...or lose a best friend? Find out in the bittersweet final volume of *Hana-Kimi!*

FINAL VOLUME!

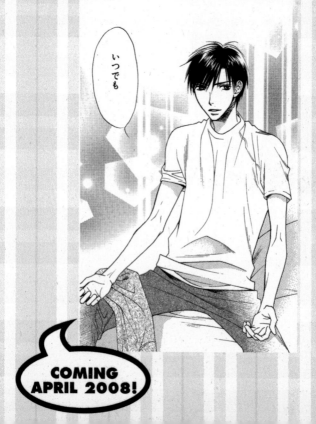

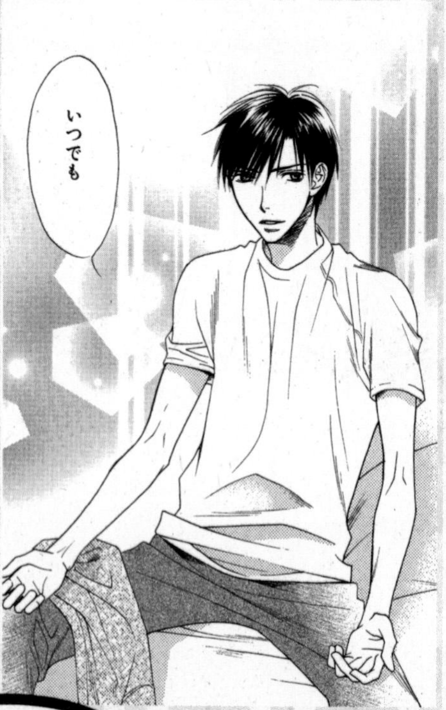
いつでも

COMING APRIL 2008!